CW00670062

THE PASTORAL
EPISTLES WITH
PHILEMON & JUDE

THE PASTORAL EPISTLES WITH PHILEMON & JUDE

RISTO SAARINEN

scm press

© Risto Saarinen 2008

The author has asserted his right under the Copyright Designs and
Patents Act, 1988, to be identified as the Author of this Work.

British Library Cataloguing in Publication data

A catalogue record for this book is available
from the British Library

978 0 334 04196 2

First published in the United Kingdom
in 2008 by SCM Press
13-17 Long Lane, London EC1A 9PN

www.scm-canterburypress.co.uk

SCM Press is a division of
SCM-Canterbury Press Ltd

Printed and bound in the United States of America

CONTENTS

Titus

Appointment of Elders in Crete (Titus 1:1–16) *169*

Virtues among Christians (Titus 2:1–15) *177*

Good Works in the Society (Titus 3:1–15) *189*

Philemon

Jude

SERIES PREFACE

Near the beginning of his treatise against Gnostic interpretations of the Bible, *Against the Heresies*, Irenaeus observes that Scripture is like a great mosaic depicting a handsome king. It is as if we were owners of a villa in Gaul who had ordered a mosaic from Rome. It arrives, and the beautifully colored tiles need to be taken out of their packaging and put into proper order according to the plan of the artist. The difficulty, of course, is that Scripture provides us with the individual pieces, but the order and sequence of various elements are not obvious. The Bible does not come with instructions that would allow interpreters to simply place verses, episodes, images, and parables in order as a worker might follow a schematic drawing in assembling the pieces to depict the handsome king. The mosaic must be puzzled out. This is precisely the work of scriptural interpretation.

Origen has his own image to express the difficulty of working out the proper approach to reading the Bible. When preparing to offer a commentary on the Psalms he tells of a tradition handed down to him by his Hebrew teacher:

> The Hebrew said that the whole divinely inspired Scripture may be likened, because of its obscurity, to many locked rooms in our house. By each room is placed a key, but not the one that corresponds to it, so that the keys are scattered about beside the rooms, none of them matching the room by which it is placed. It is a difficult task to find the keys and match them to the rooms that they can open. We therefore know the Scriptures that are obscure only by taking the points of departure for understanding them from another place because they have their interpretive principle scattered among them.[1]

As is the case for Irenaeus, scriptural interpretation is not purely local. The key in Genesis may best fit the door of Isaiah, which in turn opens up the meaning of Matthew. The mosaic must be put together with an eye toward the overall plan.

---

1. Fragment from the preface to *Commentary on Psalms 1–25*, preserved in the *Philokalia* (trans. Joseph W. Trigg; London: Routledge, 1998), 70–71.

Irenaeus, Origen, and the great cloud of premodern biblical interpreters assumed that puzzling out the mosaic of Scripture must be a communal project. The Bible is vast, heterogeneous, full of confusing passages and obscure words, and difficult to understand. Only a fool would imagine that he or she could work out solutions alone. The way forward must rely upon a tradition of reading that Irenaeus reports has been passed on as the rule or canon of truth that functions as a confession of faith. "Anyone," he says, "who keeps unchangeable in himself the rule of truth received through baptism will recognize the names and sayings and parables of the scriptures."[2] Modern scholars debate the content of the rule on which Irenaeus relies and commends, not the least because the terms and formulations Irenaeus himself uses shift and slide. Nonetheless, Irenaeus assumes that there is a body of apostolic doctrine sustained by a tradition of teaching in the church. This doctrine provides the clarifying principles that guide exegetical judgment toward a coherent overall reading of Scripture as a unified witness. Doctrine, then, is the schematic drawing that will allow the reader to organize the vast heterogeneity of the words, images, and stories of the Bible into a readable, coherent whole. It is the rule that guides us toward the proper matching of keys to doors.

If self-consciousness about the role of history in shaping human consciousness makes modern historical-critical study critical, then what makes modern study of the Bible modern is the consensus that classical Christian doctrine distorts interpretive understanding. Benjamin Jowett, the influential nineteenth-century English classical scholar, is representative. In his programmatic essay "On the Interpretation of Scripture," he exhorts the biblical reader to disengage from doctrine and break its hold over the interpretive imagination. "The simple words of that book," writes Jowett of the modern reader, "he tries to preserve absolutely pure from the refinements or distinctions of later times." The modern interpreter wishes to "clear away the remains of dogmas, systems, controversies, which are encrusted upon" the words of Scripture. The disciplines of close philological analysis "would enable us to separate the elements of doctrine and tradition with which the meaning of Scripture is encumbered in our own day."[3] The lens of understanding must be wiped clear of the hazy and distorting film of doctrine.

Postmodernity, in turn, has encouraged us to criticize the critics. Jowett imagined that when he wiped away doctrine he would encounter the biblical text in its purity and uncover what he called "the original spirit and intention of the authors."[4] We are not now so sanguine, and the postmodern mind thinks interpretive frameworks inevitable. Nonetheless, we tend to remain modern in at least one sense. We read Athanasius and think him stage-managing the diversity of Scripture to support his positions against the Arians. We read Bernard of Clairvaux and

---

2. *Against the Heresies* 9.4.
3. Benjamin Jowett, "On the Interpretation of Scripture," in *Essays and Reviews* (London: Parker, 1860), 338–39.
4. Ibid., 340.

assume that his monastic ideals structure his reading of the Song of Songs. In the wake of the Reformation, we can see how the doctrinal divisions of the time shaped biblical interpretation. Luther famously described the Epistle of James as a "strawy letter," for, as he said, "it has nothing of the nature of the Gospel about it."[5] In these and many other instances, often written in the heat of ecclesiastical controversy or out of the passion of ascetic commitment, we tend to think Jowett correct: doctrine is a distorting film on the lens of understanding.

However, is what we commonly think actually the case? Are readers naturally perceptive? Do we have an unblemished, reliable aptitude for the divine? Have we no need for disciplines of vision? Do our attention and judgment need to be trained, especially as we seek to read Scripture as the living word of God? According to Augustine, we all struggle to journey toward God, who is our rest and peace. Yet our vision is darkened and the fetters of worldly habit corrupt our judgment. We need training and instruction in order to cleanse our minds so that we might find our way toward God.[6] To this end, "the whole temporal dispensation was made by divine Providence for our salvation."[7] The covenant with Israel, the coming of Christ, the gathering of the nations into the church—all these things are gathered up into the rule of faith, and they guide the vision and form of the soul toward the end of fellowship with God. In Augustine's view, the reading of Scripture both contributes to and benefits from this divine pedagogy. With countless variations in both exegetical conclusions and theological frameworks, the same pedagogy of a doctrinally ruled reading of Scripture characterizes the broad sweep of the Christian tradition from Gregory the Great through Bernard and Bonaventure, continuing across Reformation differences in both John Calvin and Cornelius Lapide, Patrick Henry and Bishop Bossuet, and on to more recent figures such as Karl Barth and Hans Urs von Balthasar.

Is doctrine, then, not a moldering scrim of antique prejudice obscuring the Bible, but instead a clarifying agent, an enduring tradition of theological judgments that amplifies the living voice of Scripture? And what of the scholarly dispassion advocated by Jowett? Is a noncommitted reading, an interpretation unprejudiced, the way toward objectivity, or does it simply invite the languid intellectual apathy that stands aside to make room for the false truism and easy answers of the age?

This series of biblical commentaries was born out of the conviction that dogma clarifies rather than obscures. The SCM Theological Commentary on the Bible advances upon the assumption that the Nicene tradition, in all its diversity and controversy, provides the proper basis for the interpretation of the Bible as Christian Scripture. God the Father Almighty, who sends his only begotten Son to die for us and for our salvation and who raises the crucified Son in the power of the Holy

---

5. *Luther's Works*, vol. 35 (ed. E. Theodore Bachmann; Philadelphia: Fortress, 1959), 362.
6. *On Christian Doctrine* 1.10.
7. *On Christian Doctrine* 1.35.

Spirit so that the baptized may be joined in one body—faith in *this* God with *this* vocation of love for the world is the lens through which to view the heterogeneity and particularity of the biblical texts. Doctrine, then, is not a moldering scrim of antique prejudice obscuring the meaning of the Bible. It is a crucial aspect of the divine pedagogy, a clarifying agent for our minds fogged by self-deceptions, a challenge to our languid intellectual apathy that will too often rest in false truisms and the easy spiritual nostrums of the present age rather than search more deeply and widely for the dispersed keys to the many doors of Scripture.

For this reason, the commentators in this series have not been chosen because of their historical or philological expertise. In the main, they are not biblical scholars in the conventional, modern sense of the term. Instead, the commentators were chosen because of their knowledge of and expertise in using the Christian doctrinal tradition. They are qualified by virtue of the doctrinal formation of their mental habits, for it is the conceit of this series of biblical commentaries that theological training in the Nicene tradition prepares one for biblical interpretation, and thus it is to theologians and not biblical scholars that we have turned. "War is too important," it has been said, "to leave to the generals."

We do hope, however, that readers do not draw the wrong impression. The Nicene tradition does not provide a set formula for the solution of exegetical problems. The great tradition of Christian doctrine was not transcribed, bound in folio, and issued in an official, critical edition. We have the Niceno-Constantinopolitan Creed, used for centuries in many traditions of Christian worship. We have ancient baptismal affirmations of faith. The Chalcedonian definition and the creeds and canons of other church councils have their places in official church documents. Yet the rule of faith cannot be limited to a specific set of words, sentences, and creeds. It is instead a pervasive habit of thought, the animating culture of the church in its intellectual aspect. As Augustine observed, commenting on Jeremiah 31:33, "The creed is learned by listening; it is written, not on stone tablets nor on any material, but on the heart."[8] This is why Irenaeus is able to appeal to the rule of faith more than a century before the first ecumenical council, and this is why we need not itemize the contents of the Nicene tradition in order to appeal to its potency and role in the work of interpretation.

Because doctrine is intrinsically fluid on the margins and most powerful as a habit of mind rather than a list of propositions, this commentary series cannot settle difficult questions of method and content at the outset. The editors of the series impose no particular method of doctrinal interpretation. We cannot say in advance how doctrine helps the Christian reader assemble the mosaic of Scripture. We have no clear answer to the question of whether exegesis guided by doctrine is antithetical to or compatible with the now-old modern methods of historical-critical inquiry. Truth—historical, mathematical, or doctrinal—knows no contradiction. But method is a discipline of vision and judgment, and we

8. *Sermon* 212.2.

cannot know in advance what aspects of historical-critical inquiry are functions of modernism that shape the soul to be at odds with Christian discipline. Still further, the editors do not hold the commentators to any particular hermeneutical theory that specifies how to define the plain sense of Scripture—or the role this plain sense should play in interpretation. Here the commentary series is tentative and exploratory.

Can we proceed in any other way? European and North American intellectual culture has been de-Christianized. The effect has not been a cessation of Christian activity. Theological work continues. Sermons are preached. Biblical scholars turn out monographs. Church leaders have meetings. But each dimension of a formerly unified Christian practice now tends to function independently. It is as if a weakened army had been fragmented, and various corps had retreated to isolated fortresses in order to survive. Theology has lost its competence in exegesis. Scripture scholars function with minimal theological training. Each decade finds new theories of preaching to cover the nakedness of seminary training that provides theology without exegesis and exegesis without theology.

Not the least of the causes of the fragmentation of Christian intellectual practice has been the divisions of the church. Since the Reformation, the role of the rule of faith in interpretation has been obscured by polemics and counterpolemics about *sola scriptura* and the necessity of a magisterial teaching authority. The SCM Theological Commentary on the Bible series is deliberately ecumenical in scope, because the editors are convinced that early church fathers were correct: church doctrine does not compete with Scripture in a limited economy of epistemic authority. We wish to encourage unashamedly dogmatic interpretation of Scripture, confident that the concrete consequences of such a reading will cast far more light on the great divisive questions of the Reformation than either reengaging in old theological polemics or chasing the fantasy of a pure exegesis that will somehow adjudicate between competing theological positions. You shall know the truth of doctrine by its interpretive fruits, and therefore in hopes of contributing to the unity of the church, we have deliberately chosen a wide range of theologians whose commitment to doctrine will allow readers to see real interpretive consequences rather than the shadow boxing of theological concepts.

SCM Theological Commentary on the Bible has no dog in the current translation fights, and we endorse a textual ecumenism that parallels our diversity of ecclesial backgrounds. We do not impose the thankfully modest inclusive-language agenda of the New Revised Standard Version, nor do we insist upon the glories of the Authorized Version, nor do we require our commentators to create a new translation. In our communal worship, in our private devotions, in our theological scholarship, we use a range of scriptural translations. Precisely as Scripture—a living, functioning text in the present life of faith—the Bible is not semantically fixed. Only a modernist, literalist hermeneutic could imagine that this modest fluidity is a liability. Philological precision and stability is a consequence of, not a basis for, exegesis. Judgments about the meaning of a text fix its literal sense, not the other way around. As a result, readers should expect an eclectic use of biblical translations, both across the different volumes of the series and within individual commentaries.

We cannot speak for contemporary biblical scholars, but as theologians we know that we have long been trained to defend our fortresses of theological concepts and formulations. And we have forgotten the skills of interpretation. Like stroke victims, we must rehabilitate our exegetical imaginations, and there are likely to be different strategies of recovery. Readers should expect this reconstructive—not reactionary—series to provide them with experiments in postcritical doctrinal interpretation, not commentaries written according to the settled principles of a well-functioning tradition. Some commentators will follow classical typological and allegorical readings from the premodern tradition; others will draw on contemporary historical study. Some will comment verse by verse; others will highlight passages, even single words that trigger theological analysis of Scripture. No reading strategies are proscribed, no interpretive methods foresworn. The central premise in this commentary series is that doctrine provides structure and cogency to scriptural interpretation. We trust in this premise with the hope that the Nicene tradition can guide us, however imperfectly, diversely, and haltingly, toward a reading of Scripture in which the right keys open the right doors.

R. R. Reno

AUTHOR'S PREFACE

Writing this commentary has been an adventure. Systematic theologians employed in a European state university do not normally write New Testament commentaries. Ecumenists and Reformation scholars too often work with issues that do not require profound biblical knowledge. Hermeneutical theologians tend to deal with philosophy rather than with concrete canonical texts. Belonging myself to all four categories, I would have had all the reason to avoid this task. But it has been a pleasant task and an exciting adventure.

Rusty Reno and Michael Root gave me a lot of good advice. At times I thought less would have been enough, but in the end it was all constructive. Antti Marjanen and Ismo Dunderberg read carefully my exposition of the Pastoral Epistles, providing an indispensable exegetical perspective. Troels Engberg-Pedersen read and commented on some crucial parts of my manuscript. Lisa Muszynski revised my English. David Aiken edited the manuscript with great care.

This book was written during a sabbatical leave at the Helsinki Collegium for Advanced Studies. I am grateful to its director, Juha Sihvola, not only for this opportunity, but also for our long cooperation in the History of Mind research project. Several scholars working with this project in Helsinki have helped me in various ways. My views on emotion and virtue are indebted to the insights of Simo Knuuttila and Richard Sorabji.

The Institute for Ecumenical Research, Strasbourg, has provided me many opportunities for ecumenical learning. Many of my colleagues and students in the Department of Systematic Theology at the University of Helsinki have commented on large portions of the manuscript. Thank you so much. All remaining faults are my own.

ABBREVIATIONS

General

ANF   The Ante-Nicene Fathers. 10 vols. Reprinted Grand Rapids: Eerdmans, 1957.

HWP   *Historisches Wörterbuch der Philosophie.* Basel: Schwabe, 1971–2004.

LCL   Loeb Classical Library. Cambridge: Harvard University Press.

LW   Luther's Works: American Edition. 55 vols. Edited by J. Pelikan and H. Lehmann. Saint Louis: Concordia/Philadelphia: Muhlenberg/Fortress, 1955–86.

NA²⁷   *Novum Testamentum Graece.* Edited by B. Aland, K. Aland, J. Karavidopoulos, C. M. Martini, and B. M. Metzger. 27th revised edition. Stuttgart: Deutsche Bibelgesellschaft, 1993.

NPNF¹   A Select Library of the Nicene and Post-Nicene Fathers of the Christian Church. First series. Reprinted Grand Rapids: Eerdmans, 1956.

NPNF²   A Select Library of the Nicene and Post-Nicene Fathers of the Christian Church. Second series. Reprinted Grand Rapids: Eerdmans, 1956.

NRSV   New Revised Standard Version

TDNT   *Theological Dictionary of the New Testament.* Edited by G. Kittel and J. Friedrich. Translated by G. W. Bromiley. 10 vols. Grand Rapids: Eerdmans, 1964–76.

WA   D. Martin Luthers Werke: Kritische Gesamtausgabe. Weimar: Böhlau, 1883–.

WADB   D. Martin Luthers Werke: Kritische Gesamtausgabe. Abteilung Deutsche Bibel. Weimar: Böhlau, 1883–.

Biblical

Acts	Acts	2 Chr.	2 Chronicles
Amos	Amos	Col.	Colossians
1 Chr.	1 Chronicles	1 Cor.	1 Corinthians

2 Cor.	2 Corinthians	Lam.	Lamentations
Dan.	Daniel	Lev.	Leviticus
Deut.	Deuteronomy	Luke	Luke
Eccl.	Ecclesiastes	Mal.	Malachi
Eph.	Ephesians	Mark	Mark
Esth.	Esther	Matt.	Matthew
Exod.	Exodus	Mic.	Micah
Ezek.	Ezekiel	Nah.	Nahum
Ezra	Ezra	Neh.	Nehemiah
Gal.	Galatians	Num.	Numbers
Gen.	Genesis	Obad.	Obadiah
Hab.	Habakkuk	1 Pet.	1 Peter
Hag.	Haggai	2 Pet.	2 Peter
Heb.	Hebrews	Phil.	Philippians
Hos.	Hosea	Phlm.	Philemon
Isa.	Isaiah	Prov.	Proverbs
Jas.	James	Ps.	Psalms
Jer.	Jeremiah	Rev.	Revelation
Job	Job	Rom.	Romans
Joel	Joel	Ruth	Ruth
John	John	1 Sam.	1 Samuel
1 John	1 John	2 Sam.	2 Samuel
2 John	2 John	Song	Song of Songs
3 John	3 John	1 Thess.	1 Thessalonians
Jonah	Jonah	2 Thess.	2 Thessalonians
Josh.	Joshua	1 Tim.	1 Timothy
Jude	Jude	2 Tim.	2 Timothy
Judg.	Judges	Titus	Titus
1 Kgs.	1 Kings	Zech.	Zechariah
2 Kgs.	2 Kings	Zeph.	Zephaniah

INTRODUCTION
TO THE PASTORAL EPISTLES

The First and Second Letters of Paul to Timothy and the Letter of Paul to Titus are usually called the Pastoral Epistles. The three epistles belong together in terms of both their style and content. It is therefore natural to treat them together in this introduction.

Although the present study uses the conventional attribute "pastoral," it can be questioned as to whether this word conveys the distinctive character of the three epistles in a proper sense. Pastoral situations are often characterized by their particularity. In the churches of today, pastoral care and counseling aim at finding solutions to the individual life situations that cannot be solved merely by looking at the general rules. But if "pastoral" is understood in this sense, then 1 Corinthians and Philemon would be pastoral epistles, whereas 1 Timothy, 2 Timothy, and Titus would not. The three epistles aim at presenting generally valid rules rather than targeted counseling.

The word "pastoral" is not, however, intended to be read in an individualistic or particularist manner. The three epistles are called pastoral because they have been read as guidance to pastors and other teachers of the church. Already John Chrysostom remarks that in 1 Timothy, Paul is "through the whole epistle adapting his instructions to a teacher" (NPNF[1] 13.408). Understood in this sense, the Pastoral Epistles can be regarded as instruction to advanced Christians, as training in leadership.

Although this interpretation has probably motivated many church leaders to study the three epistles with special intensity, there is no indication that the Pastoral Epistles would have enjoyed a particular prominence in the history of Christianity. The three epistles are missing from one important manuscript, that is, Papyrus 46, as well as from the canon of Marcion. But they are known to Christian writers of the early second century and are used by Polycarp. According to Canon Muratori,

"[Paul writes] one [letter] to Philemon, one to Titus, and two to Timothy in love and affection; but they have been hallowed for the honor of the Catholic church in the regulation of ecclesiastical discipline." Generally speaking, the use of the Pastoral Epistles in early Christianity is similar to other epistles of the Pauline corpus (Marshall 1999: 2–8; Mounce 2000: lxvii–lxviii; Johnson 2001: 20–26; Bruce 1988; Tertullian, *Marcion* 5.21 [ANF 3.473–74]).

In patristic, medieval, and early modern periods, the Pastoral Epistles were commented upon regularly, though less frequently than the most popular New Testament books. From patristic times to the nineteenth century, the three epistles were understood as Paul's personal instructions to Timothy and Titus, who, according to Eusebius (*Ecclesiastical History* 3.4.5 [NPNF[2] 1.136]), were the first bishops of Ephesus and Crete. Thus 1 Timothy especially came to be read as Paul's handbook on the office of bishop (so Wengert 2005: 70).

Not many patristic commentaries have survived.[1] Augustine wrote no treatises on the Pastoral Epistles, but we do have Jerome's exposition of Titus (Patrologia latina 26.589–636). By far the most interesting and influential commentary, in both East and West, is the extensive work of John Chrysostom, consisting of eighteen homilies on 1 Timothy, ten on 2 Timothy, and six on Titus (Patrologia graeca 62.501–700; NPNF[1] 13.407–543).[2] Chrysostom proceeds verse by verse, focuses on the literal meaning of the text, and avoids allegorical interpretations. In the concluding parts of the homilies he often presents moral conclusions and applications. The Latin translation of Chrysostom's commentary was printed in Basel in 1536 and used, among others, by Calvin in his detailed commentaries on the three epistles (Wengert 2005: 71; see Calvin 1996: 77, 84, 201; and Corpus reformatorum 52). Among medieval commentaries, Thomas Aquinas's exposition (1888) of all the Pauline Epistles remains influential.

Martin Luther lectured on 1 Timothy in 1528. Although Luther's lectures were not printed until 1797 (Wengert 2005: 87; WA 26.1–120; LW 28.217–384), they were used by his students, for instance, by Georg Major in his 1563 commentary on 1 Timothy. Other early Lutheran expositors of 1 Timothy include Caspar Cruciger and Philipp Melanchthon.[3] Luther also lectured on Titus in 1527 (LW 29.4–90; WA 25.1–69).

---

1. Spicq 1969: 11–16 lists the patristic and medieval commentaries. The complete interpretation history of the Pastoral Epistles remains to be written. Johnson 2001: 20–54 offers a compact overview of the interpretation of 1–2 Timothy from early Christianity to the early twentieth century. Schenk 1987 covers the research history of the Pastoral Epistles from 1945 to 1987. The interpretation history of some passages has been studied in detail; for instance, the role of women in 1 Tim. 2:9–15 (Doriani 1995; Mounce 2000: 94–102) or the inspiration of Scripture in 2 Tim. 3:16 (Weiser 2003: 286–92).

2. Although Johnson 2001: 27 calls this commentary "moralistic," it is not. As we will see below, Chrysostom employs sound doctrine for the purposes of Christian character formation.

3. Melanchthon's 1550–51 *Enarratio epistolae prioris ad Timotheum, et duorum capitum secundae* may be found in Corpus reformatorum 15.1295–1396. Cruciger's 1540 *In epistolam Pauli ad Timotheum priorem* is edited in Burigana 1986. For Major's 1563 *Enarratio epistolae Pauli primae ad Timotheum*, see Wengert 2005, which offers an excellent overview of the Reformation period.

The designation "Pastoral Epistles" stems from the eighteenth century,[4] but already Thomas Aquinas called 1 Timothy "a rule . . . for pastors" (*quasi regula pastoralis*) (*Super 1 Timothy* lecture 2 on 1:4 [Quinn and Wacker 2000: 1; Collins 2002: 1]). Calvin begins his commentary on 1 Timothy by stating that "this Epistle appears to me to have been written more for the sake of others than for the sake of Timothy. . . . It contains many things which it would have been superfluous to write, if he had had to deal with Timothy alone" (1996: 13; cf. 19).

In the era of historical-critical exegesis, the Pastoral Epistles have often fallen into disgrace. Because their style, content, and presupposed ecclesiastical situation differs from other epistles of the Pauline corpus, the Pastoral Epistles are considered to have emerged only after the time of Paul. Their pseudonymity, late date of writing, and "early Catholic" emphasis have been taken as indications that they are less important than other canonical writings.[5] There are exceptions, most notably Heinrich Schlier (1958: 129–47), who argue that the Pastoral Epistles allow us to see the normative direction of ecclesiastical development within the canon. With the help of the Pastoral Epistles, it can therefore be claimed that the emergence of early Catholicism is biblically grounded. More often, however, this development has been interpreted as departing from the original message of Jesus and Paul.

During the last twenty years, new major commentaries have been published, which are no longer hampered by the polemical discussion on pseudonymity and late date of composition. Especially the German commentaries of Jürgen Roloff (1988), Lorenz Oberlinner (1994, 1995, 1996), and Alfons Weiser (2003) manage to create a synthesis in which the theology of the Pastoral Epistles becomes important in its own right. All these commentaries assume that the epistles are post-Pauline. They are also critical with regard to the identity of "Timothy" and "Titus" and proceed from the assumption that the author intends to defend the Pauline tradition to a broader audience. But these historical presuppositions are not employed to downplay the importance of the theology of the three epistles.

There are also erudite new British and American commentaries. The most important commentary available in English is that of I. Howard Marshall (1999). He defends moderate evangelical positions and manages to show in many cases that the early Catholic frame of the Pastoral Epistles is not as rigid as many interpreters have assumed. Marshall also reports conscientiously on the results of German scholarship (i.e., on Roloff 1988 and Oberlinner 1994–96, but not on Weiser 2003); his work contains many useful excursuses. The extensive 2000 commentary of Jerome D. Quinn and William Wacker is rich in linguistic detail, but it does not offer comprehensive theological interpretation. The 2002 commentary of

4. According to Collins 2002: 1, B. D. P. Anton's 1753 commentary on the three epistles carries this name. Already in 1703 D. N. Bardot calls 1 Timothy a pastoral letter.

5. See, e.g., Käsemann 1964: 63–94 and Schulz 1976. For critical reviews, see Hahn 1986: 39–56 and Mounce 2000: cxviii–cxix. For research history from 1945 to 1987, see Schenk 1987. Among the first skeptics with regard to Paul's authorship was Friedrich Schleiermacher; see Collins 2002: 3.

Raymond F. Collins is concise but presents useful parallel material from Jewish and Hellenistic sources. William D. Mounce's 2000 commentary is an attempt to argue in favor of Paul's authorship; Mounce also offers excellent bibliographies on many particular topics. Luke Timothy Johnson likewise defends Pauline authorship. His 2001 commentary offers the best interpretation history and pays some attention to the medical imagery of 1–2 Timothy.

Given this state of scholarship, it would be misleading to say that the interpretation of the Pastoral Epistles suffers from a lack of theological interest or an absence of sophisticated academic discussion. It is difficult to present any plausible interpretation that has not already been competently discussed in the above-mentioned commentaries. At the same time, it can be added that the secondary literature on the Pastoral Epistles is not as vast as on most other New Testament writings. It is possible to follow the ongoing discussion and to master at least the most important secondary works. In this quantitative sense the Pastoral Epistles are still considered today to be less important than most other New Testament books.

While a theological interpreter of the Synoptic Gospels has many good reasons to bypass the enormous existing secondary literature, the author of the present commentary cannot do this for two reasons. The first reason is simply that with the help of the above-mentioned new commentaries the most important trends of the exegetical research can be taken into account. The second reason has to do with the specific nature of the Pastoral Epistles. These epistles deal with theological issues, and we do not know much about their historical background. Thus the exegetical scholarship on the Pastoral Epistles concentrates on issues that are fundamentally theological. The most important issues have already been discussed in the commentaries, and a theological interpreter has to show his or her awareness of them.

Since this task already demands many pages, I will only briefly mention my basic decisions with regard to the introductory issues. These issues are discussed in much detail in the above-mentioned commentaries, and my decisions, for the most part, follow the majority opinion. Therefore I will not return to them in my exposition.

All three epistles are written by the same author. He defends the legacy of Paul and quotes many epistles of the apostle. The style, vocabulary, and situation make it nevertheless improbable that the author could be Paul (see Marshall 1999: 57–92, whose reflections are exemplary in showing why even rather conservative exegetes today take this position). The option outlined by Marshall that the author of 1 Timothy is Paul's "close associate in the immediate post-Pauline period via a letter intended to maintain Paul's influence without any attempt to deceive readers" (I. Howard Marshall in Vanhoozer 2005a: 801) seems fitting with regard to all three epistles. As the leading Lutheran (Roloff), Catholic (Oberlinner, Weiser, Collins), and evangelical (Marshall) commentators can all combine pseudonymity with their own high appreciation of this Pauline legacy, I can side with them on this issue.

For the sake of convenience, the author in my text is called "Paul" and "the apostle." Those readers who are committed to the immediate authorship of Paul can find some consolation in the observation that, given the concentration on theological exposition, my commentary would not be dramatically changed even if I would affirm Paul's authorship. The most demanding task would then be that of connecting the Hellenistic philosophical and therapeutic terminology of the Pastoral Epistles with the theology of the other Pauline epistles. Another difficult task would concern Paul's view of women.

All three epistles are written toward the end of the first century. It is obvious that they contain many mutual dependencies, but they do not allow us to decide in which order the epistles were composed. The canonical order follows the length of the texts (Marshall 1999: 2). This order has been preserved in many commentaries, and I see no reason for changing it. The place of writing remains uncertain and has no theological consequences. Timothy and Titus are historical figures who are connected with Paul's missions as well as with the churches in Ephesus and Crete.[6] They are church leaders, but the epistles do not mention their precise titles. Although the epistles are addressed to Timothy and Titus, the author presupposes that the epistles will be read and circulated in the churches.

I use the standard *Novum Testamentum Graece* (NA[27]) and prefer in most cases the NRSV. As a nonnative speaker of English I do not feel competent enough to compare different translations extensively. But I do mention the Vulgate translation quite often, since it is highly influential for the theological reception of the epistles. Sometimes theologians still instinctively read the Pastoral Epistles through the lenses of Vulgate.[7] My exposition proceeds verse by verse, and a reader who is interested only in the explanation of a particular passage can consult it without problems.

Although I am indebted especially to the above-mentioned commentaries of Roloff, Weiser, Oberlinner, and Marshall, my exposition aims at accomplishing a distinct profile. I have attempted to construct this profile so that it would be intelligible for both exegetes and systematic theologians and could be discussed both historically and theologically. One way of explaining my strategy is to say that I aim at avoiding two fallacies: (1) the fallacy of downgrading Greco-Roman topics and (2) the fallacy of preferring the extreme options.

Concerning the first fallacy, the perpetual problem in the theological evaluation of the Pastoral Epistles has been that they remain secondary to other Pauline writings. The Pastoral Epistles also seem to be dependent on Greco-Roman thought in ways that are not proper in a canonical text. In order to meet these problems, different ways of downgrading the philosophical and cultural background have

---

6. On Timothy, see Weiser 2003: 44–51; on Titus, see Barrett 1969. Later tradition (Eusebius, *Ecclesiastical History* 3.4.5 [NPNF² 1.136]) mentions Timothy and Titus as the first bishops of Ephesus and Crete.

7. The words *regeneratio* and *renovatio* in the phrase "water of rebirth and renewal" in Titus 3:5 are a good example. While the Greek words are probably synonymous, the Latin terms involve two stages.

been adopted by interpreters. Their common denominator is that the Hellenistic influences can be bracketed or counteracted so that the distinctive theological profile of the epistles can emerge.

My exposition aims at treating these features (see appendixes A–C) as an integral part of the epistles (for the exegetical assessment of Hellenistic philosophy, see Malherbe 1989: 1–9). The distinctive message of the Pastoral Epistles is, therefore, not found in verses that deviate from popular philosophy and cultural encounter, but the Pastoral Epistles are distinctive in the canon precisely because they witness to the first constructive encounters between "Jerusalem and Athens," that is, between the proclamation of the gospel and the ideals of the surrounding culture. This distinctive feature does not mean problematic accommodation or the watering down of the gospel, but it is an attempt to express sound doctrine and the Christian life with a terminology that is distinct from, but nevertheless commensurable with, other ideals of character formation. Following this lead, my exposition often aims at finding the distinctive profile in verses that have been downgraded as mere Hellenisms.

Concerning the second fallacy, the expositors have often considered the great problem of the Pastoral Epistles to consist in their lukewarm and compromising answers to the pressing issues at hand. The author seems to be worried about the reputation of Christians among non-Christians. Therefore he recommends civil virtues. The commentators ask "whether the life-style in the [Pastoral Epistles] is over-concerned with a dull respectability" (Marshall 1999: 189). As our late modern era praises original ideas, it also embraces the extreme options and considers them to be more committed and serious than their alternatives. Religion in particular is considered to be the forum of extreme commitments.

In the world of the Pastoral Epistles, however, the habit of preferring extreme options is symptomatic of the lack of good judgment. A virtuous person who can exercise moderation and self-control seldom prefers the extremes. The capacity to discern and to avoid the harmful extremes is a sign of moral and intellectual progress. The Pastoral Epistles argue that the doctrine of a moderated mean is the Christian ideal. The fallacy of preferring the extreme options prevents many expositors from seeing this ideal (Käsemann 1964: 63–94 and Schulz 1976 are symptomatic of this problem). Given this, the Pastoral Epistles are not concerned with compromises and dull respectability, but their distinctive message relates to the ideal of moderated mean. Such a mean is not primarily a civil virtue, but it receives its deeper meaning from the tradition coming from Jesus and the Jewish Bible. In some cases, for instance, with regard to the virtue of being "gentle" (*praus, prautēs*), the radical virtue of Jesus (Matt. 5:5; 11:29) and Moses (Num. 12:3) also expresses a proper mean to be followed by the church leader (1 Tim. 6:11; 2 Tim. 2:25; Titus 3:2).

In our age of different extremisms, the ideal of a moderated mean has new actuality, not only among ecumenists like myself, but also among other committed Christians (as well as among people of other faiths) who train their judgment. In the history of Christian theology, Thomas Aquinas is the most prominent representative of the view that virtue can be identified as a mean between problematic extremes (*Summa theologiae* 2/1 Q. 64).[8] At the same time theologians must ask whether the view of virtue as mean provides a too narrow description of the ideals of Christian life. As the Christian faith is an unconditional commitment to God through Jesus Christ, does it not lose something essential when it is interpreted as proper moderation? To answer this question, the Pastoral Epistles should be set against the background of the emerging early Christianity as portrayed in other canonical texts of the New Testament.

We may characterize this theological horizon of the Pastoral Epistles with Tertullian's question: "What has Athens to do with Jerusalem?" (*Against Heretics* 7 [ANF 3.246]).[9] In this paradigmatic question, Jerusalem stands for the core of the Christian faith: the proclamation of Jesus, his death and resurrection, the inner life of the emerging church, as well as the act of faith itself in distinction from reason. Jerusalem further points to the fundamentally important background of Judaism and the Jewish Bible, mostly read through the Greek Septuagint, as the cradle of Christianity. Athens stands for the cultural context of Christianity, the Greco-Roman world in which not faith but reason provides the tools for arguing the personal conviction. In Athens, the individual is primarily surrounded by his or her own household, the *oikos*. The household provides the material basis for individual learning, growth, and flourishing. The broader social circle is that of a *polis*, a city-state that is finally subordinated to the Roman Empire.

The Christian church needed to find its identity vis-à-vis the secular realms of household, *polis*, and empire. It also needed to spell out why and in which sense faith is more important than reason and philosophy. The proclamation of Jesus and the understanding of his life, death, and resurrection as that of the Christ, the Messiah promised by the God of Israel, provided the constitutive understanding of the Christian faith. This essence of Jerusalem is codified in the Four Gospels. The longest and most comprehensive of the Pauline epistles—most notably Romans, 1–2 Corinthians, Galatians, and Ephesians—also witness to this self-understanding of the earliest Christian churches.

These early witnesses are primarily concerned with the basic identity of Christianity as the narrative of God's salvation history fulfilled in Jesus Christ and the proclamation of this gospel message. They exemplify the radical commitment to Christ rather than the cultural contextualization of Christianity. In performing this task they, for the most part, remain in Jerusalem and do not visit Athens.

And yet, even this first phase of doctrinal development had to borrow words and phrases from the surrounding world. The very word for the church, *ekklēsia*, is homonymic with the secular legal organ responsible for important decisions in the

---

8. The only exception for Thomas Aquinas is that the divine side of theological virtue cannot be in excess. But even the human side of theological virtue consists in proper measure (Q. 64a4).

9. The following reflections broaden the original scope of Tertullian, which focuses on the relationship between philosophy and scriptural authority.

polis. The homonymy, however, does not imply synonymy: the church functions in many respects very differently from political meetings. But in order to define the meaning of this word in Jerusalem, the ecclesiologist needs to recognize the existence of the concept of *ekklēsia* in Athens.

In the Pastoral Epistles, the interaction between Jerusalem and Athens becomes more complex. The gospel narratives and the major Pauline epistles are taken for granted. They provide the essence of Jerusalem in the sense of an authoritative story of God's plan of salvation in Jesus Christ. This narrative is not in need of moderation: Christians are expected to have full faith and unconditional commitment to this divine economy (1 Tim. 1:4). At the same time, Christians have begun to realize that they live in two kingdoms at the same time. While their whole heart may already be in the heavenly Jerusalem, their bodies, minds, and external conduct remain in their earthly city and *oikos*. Even their gathering in the church occurs in the material and political reality of the Greco-Roman world.

The Pastoral Epistles are often concerned with the life and conduct of the church, its leaders, and its members in this external reality of Athens. While the Pastoral Epistles do not lose sight of Jerusalem as the eschatological fulfilment, they are "pastoral" epistles in the sense that they deal with the concrete life of the church and its members. The virtuous life of bishops, deacons, rich and poor people, teachers and presbyters, young and old widows, and other women is discussed so that the signal value of their concrete life within the *polis* is taken into account. In other words, the church needs to pay attention to the signals that it gives to people outside Christianity. The church also needs to elaborate its stance with regard to various philosophies and other ideologies that are effectively taught by the so-called false teachers who often promote ascetic practices.

With regard to the false teachers as well as with regard to the reputation of Christians in the eyes of the surrounding society, the Pastoral Epistles often recommend moderation. Christians should witness by their conduct, but exaggerated ascesis is problematic. Christianity offers a new way of life, but the Christian virtues are not totally different from the surrounding society. It is rather the case that the virtues of godliness, self-control, and the genuine care for others affirmed by the philosophers are more effectively practiced by Christians than by the rest of society. Christians should therefore show the distinctive character of their faith through the display of these generally accepted virtues that normally require moderation and peace of mind. Although their heart and spiritual eyes look toward the heavenly city, the civil life of Christians in their earthly *polis* is characterized by the striving after virtues that set an example for everyone.

The frequent use of materials that stem from the older canonical tradition underlines this twofold aim: the Pastoral Epistles want to continue the apostolic tradition of sound doctrine, but they also want to argue in which ways Christians can live in the broader society so that their conduct can witness to their faith in a constructive manner.

Given the overall theological dynamic between Athens and Jerusalem, it is necessary to add some words about the genre and structure of the Pastoral Epistles. Traditionally, the three epistles have been understood as Paul's handbook for pastors and church leaders. In addition to the discussions pertaining to character formation, the Pastoral Epistles employ materials from church tradition. This material underlines the theological and canonical continuity between the Gospels and the earlier Pauline texts and the Pastoral Epistles. Hanson (1982: 42–47) and Marshall (1999: 14) mention no less than nine groups of such materials:

1. extracts from church order (1 Tim. 3:1–7, 8–13; 5:3–16, 17–24; Titus 1:5–9)
2. domestic codes (1 Tim. 2:9–15; 6:1–20; Titus 2:1–10)
3. liturgical fragments (1 Tim. 3:16; 2 Tim. 2:11–13; Titus 2:11–14; 3:3–7)
4. confessional or homiletic statements (1 Tim. 2:4–6; 6:11–16)
5. lists of sinners or sins (1 Tim. 1:9–10; 6:4–5; 2 Tim. 3:2–5; Titus 3:3)
6. historical details about Paul's life (1 Tim. 1:3, 20; 5:23; 2 Tim. 1:5, 16; 2:17; 4:9–21; Titus 3:12–13)
7. Pauline passages transposed (1 Tim. 1:12, 20; 2:13–15; 3:15–4:10; 4:12; 5:18, 19; 6:3–5, 12; 2 Tim. 1:3–4, 6–8, 8–9, 9–10; 2:1–3, 8–13, 20–21; 3:2–4, 16–17; 4:6–8, 8, 11b)
8. midrash or haggadah on Scripture (1 Tim. 1:13–16; 2:3–4; 3:15; 2 Tim. 2:19; 3:7; 4:16–18)
9. direct exhortation and instruction (1 Tim. 2:1–2, 8–9; 5:1–2; 6:6–10, 17–19; 2 Tim. 2:2; 3:16; Titus 1:5, 12, 14; 3:10)

It is important that the distinct character of such materials is respected. They reflect doctrines, opinions, and practices that go back to the times of the Apostle Paul.

At the same time this traditional material becomes integrated into the network of character formation, and it appears in the context of philosophical and therapeutic insights. This state of affairs makes it difficult to discuss the overall aim and inner coherence of each epistle. The table of contents of this volume and the introductory paragraphs to the main parts of each epistle elucidate the structural decisions made in my exposition. In keeping with the distinctive profile of this commentary, the overall aim of all three Pastoral Epistles is considered to be educational and therapeutic rather than pastoral in the sense of church order or as a handbook for pastors.

The meaning of "educational" and "therapeutic" should be neither exaggerated nor downgraded. The Pastoral Epistles deal with sound doctrine and connect the word "sound" with health and the presence of judgment. This usage is not merely metaphorical imagery, but the author thinks in a strong sense that false teachers are mentally ill and in need of a strong cure. This conviction should not, however, be read in terms of modern medical science. The view of philosophical therapy and proper moderation of emotions assumes that mental disorders can be cured with dialogical discussion and persistent character formation. In this sense the Pastoral Epistles discuss the formation of Christian character and especially the character of various groups, such as bishops, widows, or rich people. Reading, listening, and practicing the advice given in the Pastoral Epistles can perhaps even be regarded as facilitating "self-help" for the groups mentioned. At the same time the Pastoral Epistles offer exemplary biographies, household codes, and models of liturgy and leadership.

In sum, the present commentary aims to present a distinct contribution to the exegetical and theological discussion, but it also aims at safeguarding the richness of traditions present in the Pastoral Epistles. Broader discussions on fundamental theological matters, for example, law and gospel, divine economy, the nature of the church and its ministries, are integrated into the commentary and can be identified from the subject index. In many cases these broader discussions appear as distinct excursuses. Sometimes I also investigate the interpretation history of crucial passages in more detail, as can be seen from the index of names. But, as the present work is a theological commentary, these discussions remain an essential part of the actual exposition.

The three appendixes aim at outlining the broader historical background of some relevant issues. Appendix A deals with the moderation of emotion; appendix B deals with the therapeutic philosophy of mental disorders; and appendix C outlines some anthropological concepts that relate to the complex idea of tradition as "keeping-while-giving."

As a last point, it should be mentioned that the Pastoral Epistles contain some difficult passages that challenge a modern theological interpreter to the utmost. The most difficult of these is 1 Tim. 2:11–15, the famous passage that speaks of the submission of women and their salvation through childbirth. It will hardly surprise any reader that the present interpreter has not found a philosopher's stone that would turn this passage into gold. In such cases my exposition can be defended only by Martin Luther's words: "Ist niemandt verboten ein besseres zu machen"; that is: "No one is forbidden to do better" or "We are all invited to give better explanations" (WA 30/2.633, 22–23; LW 35.183).

FIRST TIMOTHY

INTRODUCTORY PART

1 Tim. 1:1–20

The first chapter of 1 Timothy is also a complete literary unit. It begins with a greeting and is continued with a description of the task of Timothy, whom Paul has left in charge of the Christian church in Ephesus. Timothy should fight false doctrines and defend sound teaching. In this introductory admonition Paul does not extensively outline the content of sound teaching, but he employs a variety of doctrinal concepts that later played a prominent role in theology. These concepts include law and gospel, the use of the law, good conscience, and divine economy. The author stresses his own authority as an apostle and delegates both his own task and his authority to Timothy.

Because of this emphasis on apostolic authority, the style of the introductory part is often official and solemn. The unity of sound teaching and exemplary moral behavior become important topics. Paul uses his own biography as an example of the grace of Christ. The introductory part concludes with a reverse example: two persons have rejected conscience, and thus the apostle has turned them over to Satan. Through this contrast the apostolic authority is again highlighted.

Apostolic Greeting (1 Tim. 1:1–2)

The greeting employs traditional formulas but also some innovative wordings. As in other Pauline epistles, the opening consists of naming the author and the addressee, followed with a blessing. Unlike most epistles of the Pauline corpus, no cosenders are mentioned, and the greeting does not include a thanksgiving.

Although the epistle is not addressed to a congregation, but to an individual, the opening phrases are more official or authoritative than in most Pauline epistles.

Paul's own role is emphasized: he is "an apostle of Christ Jesus by the command of God." With the exception of 1 Thessalonians and Philemon, Paul in all his epistles calls himself an apostle of Jesus Christ. The phrase "by the command of God" (*kat' epitagēn*; cf. Titus 1:3) is more official and solemn than "by the will of God" (e.g., 1 Cor. 1:1). The phrase appears in many administrative letters of Hellenistic rulers (Roloff 1988: 54; Marshall 1999: 130–31), but here Paul simply stresses the plan of God for the salvation of humankind.

God is called "Savior" (cf. Luke 1:47; Jude 25). Hellenistic gods and rulers, and even other generous people, like mecenates, were called *sōtēr*. The designation may therefore have a polemical edge, namely, that only the Christian God can legitimately be called Savior. The characterization of Christ as "our hope" does not reflect any earlier source, and it may be an innovation of 1 Timothy. The word "hope" is employed in a comprehensive manner, alluding to the eschatological salvation that will be realized in Christ Jesus. The Pauline Epistles express Christian hope as a major virtue connected with salvation history.

Describing Timothy as "my loyal child in the faith" alludes to 1 Cor. 4:17 (maybe also Phil. 4:3), but here the tone of the apostle is again more official. The word "loyal" (*gnēsios*) can also be translated "legitimate" or even "real," though not in any biological sense but rather in true faith. Timothy is a legitimate child of the apostle. He has the right and power to defend the apostle's cause in all matters; he has inherited the right faith and will spread it further. The phrase *en pistei* ("in the faith") is not found in earlier Pauline epistles, but it appears also in 1 Tim. 1:4; 2:7, 15; and Titus 3:15. The phrase does not refer to subjective faith but to the heritage of faith and sound doctrine that Timothy defends.

The high rank of the Apostle Paul becomes emphasized through the claim that he is, in this sense, the father of Timothy. The command of God is realized in the very words of the apostle. Paul normally uses the bipartite phrase "grace and peace," but here the blessing is tripartite, including mercy. Mercy can be understood as a summarizing notion that characterizes God's salvatory action in Christ. Whereas grace points to this salvific action, mercy refers to its motivation and peace to its effects in the life of God's people. Christ and mercy are mentioned together in 1:16.

False Doctrines, Divine Economy, and Timothy's Task (1 Tim. 1:3–7)

The epistle presupposes that Paul writes to Timothy from Macedonia. After working together as missionaries in Ephesus, Paul has left Timothy there to lead and instruct this important congregation. Leaving the historical problems of this description aside (Roloff 1988: 62–63; Oberlinner 1994: 10–11), we can say that the author knows other Pauline epistles and Timothy's role in the history of Paul's missions (e.g., Acts 19:21–22; 1 Thess. 3:2; Phil. 2:19–22). As in other Pauline epistles, Timothy is a trusted figure who can be sent to solve problems and to teach the right doctrine during the absence of the apostle. Ephesus was a prominent place of Pauline missions and serves well as a paradigmatic case of handling problems related to the heritage of Paul and to the leadership of the church.

In 1 Tim. 1:3–4 the sentence beginning with *kathōs* ("as") is incomplete so that 1:5 begins a new sentence. The grammatical incompleteness need not be explained with conjectures, since the flow of thought is clear. Timothy is given the task of instructing "certain people" who occupy themselves with false and secondary thoughts. The verb "to instruct" (*parangellō*) appears in Paul's Epistles as a characterization of binding instructions that can be understood as the commands of the risen Lord Jesus (1 Cor. 7:10; 1 Thess. 4:2, 11). These instructions are contrasted with the "different doctrine" (*heterodidaskaleō*) mentioned in 1 Tim. 1:3. They represent the "sound teaching" (*hygiainousa didaskalia*) spoken of in 1:10.

Both the *heterodidaskaleō* (1:3) and the *hygiainousa didaskalia* (1:10) refer to the teaching of church doctrine. A third related phrase is the "teachers of the law" (*nomodidaskaloi*) in 1:7. Timothy is given the task of teaching sound doctrine, which is closely related to the right conduct. Right instruction and sound doctrine thus concern both the content of faith and the right moral conduct.

In 1:4 the different or false doctrine is concerned with "speculations" (*ekzēteseis*), whereas true faith and sound doctrine express the "divine training" (*oikonomia theou*). The Greek word employed for "speculations" does not appear anywhere else in the New Testament or in the Hellenistic literature, but it is obviously an emphatic form of *zētēseis* ("philosophical inquiries") (Marshall 1999: 362; Bauer 2000: 303). The author is critical of speculative philosophy, having perhaps 1 Cor. 1:18–21 in mind. He has a specific genre of speculation in mind, namely, "myths" and "genealogies." The word *mythos* may refer to many kinds of Hellenistic myths, for instance, pagan gods, stories of the origin of the world, esoteric and gnostic teachings in both Judaism (Titus 1:14) and other circles.

"Genealogies" refer to the speculative and allegorical interpretations of the catalogues of generations in Genesis. Such interpretations were popular in the esoteric circles of the first century, as we know from the Dead Sea Scrolls (1QS 3.13–15 [Vermes 2004: 101]) and some church fathers (see Gorday 2000: 131–32). Origen (*On First Principles* 4.3.2) and Theodore of Mopsuestia (*Commentary on 1 Timothy*) connect the genealogies mentioned here with Jewish teachers, whereas Irenaeus (*Against Heresies* 1.1) has the gnostic demiurge and creation myth in mind. Today's exegetes continue to discuss both sources, with an emphasis on Jewish genealogies (Roloff 1988: 64; Oberlinner 1994: 13–16; Marshall 1999: 366). The apostle's warning against myths and genealogies is directed against the intellectual and imaginative stimulation they provide: one should not believe in imagined stories, but had better trust the sound doctrine handed over by reliable witnesses.

"Divine training" means both God's plan for the universe and the execution of this plan. *Oikonomia* may be translated "training" in the sense of education, but in Hellenistic Greek the divine economy normally means the order established by God, who steers the universe according to the divine plan. This meaning is connected with the Christian view of salvation history. It is Timothy's task to instruct his fellow Christians of the divine plan that finds its expression in "sound teaching" (1:10) and is referred to as "the glorious gospel" (1:11).

Both this *oikonomia* and the idea that it is "known by faith" (1:4) contain a variety of intentions. Timothy is the master of the household, a church or parish. As such he is an *oikonomos*, a steward of God's salvific economy (Titus 1:7). In this economy faith cannot remain a personal or subjective faith, but it is loyalty to the message entrusted to him by the apostle. Thus faith in 1 Tim. 1:2 and 1:4 approaches the notion of orthodoxy, the right faith that becomes expressed in sound doctrine. Timothy's stewardship consists in this loyalty in which he is supposed to know and follow the divine economy.

In this manner divine economy and right faith become key concepts that set the tune for Timothy's activities. The larger part of 1 Timothy is concerned with right conduct and different concrete problems. Taking care of these problems should finally be measured against the background of the divine plan, the salvation history that is known by faith. The concept of *oikonomia* relates to the manifold reality of the communities in which the Christian individual lives and that are discussed throughout the Pastoral Epistles. The smallest community is that of an *oikos* ("household"). An individual learns the taking care of others within this social reality. The church and its various functions are often compared to the household (3:4–5, 15; 2 Tim. 2:20–21). Bishops and other stewards take care of this larger Christian community. The divine plan of salvation is the most comprehensive economy in which God steers the universe according to his will.

In the history of interpretation, this interplay of divine economy (sometimes translated "dispensation" or "edification") and personal faith has often yielded the conclusion that salvation is by faith. This is expressed by Chrysostom as follows: "For what is dispensed by faith? To receive his mercies and become better men; to doubt and dispute of nothing; but to repose in confidence.... Christ has said that we must be saved by faith; this these [false] teachers questioned and even denied" (NPNF[1] 13.410). In a similar vein Calvin concludes: "Knowing that all the worship of God is founded on faith alone, [Paul] therefore reckoned it enough to mention 'faith,' on which all the rest depend" (Calvin 1996: 25).

In 1:5 the opening phrase begins a new sentence that continues the theme of right instruction, pointing out its aim. *Agapē* ("love") is characterized by the three sources from which it is said to come: "pure heart," "good conscience," and "sincere faith." If the three gifts of God were "grace, mercy, and love" (1:2), these three human characteristics round out the Christian *agapē* that emerges as a result of instruction. In the Pastoral Epistles, Paul repeatedly employs similar tripartite groups (1 Tim. 2:15; 4:12; 2 Tim. 2:22; Titus 3:15). They should not be understood as permanent systematic topics. But it would also be misleading to treat them as merely pedagogical or rhetorical instruments. They are theological concepts that can be employed in several different but related ways.

Faith and love become almost synonymous in 1 Tim. 1:4–5, 14; 2:15; and 4:12. Theologically, 1:5 is not a sufficient picture of *agapē*, but only a description of the human, or subjective, affirmation of Christian love. Due to this subjective emphasis, *agapē* here resembles *pistis* ("faith"). In order to get a full picture of *agapē*, the Johannine ideas of God as love should be considered in a more comprehensive manner than is done in 1 Timothy. Pure heart and good conscience are here presented as the integral outcome of right instruction. But they do not define the content of sound doctrine. They witness to the theological truths without actually making them explicit.

"Pure heart" may reflect some aspects of Hellenistic ethics, for example, freedom from sinful passions, but it primarily alludes to the Jewish Bible, especially Ps. 51:10, which is also presupposed in Acts 15:9. The attribute "pure" may also contain a reference to baptism. Given the context of sinful deeds that are to be avoided (1 Tim. 1:9–13), pure heart and good conscience do not here refer to mere inner attitudes in the sense of Stoic inner life, but they comprise the actual conduct of well instructed Christians.

The same consideration pertains to the term "conscience" (*syneidēsis*). Paul and Pauline Christianity adopted this term from the Hellenistic world. *Syneidos* generally means the voice that points out the guilt or debt, being a reflection of the past. In addition to this, Paul also understands conscience to be capable of clarifying the existing norms and understanding the future (Rom. 2:15; Roloff 1988: 68–69; Plutarch, *On Tranquility* 19 [LCL 337.235–37]; Euripides, *Orestes* 391–97 [LCL 11.157]). The "good conscience" of 1 Tim. 1:5, 19 is again different from this Pauline meaning.

In 1:5, "good conscience" is a moral predicate that designates the right conduct of the well-instructed Christian. The phrase corresponds to the "pure heart" as a description of the good Christian existence. It may reflect early Christian baptismal formulas in which people were asked to have a "pure heart" (Roloff 1988: 67). Given this, the three virtues mentioned in 1:5 would be primarily connected with Christian initiation. This begins with a catechetical instruction and is followed by baptism that purifies the heart, gives a good conscience, and presupposes a sincere faith.

Paul thus stresses the right conduct but does not give an account of the content of sound doctrine. The content of sound baptismal instruction was probably known to the recipients of the epistle. But 1 Tim. 1 also avoids elaborate verbal formulations of sound doctrine. Myths and genealogies are criticized as empty speculations, and in 1:6–7 we again hear of "meaningless talk" (*mataiologia*; cf. 6:20 and Titus 1:10) performed by the people who desire to be teachers but have no understanding.

We are not informed of the actual position of the false teachers but learn only that they are wrong. Also in other parts of 1 Timothy (4:3; 6:4–10), their position is not explained in detail. Paul clearly disapproves that some baptized Christians do not find the instruction given to them to be sufficient. They want to speculate and practice empty or meaningless talk that leads to the loss of sincere faith and other basic virtues. These virtues are in 1:5–7 contrasted with examples of meaningless talk. Thus an ideal of simplicity emerges, an idea that prefers purity and sincerity and turns away from unnecessary commentaries and expositions.

In this undertaking of the apostle we find terminology that is also employed by the Hellenistic philosophers. The verb *ektrepō* means "to deviate or turn away" from the right way. The word *mataiologia* appears in Plutarch meaning "vain discussion" (*On Bringing Up Children* 9 [LCL 197.31]). In Hellenistic philosophical schools one also encounters the idea that a wise man should not talk too much (e.g., Epictetus, *Encheiridion* 33 [LCL 218.517]: "Be for the most part silent, or speak merely what is necessary, and in few words"; see Bauer 2000: 621 and G. Wohlfart and J. Kreuzer in *HWP* 8.1483–95).

Paul's critical attitude to idle talk is connected with other similar passages in the New Testament. Jesus reminds that "by your words you will be condemned" (Matt. 12:37). According to Jas. 3:6 the tongue "stains the whole body" and "is itself set on fire by hell." In keeping with this paradigm, 1 Timothy also considers silence to be a virtue. Still another perspective to the issue is offered by 6:4–5, where Paul again says that the false teachers "understand nothing" and even that they are "depraved in mind." Already in 1:6–7 one can read the text as saying that the turning to meaningless talk and the lack of understanding reflects a sort of psychopathology. People who are obstinately engaged with genealogies and who love meaningless talk have turned away from the ideals of clarity, sincerity, and silent learning (see appendix B).

The identity of "some people" described in 1:6–7 remains unclear. On the one hand the phrase "teachers of the law" clearly alludes to Judaism (as in Luke 5:17; Acts 5:34; 22:3). On the other hand, one can also think of talkative gnostics (1 Tim. 6:20) and, more generally, Christians who can master neither their tongue nor their moral conduct, although they desire to be teachers. The description of these people in 1:6–7 is not without sarcasm. Although the picture of the opponents remains vague, the ethos of a good Christian is portrayed in clear terms of purity and sincerity.

Law and Gospel, Doctrine and Conduct (1 Tim. 1:8–11)

In contrast to 1:6–7, Paul now outlines his authoritative view of the law. As in Rom. 7:16, the law is called "good" (*kalos*). The word *kalos* can also mean "fine" or "attractive." The Pauline writings employ both *kalos* and *agathos* of the law, its commandments, and the corresponding good works (Rom. 7:12, 16; Titus 1:16; 2:7). The added qualification "if one uses it legitimately [*nomimōs*]" is somewhat enigmatic, especially because 1 Tim. 1:9 seems to undermine the value of the law for pious persons. If the law actually concerns only the "lawless and disobedient" persons, does its "lawful use" mean punishing them? What would be the elegance or goodness of such use? If one reads 1:8–11 as a unity, there seems to be a gap between the two issues: the good use of the law and the glorious gospel (1:8, 11) on the one hand and the control of sinful people (1:9–10) on the other.

The Reformation, in particular Lutheranism, made "the use of the law" (*usus legis*) a prominent theological topic. It was 1 Tim. 1 that prompted Martin Luther to highlight this terminology. On the basis of Reformation theology and 1 Timothy it is possible to construe distinctions among punitive, civil, and parenetic uses of the law (Roloff 1988: 81–83, referring to Ebeling 1982: 282). Before doing that, however, the immediate context of Paul needs to be deepened.

The meaning of *nomimōs* in 1:8 can be connected with the verb *nomizō* in the sense "to consider as" in 6:5 ("creating a custom or making a law," according to Collins 2002: 156). The two terms are related to the ability to judge the situation in a customary manner. In 6:5 an idiosyncratic and false custom is described, but in 1:9 the law is put into practice in keeping with its own intentions. The good, or well-considered, use of the law is connected with the ability to judge the situation properly. Law is to be used in a "prudential" fashion, namely, so that it becomes "considered as" pertaining to the particular circumstances. A prudential person can apply moral rules to particular cases and has social skills in this manner (F. Wiedmann and G. Biller in *HWP* 4.857–63; P. Aubenque in *Der Neue Pauly* 6.608–9; and appendix B).

For a proper understanding of 1:8–11, it is illuminating to read the individual claims as units that are only loosely connected with each other. Without being actually incoherent, the apostle makes several different claims. In 1:8 he takes over the view of Rom. 7:16 but qualifies it in his own way. The goodness of the law consists in the right conduct of the good people. In our right conduct the law is tacitly employed as a social capital that allows people to live together. This life-form, or a rule of law, is not thought of as a series of commands, but losing this social capital leads to the vices mentioned in 1 Tim. 1:9–10.

Although 1 Timothy shows an awareness of Romans and other Pauline writings, it broadens the scope of the law in comparison with earlier Pauline epistles. In Romans and Galatians the law is above all the Torah of Israel. It was considered good because it contains God's promise and covenant with God's people as well as moral guidelines. Paul's criticism of this law in Romans and Galatians is motivated by the need to formulate a specific Christian soteriology in conscious distinction to Judaism (for the theological problems related to this complex issue, see Westerholm 2004). The Jewish law was not a way of salvation. In Pauline soteriology, the Jewish law can point out our sin, but it cannot heal it. Only in Christ do we have access to the reality of salvation.

In the Pastoral Epistles the situation is different. Pauline soteriology and the distinction from Judaism are taken for granted. New challenges are offered by the popular Hellenistic philosophy that taught that all people are aware of the basic moral laws that enable them to live together in a society. It would be pointless or very strange to criticize these basic natural laws in the way that Paul criticized the

Jewish law in Romans and Galatians. Romans 7:16 offers a bridge to affirm the basic moral laws as positive reality: even those who miss the ultimate moral mark may agree that the law is good. At the same time, the new context of 1 Timothy influences the understanding of *nomos*. The law is no longer primarily the Jewish Torah. The good law that is known is the natural order of the world; in Hellenistic philosophy, this *nomos* is accessible to reason (Roloff 1988: 72–74; Oberlinner 1994: 23–26).

Obviously, the Jewish Torah is not completely different from the Hellenistic *nomos*. In both, similar guidelines of right conduct are taught. Although the motivation to the right conduct and the background story related to the law may vary, the actual definitions of the good life remain similar. Paul therefore here stresses the "lawful," in the sense of well-considered or prudential, use of *nomos*. He presupposes a partial merger of the Jewish Torah and the Hellenistic moral law.

The *nomos* of 1:8–11 is not merely a natural moral law, but a law given or "laid down" (*keimai*; 1:9). This verb is employed when the validity and range of Jewish law is discussed. First Timothy 1:8–9 therefore preserves the Jewish background of *nomos*. In addition, as 1:5 points out, the actual good behavior stems from a pure heart and sincere faith that emerge as a result of sound doctrine. Thus we are in 1:8–11 concerned with theological ethics, not only with the Hellenistic understanding of *nomos*.

With the help of these observations, the theological distinction between law and gospel can be elaborated. Although law punishes the wrongdoers, it is important to realize that the law has many uses. In both Judaism and Hellenism, we can discern the "good law" that conforms to sound doctrine and the gospel (cf. 1:11). This good law can be used in punitive justice (1:9–10). Given the criticism of the law in Romans and Galatians, it would be misleading to see the law as a way of salvation, but it is nevertheless important that in 1 Tim. 1:8–11 the good law, the sound doctrine, and the glorious gospel are on the same side, in contrast to the wrongdoers and false teachers (1:7). This means that the Lutheran distinction between law and gospel should not be interpreted in terms of radical separation. As recent studies point out, Luther did leave room for a positive understanding of "good law" (Wöhle 1998; Raunio 2001; Saarinen 2006). To obtain a full picture, we need to see first how 1:9–11 relates the broader reality of divine economy.

The partial merger of Jewish and Greco-Roman ethics is clearly visible in the list of vices catalogued in 1:9–10. Paul does not here report the actual vices of the "certain people" (1:3) in Ephesus, but he describes the ultimate negative alternative: the imagined case of totally lawless people who emphatically act against the law and sound doctrine. The vices listed here break down the natural order and social capital available in human societies. As radical crimes against basic moral codes the fourteen vices identify the external boundaries of Hellenistic *nomos*.

At the same time, the fourteen vices display an affinity to the Jewish Decalogue. "Lawless and disobedient, . . . godless and sinful, . . . unholy and profane" commit sin against the first table of the Decalogue. "Those who kill their father or mother, . . . murderers, fornicators, sodomites, slave traders, liars, perjurers" act contrary to the second table. While this catalogue displays a proximity to both Hellenistic and Jewish ethics, it is also original. Only four of the fourteen vices appear in similar catalogues of popular philosophy (Roloff 1988: 75). The list also differs significantly from other lists available in the New Testament (Rom. 1:29–31; Gal. 5:18–21; 1 Tim. 6:4–5; 2 Tim. 3:2–5; Titus 3:3).

The originality of this particular list probably reflects its dramatic purpose: it is not given for moral guidance, but in order to identify the most terrible forms of lawlessness that are condemned in every society. Especially the crimes against the second table clearly mirror this purpose. The six vices mentioned first are more diffuse. In them Paul gives a general characterization of lawlessness as disobedience to God before proceeding to particular crimes. The closing phrase "and whatever else is contrary" (1 Tim. 1:10) stresses that the list is exemplary rather than complete.

Without going into the particular vices in detail, one may say that their theological understanding should pay attention to their content and purpose. The vices identify basic laws without which human dignity is lost and society cannot exist. When "the rule of law" in its most basic sense is lost, human beings become objects that can be traded, destroyed, and utilized in all possible ways. The list displays a certain affinity to the modern theories that relate the birth of human society to patricide, incest taboos, or successful control of violence (Girard 1977). In this sense the apostle is not only merging the Decalogue with philosophical ethics, but he also radicalizes the Decalogue to make visible the moral roots and taboos of human society.

First Timothy 1:10b–11 returns to the actual topic of the first chapter, namely, instruction, divine training and sound teaching. "Sound teaching" (1:10b) can often be translated "sound doctrine," which matches the NRSV's "different doctrine" in 1:3. *Hygiainousa didaskalia* clearly refers to an established body of teachings that Paul has handed over to Timothy and is now asking him to teach in Ephesus. We know only imperfectly what this body of doctrine actually says, but at least the gospel in Jesus Christ is meant (1:11).

In the New Testament, the distinct phrase "sound doctrine" is established only in the Pastoral Epistles (2 Tim. 4:3; Titus 1:9; 2:1). The adjective "sound" means literally "healthy" and could be so translated, as in the related phrases "healthy words" (1 Tim. 6:3; 2 Tim. 1:13; Titus 2:8) and "healthy in the faith" (Titus 1:13; 2:2). The Vulgate uses the Latin word for healthy in these places: *doctrina sana, verba sana, sani in fide.* Such phrases essentially belong to the language of the Pastoral Epistles. They witness that for the senders and recipients of these epistles an established set of criteria already existed for judging sound teaching.

The health metaphor is instructive when we tackle the difficult issue of the relationship between law and gospel, or more precisely: right conduct and sound doctrine. A contemporary reader of 1 Timothy is, to an extent, puzzled that sound doctrine is not opposed to the false doctrine but rather to the dramatic moral crimes. Obviously, sound doctrine is contrary to criminal acts, but 1:10–11, if taken literally, seems to imply that sound doctrine and the gospel would be concerned with the requirements of the law. This is, however, not the point. What the apostle claims is that the "good law" (1:8) is on the same side as what is held to be gospel and sound doctrine.

Although *hygiēs* ("healthy") can also mean reasonable and sound, the word in 1 Timothy points toward practical and behavioral components of doctrine (Oberlinner 1994: 28–30; Johnson 2001: 393–94). Becoming instructed in "healthy doctrine" and holding this doctrine in faith implies a healing of moral practices. The reality of salvation becomes transmitted in healthy doctrine, and this doctrine brings about the right conduct that is characteristic of Christian life. As we will see later (6:4–5), this view does not exclude the idea of reasonable doctrine, but integrates it into the more comprehensive picture of mental and intellectual health.

Such a behavioral or action-oriented interpretation of doctrine may be difficult for some Protestant denominations, for instance, the Lutheran churches, which traditionally distinguish between law and gospel, or faith and conduct, and hold that the Christian truth is not primarily an ethical view. But the Pastoral Epistles are not questioning that fundamental position. What is referred to as healthy doctrine does not receive its legitimation from morals, but from its being apostolic, namely, that it is handed over by Paul, an apostle of Christ Jesus (1:1). The Christian truth is not primarily an ethical matter.

At the same time, in 1:10 the doctrine is described as being in integral connection with law and morality. The apostle is not, however, primarily concerned with morals but rather with the divine *oikonomia* or "training" as a whole. This training proceeds through healthy doctrine. It is visible through the right conduct of the Christians, but at the same time it stems from a pure heart and sincere faith. It is therefore more of a life-form or cultural performance than a moral guideline or ethical conviction. In this sense "healthy doctrine" may perhaps be compared with some modern views of doctrine as a cultural-linguistic code that is expressed in conduct rather than in verbal sentences (see Lindbeck 1984; Vanhoozer 2005b; and the postscript).

The full picture of "law and gospel" that we can obtain from 1:8–11 is thus as follows: this Lutheran distinction points to the essential view that the Christian truth, the gospel, cannot be reduced to ethical matters. At the same time the distinction can be potentially misleading, if it entails the idea that the law would always remain in a contraposition to the gospel. The "good law" of 1:8 is on the same side with sound doctrine and the gospel. The divine economy, or the salvation history, entails the idea that Christians are educated in healthy doctrine that manifests itself as right conduct. Thus Christians can be expected to manifest their faith in their conduct. Affirming this to be the case does not, however, reduce gospel toward law or moral conduct. The legitimate use of the law needs to pay attention to this many-sided dynamic. The idea of "health-bringing doctrine" captures this dynamic.

Let it be just briefly noted that the practical dynamics of "law and gospel" is not so many-sided as its theoretical analysis. Most religious and other convictions consider it as self-evident that a firm conviction manifests itself as honorable public conduct. Moreover, they do not confuse the inner conviction with the external conduct merely because of this connection. It may rather be the Enlightenment view of "Hume's guillotine," that is, a philosophical separation of facts and values that lurks behind some modern ideas of religious conviction that is claimed as being totally separate from concrete character formation.

First Timothy 1:11 is liturgical in its use of *doxa* ("glorious") and *makarios* ("blessed"). The verse rounds out the first unit by using these terms, in particular through the emphasis that God has entrusted the gospel to Paul who has the authority to hand over this doctrine. For a deeper understanding of this verse one must define the relationship between sound doctrine and the gospel. The verse holds that the "glorious gospel" is the highest instance of Christian truth against which all teaching and doctrine is measured and to which it should conform.

Although the gospel is a higher and greater reality than our teaching, however healthy it may be, the presupposed view of *euangelion* in the Pastoral Epistles is many-sided. The term appears four times (1 Tim. 1:11; 2 Tim. 1:8, 10; 2:8), always denoting the revelatory event of God in Jesus Christ. Also in 1 Tim. 1:11 the word "glorious" points toward revelation. This gospel is entrusted to the apostle to the extent that he may speak of "my gospel" (2 Tim. 2:8). As Paul's theology of handing over the gospel entails both the idea of "giving" and the idea of "keeping" (see excursus 6 and appendix C), such phrases should not be read as meaning that Paul would develop a particular understanding of his message. He is always handing over the gospel of Christ.

Whereas earlier Pauline epistles speak of the "gospel of Christ" (e.g., Rom. 15:19) that is proclaimed by the first Christians, the Pastoral Epistles connect the gospel strongly with the authority and legitimacy of the apostle. In this sense the term "gospel" approaches "sound doctrine." Although the gospel is introduced in 1 Tim. 1:11 as fundamental reality and the criterion of healthy doctrine, it is also an established body of Christian truths entrusted to the teaching authority.

For these reasons it would be exaggerated to make a systematic distinction between "doctrine" and "gospel" in 1:10–11. One can say that "healthy doctrine" is a behavioral reality transmitted through instruction, whereas the "glorious gospel" is the fundamental truth available in Jesus Christ. In concrete reality, both go hand in hand (for the mutual relationship of "gospel," "apostolic deposit," and "scripture," see excursus 8).

Commission of Paul as Apostle (1 Tim. 1:12–17)

After this outline of healthy doctrine, Paul undertakes a self-description of his own task as apostle. A modern reader easily doubts whether this passage is a self-portrait or a portrait drawn by an admiring follower. I will not investigate such historical issues in detail but will simply speak of "Paul," meaning both the author and the model of this portrait (for the issue of authorship, see the introduction to the Pastoral Epistles).

In this self-portrait Paul is depicted as a model Christian who is made "an example to those who would come to believe" (1:16). At the same time, the passage is a small treatise of Christology, describing the work of Christ in simple terms. As in 1:1–11, the passage begins (1:12) and ends (1:17) with solemn, liturgical, and official statements that underline the divine calling of the apostle. At the same time these statements imitate other Pauline writings in which giving thanks to God is typical of Paul's style.

Christ Jesus is again (1:2, 14) called our Lord. In this typical confessional formula the word "our" marks a distinction to the people criticized above. The idea of strengthening echoes Phil. 4:13. At the same time it relates to healthy doctrine. This doctrine has healed the apostle, who was earlier, as 1 Tim. 1:13 points out, an impious and lawless person. But now Paul is appointed to the "service" (*diakonia*) of Christ. Although this *diakonia* is not a distinct position, 1:12 probably presupposes some kind of ministry (Vulgate: *ponens in ministerio*). God has instituted or appointed Paul to this ministerial task or service, and as such it represents an apostolic ministry.

The view that God "judged me faithful" may be loosely connected with the justification of the sinner in other Pauline epistles (Romans and Galatians). The event of judging is not merely forensic, but it also creates justice or faithfulness. At the same time, as John Chrysostom points out, the judgment of divine forgiveness contains the idea of remembering the sins: "Although I have received the remission of sins, I do not reject the memory of those sins" (*Homilies Concerning the Statues* 12.1 [Gorday 2000: 141]; Roloff 1988: 92; Spicq 1969: 340–41).

In a way, precisely this is done in 1:13, in which Paul recollects his pre-Christian sins. The verse is difficult, since Paul here identifies his former self with the false teachers criticized above. In Phil. 3:6 he describes his own former existence as that of a "blameless" Pharisee whose faults were not of a moral nature but consisted in seeking righteousness under the law. It may be granted that he, as Saul, was a persecutor of some Christians (Gal. 1:13), but hardly a blasphemer or an arrogant wrongdoer, a *hybristēs* ("a man of violence"). The verse should not be read as a part of the apostle's biography but as a paradigmatic example of how a Christian improves after meeting Christ and receiving mercy.

The difficult end of 1 Tim. 1:13 seems to relativize this picture to an extent. "Act[ing] ignorantly in unbelief" should not, however, be regarded as an excuse for Paul's former sins, but it belongs to the paradigmatic picture: a godless and faithless person is also ignorant. The fact of "receiv[ing] mercy" (1:13) or of being "judged . . . faithful" (1:12) is not founded on any hidden quality or excuse visible only to God, but God in these acts anticipates the future improvement of Paul and his future role as apostle. After receiving God's mercy, Paul may be able to see his own past both as sinful and also in a somewhat better light, admitting that ignorance had something to do with his earlier sinfulness. It is not an excuse, but an aspect to be mentioned together with the memory of those sins.

Although this may be the actual flow of Paul's thought in 1:13, a reader who needs theological consistency may still ask whether Paul actually makes two different and unrelated points: (1) that he was a very bad person, and (2) that he was ignorant and was therefore granted mercy. In 1:16 Paul says that he "received mercy" not because of his ignorance but "for that very reason"—meaning that he was a sinner.

For the paradigmatic purposes of this conversion story, it is important to realize that God in Jesus Christ acted out of grace and mercy with regard to Paul. The idea of "receiving mercy" appears in both 1:13 and 1:16. In both verses, God's mercy appears to be a preparatory stage in the process of salvation. It is a divine attitude in which God does not proceed to punitive justice but allows room for other considerations. Readiness to help people who have no lawful right to such help essentially belongs to the attitude of mercy. Loyalty and solidarity with the helpless people are also presupposed. At the same time, God's mercy is a prerequisite of salvation rather than salvation itself.

In 1:14 Paul describes the positive change that occurred when he became a Christian. Grace is here, as elsewhere in Pauline theology, an eschatological reality of salvation that already here and now permeates and improves the life of a human being. Paul speaks of the "flow" or "fullness" of grace in Rom. 5:20; 6:1; and 2 Cor. 4:15; here the term "overflowed" (*hyperepleonasen*) stresses the fullness of grace in a superlative manner and in dramatic contrast to his earlier sinfulness.

Faith and love are the primary gifts of this grace. Using the Pauline idiom "in Christ," the apostle stresses that these two are gifts in the sense that they are given to us. The verse also relates to 1 Tim. 1:5: the apostolic instruction aims at bringing forth love that comes from sincere faith. But whereas faith and love in 1:5 are displayed as human virtues, in 1:14 they are characterized as gifts of grace. There is no contradiction between the two, since the exemplary Christian receives everything from God in Christ. Through this reception process, he becomes a participant of a new reality and a new communion.

As elsewhere in the Pauline writings, the phrase "in Christ" has an ecclesiological aspect. Faith and love characterize the new community of Christians. Later in 1 Timothy, Paul turns to the concrete instructions regarding church life, but already here he paints an ideal picture of faith and love that should characterize every Christian living in the new community.

In 1:15 Paul turns away from self-description and recites an elementary confession: "Christ Jesus came into the world to save sinners." The grace that is operative in Paul is thus declared to be universally valid. The confession presupposes some important doctrinal motives of salvation history, at least the incarnation and maybe the preexistence of Christ. Paul is most probably employing an already existing confession that resembles some sayings of the Synoptic Gospels (e.g., Luke 19:10) (Oberlinner 1994: 43).

More importantly, 1 Tim. 1:15 continues the overarching theme of divine economy as salvation history. Within this economy, Jesus Christ receives many different but related roles in the Pastoral Epistles. He is depicted as "mediator" and as human being (2:5). He is addressed as "great God and Savior" (Titus 2:13). The coming of Jesus Christ is often called "epiphany" (1 Tim. 6:14; 2 Tim. 1:10; 4:1, 8). This term can relate to both the recent past, meaning incarnation, or the future, underlining the eschatological expectation. The Pastoral Epistles thus already contain a rich Christology in which Jesus Christ becomes described as God and human, as mediator who came into the world and will come in the future "to judge the living and the dead" (2 Tim. 4:1).

Although these aspects are probably assumed in 1 Tim. 1:15, I will leave their treatment to the verses in which they are explicitly mentioned. In 1:15 the focus is on salvation as the fulfilment of the divine plan. Paul has expressed above (1:5, 8) his appreciation of the good law and good conscience, but he nevertheless emphasizes that salvation concerns sinners. The way of salvation that Jesus Christ has opened is not the way of the law, but it has to do with mercy and *makrothymia* (1:16), which are divine rather than human attributes.

The vocabulary of salvation and Savior further employs the medical metaphor of sickness and healing and is thus connected with "healthy" doctrine. This vocabulary is carried over to later Christian expositions. Augustine, for instance, interprets this verse in using a medical view of incarnation: "If a great doctor has come down from heaven, a great invalid must have been lying very sick. . . . This invalid is the whole human race" (*Sermons* 175.1 [Gorday 2000: 144]).

The end of 1:15 returns to Paul in a somewhat puzzling manner. Why is Paul the "first" (*prōtos*) sinner? He is a prototype of the sinner who receives grace, as the paradigmatic story of 1:12–17 tells us. The phrase is also connected with 1 Cor. 15:9: Paul is the least of the apostles, the foremost of the sinners. In addition to these motives, 1 Timothy also wants to say that Paul is the first sinner to be saved. Thus he represents a direct apostolic line from the salvation event to Timothy and his church.

It is also remarkable that Paul now speaks in the present tense. Does he consider himself still as sinner, in keeping with the Lutheran idea of "justified and sinner at the same time"? Or is this a sort of dramatic emphasis in order to say that God's saving work is not only history, but takes place here and now? Since in 1:16 Paul again moves to the past tense, it may be inadequate to speak of the Christian Paul as the prototype of a sinner.

The "reason" (*dia touto*) for Paul's receiving mercy is not some hidden quality or ignorance (as noted in 1:13), but simply the sinner's need for mercy. In 1:13

and 1:6 the reasons and causes mentioned may confuse a modern reader. Paul is not seeking an argumentative foundation for God's mercy, but he simply points out the causative sequence. God sees that this person can be made good only through mercy and grace. This need moves God in Christ to give the gifts of grace to Paul, the sinner. The word *makrothymia* ("utmost patience") in 1:16 employs the same logic.[1] This word is sometimes employed in the New Testament of God (Matt. 18:26; 1 Pet. 3:20), but Paul here thinks that Jesus Christ participates in the divine judgment, acting as a judge who exercises *makrothymia* instead of punitive justice. First Timothy 1:15–16 thus employs a rich Christology that stretches from possible preexistence through incarnation to the eschatological, but also present, judgment. The use of *makrothymia* lends Christ a divine attribute.

God is called *makrothymos* already in the Septuagint (e.g., Exod. 34:6). Given the nature of mercy as God's free decision to show sympathy and even *makrothymia*, one does not need to seek reasons for why mercy is shown. But, as in 1 Tim. 1:13, Paul wants to elucidate the general significance of this mercy. Through the merciful act Jesus Christ makes Paul a *hypotypōsis* ("example") in the sense "model, paradigm, prototype" for other Christians. *Hypotypōsis* is not primarily a moral example; it is rather the life story of Paul, which can be employed as an illustration of how the gospel is operative.

The paradigmatic story does not primarily depict Paul or his qualities, but it witnesses to the utmost patience of God in Jesus Christ. It is further meant to reflect God's mercy and the grace of God that brings forth the gifts of faith and love. Above all, it witnesses to the salvation in Jesus Christ. In this sense the story told in 1:12–16 should be employed as a paradigm for "those who would come to believe in him for eternal life."

The story narrated in 1:12–16 is clear in its theological purpose: through presenting an autobiography of Paul, some central insights of Christology and soteriology are highlighted. The story also strengthens the authority of Paul as an apostle. The most important purpose of this story is to present a paradigm of Christian existence based on mercy, grace, faith, and love, all of which are provided to sinners through the utmost patience of God in Christ.

The doxology that appears in 1:17 is most probably taken from early Christian liturgical practice. Its vocabulary resembles Jewish and Greco-Roman counterparts. "King of the ages" appears in Jer. 10:10; Tobit 13:7, 11; and Rev. 15:3. "Immortal" and "invisible" resemble philosophical language, but are also compatible with Judaism (Philo, *Moses* 2.171 [LCL 289.533]; *Cherubim* 101 [LCL 227.69]; see Marshall 1999: 405). "The only God" is a general biblical phrase that connects the doxology with the universalist view expressed in 1 Tim. 2:5.

---

1. Although this concept has Jewish/Septuagint origins (see J. Horst in *TDNT* 4.374–87), it may be said that it connotes a "positive" suffering or passion of God. See also the positive *epithymia* in 3:1 and appendix B.

Given that the significance of Jesus Christ is emphasized in the preceding passages, one may wonder why this doxology employs many Greco-Roman predicates. Since 1:12–16 speaks of Christ without mentioning God, it may be proper to address God in 1:17. And since 1:12 marks the beginning of the autobiographical story that is essentially christological, a theological balance is achieved by 1:17.

Admonition to Timothy (1 Tim. 1:18–20)

First Timothy 1:18–20 concludes the introductory part. These verses also prepare for the actual instructions that begin in 2:1. The key word is *parangelia* ("instructions"), relating to both 1:3–5 and the particular teachings given below. The instructions are not simply "given," since the verb *paratithēmi* here means that the recipient is endowed with responsibility and power over the instruction received. The apostle solemnly hands over his message as well as his authority and responsibility to Timothy. The recipient is again (cf. 1:2) called "my child," which may imply the idea of legal heir.

What are the "prophecies made earlier" about Timothy? A possible clue is given in Acts 13:1–3, in which the ordination of Barnabas and Saul is described and the ministry of prophets is mentioned. Similar allusions can be read from 1 Tim. 4:14. We do not know for certain whether the ordination liturgies of the early church included or presupposed prophets and prophecy, but it is likely that 1:18 refers to Timothy's ordination, in which at least prophetic texts were read and their message was applied to the ordained persons. It is even possible that the Latin term *praefatio* in the ordination liturgy comes from "prophecy." The two terms are coined already in Tertullian (*Apology* 18.5 [ANF 3.32]; Roloff 1988: 101–2). In speaking of Timothy's ordination, I will simply leave open the complex historical discussion whether and in what sense this ritual contained more than the commission present in Act 13:1–3 (see Marshall 1999: 409–10 and excursus 2). In keeping with this decision, I will not label Timothy as "bishop," but will speak of him as "church leader."

When Timothy follows the prophetic prayers recited in his ordination, he may "fight the good fight." In this phrase we again meet the metaphoric language of the Hellenistic world, this time transferred from warfare and sport. This language is taken over from other Pauline epistles in which it is extensively used. Paul does not, however, apply this imagery to moral life in general, but concentrates on the tasks of apostolic service and church leadership (e.g., 1 Cor. 9:24–27; 2 Cor. 10:3–6; Phil. 1:27–30). The minister's task is described in terms of athletics and warfare. A Christian leader is called to compete with others and to fight against those people and circumstances that prevent the proclamation of the gospel.

In his task as church leader, Timothy participates in the same fight as the apostle. In order to fight a good fight he also needs "faith and a good conscience." These were already mentioned in 1 Tim. 1:5, but in 1:19 the phenomenon of conscience is particularly highlighted. Faith comes from our Lord Jesus Christ and remains loyal to the good instruction received (1:5, 14). As in 1:5, the good conscience is here a moral term denoting the right conduct of the Christian. As faith and love are very closely connected in 1 Timothy, so too is good conscience an indication that the faithful persons have preserved their integrity in actual moral conduct.

In this moral sense conscience is self-consciousness, "knowing with" oneself. An ordained leader like Timothy who is entrusted with authority and healthy doctrine must be able to consider himself as "healthy" not only in terms of pure doctrine but in his moral conduct. Faith is the believer's attitude; good conscience is the ability of one's self-consciousness to affirm this attitude without inner doubts or misgivings. Because people are endowed with conscience, they cannot simply believe and act contrary to this belief at the same time. In this way the phenomenon of conscience preserves the personal integrity.

The picture of "shipwreck" is taken from Greco-Roman imagery, in which it is a general metaphor of human failure (Marshall 1999: 412). People who "reject conscience" are Christians who in their moral conduct have not followed the "healthy" path of doctrine. Hymenaeus and Alexander are portrayed as examples of shipwrecked people. Their names also appear in 2 Tim. 2:17 (Hymenaeus) and 4:14 (Alexander), but otherwise they remain unknown. Given the context of ordination and leadership, they may have been ordained leaders.

Theologically more interesting and challenging is the statement that Paul has turned these two over to Satan "so that they may learn not to blaspheme" (1 Tim. 1:20). The verse alludes to 1 Cor. 5:5. In both verses, the event of handing over is not merely a punishment or a final destruction, but Paul attaches some educational value (*paideuō* in 1 Tim. 1:20) to this act. In 1 Cor. 5:5 the act is performed to save the sinner; here, Hymenaeus and Alexander are expected to learn better. The imagery of pedagogical and medical hell, in which the sinners were healed or learned to be better, was surprisingly common in patristic times and still later played a certain role, especially in Eastern Christianity. Although it sounds very strange that Satan could teach the heretics to learn better, such ideas were extensively applied by later and more speculative Christian theologians (Vorgrimler 1994 offers an abundant supply of patristic material on medical and pedagogical hell).

On a more concrete and everyday level, 1 Tim. 1:20 and 1 Cor. 5:5 probably describe some disciplinary acts in metaphorical terms. Sinners and heretics were to be excommunicated from the church in order that they may repent and return to faithful doctrine and a morally good life. Given this concrete meaning, one can pay attention to some differences between the two verses. In 1 Cor. 5:5 it needs the decision of a church assembly "with the power of our Lord Jesus" to execute the act of excommunication. But here Paul is performing this act by himself. The recipients of 1 Timothy nevertheless may have understood this act to have required more decision-making bodies. But as it stands, the text clearly ascribes more disciplinary power to the apostle than most other Pauline writings. This is in keeping with the high rank of the apostle throughout 1 Timothy.

A mature theological understanding of 1 Tim. 1:20 would require some answer to the most difficult question, namely, whether this kind of solitary authority is a model to be followed in the Christian church. The author clearly intends his behavior to incorporate such a model. In order to decide otherwise, a theologian needs to relativize the role of this text by other canonical texts. In addition, one needs to question the sense in which contemporary church leaders have an apostolic authority to perform disciplinary measures. At the same time, one should see that in both 1 Corinthians and 1 Timothy the intention is not to punish or to destroy, but to educate and finally to save the person in question. Harsh language is thus connected with the optimistic ideas of a pedagogical (1 Tim. 1:20) or purifying (1 Cor. 5:5) Satan.

WORSHIP, LIFE, AND ORDER IN THE CHURCH

1 Tim. 2:1–3:16

After the introductory part Paul moves to his actual instructions. As he writes in 3:14–15, these practical guidelines are given in order that the recipients know "how one ought to behave" in the church. Although the NRSV adds "instructions" in 3:14, one cannot simply identify this teaching with the *parangelleō* of 1:3–5 and still less with the "healthy doctrine" of 1:10. Doctrine and teaching are generally concerned with the "glorious gospel" (1:11) expressed in the salvific mission of Jesus Christ, whereas 2:1–3:16 describes the behavioral guidelines for men, women, bishops, and deacons. They can also be called "instructions" (1:18), but such guidelines tell us rather how orthodox Christians ought to look and act rather than what they teach.

Paul wants to say that doctrine and external behavior are closely related. In their worship and moral life Christians should display certain characteristics. They are an aspect of the legitimate, or well-considered, use of the law (1:8). If someone teaches otherwise, a case of *heterodidaskaleō* emerges (6:3). At the same time, the guidelines clearly concern the church order. An interpreter of 1 Timothy should reflect the relationship between the concrete church order and the foundational gospel message of salvation in Jesus Christ. Such hermeneutical considerations are of particular importance because the passage contains views that are neither shared by many other early Christian writings nor adopted by later churches.

For the understanding of this passage it is important to notice that the behavioral instructions are motivated by the absence of Paul. As 3:15 clearly points out, the truth of the Christian message is endowed to the *ekklēsia* ("church"). In this way, the apostolic instruction remains among the faithful even during the absence of the apostle. Tradition thus begins to take the place of immediate apostolic proclamation. The abstract use of the concepts "truth" and *ekklēsia* in 3:15 underline the issue that Paul is not only giving particular instructions to Timothy but intends to express universal truths relevant to all congregations, pastors, and bishops in his own times and after him.

As in 1 Tim. 1, a liturgical and official statement is made before and after the actual instructions. These statements (2:1–7; 3:15–16) are particularly elaborate and solemn. They reveal many aspects of the doctrine and liturgy of the early Christians, to the extent that one may discuss whether the whole of 2:1–3:16 is more concerned with worship and liturgy than with church order. An interpreter needs to make some hermeneutical decisions concerning the mutual relationships among (1) the order of worship, (2) moral discipline, and (3) other rules regulating the life of the church and its ministers. The text makes clear that these three realities do not exist in separation from one another or from the underlying sound doctrine. At the same time, conceptual distinctions among all these different ways of ordering church life remain necessary.

Pray for Everyone: Christianity Is Universal (1 Tim. 2:1–7)

The solemn beginning of the passage is not only a liturgical ornament or a theological foundation, but also a concrete instruction and advice. The Christian church ought to pray for everyone, including kings and other rulers who are not themselves Christians. A theological and moral issue was faced by the early congregations: may a Christian pray for a pagan ruler, in particular if such a prayer is required as an act of obedience and good citizenship? Paul's answer is positive: yes, you may do that. If you have conceded to such prayer in order to show honor or gratitude and to live in peace, you have done nothing wrong. God wants everyone to be included in the prayer, since God wants everyone to be saved.

Paul here uses four different terms denoting prayer and claims that they can all be said "for everyone." In a "supplication" (*deēsis*) a person simply brings his or her issue before God, whereas a "prayer" (*proseuchē*) generally means an act of a worshiping group. Given their synonymous use in 5:5, they may also here synonymously denote the prayers said in a Christian worship. The third term, *enteuxis*, which in Greek simply means asking for something, is probably synonymous with the fourth one, *eucharistia* (1 Tim. 4:4–5). This last term means "thanksgiving" and "praise," and it is often connected with the Eucharist (see Roloff 1988: 113–14; Johnson 2001: 189).

Although *eucharistia* does not here technically refer to the Eucharist, the context makes it likely that the author is speaking of various prayers said during the worship. Matthew's words of institution (26:28) employ the phrase "for many" (*peri pollōn*), which ascribes an extended, if not universal, significance to the Eucharist. The different prayers said "for everyone" (*hyper pantōn*) thus do not only refer to a general intercession, but the author ascribes to them a rich theological significance that is developed further in 1 Tim. 2:3–7.

In 2:2 Paul introduces several concepts that have played a prominent role in Christian spirituality. A "peaceful and quiet" life does not primarily mean that one complies with rulers to avoid trouble, but the two virtues belong to the broader Christian ideal of life. As elsewhere in his epistle, Paul is interested in the outward behavior of Christians: they should look calm and keep quiet. The word *hēsychios* ("silent") later came to mean a specific Eastern spirituality in which one refrains from talking. Already in 2:2 the description bears similarities to the Stoic philosophical therapy in which one becomes virtuous through the mastering of one's own emotions and the ability to not waste words (F. von Lilienfeld in *Theologische Realenzyklopädie* 15.282–89 and appendixes A–B). Earlier Jewish and Christian texts (Isa. 66:2; 2 Thess. 3:12; Matt. 5:5; Jas. 3:6), which are similar, are also taken into account. The ideal of silence is later applied to women (1 Tim. 2:11–12; see also 2:8); but here, as in Matt. 12:36, it concerns everyone.

The word *eusebeia* ("godliness") is introduced as a Christian virtue in 1 Tim. 2:2. Its background is found in Hellenistic ethics, in which it means the proper respect of gods.[1] This virtue appears often in the Pastoral Epistles, but is only sporadically mentioned elsewhere in the New Testament (Acts 3:12; 10:2, 7; 17:23; 2 Pet. 1:3, 6–7; 2:9; 3:11). The virtue of proper respect fits well with the official tone of the apostle. Although the notion of God is connected with this virtue, it is not of Christian but of Greco-Roman origin. The context generally advises Christians to an external behavior that creates public trust through a display of proper moral qualities. Thus a "civil religion" visible in *eusebeia* is recommended. Theologically, however, the term evokes the issue of whether Christians just exercise the same kind of civil godliness as other people.

On the one hand, *eusebeia* belongs together with quietness and *semnotēs* ("dignity"), another Hellenistic virtue denoting serious and well-ordered behavior. Christian behavior is here connected with the civil virtues and values of the surrounding society. This may reflect Paul's antignostic attitude: the virtues of faith are not esoteric and hidden, but they belong rather to the public sphere and are manifested in the everyday behavior among all people. The theme of godliness thus continues the view discussed above (1:8–11) as the dynamics of law and gospel: the public nature of Christian virtue.

On the other hand, Christian godliness does not indicate only a civil virtue. As 2 Tim. 3:5 points out, one may have the external form of *eusebeia* without true conviction. Genuine *eusebeia* is characterized as "knowledge of the truth" in Titus 1:1. Healthy doctrine is in accordance with true godliness (1 Tim. 6:3). The Hellenistic virtue thus has a specific content in Christianity: it manifests the

---

1. Marshall 1999: 135–44 offers a useful survey of the history of interpretation of this concept. While he stresses the distinctively Christian features of the concept, Roloff 1988: 117–19 connects *eusebeia* more strongly with Hellenism. See also Collins 2002: 122–26.

healthy doctrine that the Christian has adopted. *Eusebeia* fulfills an important argumentative role in 1 Timothy: it is the virtue that connects healthy doctrine with right conduct.

Extending this thought, one may say that the role of *eusebeia*—in theological ethics to an extent at least—resembles the function of prudence (*phronēsis*) in Aristotelian ethics. As prudence is the virtue of finding the concrete particular acts that correspond to the general moral truths (F. Wiedmann and G. Biller in *HWP* 4.857–63), so *eusebeia* denotes a skill of actually behaving in a way that communicates the adoption of healthy doctrine in right conduct. One probably cannot read too much into this analogy, but it is important to see that the Vulgate, and thus later Western Christianity, translates *eusebeia* with *pietas* and *semnotēs* with *castitas*. *Pietas*, too, was a civil virtue, but in Christianity it became a generic term for spirituality. This has remained a valid rendering; many new translations employ words corresponding to Latin *pietas* (e.g., German *Frömmigkeit*). *Eusebeia* is thus not only proper respect, but it expresses an inner spiritual conviction formed by healthy doctrine.

In spite of this Christian specification, the phrase "for everyone/all" (2:1, 6) and the term "everyone/all" (2:2, 4) remain the key words of 2:1–7. Paul wants to stress the universal or "ecumenical" nature of the gospel message: God wants "everyone to be saved" (2:4).[2] As in Titus 1:1, *eusebeia* is connected in 1 Tim. 2:4 with "the knowledge of the truth" (*epignōsin alētheias*; cf. 2:7). The universality of Christian truth thus concerns everyone. In 2:4–7 Paul is not primarily defining the relationship between the Jewish and the Christian faith, but a universal context is presupposed.

The repetition of the words "everyone" and "truth" ascribes a very public and an almost philosophical significance to the Christian message. God is not interested in saving a particular group of people who claim an esoteric *gnōsis* (6:20), but God's truth is public and concerns everyone. Paul's being a "herald and apostle" (2:7) is motivated by the universality of his message. The central phrase "knowledge of the truth" (2 Tim. 2:25; 3:7; Titus 1:1) says two things: (1) the message must be known, that is, understood personally and in a communicative manner; and (2) through employing the word "truth" instead of "faith" or "doctrine," the author stresses the objective and universal counterpart, the object of this knowledge. It is thus not faith as an imaginative construct that is required, but rather a trustful understanding of objective facts and events.

A comprised outline of these facts and events is given in 1 Tim. 2:5–6a. These two verses are composed in a liturgical fashion that connects them with many other liturgical and otherwise solemn or official parts of 1 Timothy. The liturgical part ends emphatically with "for all," which, as noted, alludes to both the eucharistic liturgy ("for many" in Matt. 26:28) and the general universalism present in 1 Tim.

---

2. As Pfnür 1970: 132–33 points out, this statement was too inclusive for Luther, who preferred to translate: "God wants to help/heal everyone."

2:1–7. In addition, "one" and "all" are here contrasted with each other. It is likely that 2:5–6a comes from an earlier liturgical source.

"There is one God" states the common starting point of Jewish and Christian faith. Given the soteriological context, it refers to Rom. 3:30. The description of Christ as "one mediator" (*heis mesitēs, unus mediator*) is a strong theological statement, especially since the word "mediator" is otherwise applied to Jesus only in Heb. 8:6; 9:15; 12:24. This word can mean many things in Hellenism and Judaism. It is often connected with different legal settings (Roloff 1988: 121–22). Here, however, no clearly forensic context is visible. As the task of the mediator concerns the relationship between God and humankind, one may reasonably assume some kind of reconciliation between the two parties. Philo can say of Moses that he was a mediator and reconciler between God and Israel (*Moses* 2.166 [LCL 289.531]).

For a theological understanding of "mediator," one must define the relationship of this term to the other two important concepts of 1 Tim. 2:5–6a, namely, that Jesus was "human" (*anthrōpos*) and that he gave himself as "ransom" (*antilytron*). Whereas Mark 10:45 says that Jesus came to give his life as ransom "for many," 1 Tim. 2:6 stresses the universality of this ransom. The prefix *anti-* does not change the nature of ransom, but emphasizes the view that Jesus gave himself as a substitute for a larger group. As a human being he belonged to that larger group and can therefore act as its representative or substitute. Thus, while "one mediator" remains a title of honor and prominence, the humanity of Jesus nevertheless connects him with the group of human beings who are in need of mediatory reconciliation.

As in many other New Testament texts that speak of the self-giving of Jesus Christ, the recipient of the ransom is not mentioned in 2:5–6a. Jesus Christ is the giver and the gift, all humans are the beneficiaries, but we are not told who is the recipient of this gift. Later developments of atonement theology have proceeded from this observation. They often aim at answering the issue to whom the payment is made, how it is made, and what it effects (see Saarinen 2005 and appendix C). This theological elaboration allows room for various theories of atonement that are compatible with 2:5–6.

In this sense, "mediator" and "ransom" in 2:5–6 define an open sector within which various more specific theories of atonement can be further elaborated. It may be safe to say that this particular passage lends some support for an Anselmian theory of atonement, for two reasons: (1) because the humanity of Christ is absolutely necessary both here and in Anselm's theory; and (2) because 2:5–6 bears no indication of the so-called devil-ransom theory that Anselm of Canterbury opposes, claiming that the ransom is to be paid to God, not to the devil (*Cur deus homo* 1.7 [Anselm 1988]). The idea of a mediation between God and humans assumes that the self-giving act of this one human, Jesus Christ, is directed to God and that no third party is involved in the mediation.

The phrase "this was attested at the right time" (2:6b) again returns to Paul's own prose. The attestation or witness (*martyrion*) here refers more strongly to

the apostle's own proclamation than it does to the act of God in Jesus Christ described in 2:5–6a. The "right time" is the time of the apostle, the last days of the
apostolic *kērygma* or teaching. The apostle is "herald" (*kēryx*) because he preaches
this truth. Mentioning "the truth" twice in emphatic terms in 2:7, Paul underlines
the authoritative character of the whole passage (2:1–7).

How Men and Women Should Behave (1 Tim. 2:8–15)

Paul now proceeds to more concrete guidelines concerning congregational life,
in particular during worship. For some reason, Paul is here and in 5:3–16 especially
interested in women's behavior. We do not know the real reasons for giving this
advice, but social differences, especially differences in wealth, probably play a role
here. Banning "gold, pearls, [and] expensive clothes" (2:9) implies that at least
some of the church members were rich and that wealthy women caused offense.

Thus the situation in 1 Timothy in a way resembles that of 1 Corinthians
insofar as differences of wealth caused problems. At the same time, however, one
cannot avoid the conclusion that 1 Timothy is misogynic not only by modern
standards, but also by the standards of many other New Testament writings. The
criticism of women in 1 Timothy is not limited to the issues of wealth, but it
concerns the alleged nature of women in general. If we compare 1 Timothy with
all four Gospels and with early Pauline epistles, the difference in the portrayal of
women is clearly visible.

The Gospels and early Pauline epistles ascribe a slightly more positive role to
women than was the standard of Judaism and Hellenism (this issue is debated; I
follow Oberlinner 1994: 88–89, 94–96). But 1 Timothy repeats many of the prejudices and convictions that we also know from non-Christian sources. A modest
housewife who remains subject to the *paterfamilias* was the Jewish and Hellenistic
ideal. In this sense Paul here accommodates Christian behavior to the existing
standards of his own society. His basic point in 1 Tim. 1–3 is to advise Christians
to behave so that other people can positively affirm their behavior. The submission
and silence of women is one part and aspect of this general program.

Men are merely advised to pray, "lifting up holy hands without anger or argument" (2:8). We know from preserved art that this posture was also practiced by
non-Christians in their prayer (Roloff 1988: 131). The advice thus accommodates
Christian prayer to what people normally considered to be a proper and respectful
piety. Paul's intention is to emphasize the calm and peaceful nature of Christian
behavior. If other religious people could exercise godliness without anger and
argument, then also Christian men should be capable of this standard of behavior.
Anger and argument characterize the conduct of false teachers (6:4–5) (for the
problem of anger, see appendix B).

In 2:8–11 both men and women are called to exhibit a calm behavior: with
regard to men, this means giving up anger; with regard to women, modest and

silent conduct is recommended. In the Pastoral Epistles, too many words and empty talk are also criticized as the vice of false teachers. In this sense, men are also advised not to waste too many words (1:7; 5:1–2; 2 Tim. 2:23; see discussion of 1 Tim. 2:2 above). This advice relates to the Jewish views of the sins of the tongue that play a role already in the Decalogue. Jesus continued this ideal in Matt. 5:37: "Let your word be 'Yes, Yes,' or 'No, No'; anything more than this comes from the evil one" (cf. Jas. 3:8). This Jewish-Christian tradition offers a point of contact with the Hellenistic world, in which silence was also considered to be a virtue of wise people. When the Pastoral Epistles recommend moderation of speech as one aspect of the general moderation of behavior, they relate to both their particular theological tradition and the philosophical ideal of the surrounding world.

In 1 Tim. 2:9 a regulation of women's dressing is given. First Peter 3:3 witnesses that such rules pertained to women in other contexts of early Christianity as well. Although the regulations primarily concern conduct during worship, they are formulated as rules to be generally followed. The phrase "modestly and decently" entails a connotation to sexual chastity. "Suitable" (*kosmios*) means organized and balanced in contrast to chaotic and uncontrolled. "Suitable clothing" means that the woman appears modest and calm in her outward looks.

One cannot, however, read this guideline in a puritanical manner, for instance, so that its purpose is not to evoke sexual desires in men. Paul rather intends to say that women should appear dignified and godly in order that they meet the general standards of the presupposed social roles. Such behavior was also the norm in Jewish and Hellenistic families. Paul aims at saying that if Christian women and men can display accepted civil virtues in an exemplary manner, they can also make their inner conviction trustworthy and appealing.

This intention is also visible in 2:10. "Good works" should be the best attire of a Christian woman. It is thus the exemplary "inner self" (1 Pet. 3:4) that should be manifested in public and outward conduct. Paul calls this virtue a "reverence for God" (*theosebeia*), a term that is more or less synonymous with *eusebeia* in 1 Tim. 2:2 (Johnson 2001: 200; Roloff 1988: 133). Through a substitution of *eu-* for *theo-*, the concept emphasizes the theological dimension of this virtue: it witnesses to one's deep religiosity. As in many religious traditions, a woman's clothing is regarded as a central manifestation of her religious virtues. A woman should not preach or witness by words, but her appearance nevertheless makes a strong statement.

The aspect of silence is made explicit in 2:11. The verse should not be read apologetically, although it contains more dimensions than one would think at first glance. "Silence" (*hēsychia*) was described as a virtue of all Christians in 2:2. Peace and calmness—an ability to read, think, and learn without saying everything aloud—was also taught in the philosophical schools (Rabbow 1954). First Timothy 2:11, moreover, may even be regarded as a positive statement: the author affirms the view that women are able to master the difficult skill of silent learning. On the other hand, the sequel makes it clear that the author wants to submit women in many different and even dramatic ways.

The verse bears an obvious resemblance to 1 Cor. 14:34. The basic exegetical problem is that Paul in 11:5 also affirms the public prayer and prophecy of women (cf. Titus 2:3). Various solutions have been offered: that Paul is speaking of different tasks, that he is simply incoherent, or that 1 Cor. 14:34 is a later interpolation, maybe even prompted by 1 Tim. 2:11. Without taking a strong stance in this extensive discussion, the following observation is noteworthy: the author of 1 Timothy argues his case with the concept of apostolicity. He hands over the true doctrine of Paul to Timothy. If this doctrine is not coherent with other canonical writings—in addition to 1 Cor. 11:5, Gal. 3:28 and Jesus's treatment of women should be considered here—we have to make some hermeneutical decisions. Given that 1 Timothy wants to make its own authority dependent on the witness it employs and, more importantly, regards the earlier witness to be the source of its own apostolicity (see the discussion of *parathēkē* and *paradosis* in the exposition of 6:20), this very understanding of apostolicity may give us hermeneutical permission to regard its witness as secondary in comparison with its own authoritative apostolic sources (I am developing here the thoughts of Roloff 1988: 147).

This may not be a compelling argument, and 2:11 can probably be consistently employed in order to argue for the silence of women in Christian churches. Then, however, a consistent interpreter must also argue in favor of the authoritative character of 2:11b–15 in a similar manner. The obvious theological and hermeneutical problem is that the apostle's misogynic attitude gradually becomes more dramatic. Already the "full submission" (2:11b) and its sequel in 2:12 are categorical statements: no woman can "teach or . . . have authority over a man." If this is taken literally and the argument in favor of silence is continued, the statement loses the ties with the worship situation and becomes applied to all of life in church and society: no woman should exercise any authority over any man anywhere in (Christian) life.

This categorical line of thought gets clear historical support from the overall intention of the apostle. He wants Timothy's parishioners to exercise civil virtues in an outstanding manner, thus witnessing to healthy doctrine. If women's submission and silence is a civil virtue, then Christian women should exercise it in an undifferentiated and even categorical manner in order to display their godliness.

The most dramatic argument promoting the categorical submission is made in 2:13–15. Here Paul makes a move that resembles the treatment of *eusebeia* elsewhere in the Pastoral Epistles. First, a civil virtue is introduced and presented as a Christian duty (2:2). Then, a theological reason is attached to the civil virtue in order to make it more persuasive (6:3; 2 Tim. 3:5; Titus 1:1). But while *eusebeia* thus becomes "spirituality" in a carefully parsed manner, the theological foundation of the civil submission of women is argued very bluntly.

In 1 Tim. 2:13 Adam is given priority over Eve because he was created first. This argument was current in Judaism (Oberlinner 1994: 97; Strack and Billerbeck 1922–61: 3.645). The claim of 2:14 cannot be founded on Gen. 3, in which both Adam and Eve are guilty of the fall. A similar interpretation appears, however, in Sirach 25:34, which states that the first sin comes from woman. The words *exapataō* ("to deceive") and *apataō* may also mean a sexual seduction (cf. the Vulgate's *mulier seducta* in 1 Tim. 2:14). A teaching circulated in Hellenistic Judaism according to which Eve was indeed sexually seduced by the serpent (Roloff 1988: 139). Paul employs this double meaning in 2 Cor. 11:3. The author of 1 Tim. 2:14 thinks that the general inferiority of the female sex was already visible in Eve and that the example of the fall proves that women should keep silent.

In 1 Tim. 2:15 Paul rounds out his discussion through an attempt to contribute a balanced and positive word about women in general. Although women are responsible for the fall and have remained weak, they participate in salvation because they can bear children. Before we can proceed to a theological and hermeneutical interpretation of 2:13–15, we must realize how difficult it is to understand the purely historical meaning of this verse. The author here wants to say something positive about women, but a modern reader has difficulties in hearing what this positive side actually is.

The following aspects are relevant for the historical understanding of 2:15:

1. Although Hellenism knew some religious positions in which childbearing was relevant to the status of women, Paul is not developing any distinct soteriology for women.
2. Although 2:15 has a connection with Gen. 3:16–17, in which the pains of childbearing appear as punishment for sin, and although there may be some "homeopathic" idea in the background, the verse does not speak of the woman "paying back" something through this punishment.
3. Although one may theologically interpret 1 Tim. 2:15 according to the so-called Eve-Mary typology (i.e., through the chain of childbearings the Messiah was finally born to heal the sinful world), this is probably not intended by the author.
4. "Childbearing" (*teknogonia*) here probably refers to marriage and family life as a whole.
5. Some antignostic allusions are involved: the author wants to say that normal family life is an ideal to be followed and can secure eschatological fulfilment.
6. The chain of childbearings and the idea of "continu[ing] in faith" may also relate to the handing over of Christianity to the next generation, especially if "they continue" is understood to refer to the children (Marshall 1999:

470–71 gives reasons for the more common view that "they" refers to women but probably not to the children).

Maybe the author wants to say that marriage and family life have mysterious powers that are even relevant for salvation (cf. Eph. 5:32). If this thought is assumed, then one may understand the catalogue of basic Christian virtues (1 Tim. 2:15b) to mean that the life in family and in the Christian church is characterized by them. "Holiness" may refer to 1 Thess. 4:7; "modesty" continues the theme of 1 Tim. 2:8–12.

A theological interpretation of 2:13–15 must first admit that this passage is incompatible with the view of women given in the Gospels and in other Pauline writings, in particular 1 Corinthians and Galatians. The passage also misunderstands much of Genesis. Second, the expression "saved through childbearing" is a highly misleading characterization of Christian salvation. The phrase can be remedied to an extent with an allegorical reading (the third point), but the problem of misogynism remains. Third, one may find some constructive insights if *teknogonia* is understood as comprehensive family life that also involves men who are active in bringing up children. Although this reading needs some interpretative effort, it may offer a picture of family in which the same virtues and values are alive as in the church.

Finally, let us return to the hermeneutical issue elaborated in the exposition of 2:11. A literal reading of 2:11 is offensive, say, for 50% of the churches. In practice, these churches ordain women and prefer the apostolicity of some other canonical texts. A literal reading of 2:12–15 is offensive for probably 90% of the churches. They also must find hermeneutical keys to cope with the situation. In practice, these churches do not teach "full submission" or salvation "through childbearing," but they apply an allegorical reading or hold that the applicative range of these apostolic words is limited. The remaining 10% of Christians may, at least in theory, teach everything that 1 Tim. 2 says. But, paradoxically, they have then lost the central issue for which Paul argues here, namely, the overall accommodation to the habits and values of the surrounding civil society.

I argue that 1 Tim. 2 is a consistent text. It recommends an accommodation to public life, the universal truth, and the civil virtues. After doing that, Paul gives theological reasons for various aspects of this accommodation. The regulations concerning women belong to this context of accommodation. Today, however, our civil society appreciates women in a very different fashion. What was accommodation for Paul would be extremely countercultural in today's Western societies. A literalist understanding of his recommendations would run contrary to his overall idea of accommodation. A theological interpreter is thus inevitably called to perform complex hermeneutical procedures. Whatever line the interpreter takes, he or she has to emphasize some aspects while leaving others in the background.

Excursus 1: 1 Timothy 2:15 in Reformation Theology

One more aspect in the interpretation history deserves attention. In his 1516 edition of the Greek New Testament, Erasmus of Rotterdam observed that the phrase "they continue in faith" in 2:15 is plural, although the Vulgate translates it in the singular. Erasmus argued that women are saved by childbearing, provided that their children, who are meant by "they," continue in faith. The Vulgate presupposes that the singular "woman" continues in the faith (Wengert 2005: 88–89). Martin Luther reacted to this controversial issue with a sort of compromise, holding that "they" includes both women and children. For Luther, the phrase points out that the act of *generatio filiorum* is not as such salvatory, since it is common to pagans and Christians alike. Only when the act of childbearing and the education of the next generation are embedded in the transmission of faith and love can they have salvific meanings: "Simple childbearing does nothing. . . . For Christian women their whole responsibility is salvatory" (WA 26.48; LW 28.279).

Luther thus expounded 2:15 with some allusions toward the idea of "keeping-while-giving" (see appendix C and excursus 6). The next generation receives the faith from their mothers, and this continuation relates to salvation. Luther further moderated his exposition by pointing out that childbearing is no exceptional instance or "work" of salvation. All acts of Christian calling or duty (*omne officium*) relate to our salvation, and thus the act of childbearing represents the basic idea of fulfilling one's Christian calling. In this sense 2:15 is not contrary to the view of justification by faith (WA 26.48). We contribute to our salvation by our faith alone, but our basic Christian duties are not irrelevant with regard to salvation.

Philipp Melanchthon opposed Erasmus's interpretation and held that the word "they" refers to the women. It is obvious that one can be saved only by one's own faith. For Melanchthon, the verse speaks of the new obedience of Christians that is in keeping with the justification by faith alone. It is necessary for salvation to practice works of obedience, although these works do not merit salvation (Corpus reformatorum 15.1324–25).

Melanchthon focuses his exposition on the four virtues mentioned in 2:15: faith, love, sanctification, and modesty. They regulate the domestic realm of childbearing and the education of children (Corpus reformatorum 15.1325–27). Thus his understanding of the phrase "she will be saved through childbearing" stresses the ethical dimension that extends over a great number of household virtues, from housekeeping and helping the poor to truthfulness, sobriety, chastity, and other virtues related to sexuality. Melanchthon was especially worried by the lack of chastity. He claimed that the domestic virtues are constantly threatened by the perturbed desires (*confusiones libidinum*) (Corpus reformatorum 15.1327). With regard to the regulation and proper moderation of sexual desires, adultery and other excesses are to be avoided. On the other hand, the monastic habits of celibacy were also criticized (Corpus reformatorum 15.1327–29).

Like Melanchthon, Calvin defended the view that the word "they" must refer to the Christian women, not to their children. Calvin sees in 2:15 an ethical ideal that he illustrated from three perspectives. First, childbearing actually refers to all adversities that a faithful Christian mother must endure in giving birth and raising up children. Second, God will value this obedience to the calling more highly than other good works that do not result from obedience. Third, the promise of salvation is particularly dramatic because it is connected with the painful event of childbearing, which in Gen. 3:16 was described as the punishment of original sin (1996: 70–71).

In keeping with Luther and Melanchthon, Calvin pointed out that childbearing cannot be regarded as a "cause of salvation." The description shows merely "in what way God conducts us to salvation, to which he has appointed us through his grace." Whereas the previous verse (2:14) speaks of Eve's sin, the remark on childbearing aims at being a consolation to women who are terrified of being guilty of "the destruction of the whole human race." Paul's consolatory remark renders "their condition tolerable" (1996: 71, 70).

In sum, the leading theologians of the Reformation agree that 2:15 does not present any distinct soteriology. The verse needs to be read as a defense of Christian obedience and established social order. The claim of Erasmus that the faith of the children is here referred to is for the most part refuted. This claim evokes, however, the important topic of keeping-while-giving with regard to Christian women: their specific role in the continuation of faith begins to be discussed. The results of this discussion are not emancipatory, but the Reformers stress the household as a woman's realm of activity. Within the domestic realm, passions are moderated and traditional virtues nurtured. This practice of virtue enables the continuation of faith and love.

Although this understanding continues the patriarchal tradition of exegesis, it may nevertheless be significant that the theologically important issues of keeping the faith and handing it over to the next generation are here particularly connected with women. The church of the Pastoral Epistles is compared to the household, but, vice versa, the inalienable possessions of the Christian household—faith, love, and holiness—begin to resemble the *parathēkē* of the church and its leaders.

Requirements for a Bishop (1 Tim. 3:1–7)

First Timothy 3:1–7 describes the morals and the character of a bishop (*episkopos*). Given that the preceding chapter presupposes Christian worship and liturgy as its context, it is surprising that the episcopal office is outlined without any connection with liturgical or eucharistic tasks. One may even say that the passage does not give any spiritual or specific Christian requirements, since the exemplary character becomes outlined in terms of civil virtues required for higher public offices in general. Another difficult task for a theological interpreter is given by the observation that this text is one of the very few New Testament passages, if not the only one, in which *episkopos* appears as a technical term, meaning a task of leadership in the church.[3]

The phrase "the saying is sure" (3:1) either ends the preceding passage or begins the treatment of episcopacy. Most translations and commentaries prefer the latter alternative. According to this reading, the conduit of Paul's thoughts is as follows: since everyone certainly thinks that episcopacy is a "noble task" (*kalon ergon*), we should see to it that the moral and public character of the person occupying this office is above reproach. The following verses (3:2–7) proceed to describe the exemplary character in more detail.

We learn many things concerning the person who is suitable for this "beautiful" task. *Kalon* is not only beautiful or fine, but something that is good and desirable. The verb *epithymeō* is positive and points out that there can be positive desires. We are not informed about the theological nature of the task at hand. For this reason, very different theologies of ministry have been formulated with the help of this passage. The *ergon*, the task itself, is an established component of the emerging church. The extensive moral requirements underline the idea that this *ergon* is not merely one functional activity among many other practical tasks, but it has a representative character.

The first theological question to ask is whether "the office of bishop" in 3:1 (NRSV) is an adequate translation of *episkopē*. This word is a *nomen actionis*: it designates a function within the community (Roloff 1988: 153; Collins 2002: 79). In Hellenistic Greek, *episkopos* ("bishop"; 3:2 NRSV) is a person who oversees different things. The Greek term does not yet determine the range of this activity and can thus be employed in a functionalist or administrative manner. On the other hand, the description of this activity in the Pastoral Epistles (3:2–7; Titus 1:7–9; cf. 2 Tim. 2:24–25) clearly underlines the representative character of *episkopos*, whose *kalon ergon* is not simply administrative but requires specific personal characteristics.

At the same time, the scope of episcopal activity is not clearly defined in 1 Timothy. An *episkopos* basically takes care of one local church or congregation: we cannot yet see a diocesan level or a clear supervision of several parishes. In many ways *episkopos* is similar to *presbyteros*. My use of the NRSV's "bishop" can nevertheless be supported by some characteristics described in 3:2–7, such as the ability to teach (3:2) and especially the ability to "take care of God's church" (3:5).

As earlier in 1 Timothy (e.g., 2:2), Paul is concerned with the public and external aspects of Christian life. For this reason, in 3:2–7 he concentrates on those characteristics of a bishop that are also visible to the non-Christians. It may seem strange or frustrating that the central biblical text on episcopacy focuses on a bishop's external behavior rather than on one's inner spirituality or the theological nature of the office. But this concentration logically continues the topic

---

3. Pelikan 2005: 91–93 discusses the terminology of offices in a helpful manner. Marshall 1999: 170–81 summarizes the exegetical discussion.

of *eusebeia*, a civil virtue that comprises both the inner and the outer sphere of life. The apostle is careful to think how people look in the public sphere, but at the same time he also thinks that a bishop must have a genuine integrity in his inner and outer behavior. The first characteristic in this list, *anepilēmptos* ("above reproach"), is a general feature or flawlessness that becomes more concrete within the other items of the list.

The phrase "married only once" (*mias gynaikos anēr*) is not clear in its meaning and has been much debated. At least since Tertullian, the traditional interpretation has claimed that this phrase basically permits a widower to become a bishop, if he does not marry again after the death of his first wife. Other interpretations include a general prohibition of polygamy and a prohibition to marry again after a divorce (Roloff 1988: 155–56; Marshall 1999: 155–59). The context of different virtues makes it evident, however, that Paul expects the bishop to be an exemplary figure in various areas of his private and public life. Thus the apostle simply says that the bishop should not cause any offense in the conduct of his marriage but that he must hold to the accepted monogamous practice in an exemplary manner. This is a part of his *eusebeia* as a public figure.

This obvious reading leaves many interesting theological and moral issues unsolved. First Timothy 3:2 neither supports celibacy nor prohibits it. The bishop is obliged to follow the same sexual ethics as any other Christian, but in addition he has to think of himself as an example and as a public figure. The verse certainly speaks against simultaneous polygamy, but whether it prohibits successive polygamy, either after the death of a spouse or after divorce, may be debatable since the apostle is not concerned with the ethics of marriage per se, but with the public image of the bishop.

For similar reasons, employing 3:2 as a proof-text against women bishops may be constrained. Obviously, Paul thinks that the bishops spoken of here are men, but he is not really making that his main point. It can be conceded that in 3:11 women deacons are mentioned, whereas women bishops are mentioned nowhere. Given this and the broader context of 2:8–15, one could claim that Paul is consciously thinking of the differences of men and women in different ministries. As a distinct theme, however, women bishops simply do not appear in 3:2.

The next three virtues—"temperate, sensible, respectable"—are closely connected with one another. Although "temperate" displays a similarity with "not a drunkard," Paul is primarily using the word *nēphalios* in a metaphorical sense, as clarity in making judgments. *Sōphrōn* means experience in life and moderation of the passions. And *kosmios* (cf. 2:9) indicates a sense of balanced control and dignity. All three virtues appear frequently in Greek philosophy. They are more related to the ideal of successful moderation of desires (*metriopatheia*) than to the goal of eradicating all passions (see appendix A and Marshall 1999: 182–91).

In the New Testament, this ideal is explicitly spelled out in Heb. 5:2, in which the high priest is said to be able to "deal gently" (*metriopatheō*; Vulgate: *condolere*) with the ignorant and the wayward, for the great high priest, Jesus Christ, is also able to "sympathize" (*sympatheō* in Heb. 4:15; Vulgate: *conpati*) with our weaknesses. In both Hebrews and the Pastoral Epistles the Christian ideal expresses a life in which emotions and desires are not eradicated, but they are moderated and nurtured so that the person can feel proper sympathy and empathy.

Being "hospitable" (*philoxenos*; lit., "friend of a stranger") is likewise both a Hellenistic and Jewish virtue. This virtue is especially emphasized in many New Testament texts, both explicitly and implicitly (Matt. 10:11; Acts 16:15; 21:7, 17; 28:14; Rom. 12:13; 1 Tim. 5:10; Titus 1:8; 1 Pet. 4:9; Heb. 13:2). This has normally been explained in terms of practices and concrete needs. Wandering preachers and guests needed shelter and hospitality. In addition, Christians needed to show their Greek and Jewish neighbors that they also practiced this well-known virtue.

Although all this is likely true, the theological weight of *philoxenia* in the New Testament also presupposes the paradigm of neighborly love that comprises the love of strangers and enemies. Here, a bishop appears as provider and giver of this comprehensive *philoxenia*. As a traditional virtue, hospitality is a skill of such moderation that makes the stranger feel grateful but not unpleasantly obliged. In this sense hospitality goes well together with the ideals of being sensible and balanced (see appendix C and excursus 3).

Given that the Pastoral Epistles emphasize sound teaching (1:10), it is obvious that a bishop ought to be an "apt teacher." The bad characteristics—"drunkard," "violent," and "quarrelsome"—belong together and become a counterpart of the episcopal virtues. A drunkard looses the moderation of passions and personal dignity; thus he is easily violent and quarrelsome. "Lover of money" is a standard Hellenistic vice (cf. 6:10). The character trait of being "gentle" (*epieikēs*) is, since Plato (*Symposium* 210b [LCL 166.203]), a traditional virtue that describes a person who is just, moderate, and kind in conduct. In later Christian tradition (Acts 24:4; 2 Cor. 10:1), *epieikeia* becomes a great virtue that can be compared with justice, fairness, and mercy (K. H. Sladeczek in *HWP* 1.939–43). Taken together, the virtues of 1 Tim. 3:3 require a disengaged attitude of impartiality or contentment (*autarkeia*; cf. 6:6).

The NRSV employs the translations "gentle" and "meek" more often with regard to the important word group *praus* (e.g., Matt. 5:5; 11:29), *prautēs* (2 Tim. 2:25; Titus 3:2), and *praupatheia* (1 Tim. 6:11). Like *epieikeia*, *prautēs* is a virtue of classical philosophy, denoting a mean between anger and indifference. Both virtues can thus be translated with the words expressing gentleness. It is important to note that the Christian virtue of being gentle creates a bridge between the radical ethics of Jesus and the more moderate recommendations of the Pastoral Epistles. Both Moses (Num. 12:3) and the coming king of salvation (Zech. 9:9–10) are depicted as being gentle and humble. In his recent exposition of the Sermon on the Mount, Pope Benedict XVI emphasizes the radical and comprehensive nature of this virtue (2007: 80–84).

The requirements expressed in 1 Tim. 3:4 belong likewise to the standard of good social conduct in the Greco-Roman world. A person who has a public office must be able to manage "his own household well." A smaller unit of the family is, according to this line of thinking, comparable to the larger unit of the *polis*, of a city or a state. This basic thought is applied to the church: a bishop must be able to cope with his own family. Only when this can be assumed may we expect him to possess the social skills required for the leadership of a larger community, the church. Thus the requirement reflects the Greek virtue of *oikeiōsis* ("attachment, familiarization, or genuine care for others") (see appendix A). An exemplary church leader displays the virtues of both contentment (3:3; 6:6) and attachment (3:4–5; 5:1–2).

The comparison with a household has its implications for ecclesiology. A church resembles the family or the household, and the office of a bishop can be understood in terms of *paterfamilias*, the responsible parent. The analogy is clearly meant to hold between family and a local parish led by the *episkopos*. But the ecclesiologically interesting issue is this: can we assume that 3:5 also applies the analogy to the church as whole, in which case a bishop would also be in charge of a larger ecclesiastical unit?

This issue is complex, since the overall context of the Pastoral Epistles often assumes an individual congregation. Here, however, three grounds speak in favor of a larger unit: (1) the phrase "God's church" (*ekklēsia theou*) can be argued to mean the whole church; (2) since the point of the comparison is that the leadership of larger units is comparable to that of smaller units, one can claim that a bishop, according to this analogy, may rule over larger units than are historically meant in 1 Timothy; and (3) the context of 3:1–7 aims at saying that the episcopal office is public and should be exemplary in the eyes of outsiders as well as insiders. For these reasons, the office is thought to exemplify the good standing of the whole church (see Roloff 1988: 159–60 and Oberlinner 1994: 124–25; Marshall 1999: 481 differs from my view and holds that the phrase refers to a local congregation).

None of these three arguments is alone compelling. *Ekklēsia theou* can be understood to mean a local congregation, and the two other arguments perform a theological extrapolation of the actual text, which may have been simply intended for Timothy's congregation. But neither can we falsify the three arguments; and, taken together, they make an episcopal understanding plausible. Thus 3:1–7 indeed gives some support for a traditional understanding of the episcopal office. A bishop is a morally and doctrinally exemplary person who is in charge of "God's church" and represents it as a public figure. At the same time, the text cannot rule out a presbyterial structure of church leadership.

The requirement of not being a "recent convert" (*neophytos*) is, unlike most preceding requirements, specifically Christian in the sense that no parallels can be found in Hellenistic ethics. The inner logic of 3:6 is, however, in keeping with the Greek idea of virtue. It takes a long time for a virtue to be rooted deeply in a person's character. Although a young or an inexperienced person may learn fast and seemingly excel in some virtue, he or she is nevertheless uncertain in the exercise of that virtue (Aristotle, *Nicomachean Ethics* 1095a1–10; 1147a20–24 [LCL 73.9, 391]). For this reason, a neophyte should not occupy positions of high responsibility, since his uncertain character may be blinded or "puffed up."

In 3:6 the apostle admonishes his readers to think about the public reputation of the bishop. The good character of the bishop is important, since outsiders make their judgment of Christianity on the basis of its public representatives. The Pastoral Epistles pay a lot of attention to this phenomenon and argue that Christians should be good, or even exemplary, citizens. Given that some earlier New Testament writings are more countercultural, this trend is theologically surprising, although sociologically understandable. One way to deepen the theological understanding of this phenomenon is to analyze the very complex nature of such moral advice.

A person's act has at least two moral dimensions: the morality of the act itself and the morality of the signal it gives to other people—with regard to their own conduct but also with regard to their later judgments of the person giving this signal. One could claim that the second dimension is hypocritical and that we should pay attention to only the first one. But such a naïvely nonhypocritical attitude is obviously false, since we educate children and other people through our own behavior and, through this activity, create the moral fiber of our communities. In the New Testament, the Gospels and Paul discuss extensively the problem of *skandalon* ("offense, bad example"). As in 1 Tim. 3:7, the *skandalon* is sometimes described as a trap of the devil (Matt. 16:23; cf. 18:6–7; Rom. 16:17–20).[4]

The moral evaluation of "giving offense" is very complex, since one sometimes may have to provoke people. Often, and probably in most cases, it is nevertheless wiser not to annoy people and to give a good example without offending anybody. Such considerations have nothing to do with being hypocritical. The second dimension of morality in this sense pertains to the educational value of role models. Christian ethics cannot escape this dimension or declare it as being secondary. On the contrary, the extensive elaboration on the topic of *skandalon* in biblical texts witnesses to its elementary importance. Bishops need to think not only whether their own actions are good but also what kind of signal or role model the bishop provides the public eye. Both aspects are of great moral importance.

In 1 Tim. 3:6–7 Paul rounds out the lurking problems by saying that they are "the condemnation of the devil" or "the snare of the devil." Historically, these pictures pertain to the role of Satan as prosecutor in God's court. Theologically, this archaic picture highlights the complex and dialogical nature of moral discourse. If a bishop teaches, for instance, in a community of alcoholics that drinking is not morally wrong, his teaching may in some abstract sense be "sound." But the

4. For *skandalon* in moral theology, see Häring 1964: 2.473–93. Girard 1996: 215–16 understands *skandalon* as the satanic strategy of deluding humans by means of mimetic rivalry.

bishop is nevertheless framed or snared by the devil, who gathers evidence to accuse him for a neglect of the second dimension of morality, namely, the signal effect of one's own behavior.

The moral problems laid bare by this analysis are complex. If, for instance, the bishop of Rome forbids the effective means of birth control and is therefore not thought well of by outsiders, how should he read 3:7? Does the trap of the devil consist in strengthening the countercultural attitude of this bishop, or should the bishop think that this particular issue is not a case of showing complicity with the civil virtues of the secular world? The text of 3:7 cannot solve the moral issue; it can only emphasize that the aspect of being "well thought of by outsiders" belongs to the features that a bishop should take into account.

Requirements for Deacons (1 Tim. 3:8–13)

To a great extent, the requirements for deacons are formulated as being parallel to those for bishops. The explicit and implicit differences are, however, of great historical interest since they display a differentiation between the two offices. Deacons, too, should possess dignity or be "serious" (*semnos*; cf. 2:2). They cannot be drunkards or greedy for money. The only characteristics in 3:8 that seems to differ from bishops is the requirement that deacons should not be "double-tongued." Maybe this corresponds to the qualification of a bishop as being an apt teacher so that it expresses a lower qualification: whereas bishops ought to be good public speakers, it is enough for a deacon that he or she is honest and speaks the truth.

The next verse (3:9) supports this reading: deacons are not public teachers but they have to be sincere believers. A "clear/clean [*kathara*] conscience" obviously corresponds to 1:5 and 1:19, but the solemn phrase "mystery of the faith" remains challenging. Its content probably matches that of the (sincere) faith of the parish leader in 1:5 and 1:19, but it also connects with Col. 2:2 and 4:3 as well as with Eph. 1:9 and 3:4 (cf. 1 Tim. 3:16). In all these verses, the word *mystērion* characterizes the eschatological secret revealed in Christ. In 3:9, however, *mystērion* appears in connection with faith and thus loses its eschatological point. The mystery of the faith, later an important liturgical and doctrinal phrase, here begins to mean adherence to healthy doctrine, which is expressed in pious behavior. It is possible but not confirmed that 3:9 forms the textual background of the eucharistic response, *mysterium fidei* (Roloff 1988: 165).

The requirement of testing the deacons (3:10) says implicitly that the congregation may not yet know their character properly. Whereas bishops have already been long acquainted with the parishioners (3:6), deacons may be fairly recent converts who, however, have been tested and found blameless. The word "blameless" (*anenklētos*) means that nobody can accuse the person in question of moral or doctrinal failures. "Tested" (*dokimazō*) need not mean any longer period, but only that the choice is made with necessary care. The requirement of holding fast to the faith (3:9) presupposes that the deacons have some experience of Christian life, but it is likely that bishops are distinguished from deacons both by their ability to teach and by their longer career as Christians.

The word "women" in 3:11 probably refers to female deacons. The issue was debated in patristic times. John Chrysostom claims that Paul speaks of deaconesses (NPNF[1] 13.441), but, according to Ambrosiaster, 3:11 refers to women in general (Gorday 2000: 175–76). Today's exegetes side overwhelmingly with Chrysostom, although they admit that the reading of Ambrosiaster cannot be falsified. The first alternative preserves the harmony between the three lists begun in 3:2, 8, 11 respectively and does not have to explain the absence of bishops' wives in this chapter. In addition, a letter of Pliny the Younger from the year 112 speaks of female *ministrae* active in these tasks (*Epistle* 10.96.8 [LCL 59.289]).

A more difficult issue is, however, whether 3:11 speaks of a distinct female office of deaconess. The character traits given in this verse are roughly similar to those of male deacons. "Not slanderers" corresponds to "not double-tongued" in 3:8; being "temperate, faithful in all things" is also required of men in 3:8–9. These requirements are, however, so general that we cannot infer much from them pertaining to women deacons.

It is only in 3:12 that Paul gives a distinctive mark, now regarding male deacons. Like bishops, male deacons should be married to one wife and should manage their children and households well. The women deacons were probably unmarried or widows, whereas male deacons were married. This order matches the general rules of a society in which a married woman was obliged to devote herself to her own household. Comparing 3:4 with 3:12, we hear that the moral rule for male deacons was slightly easier than for the bishops, signaling that the role model given by the bishop was a more important one.

The concluding verse of this passage (3:13) again pertains to both men and women. It is in parallel with 3:1: as the bishop's office is a "noble task," the office of a deacon is a task that gives the person a "good standing" (*bathmos kalos*). *Bathmos* can mean a stage or a step, but one cannot infer from this word the idea that deacons would be on their way toward episcopacy, and maybe not even the view that different offices could be understood as successive stages. The plain and obvious meaning of this verse is that if a deacon serves well, this position is good and proper as such. The author is not primarily thinking of eschatological fulfillment, but simply that a good deacon is respected by the parish members.

In addition, the deacon is meant to obtain a great "boldness" (*parrēsia*), one of the great Hellenistic virtues and also prominent throughout the New Testament (H. Schlier in *TDNT* 5.871–86). Meaning "openness, boldness, freedom of speech, trust," *parrēsia* is thus a self-assurance that makes the person free of superiority and inferiority complexes vis-à-vis his or her neighbors. Given this, we can understand that "*parrēsia* in the faith" does not pertain to the boldness of proclamation. Paul is rather aiming to say that the deacon can achieve the same moderation of character and the same respectable posture as the bishop. It is this character that is his or her "good standing."

Church of the Living God (1 Tim. 3:14–16)

The concluding section of 1 Tim. 2–3 begins with an emphatic repetition of the overall aim of the epistle. The apostle is absent and hopes to be present. But if his coming is delayed or if he remains absent, the church nevertheless has "these instructions" and therefore knows "how one ought to behave" (3:14–15; cf. 1:3, 18). This aim reflects the historical situation in which the first generation of the apostles was no longer present. It was most important that their instruction was preserved and employed in the emerging church. A written form of instruction gave the bishop the necessary authority to guide his church on the apostolic path.

At the same time, this concluding passage remains solemn and does not actually reveal any concrete historical details. Remembering Paul and his instruction is only the introductory issue in this passage; with its help the author leads his readers into a solemn ecclesiological and christological treatise (3:15–16). It is revealing that the author explicitly says that his instructions pertain to the right conduct in the house of God (3:15).

The apostle now compares this state of affairs with a house or a household. It is customary to follow a certain code of conduct in a house, and this code can be assumed to stem from the lord of the household. In the church we are supposed to follow the rules of God's household. In this way Paul brings the topic of *oikonomia theou*, begun in 1:4, to an end. Given this, the *oikos theou* of 3:15 becomes connected with the comprehensive "divine training" or plan of 1:4.

This *oikos* is "the church of the living God," a phrase that obviously witnesses to 2 Cor. 6:16, in which "the temple of the living God" is mentioned. This eschatological picture alludes to Mark 14:58, in which Jesus says that he destroys the temple and builds another, not made with hands. In 1 Tim. 3:15 the church in this sense is described as a sacred space in which the living God dwells. It is difficult to say whether this ecclesiological statement refers to the local church and in which sense it presupposes a universal church. But in any case, church is here being described as a theological abstraction that preserves the truth in a universal and absolute sense.

The phrase "pillar and bulwark of the truth" strengthens this abstract ecclesiology. The phrase grammatically refers to the church, not to God or to Timothy. It may be connected with 1 Kgs. 8:13, in which the Lord dwells in an exalted house; the word *hedraiōma* ("bulwark, foundation") appears in the Septuagint (Marshall 1999: 510). In this sense the phrase continues the topic of the church as the house of God.

For a theological and doctrinal understanding of this verse one should define the relationship between "the truth" and "the church." If the church is seen as the foundation of the truth, then one gets a very strong ecclesiology and a strong *magisterium*, since according to this reading the church can be understood to safeguard the truth. But if the truth is understood as indwelling in the church, then the truth would preserve a more independent role and does not become conditioned by the foundational importance of the church.

Both readings are linguistically possible and, as is to be expected, Catholic exegetes often prefer the first alternative (Oberlinner 1994: 152–62), whereas Protestant scholars are more inclined toward the second (Roloff 1988: 197–201; 1985). Already Calvin leans toward the Protestant view when he states: "The reason why the Church is called the 'pillar of truth' is, that she defends and spreads it by her agency. God does not himself come down from heaven to us, nor does he daily send angels to make known his truth; but he employs pastors, whom he has appointed for that purpose" (1996: 90). John Chrysostom leans more toward the Catholic view when he states that "the church is the pillar of the world" (NPNF[1] 13.442).

The Catholic reading in many ways corresponds to the plain and literal meaning of the text. The church is here represented as the foundational reality that preserves and keeps the truth. This meaning also corresponds to the more general intentions of the Pastoral Epistles: the author often stresses the importance of safeguarding the Christian message through institutionalized powers, especially through the apostolic office of the bishop. Given this reading as the most plausible alternative, we cannot, however, draw the conclusion that the relationship between the church and the truth should generally be understood in this manner. The foundational role of the church in discerning and safeguarding the truth is expressed here, but it must be put in proportion with the overall witness of the New Testament (Grosshans 2003 is a recent theological attempt to deal with this issue).

Excursus 2: Ecclesiology and Ordained Ministry, Part 1

Here is the proper place to review the different prevailing views with regard to ecclesiology and ordained ministry. In his highly useful survey of the recent research on ecclesiology in the Pastoral Epistles, I. Howard Marshall distinguishes among three basic positions (1999: 512–21). There is, first, the so-called early Catholic interpretation of which Heinrich Schlier (1958: 129–47) is an influential example. Schlier sees the ecclesiological development within the New Testament as a necessary unfolding of the gospel message. Timothy and Titus are no longer called to their tasks directly by Christ but indirectly by the apostles. The authority and the institutional structure of the congregations are no longer charismatic, but they rest on an established office. The office is based on apostolic succession and it is hierarchically organized. Thus we can see a rather determinate church order at work in the Pastoral Epistles.

Schlier, a Lutheran exegete who converted to Catholicism, does not regard this development as degeneration or alienation from the original message of Jesus and Paul. On the contrary, the ecclesiological development in the canon shows an organic continuity and witnesses that the institutional office and the hierarchical structure of the church in a genuine manner unfold the proclamation of earliest Christians. Basically same exegetical findings can, however, also be employed to support a thoroughly Protestant interpretation in which the development toward the early Catholic church is regarded as problematic. Ernst Käsemann, among others, argues that the ecclesiology of the Pastoral Epistles is actually an antithesis of Paul's views (1964: 63–94; cf. Schenk 1987).

The second position is labeled by Marshall as "the current consensus." It is exemplified by the major commentaries of Roloff (1988) and Oberlinner (1994–96). The current consensus moderates and differentiates the ideas of hierarchy and institution. It emphasizes the view of the church as a household. While a household is stable and rests on a firm foundation, it is also flexible and can adapt itself to meet various needs. A household is, to a great extent, defined by its members rather than by abstract and impersonal structures. At the same time, a household defines its members in opposition to outsiders and relies on the ideas of obedience and subordination. Thus the basic distinctions between orthodoxy and heresy, insiders and outsiders, exemplary leaders and obedient followers, also prevail in the church as household.

The third position is Marshall's own. He argues that the ecclesiology of the Pastoral Epistles is actually far less early Catholic than the first and second positions assume. Marshall points out that the existing evidence does not allow us to draw many of the conclusions that support the early Catholic paradigm. For instance, that the Pastoral Epistles are written to church leaders does not tell anything about the relative importance of such congregational matters that were crucial in earlier Pauline writings. The different style and vocabulary of the author do not prove that the content of his theology would differ from Paul. It is beyond doubt that a lot of Pauline material is employed throughout the Pastoral Epistles (Marshall 1999: 516–18).

Marshall argues that although the emphasis on teaching is stronger, the ecclesiology of the Pastoral Epistles in many respects closely resembles earlier Pauline epistles. Paul regards the church to be God's household (Gal. 6:10; Eph. 2:19). The role of the Holy Spirit and charismatic features are also emphasized in the Pastoral Epistles. Although the style of the Pastoral Epistles is official, the picture of the church and its offices remains vague. The terminology of the offices is not so consolidated as the early Catholic view assumes. Church meetings, liturgies, and even church discipline remain only loosely structured; many issues and practices are debated. Thus, Marshall concludes: "The structures in the [Pastoral Epistles] are much looser and less 'official' than the consensus might lead us to suppose" (1999: 521).

If Schlier fifty years ago made a strong claim in favor of the "Catholic" ecclesiology of the Pastoral Epistles, Marshall recently argues powerfully for the "evangelical" ecclesiology inherent in these texts. At the same time it should be admitted that the Pastoral Epistles pose greater problems for Protestant interpreters than for Catholic ones. The studies and hermeneutical decisions of Schlier remain persuasive, and the current consensus can be regarded as a moderated version of the early Catholic view. Many Protestant exegetes therefore choose the option of regarding the Pastoral Epistles as secondary texts within the canon.[5]

---

5. See the research history of Schenk 1987 and the introductory sections of Mounce 2000 and Johnson 2001, who argue against this view.

My commentary does not offer a fundamentally new way to treat ecclesiology. Nor do I take a particularly strong position with regard to the perennial issues discussed by Schlier, Käsemann, Marshall, and others. I am basically arguing that the Pastoral Epistles contain an ecclesiology that is both Catholic and evangelical and cannot be reduced to either of these basic alternatives. In this sense my view is close to Marshall's second position, as the following list of particular ecclesiological matters shows.

In the exposition of 3:5 I interpreted *ekklēsia theou* to refer to the whole church rather than to an individual congregation. Thus the metaphor of the household and the task of *episkopos* in this context also relate to the larger church. In a similar manner, the "household of God" and the "church of the living God" in 3:15 concern the comprehensive divine plan of salvation history and are dealing with a church that is, theologically speaking, Catholic.

The ecclesiological phrase "pillar and bulwark of the truth" (3:15) evokes the difficult issue of the relationship between the church and the truth. It is important to see both the Catholic meaning, according to which the church keeps and safeguards the truth, and the evangelical meaning, namely, that the church is dependent on the foundational truth that it serves.

Much of the ecclesiological reflection in the Pastoral Epistles has to do with the issue of ministry. Here the discrepancies between the early Catholic and the evangelical view are particularly visible. The theological tradition from Eusebius to the Reformation held that the Pastoral Epistles, in particular 1 Timothy, are a mirror for the bishops and that Timothy and Titus are bishops (see introduction to the Pastoral Epistles). Since the Reformation, the translation of *episkopos* and other titles has continued to be debated. Contemporary exegetes point out that although Timothy and Titus are links between the Apostle Paul and later bishops, we do not know their precise titles (Weiser 2003: 44–50; Marshall 1999: 52).

In this commentary, I follow the NRSV in translating *episkopos* as "bishop." As mentioned above, 3:5 probably presupposes that the bishop oversees a significant portion of God's church. With regard to Titus 1:5–9, I consider that a bishop (1:7–9) can be distinguished from the elders (1:5–6). At the same time, I have not drawn too many conclusions from these interpretatory matters. The tasks of elders and bishops seem to overlap in Titus 1:5–9. From 1 Tim. 3:1 we can read that there were episcopal functions (*episkopē*) to which capable leaders aspired.

Timothy is said to have been ordained by the council of elders (1 Tim. 4:14), but also by Paul (2 Tim. 1:6). Timothy is further supposed to ordain new elders (1 Tim. 5:22). No clear differentiation between episcopal and presbyterial ordination can be assumed. The ordination transfers a special gift to the ordained person (4:14; 2 Tim. 1:6). The person who ordains has to consider his decision carefully (1 Tim. 5:22). The laying on of hands (4:14; 2 Tim. 1:6) shows that the ideas of collegiality and succession are present. While no detailed church order can be constructed on the basis of this evidence, the ordination practices described in the Pastoral Epistles witness to the established practices of early Christianity. As these textual witnesses are, for the most part, compatible with later Catholic and evangelical theologies of ordination, later doctrinal differences related to ordination and ordained ministry can hardly be solved by exegesis of these passages. In this limited sense the texts on ordination remain both Catholic and evangelical.

Similar conclusions can be drawn with regard to other offices. Deacons (1 Tim. 3:10–13) are clearly distinguished from bishops. Requirements for deacons are not as demanding as those for bishops. On the basis of 3:11 it is plausible to think that there were also women deacons. Widowhood (5:3–16) was an established Christian institution, but not an office. The office of elder required ordination and elders received some remuneration (5:17–22), but we do not know whether this meant full-time employment. Elders were to be appointed in every town (Titus 1:5), and their council was in charge of ordination (1 Tim. 4:14). An emerging institutional structure of the church can thus be assumed, but Marshall is also right in holding that this structure remained loose. No such church order comes into focus that would justify a particular institutional structure of various ministries.

The role of women in ministry remains a difficult issue. The Pastoral Epistles are critical of women's public role in general, and this criticism is motivated by the need to adapt to the patriarchal structures of the surrounding society. A modern interpreter can very plausibly argue that a similar adaptation to today's society requires a totally different view of women's public role. Attitudes and actions that are described as virtuous—for instance, silence and submission (2:11) or salvation through childbearing (2:15)—are today considered problematic and even harmful.

In the ideal community of the household, women can "teach what is good" (Titus 2:3); they can be active as widows (1 Tim. 5:5), managers of household (5:14; Titus 2:5), and probably deacons (1 Tim. 3:11). The active role of Christian women in spreading the gospel was debated in the congregations. In the household, women participate actively in the handing over of Christian tradition to the next generations. In this sense they are also active guardians of the *parathēkē*. In order to apply these guidelines to contemporary contexts, the extension and partial synonymity of the theological concepts "household," "church," and "public life" should be elaborated in detail.

In 3:16 Paul first speaks of the "mystery of our piety" (*to tēs eusebeias mystērion*). The civil virtue of *eusebeia* is here given a strong theological use as a comprehensive description of Christian spirituality or "religion," as the NRSV translates. Because Paul has spoken so much of Christian behavior as the proper expression of faith, this choice of wording is understandable. At the same time, the phrase appears very solemn and matches the preceding pictures of the church as God's temple. The ecclesiological context may also explain why the author does not speak of "mystery of the faith" (3:9) or "God's mystery" (Col. 2:2). Since *eusebeia* is proper Christian conduct that gives an example to the outsiders, it in many ways belongs to the institutional reality of the church.

The passage ends with a solemn hymn that describes the work of Christ in liturgical and creedal terms. The hymn is evidently taken from some already existing source and written down here in order to round out the passage. Its beginning, literally "who [*hos*] was revealed," has given rise to christological debates. Some old manuscripts and the Textus Receptus prefer *theos* instead of *hos*. The obvious grammatical problem is that the relative pronoun *hos* does not have a proper correlate. The decision of the NRSV matches the opinion of most scholars: the "mystery" is expressed by the hymn as a whole, and *hos* refers to God or Jesus (NRSV: "he") (Oberlinner 1994: 150–51; Marshall 1999: 523).

The hymn itself is carefully composed. It makes three distinctions: flesh-spirit, angels-Gentiles, world-glory. In all of them, a worldly reality is contrasted with a heavenly reality. A passive verb, describing God's activity, precedes all six realities (Roloff 1988: 192–93; but Marshall 1999: 501–2 expresses some doubts).

The first phrase, "revealed in flesh," describes the incarnation. In a purely historical exegesis, it is debatable whether a mere appearance of Jesus as human can be called incarnation and whether this phrase presupposes the preexistence of Christ. The phrase is nevertheless easily compatible with the classical idea of incarnation. Its emphasis lies in the salvific appearance of Jesus Christ as a human being (cf. 2 Tim. 1:9–10; Titus 3:4–7).

The second phrase is not obvious. What does it mean that Jesus was "justified in Spirit" (NRSV: "vindicated in spirit")? Exegetes and churches have considered various interpretations, some stressing the victory of Christ, others his divine epiphany. The most obvious reading is, however, a forensic one: in the heavenly reality of the spirit, Jesus was given justice and his right due.

Jesus was "seen by angels"; the phrase can also be interpreted "appeared to the angels." The risen and glorified Jesus is presented in heaven to the heavenly powers as a part of his enthronement ceremony (cf. Phil. 2:9–10; Matt. 28:18; Rev. 5:6–14). The proclamation to all the world is an essential part of this ceremony: in the enthronement Jesus is given all power, and all the world should hear this (Roloff 1988: 206–9; Oberlinner 1994: 166–68). Whereas "flesh" and "spirit" in the first strophe remain distinct, the process of enthronement connects heavenly and earthly reality with each other in the second strophe. The whole universe becomes under the power of the new ruler.

The third strophe describes the recognition and final reality of this process of enthronement. After the proclamation, Jesus is "believed in throughout the world." He is "taken up" by God to the heavenly glory. The third strophe thus characterizes the contemporary situation in idealized terms. Christ sits on his throne in glory, whereas believers all over the world have received the proclamation of his enthronement. In the third strophe, "world" and "glory" in some way remain distinct. At the same time, the believers' confession of their faith, expressed in this christological hymn, let them be partakers of the eschatological glory. In this way the liturgical hymn connects the believers' reality with life in the spirit and in glory.

INSTRUCTIONS FOR THE PASTORAL WORK OF TIMOTHY

1 Tim. 4:1–6:2

In the next section of the epistle, Paul gives instructions pertaining to the pastoral leadership of Timothy. Whereas the earlier instructions (2:1–3:16) were given in a direct fashion to the persons concerned, Paul now more often addresses Timothy as "you" and tells him how to instruct the members of congregation. Paul gives advice on ordination, right moral conduct, and adequate social work.

Several problems and groups of people are addressed successively. The section opens with a warning of false teachers who proclaim ascetic habits (4:1–5). As a counterpoint to this false ascesis, Paul describes the godliness (*eusebeia*) that corresponds to sound doctrine (4:6–11). After this, Timothy is given more detailed orders concerning the right conduct and tasks of a church leader (4:12–5:2). A lengthy part of the section is devoted to various problems concerning widows (5:3–16). Several instructions about the treatment of elders and teachers constitute another list of advice (5:17–22). The section closes with a brief remark on the right conduct of Christian slaves (6:1–2).

The instructions do not only concern Timothy in his concrete situation, but they represent the general norms of apostolic teaching. This intended general validity of the epistle is very clear in the treatment of false teaching (4:1–5) and ordination (4:14; 5:22). It is less evident but still visible in the treatment of widows (5:3–16).

False Teachers of Ascesis (1 Tim. 4:1–5)

Paul opens the section with a reference to the Spirit. Such a reference is typical of prophetic and eschatological texts (Mark 13:11; Acts 8:29; Rev.

3:6), and 1 Tim. 4:1 actually refers to "later days/time" (*en hysterois kairois*). The Pastoral Epistles are by no means apocalyptic texts, but they do make occasional references to the last days (cf. 2 Tim. 3:1). This may be motivated by the traditionalist leaning of the Pastoral Epistles: they want to show that they belong to the apostolic tradition and therefore employ expressions from other and more eschatological texts. Here, however, another motif is evident. The eschatological time is characterized by temptations and apostasy. "Faith" here refers to the content of faith, the sound doctrine, which is renounced when people listen to the demons. The eschatological phrase underlines the importance of sound doctrine.

Mentioning "deceitful spirits" and "demons" as the cause of renouncing the faith gives the passage a dualistic tone. Parallels to this dualism are found in the Qumran writings (1QS 3.18–22 [Vermes 2004: 101]; Roloff 1988: 220). On the other hand, no metaphysical dualism is here at stake, as 4:2 shows. The demonic powers have no reality of their own, but they operate with lies and hypocrisy, thus leading the believers away from the truth. The claim that the conscience of liars is "seared with a hot iron" may mean two things. More likely it refers to a shameful mark branded on these people. Since patristic exegesis, however, it has also been taken to mean the deadening of conscience through branding with a hot iron (cf. Eph. 4:19), as was done in Hellenistic medical practice (Marshall 1999: 540). Given that conscience in Pauline writings means a moral-anthropological reality that enables the understanding of the future (cf. 1 Tim. 1:5), the idea of deadening the conscience matches well with the eschatological horizon. Those people who renounce the true faith cannot any longer make sound judgments concerning right conduct and their own future. For this reason they also impose false ascetic practices.

These practices are described in 4:3. The false teachers forbid marriage and practice a certain diet. Similar passages from Clement (*Stromata* 3.17 [ANF 2.400–401]) and Irenaeus (*Against Heresies* 1.24.2 [ANF 1.349]) say that gnostic teachers renounce marriage and the begetting of children. According to the gnostics, the old world is ruled by lower powers. The people who serve the highest God should not live according to the old world. Since 4:3–4 emphasizes, contrary to such views, that all that God has created is good, one can assume that the false prophets are in many respects similar to the gnostics described by Clement and Irenaeus (cf. 2 Tim. 2:18).

The theological interpretation of these ascetic practices must take into account the eschatological saying of Jesus in Matt. 19:10–12 and the recommendation of Paul in 1 Cor. 7:7. Both texts seem to prefer celibacy. It would be premature to blame the gnostics for the neglect of good creation, since Christian striving for perfection can also lead to ascesis. First Timothy 4:3–4 offers a balancing statement, recommending to believers that ascetic practices may be misleading and that the practice of ascesis should be subsumed under the overall perspective of *eusebeia*. Thus 4:3–4 seeks a moderated mean between lazy indifference and exaggerated ascesis (see appendix A).

The argument from creation in 4:3–4 particularly concerns food, but in 5:14 Paul also moderates the teaching of marriage. With regard to fasting, Paul generally follows Jesus, who criticizes Jewish practices and who eats and drinks (Matt. 11:19). Earlier Pauline epistles express tolerant views with regard to various foods while remaining open to the practices of fasting (e.g., Rom. 14:14–20). Later Christian practices of fasting may be seen as attempts to commit oneself to a temporary ascesis, following the example of Jesus (Matt. 4:2), while approving the basic principle that all food belongs to God's good creation.

In 1 Tim. 4:3–4 both creation and receiving with thanksgiving are mentioned twice and thus underlined. Mentioning creation here serves the purpose of criticizing the gnostic views that downplay the goodness of creation. Less clear, however, is the purpose of the phrase that the believers should receive the food "with thanksgiving" (*meta eucharistias*). Judging from the context, the phrase is not directly related to the Eucharist, but rather to the blessing expressed at the daily meal. The Vulgate translation *cum gratiarum actione* also relates the phrase to the saying of grace at the meal. God as creator is remembered before the food is received. An allusion to the eucharistic table may nevertheless be present in the Greek original (so Roloff 1988: 226, whereas Marshall 1999: 543 remains doubtful).

Excursus 3: Hospitality and Gratitude

Giving and receiving in the first century were accompanied by an established code of conduct. This is witnessed not only in Jewish prayers at the meal, but also in philosophical works like Seneca's *On Favors* (e.g., 2.22.1).[1] Seneca underlines "receiving with thanksgiving" as the proper and virtuous attitude of the recipient. The recipient of a beneficiary act is not supposed to pay back, but is supposed to give proper thanks. Seneca points out that food is in fact given by God as the highest benefactor, whom the human benefactors imitate in their acts of benevolence and hospitality. "Receiving with thanksgiving" is thus not only a sporadic matter of politeness, but an established virtue of the recipient of good gifts (Roloff 1988: 223–26 and Oberlinner 1994: 181–82 discuss the Jewish background; see further appendix C).

In the Pastoral Epistles, the phenomenon of giving and receiving should be seen in the broader context of different favors of which hospitality (the third category of favor: consumable and freely circulated aid) is a prominent example (see appendix C). As already noted, "hospitality" (*philoxenia*) is a basic virtue required from different Christians. A bishop is to be hospitable (1 Tim. 3:2; Titus 1:8), and widows are to prove that they have shown hospitality (1 Tim. 5:10). The idea of a "stranger" (*xenos*) need not be exaggerated. If a person offers food and shelter to the members of one's own household, no special favor or hospitality is shown. A stranger is simply somebody who is not normally entitled to enjoy these services, but they are offered to him or her as a favor. It is important to note that two opposite vices are related to hospitality:

1. Quotations of Seneca's *On Favors* are taken from Seneca 1995: 193–308.

refusing to give to the needy and the practice of "bribing" the recipient so they would feel too strong an indebtedness. All interests of the giver are to be put aside when a favor is offered.

Another category of favors is relevant with regard to the issue of aiding the widows in 5:3–16. This discussion does not concern hospitality but social aid (the fourth category of favor: consumable and targeted aid; see appendix C). On the first look, the discussion seems to serve the interests of the giver, namely, the local church, which is not to be burdened unnecessarily (5:16). Paul is, however, also trying to argue in which sense the policy he advocates can serve the interest of the recipients. A too liberal policy of aiding makes young widows idle and risks their status as good Christians (5:6–7, 11–13). It further risks the ability of the church to aid those who are in real need (5:16). Carefully targeted giving enables the relatives to practice the virtue of providing for relatives (5:8, 16). In these ways Paul follows the maxim of Seneca, according to whom proper favors are disinterested but targeted so that the real interest of the recipient becomes the criterion. We may discuss whether Paul accomplishes his aim in a rhetorically convincing manner, but it is plausible to interpret 5:3–16 so that he at least attempts to modify the policy of aiding so that the real interest of the recipients is taken into account.

The practice of distributing favors concerns rich people in a particular way. The duties of the rich Christians are dealt with in 6:17–19. This passage is instructive not only because of its thematic affinities with Seneca's discussion, but also because riches are so heavily criticized by Paul elsewhere (6:5–10). The apostle assumes that rich Christians can remain on the path of healthy doctrine. In order to do this, they ought to moderate their emotion so that they are not haughty but behave humbly. As God richly provides us with everything, rich people ought to practice good works, generosity, and sharing. The same virtues appear in Hellenism, and the parallel to divine giving also appears in Seneca (*On Favors* 4.9.1). Rich people ought to give in a liberal and generous manner since they can afford it. Unlike in 1 Tim. 5:3–16, Paul is not worried here for the interest of the recipients. This is not a contradiction: whereas the moral focus in 5:3–16 is on the recipients, in 6:17–19 it remains on givers.

The other side of favors is gratitude or "giving thanks." The most important text is 4:3–4, in which the phrase "received with thanksgiving" (*metalēmpsin/apoblēton meta eucharistias*) appears twice. The phrase may refer to the event of saying grace at the meal. Orthodox Christians, that is, "those who believe and know the truth" (4:3), are expected to give thanks for food. They can believe that all food is created by God and thus good.

Seneca also teaches that one must give thanks. At the same time, one should not and need not become too indebted. Seneca advises the recipient to be careful and discriminating in receiving gifts and favors. A basic rule is to accept favors from those to whom we also would like to do a favor (*On Favors* 2.18.3). The recipient should be willing to receive the favor. If it is received under obligation, it does not bind the recipient to a real gratitude (2.18.7–8; 2.21.1–2). But "when we have decided to accept, we should do so cheerfully" (2.22.1). As in showing hospitality, so also in receiving a favor two opposite extremes are to be avoided: ingratitude and indebtedness against one's own will. If either of these reactions is to be expected, it is better to refuse to accept a favor.

The phrase "received with thanksgiving" (1 Tim. 4:3–4) is somewhat enigmatic and can be interpreted in various ways. A straightforward interpretation can be offered along Seneca's lines of receiving a favor. We should not, for ascetic reasons, refuse food that we would normally accept with gratitude, for the presence of such gratitude signals that the gift of food—and marriage (4:3)—is offered to us by a giver from whom we like to receive things and whom we like to serve. Thus the phrase on the one hand can be taken as a command to say grace. But, at the same time, the established practice of saying grace at meals witnesses to the virtue of gratitude that, in turn, points toward a giver from whom we would like to accept favors. Therefore, the false teachers do not follow God but demons (4:1) when they demand abstinence from foods. In this way, the act of thanksgiving is not merely an additional command or a hidden reference to the Eucharist, but it serves an argumentative purpose. This interpretation may not exhaust the meaning of 4:3–4, but it is probably assumed as part of the meaning.

In 1 Tim. 1:12 and 2 Tim. 1:3 Paul expresses his gratitude (*charin echō*) to Christ and God in a manner that is conventional but also makes explicit the need to display a proper amount of gratitude. The view that prayers of thanksgiving should also be made for non-Christians (1 Tim. 2:1–3) expresses a similar point: earthly rulers do a favor to Christians when they leave them in peace; Christians should express their proper thanks for this favor.

Although the minds of the giver and the recipient should remain in the focus of the attention when favors are discussed, we may also note that some material items exemplify the theme of favors. Among material gifts, food is discussed in some detail. Basically, food is to be consumed and circulated so that the virtues of hospitality and gratitude are practiced. Both the relative importance and the transitory nature of food are described: the good teachers need food and clothing as basis of their *autarkeia* (6:8). Richness is falsely supposed to be more stable, but it also vanishes in death (6:6–10). Wine is not to be completely avoided (5:23), but drinking is clearly a vice (3:3, 8). Food is created by God (4:3) and may contribute to one's health (5:23). In these ways food exemplifies the third category of favors.

If the noun *eucharistia* in 4:3–4 contains a reference to the Eucharist, we may have an interesting case of the fourth category of favors that are consumed and have a limited circulation among "those who . . . know the truth." The word "truth" may refer backward to the church as the "pillar and bulwark of the truth" (3:15). A clear example of a fourth category of favor is the social aid distributed to the widows enlisted in the catalogue of the local church (5:3, 9).

Clothes are an interesting group of material items in the Pastoral Epistles. Together with food, they are necessary for *autarkeia* (1 Tim. 6:8). Paul needs his cloak (2 Tim. 4:13) for unnamed reasons: maybe to keep himself warm, but maybe for reasons of symbolic authority. Decent clothing is exemplary, but expensive clothes are to be avoided (1 Tim. 2:9). Anthropologists often attach great value to clothing. One reason for this is their position between consumable and nonconsumable goods (Weiner 1992: 51–52). The textual evidence of the Pastoral Epistles is, however, too scarce to draw far-reaching conclusions regarding this matter.

Because money and expensive clothes are despised in the Pastoral Epistles, it is understandable that the most concrete category of favors, namely, nonconsumable material items that are freely circulated as gifts or presents, does not play any positive role. There is, however, one more category that is extremely important in the Pastoral Epistles: the immaterial deposit (*parathēkē*) that Paul is leaving to Timothy and to the church. The deposit contains Paul's sound teaching, his legacy. It is nonconsumable and needs to be circulated in a specially controlled manner (the second category of favor) (see excursus 6).

The closing remark 1 Tim. 4:5 shifts the perspective from the recipient to the giver. In the act of giving, God blesses or sanctifies the gift of food by the word. No ontological change is meant, but rather an idea that is also present in Seneca and belongs to the logic of the gift. Seneca stresses that the gift is identified as a gift by the intention and will of the giver rather than by the external and material circumstances (*On Favors* 1.5.2–3; see appendix C). These intentions can be understood through the words of the giver and the thankful prayer of the recipient. Sanctifying the gift in this sense repeats the event of 4:3–4 from a slightly different perspective. In the word of God, the believers hear the intention of God in the creation. This intention is benevolent and becomes expressed in the giftlike event of meals. The food eaten is sanctified by its giver and received with the proper attitude of thanksgiving.

Value of Godliness (1 Tim. 4:6–11)

Whereas 4:1–5 warns of false teachings, 4:6–11 outlines a positive portrait of the church leader who follows sound doctrine and is trained in godliness. Timothy is first asked to follow the apostolic instructions given above. The expression "giving instructions" (*hypotithemenos*) means general admonition rather than doctrine. Following the indirect rhetorical strategy of the second part of 1 Timothy, Paul gives the instructions to Timothy in order that he would put them into practice. When Timothy does this, he is a "good servant [*diakonos*]" not only of the apostle but of Jesus Christ. The apostolic authority becomes emphasized. *Diakonos* does not here refer to a specific ministry, but the term expresses the christological dimension of service in a solemn manner.

This service is intimately connected with true faith and doctrine. A worthy service is nourished by "the words of the faith and of the sound teaching." Although the two expressions are in many respects synonymous, the substantive *logos* ("word") expresses the content of faith, whereas the adjective *kalos* ("good, sound") refers to the "goodness" of teaching (cf. 1:8–10) in the sense of being "fine," that is, legitimate and trustworthy. One should be nourished by the true content of faith, which is handed over in a trustworthy and legitimate manner. When true faith and good tradition are adopted in this way, the church leader is a good servant of Christ. He keeps himself away from "myths" (4:7a; cf. 1:4). The term "myth" is here strongly pejorative: it means fictitious tales and fables that old people sometimes tell.

After saying this, the apostle begins to describe the spiritual training of Christians, in particular Timothy. In the Greco-Roman world, a virtue is learned by training. Like the skill of a musician or sportsman, the emergence of moral virtue demands continuous exercise. Given this, it is understandable that in Hellenistic philosophy comparisons between the training of athletes and the practice of moral virtues were commonly made. It was also common to say in the manner of the Stoics that the control of one's own desires required an even harder training than the physical games.[2] In 4:7b–10 Paul applies this idea to the spiritual virtue of *eusebeia*.

The obvious theological problem of interpreting this passage is given by 4:1–5. The false teachers demand ascesis. Paul rejects it and presents his own alternative of the proper Christian struggle. How can he himself avoid the problem of ascesis? He admits that "physical training is of some value," whereas "godliness is valuable in every way." So, while rejecting the false ascesis, Paul appreciates training (*gymnazō, gymnasia*) and wants to emphasize the spiritual training that is characterized by the word, which literally means "gymnastics."

Paul here regards godliness in terms of moderation of emotion (*metriopatheia*). If desires are regarded as harmful, one can apply two different strategies to overcome the harm. The best known Stoic strategy is to eradicate the harmful desire and to reach the state of *apatheia* ("freedom from desires"). Another widespread strategy is linked to the Aristotelian idea that a virtue is a mean between two extremes. If the harmful extremes are two opposite desires, then the virtue represents a mean between them. Aristotle, for instance, describes a brave person as representing a virtuous mean between the coward and the rash person. The virtue of *metriopatheia* was a common alternative to the ideal of *apatheia* in Hellenistic philosophical discussion (Aristotle, *Nicomachean Ethics* 1116a [LCL 73.161]; see appendix A).

In 1 Timothy, the virtue of godliness is, as we have seen, depicted as a civil virtue applied to Christianity. Especially in 2:1–4, *eusebeia* is a virtue that connects Christians with the society as a whole. It moderates radicalism and adjusts Christian ideals to the social circumstances. With the help of *eusebeia*, the ascetic lifestyle, the eschatological zeal, and the public role of women become viewed with suspicion. On the other hand, godliness does not mean that Christians should simply live as all other people. Christians must be thought well of by

---

2. Roloff 1988: 243–44, quoting Epictetus, *Discourses* 2.18.22 (LCL 131.354); Seneca, *On the Constancy of the Sage* 2.2 (LCL 213.51, 53); *Epistle* 78.16 (LCL 76.190).

outsiders, and their moral standard ought to be high. In this sense *eusebeia* represents a virtuous mean between excessive radicalism and lazy accommodation (see appendix A).[3]

As a virtue of moderation, *eusebeia* holds "promise for both the present life and the life to come" (4:8b). This key phrase in 4:7b–10 defines the core idea of godliness and explains why it is "valuable in every way" (4:8a). Being valuable (*ōphelimos*) here means being useful; whereas bodily training is useful for some purposes, the finding of the right mean between radical zeal and total accommodation is useful for most, if not all, purposes. Being *ōphelimos* is employed in philosophy as criterion of moral doctrine (Marshall 1999: 333; see also Cicero, *De finibus* 3.33 [LCL 40.253]). Practicing *eusebeia* in this way benefits the person and the Christian community in this life, since Christians are then thought well of by the society at large. It also benefits Christians with a view of the life to come, since godliness keeps the person on the right path, showing respect to the living God.

The phrase "promise ... for life" (*epangelia ... zōēs*; cf. 2 Tim. 1:1) also connects godliness with the life of salvation. This life comes from God. The human being participates in this salvific life already in the present life and also in the life to come. In this way the present life already has something of the promise. The ascesis of false teachers (1 Tim. 4:3) does not realize this theological truth. As in 1:15 and 3:1, the point of 4:9 is to emphasize the message and to give it apostolic authority.

"To this end" in 4:10 refers back to the description of godliness in 4:8. The "toil and struggle" of hard training serves the emergence of the virtue of godliness. The closeness to Col. 1:29 need not be a conscious allusion, since the contexts of the two verses differ considerably. It is obvious, however, that 1 Tim. 4:10 wants to highlight the theological and soteriological perspective of godliness. Christians endure the hard training for this virtue because their hope is set on God, who gives life and salvation. Other people also exercise *eusebeia*, but Christians have a specific promise and therefore a specific motivational hope. For these reasons Christians ought to excel other people in the practice of godliness.

As in 2:3–4, in 4:10 the dual perspective of Christianity becomes evident. God is the Savior of all people and wants everyone to be saved. At the same time, God is "our God" who is the Savior of the believers. The moderated virtue of *eusebeia* keeps both perspectives alive: one is called to appreciate all creation and the whole of humankind, but one is also called to build a specific community of believers that sets its hope in the promise of life to come rather than in the present life. This attitude is no compromise but an attempt to find a virtuous mean between exclusivism and inclusivism. Both ascetic zeal and dull indifference can lead people astray.

3. Given this, godliness and related virtues need not be seen merely as a conservative defense of the status quo or watered-down compromise. See Oberlinner 1994: 184–86.

Again, 4:11 marks the closing of the passage (cf. 1:18; 5:7). Emphasizing his apostolic authority with two imperative forms (*parangelle, didaske*), Paul hands over a body of sound doctrinal teaching to Timothy.

Conduct of the Church Leader (1 Tim. 4:12–5:2)

This passage offers advice to Timothy as a church leader. The advice concerns both moral conduct and the tasks of leadership. A central argumentative role is given to Timothy's ordination, which enables him to perform the tasks at hand. It is not Timothy's personal properties but rather the apostolic task or office that gives him the necessary authority.

First Timothy 4:12 makes an unexpected remark concerning Timothy's age. Also elsewhere (2 Tim. 1:5; 2:22) Timothy is assumed to be a relatively young man. The advice to respect young leaders is actually given to the congregation and intends to have a more general validity. In both Hellenism and Judaism a man under forty was still considered to be young. Jesus and many apostles were young people in this regard. As a new movement, Christianity had many young people in positions of responsibility (Roloff 1988: 251–52; cf. Ignatius of Antioch, *To the Magnesians* 3 [Ehrman 2003: 1.243–45]).

The remark can also be employed as evidence of the new form of leadership emerging in the church. If the earliest form of parish governance was practiced by the elders and the episcopal order begins to replace this form in Timothy's times, then it is natural to argue that the physical age of the leader is not decisive, but rather the valid ordination. At the same time 4:12 does not downplay the personal charism. Although the ordination by the elders is central, the leader has to "set . . . an example in speech and conduct, in love, in faith, in purity."

"In speech" (*en logō*) does not refer to the rhetorical skills but to the content of the *logos*, the sound doctrine. "In conduct" (*en anastrophē*) refers to the moral guidance of life. As elsewhere in 1 Timothy (e.g., 1:9–11), sound doctrine goes together with the right conduct. "In love, in faith, in purity" makes the ethical point of right conduct more concrete. Purity of thoughts and unselfish neighborly love are here accompanied with faith.

The proper tasks of leadership begin to be explained in 4:13. The opening phrase "until I arrive" memorizes Paul's situation (1:3) but it also has a theological function. Public reading and teaching make the apostolic message present even during the absence of the apostle. When Timothy performs these functions, he is linked to the apostolic heritage. "The public reading of scripture" refers to the Jewish and early Christian habit of reading texts of the Jewish Bible in the worship. One can assume that Timothy was expected to read some Christian texts, since they preach the good news and make the apostolic message present, as Paul here presupposes.

We know from other Pauline texts (1 Thess. 5:27; Col. 4:16) that Paul's Epistles were read aloud in Christian gatherings, but here the public reading already takes place in a regulated fashion and is called *anagnōsis*, a term that is employed of the public reading of the Jewish Bible (Acts 13:15; 2 Cor. 3:14). In this important sense we find here a first step toward the canonization of Christian texts being taken (so Roloff 1988: 254–55 and Marshall 1999: 563; see exposition of 1 Tim. 5:18b). We do not know whether the public reading of apostolic texts already follows a certain pattern or a fixed corpus of texts, but the reference to ordination and the formal duty of a parish leader to read these texts reveals that some regulation has occurred.

Paraklēsis ("exhorting") and *didaskalia* ("teaching") may refer to two different activities, but the two terms may also be synonymous. Teaching is related to both sound doctrine and right conduct, whereas exhortation may denote pastoral work in the sense of giving hope and encouragement. Most likely the two words denote different aspects of the same activity: preaching, for instance, consists of both faithful teaching and hopeful exhortation.

First Timothy 4:14 breaks the list of concrete advice and recollects the event of Timothy's ordination. The "council of elders" (*presbyterion*) has ordained Timothy. This remark entails a strange discrepancy with 2 Tim. 1:6, in which Paul laid hands on Timothy. Judging from the immediate context of 1 Tim. 4:14, the ordination described here resembles the Jewish practice of ordaining new teachers by established rabbis with the laying on of hands (see Lohse 1977). The aim of this practice is to preserve the right interpretation of the texts and to display continuity from the teacher to the pupil. Calvin's explanation, according to which *tou presbyteriou* means "ordination to the ministry of presbyter," is hardly possible (1960: 4.3.16).[4]

Another textual difficulty is given by the phrase "through prophecy" (*dia prophēteias*). The NRSV follows the more likely reading, which means that the prophetic word is spoken during the process of ordination. A less likely translation of *dia* is "on the basis of prophetic words." This translation would increase the weight of prophetic predictions concerning the person to be ordained (cf. 1:18), as well as the charism of this person. Although grammatically possible, this translation would be in tension with the otherwise institutional, rather than personal, features of the ordination process described here.

The "gift" (*charisma*; 4:14) of Timothy is not his personal property, but it was given institutionally in the act of ordination. The charism does not come from God immediately, but it is mediated by the elders in the laying on of their hands. The charism is nevertheless prophetic in the sense that the ordination employs prophetic texts and thus connects the ordained person with the prophetic task. This broader context of the gift given to the ordinand makes it more likely to translate *dia* as the NRSV does.

The beginning of 4:15, "put these things into practice," emphasizes the central place of ordination in the list of duties. The ordained person conducts the life

4. I follow Roloff 1988: 258–59. Marshall 1999: 569 finds that 4:14 "supports presbyterian rather than episcopal ordination."

of the local church. He has the authority and the charism needed. These gifts are prophetic gifts of God, but at the same time they are mediated through the ordination process that preserves the institutional continuity of the church.

The next sentences (4:15b–16) shift the focus again to Timothy's person. When Timothy devotes himself to the duties and tasks at hand, the parish members and "all," even the outsiders (3:7), can see his progress. In this way his character compensates his young age. The "progress" (*prokopē*) mentioned primarily pertains to the virtue of godliness. *Prokopē* is a philosophical term that means approaching the goal aimed at through education and training (see appendix A and Epictetus, *Discourse* 1.4 [LCL 131.27–37]). In the context of 1 Timothy this means the striving after *eusebeia*. False teachers also make progress, but toward the false goal of impiety (*asebeia*; 2 Tim. 2:16; 3:13).

Since godliness consists of both sound doctrine and right conduct, Timothy needs to "pay close attention" to his teaching and personal behavior (1 Tim. 4:16). The closing phrase of this admonition gives a theological reason to the practice of these duties. When Timothy continues to do the things Paul advises him to do, he will "save [*sōzō*] both [him]self and [his] hearers." This does not mean synergism or "saving oneself" in any problematic sense. Teaching and proclamation bring the gospel of salvation to other people. In this sense Paul can describe the apostolic ministry as "saving" (cf. 1 Cor. 9:22). The point of 1 Tim. 4:16 is to claim that not only teaching, but also right conduct and the practice of godliness, are essential to this ministry. Through their virtuous conduct, ministers participate in the salvatory reality that is not only essential for their own salvation, but also sets an example for other people and thus contributes to their understanding of Christianity.

The next verses (5:1–2) are connected with this flow of thought. When the church leader wants to set an example, he should follow certain rules in dealing with other people. These rules are common in Hellenistic moral philosophy. Timothy deserves respect from all parish members (4:12), but he must also show respect to the different groups of people. Older men are to be addressed with the same respect as one's own father. Younger men should be treated as brothers. The Christian community follows the ideal of good family relationships. The ideal of "attachment" or "familiarization" (*oikeiōsis*) is visible (see appendix A).

In the same spirit of family resemblance, older women are to be treated like one's mother and younger women like sisters. Mentioning "absolute purity" here does not refer to celibacy or ascesis, since such an interpretation would conflict with 4:3. Paul means simply that sexual aspects in dealing with women compromise the godliness of the church leader. In addition to familiar attachment, some detachment or contentment (*autarkeia*) is also necessary for a leader. According to 5:1–2 men and women are to be treated with equal respect and honor. This is significant in view of women being criticized in other passages (2:14; 5:3–16).

Dealing with Widows (1 Tim. 5:3–16)

A lengthy passage is devoted to the particular problem of aiding the widows in the congregation. The guidelines are relatively clear, but the passage is nevertheless difficult to interpret. At least three related problems precipitate these difficulties:

1. The guidelines give the impression that whenever possible the widows should not receive help from the parish. This feature is difficult to combine with the virtues of Christian love expressed elsewhere in the Pastoral Epistles and the New Testament as a whole.
2. The apostle seems to have an extremely negative opinion of the behavior and moral standard of many Christian widows.
3. The social problems related to widowhood in Hellenistic times need closer examination.

It is easiest to begin with the last point. In Roman cities, many men died relatively early and no social security was provided by the society. Thus the larger family with relatives, the *oikos*, provided for the needs of widows and orphans. In most cases, their legal and social rights remained weak. In Judaism, many biblical texts defend the rights of widows and orphans (e.g., Exod. 22:22; Deut. 24:17, 19–21; Isa. 1:23; Ezek. 22:6–8), but their concrete situation remained weak in first-century Judaism.[5]

In Acts 6:1 we read that "the Hellenists complained against the Hebrews" that their widows did not receive food. This criticism led to the installation of seven deacons, whose task it was to distribute food (6:2–6). The same kind of institutional help, apart from the *oikos*, is described in 1 Tim. 5:3–16. In the Pauline Epistles we see that not only did widows receive social help, but also that the position of widow was institutionalized in early Christianity. Institutional widows are expected to remain unmarried (1 Cor. 7:8–9). According to the idealized picture of Luke 2:36–38, which is echoed in 1 Tim. 5:5, a widow worships with fasting and prayer night and day. Since we cannot, however, see any established rules of tasks pertaining to widows in the New Testament, one cannot speak of a distinct ministry of widows.

At the same time, widows are not only passive recipients of help, but they appear as active moral subjects. Paul recommends that the widows should remain unmarried (1 Cor. 7:8–9, 39). Tabitha, the woman disciple, practices charity among a group of widows (Acts 9:36–37, 39). In 1 Tim. 5:3–16 widows are depicted as passive recipients of help (5:5), but at the same time they are described as being active in doing both good and bad (5:10–15). When widows say "what

---

5. Marshall 1999: 574–80 lists literature pertaining to social history. Cf. Thurston 1989 and Schüssler Fiorenza 1983: 309–15.

they should not say" (5:13), they even appear as active propagators of heresy. Although widows are portrayed as a group in society, careful differentiation among the members of this group is necessary, depending on their age, wealth, duties, and moral character.

In 5:3 this differentiation is begun with the introduction of the concept of a "real widow." A real widow is a person who should be supported by the institutional poor relief of the congregation. She is "on the list" (5:9) of persons to be aided. "Honoring" a real widow is not only a matter of respect but of material aid. A similar act of material "honoring" is due to elders (5:17–18).

The civil duty of one's own family or household is explained in 5:4. If the widow has children or grandchildren, they should take care of her. This is the common "filial piety" that we know from many cultures. The verb *eusebeō* ("to do the religious duty") connects the moral norm with Paul's general idea of civil godliness. The assumption of the NRSV that the phrase "they should . . . learn" pertains to children and grandchildren is logical and preserves the general flow of the advice given here. It is also possible to translate "they" as pertaining to the widows who, according to that translation, should pay their first duty to the family. In any case, the social role of family ties is seen as "pleasing in God's sight." As in 3:5, the household has in 5:4 some kind of theological significance.

The real widow is depicted in idealistic terms (5:5) and contrasted with the widow who "lives for pleasure" (5:6). The description of a real widow is influenced by Luke 2:37. That she is praying continuously does not need to refer to any specific liturgical office of widows. The contrast to the earlier active and exemplary life (1 Tim. 5:10) may simply mean that the real widow who is at least sixty years old (5:9) can or should no longer do physical work but nevertheless has the important task of praying. At the same time, the continuous prayer is mentioned in order to remind the other prospective applicants for the "list" that the institution of widowhood should not be used as mere social security but is reserved for those old women who are entirely "left alone."

In addition to this admonition, 5:6 describes the life of richer widows as miserable. Reasons for this portrayal are not given. It seems obvious that the apostle regards some female lifestyles as compatible with the ideal of godliness, whereas others do not receive his appreciation. Younger Christian women should marry, work hard for the household, and remain submissive to their husbands, whereas older women can be pious within the institution of widowhood. Younger unmarried women as well as all elderly women who do not qualify as real widows remain suspect. In general terms, independent women and women who control their own property are met with criticism in both 5:6–16 and 2:8–15. They spread gossip (5:13) and have illicit sensual desires (5:11).

A responsible theological interpretation of such passages should see various patterns at work at the same time. The apostle wants to promote godliness, and his concept of proper civil godliness is threatened by such female behavior. If a modern, Western interpreter would claim that women should not have rights of property or that rich elderly ladies should be regarded as "dead" even while living (5:6), this interpreter would seriously conflict with the *eusebeia* of our own society. As in 2:12–15, a literal understanding of the text within the conditions of modernity would violate the author's basic intention to improve the reputation of a certain part of his flock in the broader society.

An opposite interpretation, taking the values of our own society for granted and understanding the text as relative to them, also has its problems. Maybe in the case of 5:3–16 these problems are not very significant and one can simply read the text as an attempt to treat elderly women in keeping with the civil virtue of filial piety and hopefully better than the rest of society. But, as a general rule, an uncritical accommodation to one's own circumstances cannot be recommended as a hermeneutical principle. One probably needs an interpretation that proceeds from the ideal of the virtuous mean: when the literal meaning of the texts applies the virtue of *eusebeia*, both the extreme accommodation to one's own society and the extremely countercultural expositions need to be avoided.

In 5:7–8 the same guidelines are emphatically repeated. The lifestyle of the real widow should be regulated as a normative code of conduct in order that nobody would criticize the widows for idleness or for seeking pleasure. In a similar manner, filial piety needs to be commanded with the authority of faith. Even unbelievers exercise filial piety. Christians should excel in the display of this civil virtue. Because the domestic sphere of the *oikos* is particularly suitable for women, widows should primarily seek security in the realm of the household.

First Timothy 5:9–16 continues to define the real widow. At the same time, various virtues and vices are mentioned that give a vivid picture of the circumstances in early Christian congregations. The concrete norms of 5:9—"sixty years old" and "married only once"—resemble the requirements for bishops, deacons, and deaconesses (3:2–12) and give some support to the hypothesis that widows have some kind of ministry (Thurston 1989). The high age and the description of the task as praying alone (5:5) make it nevertheless more probable that the life of real widows resembles retirement rather than any kind of ministry. The requirement of having been married only once, although similar to 3:2 and 3:12, may have concerned women in a more consistent manner. In the Roman world it was considered virtuous to remain a widow and thus to earn the title *univira* (Roloff 1988: 293–96).

The impression of quiet retirement is to an extent questioned by 5:10, in which the active virtues of the real widow are described. Although the description moves to the past tense, one can read the virtues as having to do with the present reality of the widow. Given the high age and the requirement of quiet life assumed in 5:5, it is most plausible to read 5:10 to the effect that the old widow has for the most part displayed these virtues in the past, although she may still continue to practice them in some way.

More interesting than this issue is the actual catalogue of virtues, since it exemplifies the life of virtuous Christian woman. Bringing up children is not a virtue of women only, but in the household this duty concerns men likewise, as 3:4 shows. Hospitality also concerns women as well as bishops (3:2), although here not the substantive *philoxenia*, but the verb *xenodocheō* ("to show hospitality") is employed. Maybe *philoxenia* (lit., "love toward a stranger") would have been too strong expression in the case of women, but the central role of good treatment of strangers is significant. Washing the saints' feet is a typical, but nevertheless limited expression of hospitality (cf. John 13:14-17), since the word "saints" does not refer to strangers but to other Christians (see appendix C and Chrysostom's comments on this passage, described in excursus 5).

Helping "the afflicted" (*thlibomenois*) underlines the active role taken by Christian women. The active service of Tabitha (Acts 9:36, 39) offers here a parallel. Paul refers to all kinds of sufferings and tribulations with the verb *thlibō* (1 Thess. 3:3-4; 2 Cor. 1:4-5). In such tribulations we participate in Christ's afflictions (Col. 1:24; 2 Cor. 4:8-11). Women play an important role in alleviating suffering. The closing phrase of 1 Tim. 5:10, "doing good in every way," rounds out the description of virtues, but it also fits well together with the thought of helping the afflicted, since in both phrases a comprehensive and active source of assistance is presupposed.

First Timothy 5:11-13 appears to be both misogynic and prejudiced. It is hard to interpret it in a constructive manner. It also seems severely inconsistent, because the apostle recommends young widows to remarry (5:14), but he also says that a wish to remarry "incur[s] condemnation" (5:12). In 5:11-12 the author has 1 Cor. 7:8, 40 in mind, in which Paul recommends that widows not marry. At the same time, the author here wants to deny access to the institution of widowhood to younger widows. The "first pledge" refers to the promise of solitude and celibacy required from institutional widows. The threat of condemnation is directed to the institutional widows who have promised to live according to the prescribed standards. The threat of condemnation is employed in order to emphasize the seriousness of becoming a real widow.

In 1 Tim. 5:13 the bad consequences of burdening younger widows with the obligations of a real widow are emphasized through examples. If young widows are given the status of a real widow, they have time and energy to devote themselves to activities that harm the congregation. Learning to be "idle" offers a contrast to learning in "silence" (2:11). Solitude serves acceptable goals only when the proper context is given. A good woman stays within her household, but these widows go "from house to house," thus breaking out from the proper context of one's own household.

In addition to idleness, such conduct makes women active talkers who do not practice the silence that is praised in 2:11. Generally speaking, this talkative behavior is described as spreading gossip (*phlyaroi*) and as being busybodies (*periergoi*). The first word means simply "talkative," whereas the second refers to curiosity and spreading rumors. More seriously, however, the apostle refers to these widows as "saying what they should not say" (*lalousai ta mē deonta*). In Titus 1:11 "what is not right [*ha mē dei*] to teach" refers to heresies, and 2 Tim. 3:6 claims that false teachers "make their way into households and captivate silly women." In 1 Tim. 5:15 it is remarked that some young widows already "follow Satan." Given these analogies, the young widows are here accused of spreading false teachings (Roloff 1988: 297–98; Marshall 1999: 603). When the proper structure of households is disturbed, false teachings begin to find supporters.

A theological interpreter has to be careful here. Taken literally, this view of women would make impossible the calling of younger nuns. It would also restrict women's role in general to the household of her own family until the age of sixty. The guidelines are motivated by the view that younger women remain captive to their "sensual desires" (5:11) and should therefore remain within their own households. Probably no church today shares this view in its totality. Without excusing the apostle, one can add that this negative view of women does not only serve misogynic purposes, but the author employs it in order to alleviate the earlier Pauline recommendation that widows should not marry.

Paul (1 Cor. 7:8, 40) recommends that widows should not remarry. But here the apostle says: "I would have younger widows marry" (1 Tim. 5:14). He does not want to conflict with his own, Pauline and apostolic, authority, and therefore he builds a somewhat odd ethical construct. Real widows should follow the advice of 1 Corinthians. Even for younger widows, the desire to remarry means an "alienat[ion] . . . from Christ," and in this sense the advice of 1 Corinthians remains theoretically correct. On the other hand, the perpetual unmarried state of younger widows would cause other and greater harm. Young widows would unnecessarily burden the finances of the congregation. At the same time, they would break the proper and godly structure of households by going from house to house and spreading rumor and even heresies. Therefore, the advice that younger women should remarry is a lesser evil. They would lose the title *univira*, but in many other respects a new marriage would benefit their godliness.

In this sense, the overall intention of 1 Tim. 5:3–16 is to moderate the earlier Pauline recommendation of 1 Cor. 7:8, 40. The desired end is more friendly to the younger widows, because they now get the permission and even recommendation to remarry. But, naturally, the desired end does not as such justify the means employed by the apostle. First Timothy 5:3–16 aims at serving the well-being of both the congregation and the younger widows, but employs misogynic arguments. The matter is complicated, since Paul in 1 Corinthians is more friendly toward women in general, but his recommendation not to remarry may have laid an unnecessary burden on young widows. In 1 Tim. 5:3–16 this burden is alleviated, but at the same time the general picture of women gets darker.

After the somewhat complicated argument, 5:14 describes the new rule given by the apostle. Widows who do not qualify as real widows may find a suitable Christian existence through remarrying. Their bearing children offers evidence of their belonging to the salvatory reality (cf. 2:15). They do not shake the grounds of household ethics, but manage their households as all housewives do. As in other places (3:4–5, 12–13), the task of "managing households" (*oikodespoteō*) is given a theological importance. When this task is performed well, the non-believing person or "adversary" (*antikeimenos* refers to humans, not to Satan) has no occasion to lead Christians astray. Like the church or congregation, the household appears to be an almost sacred space in which people remain in the sphere of salvation.

One needs to see that this character of household does not relate to women in any particular sense. "Managing households" is the task of both women and men, as the use of the verb *proistēmi* in 3:4 and 3:12 shows. The verb *oikodespoteō* employed of women in 5:14 carries strongly the idea of being the "master of the house." The apostle may here think that the young widows want to be active subjects of their life, but instead of seeking the fulfilment of this calling in talking "from house to house," they can find it through remarrying into a new household. The secular and at the same time theological duty of taking care of one's own household applies to both men and women alike (for the "handing over" of Christianity as a duty of both sexes, see appendix C and excursus 6).

The closing remarks do not add much to the actual topic. The statement that "some have already turned away" (5:15) strengthens the assumption (5:13) that some young widows have been among the false teachers. The denial of marriage (4:3) by the false teachers fits well with this picture. The last remark (5:16) is another attempt to have as few real widows on the list of the congregation as possible. As in 5:4, the duty of relatives to help widows is emphasized. Church members can help both the widow and their church by taking responsibility of the relative in question. Although some manuscripts say "believing man or woman," it is more likely that 5:16 is addressed to the wealthy women in the congregation. Although the economic point "let the church not be burdened" appears only here, it is in some way presupposed throughout 5:3–16.

In sum, the narrow definition of real widows serves a dual purpose. It allows many, if not most, widows to remarry, and it keeps the financial burden of the church within limits. One may find both of these ends, as such, fully legitimate and nevertheless think at the same time that the arguments used to promote them needlessly oppress women, especially young widows.

Three theological concerns emerge from this difficult passage. First, it shows that the Christian church wants to promote institutional aid that is available outside one's own family. Second, the passage witnesses to the many-sided activities of Christian women in the early church. Although the institution of widowhood probably cannot be regarded as a ministry, it ascribes many important tasks to elderly widows as well as to younger ones. Third, in spite of institutionalized assistance the primacy of the household is underlined. Both men and women are called to manage their own household well. This task is primary and shapes the person's activities in other social arenas.

Position of Elders in the Church (1 Tim. 5:17–20)

Earlier in 1 Timothy, the word *presbyteros* appears both referring to a certain position or ministry (4:14) and as a characterization of an elderly man (5:1). Since this passage follows the treatment of elderly women, one could try to interpret the term as simply meaning "elderly man." In 5:17–25 such an interpretation would nevertheless remain highly unlikely, since the passage speaks of "preaching and teaching" (5:17), of ordination (5:22), and of the public discipline of elders exercised by Timothy (5:20). The passage needs to be understood as speaking of the ministry of elders, and it cannot be read as a counterpart to the treatment of widows. I will divide the passage into two parts: whereas the first part (5:17–20) treats the position of the presbyters in the church, the second part (5:21–25) is meant to serve as direct advice to Timothy to develop his judgment and skills in his position of leadership.

Another and more difficult general problem pertains to the authority of this presbyterial ministry in running the congregation or the local church. In 4:14 a collegium of presbyters is mentioned. This collegium has ordained Timothy, and now Timothy is said to be in charge of further ordinations (5:22). It is evident that Timothy is in charge of the presbyters. But the nature of presbyterial ministry remains less clear. According to the standard picture of historical scholarship, the elders formed the oldest structure of parish leaders. In the time of Timothy, the episcopal ministry gains in importance. Although I argued in the exposition of 3:5 that a bishop can oversee a larger unit of "God's church," the evidence of the Pastoral Epistles as a whole does not allow us to take a strong stance with regard to the mutual relationship of the two ministries (see excursuses 2 and 7).[6]

In 5:17 "the elders who rule well [*kalōs proestōtes*]" are worthy of "double honor." As in 3:4 and 3:12, the verb *proistēmi* is employed of good leadership. Presbyters are thus connected with bishops and deacons in the task of leadership. The word for "honor" (*timē*) cannot mean only praise, since 5:18 speaks of payment. It is probably not a regular salary, but some other kind of remuneration. If we assume that the elders in the earliest Christian congregations were not full-time pastors but representatives of the local congregation (Acts 11:30; 15:2–4; 21:18), we can see here a development toward the profession of a presbyter or even a parish pastor.

Some people among the collegium of presbyters labor "in preaching and teaching" (*en logō kai didaskalia*). As elsewhere in 1 Timothy (1:3, 10; 3:2; 4:16), leadership occurs through teaching and doctrine. It is assumed that Timothy has the authority over these persons. The passage, together with 3:1–13, thus gives some support to the "threefold ministry" of church leaders, presbyters, and deacons. But it does not rule out the view that the ministry of doctrinal teaching is essentially one and that church leaders, bishops, and presbyters participate in

6. Marshall 1999: 512–21 offers noteworthy evidence in favor of "low-church" views.

the same ministry. The circumstance that Timothy was himself ordained by the presbyters (4:14) as well as the mention in Acts 20:28 that some presbyters were made bishops give further support to the view of "one ministry" (Pelikan 2005: 91–93; Marshall 1999: 170–81; Roloff 1988: 263–81).

The following argument in support of remuneration is theologically remarkable for a specific reason. The apostle refers not only to Deut. 25:4 but also to Luke 10:7 (and 1 Cor. 9:9, 14; cf. Matt. 10:10) as "scripture" (*hē graphē*). This would mean that in Timothy's time the church already had some texts that could be referred to as Christian Scripture. We met this assumption already in 1 Tim. 4:13. The assumption is heatedly debated in exegetical literature. It has been suggested that 5:18b must be a gloss, since for the early Christians "scripture" meant the Jewish Bible until the end of second century. One can also claim that the term "scripture" here pertains only to Deut. 25:4 and its quotation in 1 Cor. 9:9. Given this, the use of the word of Jesus would be only an allusion through 1 Cor. 9:14. On the other hand *Barnabas* 4.14 and *2 Clement* 2.4 (Ehrman 2003: 2.25; 1.167) already refer to the words of Jesus as Scripture (Marshall 1999: 615 gives a brief overview of the debate).

The theological interpretation here can follow the plain meaning, which regards the words of Jesus as Scripture. This understanding receives support from *2 Clement* and *Barnabas*, but also from the general intention of the author to give Paul a special weight as apostle and to treat his teaching as highly normative. When 1 Cor. 9:14 says that "the Lord commanded" that preachers should be rewarded, it is not unnatural to assume that the same words of Jesus were later quoted with scriptural authority. We cannot say that *hē graphē* would here refer to an established body of Christian texts, but we can say that such collections existed, were publicly read in the congregations, and could thus be referred to.

Similarly to 1 Cor. 9:9–14, the two references serve in 1 Tim. 5:18 as an argument in favor of paying double remuneration to some elders. We know nothing about the quantity of such payments but can assume that a double payment qualifies the presbyter as a "laborer." In 5:19 further security is given to presbyters. Accusations against them should be backed by a sufficient number of witnesses. The apostle here thinks of Deut. 19:15 and maybe Matt. 18:16, but he is actually stricter than the Mosaic law. In Deut. 19:15 a person can be convicted on the basis of two or three witnesses, whereas in 1 Tim. 5:19 they suffice only for the serious hearing of the accusation. This reflects the apostle's intention to safeguard the position of elders in a congregation.

The strong position of elders is also visible in 5:20. When a presbyter has been found guilty of sin (the NRSV's "persist in sin" may be too strong), he is to be publicly "rebuked" or corrected (*elenchō*). Although this disciplinary act is supposed to awake fear in other people as well, it is more moderate than the church order described in Matt. 18:15–20. No possibility of excommunication is mentioned, and the presbyter can continue in his ministry after the disciplinary act. It seems that the apostle is here, as in the case of widows (1 Tim. 5:3–16), carefully alleviating earlier practices. Presbyters are entitled to remuneration, they should be protected against accusations, and public rebuke does not lead to the loss of office.

This tendency fits well together with the overall virtue of *eusebeia*, which can be understood as moderation between religious zeal and secularized indifference. The church and its leaders need to affirm the world with its civil habits and virtues, for instance, marriage and magnanimity, while nevertheless striving after Christian "progress" (4:15) and "purity" (5:22).

Instructions Concerning Right Judgment (1 Tim. 5:21–25)

In 5:21 Paul suddenly refers to God, Jesus Christ, and the angels in order to underline the authoritative character of the preceding statements. As we have seen, similar emphatic reminders are scattered in many places (e.g., 1:18; 4:11; 5:7), but this time the statement has a particularly solemn, liturgical tone (cf. 2 Tim. 4:1). Reasons for this tone are not obvious, but one is tempted to think that after the apostle has moderated some traditional guidelines pertaining to widows (1 Cor. 7:8, 40) and sinful church members (Matt. 18:15–17), it is necessary to emphasize that the new policies are meant to be taken seriously. At the same time, the solemn tone initiates a new section that deals with the divine and human capacity of judgment.

The apostle claims that the instructions should be followed "without prejudice" (*chōris prokrimatos*). This expression is a Latinism (*absque praeiudicatio*) that, employed as a legal term, refers to the hearing of witnesses (Roloff 1988: 312). The Latin *praeiudicatio* can refer to both positive and negative attitudes preceding the judgment. The other qualification of judging without "partiality" (*proklisis*) is more closely related to the vice of favoring the accused person.

Commentators tend to regard the two phrases as synonymous, meaning favor toward the accused. The Vulgate translates the phrases *sine praeiudicio nihil faciens in aliam partem declinando*. It would also make sense to say that whereas the first phrase refers to negative prejudices toward the accused, the second speaks of positive favor toward them.[7] In any case, Timothy is reminded to be a fair judge with regard to controversial issues. Given that the new instructions moderate the earlier practice, possible conflicts may involve either the hard-liners or the liberals. A careful and impartial attention to the new guidelines is thus necessary.

Apart from this disciplinary intention, the liturgical phrase may refer to the presence of "two or three witnesses" required above, but the phrase is probably also connected with Dan. 7:13 and Mark 8:38. Connecting many issues in this way, the construction reflects the literary skill of the apostle. When the Son of

---

7. Marshall 1999: 620 has a slightly different exposition: the first phrase indicates no preformed opinions, the second phrase speaks of no partiality. Roloff 1988: 312 and Oberlinner 1994: 258 prefer to speak of synonymous phrases.

Man comes in the glory of his Father and with angels in Mark 8:38, he appears as the judge. It is also important to note that this section closes (1 Tim. 5:24–25) with another solemn reference to the last judgment. Timothy's impartiality in judging the presbyters with the help of "these instructions" is thus compared with the divine judgment.

The next two verses (5:22–23) spell out four guidelines that seem to have little to do with each other or with other matters in the context. On a closer look, however, they can all be read as descriptions of finding a virtuous mean and of making an impartial judgment between two extremes.

The first advice, acting "hastily," can be regarded as a typical mistake of young or inexperienced persons. Aristotle says that young people pursue what is immediately before them. They tend to follow their passions and therefore go wrong (*Nicomachean Ethics* 1156a34–35; 1095a2–5; 1128b17–18 [LCL 73.461, 9, 249]). Delay and hesitation are also vices, but young people are more likely to go wrong in haste. Aristotle's description of youth as quick-tempered and sanguine people who are easily cheated and overdo everything in their haste captures the Greek paradigm of the vice of acting hastily (*Rhetorics* 1389a2–b11 [LCL 193.247–51]). Such an ideal of *metriopatheia* may be connected with the advice of not ordaining people hastily in 5:22. As a young church leader Timothy may be too rash in his attempt to serve the church well, in particular in dealing with the more experienced "elders."

The precise meaning and context of the laying on of hands continues to be discussed extensively in the exegetical research. Already in patristic times, some fathers interpreted it as referring to the absolution after repentance, whereas others connected it with ordination. Nowadays most interpreters and Bible translations find the second meaning to be more plausible.[8] But who is ordained and to which office? We do not obtain all answers to these good questions.

My interpretation proceeds from the premise that 5:22–23 constitutes a series of this type of advice to Timothy that applies the ideal of moderation of emotion. The first advice simply says that the church leader, in this case Timothy, should carefully examine the person to be ordained. The needs of church life may demand a rapid series of ordinations, but the church leader should nevertheless avoid making hasty decisions. The laying on of hands endows the ordained with a specific gift (4:14), but careful examination of the person's own properties and of external circumstances always remains necessary.

The second and the third advice of 5:22 belong together and aim at supporting the impartiality (5:21) of the church leader. A responsible leader ought to be "above reproach" (3:2) and "well thought of" by outsiders (3:7). Therefore it is obvious that he should "not participate in the sins of others" and that

---

8. Oberlinner 1994: 259–60 and Roloff 1988: 313–14 are in favor of ordination, as is John Chrysostom, *On the Priesthood* 4.1 (NPNF¹ 9.61). So is Marshall 1999: 620–21, although he speaks of the "appointment of church leaders."

he should "keep [him]self pure." But it is also important to see the virtuous mean that lies between alienation and extreme attachment. The leader ought to pay attention to all parties in his church, but at the same time he should keep himself pure (cf. 5:1–2). Active involvement in the matters of the church members should not compromise the impartial character of the leader. In this sense 5:22 does not speak only of high moral standards, but also of the right distance necessary for a position of leadership. Both attachment and detachment are needed.

The fourth advice of "tak[ing] a little wine" (5:23) is often regarded by the commentators as an unexpected remark that breaks the flow of the text. But the advice can be understood as another recommendation to moderate one's own standards. A person with ascetic leanings hesitates to drink wine. But the body consists of many different elements that ought to stay in balance. Ailments may follow from an imbalance in diet. Virtue and purity do not consist in cultivating one extreme, but rather in achieving the right mean between the extremes. Health and right judgments likewise presuppose an impartial balance. Both unnecessary hesitation and rigid absolutism may be symptomatic of false ascesis (cf. 4:3). Too much wine is harmful, but a little wine may help to achieve the balance.

The four pieces of advice in 5:22–23 thus pertain to the training that aims at the formation of right judgment. In this way the advice is connected with the virtues of impartiality and godliness. In 5:24–25 the apostle shifts the perspective to other people and instructs Timothy about making the right judgment of their behavior. Timothy should be aware of the issue that some sins are manifest, whereas others remain hidden. At the same time, *krisis* refers to the eschatological judgment already alluded to in 5:21. Thus 5:24–25 rounds out the section.

The content of the two proverbial sentences is obvious: it is easy to judge some people because their sins are "conspicuous" (*prodēloi*; Vulgate: *manifesta*). But the hidden sins of other people also follow them to the last judgment. To see this, however, we must wait for God's judgment. Human judgment is important and should be trained, as 5:21–23 teaches, but the final *krisis* is left to God. The last verse of this passage, 5:25, is constructed as a counterpart to the preceding sentence. "Good works" are normally manifest. But even when they are not, they will not remain hidden for ever.

In sum, I argue that 5:21–25 forms a consistent and carefully planned literary unit. In its beginning and end, a strong reference to the last judgment is made. Between these references, the church leader is advised to make right judgments on the basis of impartiality. With the help of four specific guidelines, he is informed of the practice of finding the right mean between harmful extremes. The balances between the extremes of rashness and hesitation, involvement and alienation, ascesis and addiction, are all important for the training of right judgment.

Duties of Slaves (1 Tim. 6:1–2)

A brief instruction concerning the slaves is included in the duties of various groups in the church. The high relevance of *oikos* ("household") for the apostle may have prompted him to mention slaves. Instructions about slaves appear in many Pauline epistles (Eph. 6:5–8; Col. 3:22–25; Philemon). The instructions given in 1 Tim. 6:1–2 follow the same ideal of household obedience present in other Pauline epistles. The social problem behind 6:1–2 is the disrespectful behavior of Christian slaves toward their masters in the congregation. Since in Christ "there is no longer slave or free" (Gal. 3:28), some slaves had obviously drawn the conclusion that an egalitarian behavior is proper in the church.

The first instruction (1 Tim. 6:1) is given to all Christian slaves irrespective of whether their master is a Christian. Taken literally, 6:1 pertains to all slaves, but one can assume that the instruction is given to Christian slaves, since otherwise the reason in the second half of the verse would not make sense. "Under the yoke" (*hypo zygon*) gives the impression that slavery is not a part of Christian personhood, but only a sociological reality. "Worthy of all honor" also pertains to the external behavior dictated by the social role rather than by the internal dignity of the person.

The point of 6:1 is that Christian slaves should not behave in an egalitarian manner toward their masters. The reason for this instruction is social rather than theological. Such behavior would be blasphemy in the sense that a non-Christian master would regard the influence of Christianity on the slave as negative. In order to respect "the name of God" and the doctrinal "teaching" (*didaskalia*), the slave should respect civil godliness and not give the master a bad impression of Christianity. The intention of the instruction is therefore more pragmatic than theological (so Roloff 1988: 321; Oberlinner 1994: 265–66 remarks that the grounds given are nevertheless theological). As in 3:7, Christianity should be well thought of by the outsiders.

In 6:2 the focus is shifted toward the situation in which both the slave and the master are Christians. The apostle argues that also in this relationship an egalitarian behavior is not proper. The NRSV's "they are members of the church" is very free. The Greek *hoti adelphoi eisin* ("because they are brothers") matches the later phrase *hoti pistoi eisin kai agapētoi* ("because they are faithful and beloved"). The argument is obvious: membership in the same group should not lessen obedience, but increase it, since the beloved master benefits from the service, and Christian love wants to help others.

The argument does not downgrade slavery, but makes a straightforward point: you should not neglect your work on the grounds that your boss belongs to the same parish. At the same time, the apostle thinks about the transitive influence of this relationship toward third parties. When outsiders see that a Christian slave works hard and conscientiously for both Christian and non-Christian masters, Christians are regarded as good practitioners of the civil virtue of godliness.

As a whole, slavery is expounded in pragmatic terms. It does not concern personhood but the social role of the person; in this sense it resembles the contracts of employment in some, though not in all, respects. The pragmatic and social emphasis of 6:1–2 gives the impression that the Christian message promotes equality and regards a person valuable irrespective of his or her social standing. Given this observation, it may be easier to interpret other texts in which the household ethics is more directly argued as the will of God (e.g., Eph. 6:6).

The final phrase "teach and urge these duties" again (e.g., 1 Tim. 1:3; 4:11; 5:21) underlines the importance of the aforesaid instructions and marks the transition to the next section.

TRUE AND FALSE TEACHERS

1 Tim. 6:3–21

The closing section of the epistle contrasts false and true teachers and their teachings or doctrines. When in the following exposition I designate *didaskalia* and *logoi* as doctrine, this occurs with the consciousness that teaching and life belong together. The closing section bears some resemblance to the introductory part (1:1–20). In both, sound doctrine is contrasted to false teaching and various catalogues of virtuous and blameworthy conduct are given. Both parts employ liturgical phrases with rich theological content. In telling Timothy to guard what has been entrusted to him, 6:20 clearly refers to 1:18. The actual instructions given in the main body of the epistle are surrounded by a discussion that underlines the importance of sound doctrine.

The closing section has three clearly distinguishable parts. First comes an extensive characterization of false teaching and its motivational background (6:3–10). Then the advancement of sound doctrine is described in theological and liturgical terms (6:11–16). In the third part (6:17–21), brief instructions for rich Christians are given and a final admonition to Timothy is formulated.

False Teachers Are Mentally Disturbed (1 Tim. 6:3–10)

Paul begins the last part of 1 Timothy by going back to the terminology of the first chapter. The false teachers do not agree with "the sound words" (*hygiainontes logoi*) of Jesus Christ or with "the teaching that is in accordance with godliness" (*kat' eusebeian didaskalia*). But whereas 1:10 gives only "sound doctrine" (*hygiainousa didaskalia*) as the norm, we can ask whether two sources of normative doctrine are mentioned in 6:3.

Although one could claim that "sound words" refer to a collection of the words of Jesus employed also in 5:18, the issue here is that the authority of the church and its teachers is based on the sound doctrine that is essentially one (Oberlinner 1994: 273). In addition, both phrases connect a cognitive-verbal component (*logoi, didaskalia*) with a behavioral-normative aspect (*hygiainontes, kat' eusebeian*). Thus both phrases are synonymous insofar as they underline that sound teaching and right conduct go hand in hand. In 6:2 Timothy is commanded to "teach and urge" (*didaske kai parakalei*) this totality of instructions.

Another disputed point in 6:3 concerns the precise meaning of *mē proserchetai*, which the NRSV translates as "does not agree with" (Vulgate: *non adquiescit*). Other possibilities include the literal meaning "does not come" (i.e., to you with the sound words) and "does not devote oneself to" (Marshall 1999: 638). Choosing among these variants is a minor issue, since in any case the point is that false teachers do not submit themselves to the apostolic authority. But it is important to hear the idea of "coming to" or "approaching" sound or "healthy" words. Doctrine is here understood as a cognitive-behavioral unity toward which the true believers are assumed to approach. Approaching the doctrine is not primarily an issue of submitting to an authority, but of readiness and the will to measure oneself on the basis of a given model. This model is essential for the comprehensive health of the person, as 6:4–10 shows in more detail.

First Timothy 6:4–5 contains slander toward persons who do not want to approach sound teaching. True doctrines are "healthy" (*hygiainontes*), but false teachers are sick or "morbid" (*noseō*). Although the series of invectives at first glance appears as an emotional outburst of the apostle, it employs a certain argumentative structure. Two points of departure are presupposed: (1) the false teachers are not content with the given model but they aim at making original contributions, and (2) this behavior is related to sickness and other comparable disturbances.

The idea of being "conceited" employs the verb *typhoomai*,[1] which in philosophical texts means the kind of stupidity in which a person obstinately remains fixed to some aspects and is blind toward others (Roloff 1988: 332; Marshall 1999: 640). "Understanding/knowing nothing" (*mēden epistamenos*) is closely related to this one-sided obsession that replaces true knowledge. The apostle aims at describing a psychopathic character whose morbid obstinacy forces him to follow the chosen path, leading necessarily to "controversies" (*logomachia*), also referred to in 2 Tim. 2:23. One can plausibly relate this quarrelsome behavior to the myths, genealogies, and other speculations mentioned in 1 Tim. 1:4.

A list of vices accompanies this psychopathic conduct. "Envy" (*phthonos*) and "quarrelsomeness" (*eris*) are connected with the struggle for power and supporters, whereas cases of "slander" (*blasphēmia*) and "base suspicions" (*hyponoiai ponērai*) refer to the unfair methods employed in such a struggle. It seems that the apostle has some concrete cases in mind, on the basis of which he describes the general

---

1. Collins 2002: 249 translates *tetyphōmenoi* in 2 Tim. 3:4 as "those surrounded by smoke."

features of dealing with people who are not happy with sound teaching but want to develop their own obsessive interpretations. The word *hyponoia* alludes to the skeptical activity of the mind (*nous*) in this process.

Two possibilities of theological interpretation can be discussed. One way is that the apostle is again, as in the case of women, blaming other parties in an unfair manner. This is, however, difficult, since we do not have any point of comparison for evaluating the false teachers, whereas in the case of Christian women we have plenty of other evidence. Another way is to think seriously about the psychological description undertaken here and to examine its background.

The apostle presupposes that the false teachers suffer from an obsessive psychopathology. Their mind is disturbed. This assumption may be one more aspect of the power struggle or a rhetorical exaggeration for the sake of slander. But the description of quarrelsome behavior could be compared with some other contemporary descriptions (e.g., Seneca, *On Anger* 3.30–31 [Seneca 1995: 105–6]; see appendix B). Psychological exegesis has its serious limitations, but here psychological knowledge of character traits can be helpful.

In 6:5 the "base suspicions" are connected with a characterization of the false teachers as those who think that "godliness is a means of gain." The strange word *diaparatribai* ("wrangling") means a provocation to lasting controversies (Roloff 1988: 332–33). This occurs through making ordinary people suspicious of everything so that the false teachers may steer the controversies to their own profit. This is not, however, a sign of skill or cleverness. On the contrary, the false teachers are described as rigidly conceited (*typhoomai*; 6:4). One can also read from 6:5 that this obsessive stupidity is contagious so that the supporters of the false teachers also become enchanted by the same obstinacy. Thus the congregation suffers from a group of suspicious people who persistently relativize all godliness and argue in terms of profit. They may themselves think that their consistently skeptical attitude is clever, but in Paul's view it is a sign of mental disturbance.

For many reasons, the overall characterization of false doctrine as a view in which "godliness is a means of gain" is highly significant. I will therefore investigate it closer on the basis of the assumption of psychopathology or mental disturbance. Commentators sometimes see in this phrase an ancient parallel to the contemporary "prosperity gospel" (Marshall 1999: 642–43). Because 6:4–5 is elliptic, that is, it does not clearly spell out all roles taken by the false teachers and their supporters, the interpreter is left to deal with a variety of options. It is possible to read the passage as warning against the prosperity gospel or as warning against false godliness, through which the false teachers aim at making profit. These interpretations can be called the "plain view." The plain view presupposes that Paul simply accuses other people of making profit with the help of religious convictions.

First Timothy 6:4–5 can also be read as a warning against such a skeptical spirit that deconstructs all sound teaching and obstinately claims that it represents only a will to power and profit. It is not only Paul who accuses false teachers of greed, but his opponents, because of their corrupted mind, can only imagine godliness as a means of gain. According to this reading, the false teachers would resemble skeptical philosophers who relativize *eusebeia* to an analysis of personal gains and losses.[2] The skeptics may claim that there is no "truth" and thus be "bereft of the truth" in the sense of 6:5.

If the skeptical person sees that the good presbyters get paid (5:17), he may feed the suspicions of parish members by saying that all this "godliness" propagated by church leaders is related to profit. Thus the maxim "godliness is a means of gain" is presented by both skeptics (as an ideological stance) and Paul (as an accusation). Such skepticism and the entailing denial of objective truth and virtue witness for Paul of serious mental disturbance that prevents the use of reason. This interpretation may be called the "mental disturbance" reading of 6:4–5. A similar kind of disturbance can be presupposed when the apostle says that the conscience of false teachers is "deadened" (4:2).

The difference between the two alternatives can be highlighted when we distinguish among Paul, his opponents, and his addressees. According to the plain view, Paul presents his addressees the accusation that the opponents aim at making profit. According to the mental disturbance reading, Paul tells his addressees that the opponents suffer from an anger-related disturbance (see appendix B) that causes them to think of everything in terms of profit. Although Paul can admit another kind of "profit" that godliness brings (6:6), he considers it pathological to think of godliness as means of gain.

The mental disturbance reading remains debatable, since one can stick to the plain view, saying that Paul simply presents the accusation that his opponents make their own profit. Following the logic of the mental disturbance reading one may, however, read 6:5 as follows: the people whose mind is corrupted (*diephtharmenōn . . . ton noun*) are habituated or accustomed (*nomizō*; cf. 1:8) to think of the virtue of *eusebeia* in a corrupt way, namely, in purely utilitarian and skeptical terms. So, when they begin to think about godliness, the suspicion of profit immediately emerges. One aspect of this psychopathology is that, according to them, no doctrinal truth is available and unselfish godliness is impossible. Given this, the suspicion and the controversies concerning the skeptical stance can always be persistently continued. The verb *diaphtheirō* here refers to a "corrupted" or even "destroyed" mind (cf. 2 Tim. 3:8). In Titus 2:7 an exemplary leader is expected to teach with "soundness" (*aphthoria*).[3]

2. According to Diogenes Laertius 9.61–108 (LCL 185.475–519), skeptics claim that "dogmaticians" are wrong in holding doctrinal positions. Arguments cannot solve cases, because arguments can be turned against the positions they are supporting (9.76). Perceptions are different, depending on the perceiving subject (9.81). The same thing appears just for some, unjust for others; it is good for one party while bad for others (9.83, 101). We cannot make judgments about the truth, since all truth depends on circumstances (9.92). A skeptic should therefore remain indifferent.

3. For the philosophically rich vocabulary of corruptible versus incorruptible, see G. Harder in *TDNT* 9.93–106. Malherbe 1989: 129 finds an important parallel in Dio Chrysostom's *Discourse* 77/78

Given the mental disturbance reading, one can interpret 1 Tim. 6:6 as a defense of the true *eusebeia* that has been questioned by the obstinate skeptics. This is an additional benefit of this reading, since the plain view gets into new difficulties in explaining why good presbyters receive payment and why Paul in 6:6 bothers to respond to the accusation of profit, if it is only he himself who presents it critically of others. If the claim "godliness is a means of gain" concerns all parties as an ideological stance, the argumentative role of 6:6 is easier to understand.

In 6:6 Paul argues that sound teaching in fact combines godliness with *autarkeia* (NRSV: "contentment"). *Autarkeia* is a concept of Stoic philosophy (Bauer 2000: 152 and appendix A). Here it does not mean only a state of satisfaction, but is strongly connected with the idea of autonomy, integrity, and impartiality (cf. 5:21). Even if the person gets paid by other people, he should not compromise his *autarkeia*. If it gets compromised, then godliness also disappears. Thus godliness helps people or is a "great gain" (*porismos megas*) only if it is connected with *autarkeia*. Paul has stated earlier that "godliness is valuable in every way" (4:8). Therefore he does not aim at denying its gain, but makes two moves: he (1) connects it with *autarkeia* and (2) distinguishes between material and immaterial gain, as 6:7–10 shows.

The next proverbial sentence (6:7) is known in many different wordings in both the Jewish and Greco-Roman worlds. The awareness of death relativizes the importance of material gain. If the skeptical argument says that all virtue and even the truth can be reduced to profit and endless controversy, Paul now responds to it by saying that the universal fact of death is stronger than personal profit. Dead people have no use for riches, but their godliness and personal integrity are remembered. In this sense *eusebeia* and *autarkeia* remain a great immaterial gain beyond death. Thus 6:7 can be seen to parallel 4:8 in the claim that these virtues are valuable beyond death.

As to material gain, food and clothing suffice to preserve a living person's godliness and personal integrity. An increase in material gain does not increase these virtues. Some material remuneration may be proper or necessary (5:18). But a moderated mean ought to be found in order that the practice of piety does not become a means of gain. In both 6:7 and 6:8 Paul is referring to Jewish and Hellenistic philosophical sources that define *autarkeia* in similar ways.[4] It is important to see that in 6:4–8 the autonomy of the person is praised. We often consider heteronomy to be a religious virtue, but here godliness is coined with

---

(LCL 385.261–301). Dio reports a soul corrupted (*diephtharmenē*) by passions. The sound (*hygiēs*) philosopher sets out to treat this soul.

4. Marshall 1999: 643–45, giving parallels from Diogenes Laertius 2.24; 6.104; 10.130–31 (LCL 184.155; 185.109, 655–57). *Autarkeia* should not, however, extinguish genuine care for others. It differs from skeptical "indifference" (*adiaphoron*), which can be exemplified in the story of Pyrrho's teacher Anaxarchus (Diogenes Laertius 9.63 [LCL 185.477]). When Pyrrho saw that his teacher had fallen into a ditch, he went by without helping him. Seeing this, Anaxarchus praised the indifference of Pyrrho. For Christians, such ideals could have approached the deadening of conscience (1 Tim. 4:2).

autarkeia. Both are important in order to exercise impartial judgment and to refute a profit-centered skepticism.

Paul makes the point that some gain or value is indeed connected with godliness, but this value is immaterial, as we can see in facing the necessity of death. Having said this, in 6:9 he throws the ball back and begins to claim that the other party, namely, the false teachers, are not concerned with immaterial gain but with concrete riches. If they had the full use of reason, they would realize already with the help of reason and philosophy that profit and riches are not everything. Virtues and the truth are higher and more permanent than profit. A rational person whose mind is not disturbed and whose conscience is not "deadened" (4:2) can see that virtues and truth are more valuable than profit. Since false teachers are not only heretics but also depraved in mind, they are not able to understand this, but analyze everything in terms of profit and changing circumstances.

In fact, the false teachers have lost their *autarkeia*. They have fallen into temptation and remain trapped. The cause for this loss of freedom is, like in Stoicism, "senseless and harmful desires [*epithymiai*]." A person who does not live according to his or her reason, but follows desires, has lost integrity and remains trapped. This description culminates in the claim that these people end up in "ruin and destruction" (6:9). Some manuscripts speak here of the "devil's trap" and thus make the connection with 3:7 even more evident. Blaming false teachers for succumbing in temptation and living under the influence of their own desires underlines the goodness of reason and the need for *autarkeia*.

In 6:10 Paul returns to the proverbial statements that are current in both philosophical and religious texts. Especially in cynical literature, greed is considered to be the root of all evil (Diogenes Laertius 6.50 [LCL 185.53]; Polycarp, *Philippians* 4.1 [Ehrman 2003: 1.337]; Johnson 2001: 298–300). The desire for riches has made the false teachers mentally disturbed and ruined their capacity for understanding. Thus they have also "wandered away from the faith" that preserves godliness and integrity.

The last phrase, "pierc[ing] themselves with many pains," remains enigmatic for the plain view. If the false teachers would simply propagate prosperity theology, they may not have ascetic leanings. The phrase probably refers back to the ascesis mentioned in 4:2–3. Maybe here one could also apply psychological exegesis. Psychopathic characters who provoke others to controversies and lasting suspicion can be inclined to exaggerate their own pains and, in extreme cases, even have self-inflicted physical injuries.[5] If the flow of thought in 6:4–10 proceeds from the idea that Paul's opponents are mentally disturbed, this would be one more

5. Cf. Pyrrho's idea of *adiaphoron*, his affinity with the ascetics of India, and his indifference to pain in Diogenes Laertius 9.62–63, 67, 108 (LCL 185.475–81, 519). Within the limits of this commentary, it is not possible to formulate a thorough hypothesis concerning Paul's opponents. The parallels from Diogenes Laertius aim at showing only that Paul's text employs Hellenistic commonplaces that can be related to skeptical views. For the Pastoral Epistles, the underlying problem is not skepticism as such, but the anger that provokes other vices. See appendix B.

symptom of their pathological behavior. Commentators tend to explain the phrase metaphorically, for instance, as the frustration caused by unfulfilled desires, but a mental disturbance reading can understand the phrase literally.

Excursus 4: Chrysostom on Self-Control

In the interpretation history of the Pastoral Epistles, John Chrysostom's homilies offer evidence of how the epistles can be read from a therapeutic point of view. Chrysostom is familiar with the Stoic ideas of eradication and moderation of emotion (Knuuttila 2004: 135–36). In his homilies on 1–2 Timothy and Titus, Chrysostom often recommends moderation and self-control. With regard to Paul's emphasis on right conduct as the indication of sound doctrine, Chrysostom remarks that "the Greeks judge not of doctrines by the doctrine itself, but they make the life and conduct the test of the doctrines" (NPNF[1] 13.533). When he explains why bishops ought to be well thought of by outsiders (1 Tim. 3:1–7), he considers this to be a mean between harmful extremes: "Let us not, on the one hand, look to human reputation; nor on the other, subject ourselves to an evil report, but on both sides let us observe moderation [symmetria]" (NPNF[1] 13.440).

Paul's criticism of too rigid ascesis (1 Tim. 4:1–3) is also explained in terms of moderation: God "created bread, and yet too much is forbidden; and wine also, and yet excess is forbidden; and we are not commanded to avoid dainties as if they were unclean in themselves, but as they corrupt the soul by excess" (NPNF[1] 13.445). Chrysostom teaches that not only women, but also young men should display moderated obedience: "Let your sons be so modest, as to be distinguished for their steadiness and sobriety. . . . Let them learn to govern their appetites, to avoid extravagance, to be good economists, affectionate, and submissive to rule" (NPNF[1] 13.437). No eradication of emotions, but their moderation is recommended.

When Chrysostom discusses 5:5, he teaches that if rich women do not practice moderation, they cause two deaths:

> Hear this, you women that pass your time in revels and intemperance, and who neglect the poor, pining and perishing with hunger, while you are destroying yourself with continual luxury. Thus you are the causes of two deaths, of those who are dying of want, and of your own, both through ill measure. But if out of your fullness you tempered their want, you would save two lives. Why do you thus gorge your own body with excess, and waste that of the poor with want; why pamper this above measure, and stint that too beyond measure? (NPNF[1] 13.452)

In this example the moderation of emotion not only serves one's own good, but it very concretely adds to the well-being of the community. The practice of *metriopatheia* thus serves the *oikeiōsis*, a genuine care for others.

The practice of *metriopatheia* presupposes that passions often disturb the soul and prevent the power of reason. Chrysostom can describe this disturbance as follows: "For there is nothing that is not spoiled by these passions. But as when violent winds, falling on a calm sea, turn it up from its foundation, and mingle the sand with the waves, so these passions assailing the soul turn all upside down, and dim the clearness of the mental sight, but especially does the mad desire of glory" (NPNF[1] 13.526).

According to the Stoic theory, passions are wrong judgments. The faculty of judging plays an essential role in cognitive therapy. Chrysostom treats extensively the problems of human judgment. Sometimes he presents a short maxim: "Cleanse your mind, and rectify your judgment, and then you will be good" (NPNF[1] 13.448). He can also describe the disordered human condition with the help of comparisons, as in his exposition of 2 Tim. 2:19: "The judging faculty of the soul is disordered. Just as balance, if its beam be unsteady, moves round, and does not show accurately the weight of things placed in it; so the soul, if it has not the beam of its own thoughts fixed, and firmly riveted to the law of God, being carried round and drawn down, will not be able to judge aright of actions" (NPNF[1] 13.494).

This anthropology presupposes that the fundamental faculty of judgment, which humans possess as rational beings, is never completely lost, although it can be disordered and perturbed. The inner conscience is the seat of judgment: "The faculty of judging is naturally implanted in us by God, and what comes from God cannot be so corrupted. But uneasy slumbers, thick-coming fancies . . . destroy our repose" (NPNF[1] 13.494). Chrysostom emphasizes the fear of death as a positive emotion that can clarify the mind so that harmful emotions are dissolved: "The fear of death . . . obliges the soul to philosophize. . . . The desire of wealth, the love of gain, and of bodily pleasures, no longer possesses it. These things passing away like clouds, leave the judging faculty clear" (NPNF[1] 13.495). In this sense the Stoic anthropology is optimistic: even the disordered heretics described in 2 Tim. 3:1–7 have not completely lost the faculty that enables right judgment.

False judgment can be compared with disease or intoxication. In the face of death, foolish people may recover so that their judgment again becomes clear. But it would be better to treat the disease of the soul without delay: "If one had a son diseased in his body, he could not refuse to take a long journey to free him from his disease. But when the soul is in a bad state, no one concerns himself about it, but we are all indolent, all careless, all negligent, and overlook our wives, our children, and ourselves, when attacked by this dangerous disease. But when it is too late, we become sensible of it" (NPNF[1] 13.539–40).

One typical feature of wrong opinion is that the desired things are evaluated not by their inherent nature, but according to their relative value. This is the case with regard to the mental disorders discussed in 1 Tim. 6:2–7:

> Thus we are everywhere under the influence of covetousness and opinion. And that is so, and that a thing is valued for its rarity, and not for its nature, appears hence. The fruits that are held cheap among us are in high esteem among the Cappadocians. . . . Such preference therefore is nothing but prejudice, and human opinion. We act not from judgment, but at random, as an accident determines.

But let us recover from this intoxication, let us fix our view upon that which is truly beautiful, beautiful in its own nature, upon godliness and righteousness. (NPNF[1] 13.470)

For Chrysostom, the Pastoral Epistles offer examples of recommending the moderation of emotion and correcting mental disorders so that clear mind and sound judgment may prevail. The church father applies Stoic philosophy in order to understand Paul. Since this philosophy is also present in the Pastoral Epistles (see appendixes A–B), Chrysostom unfolds and develops ideas that are present in the text. As a prominent exegete of the Antiochian tradition, Chrysostom lays out a historically adequate understanding of the epistles.

Exemplary Life and Teaching (1 Tim. 6:11–16)

After the harsh criticism of false teachers, Paul turns back to the description of the exemplary life and "teaching that is in accordance with godliness" (6:3). This section uses extensively liturgical and doctrinal sentences that come from the tradition of the church. Exegetical discussion has concentrated on the question of whether this traditional material is taken from early ordination formulas (Marshall 1999: 654–55). Especially 6:13–14 sounds like a solemn admonition that a bishop addresses to the person to be ordained.

Materials related to ordination are found throughout 1 Timothy (1:18; 4:14; 5:22). The task of Timothy as described in 6:13–14 refers to his ministry; at the same time, the admonitions of 6:11–16 are quite broad and encompass the whole life and teaching. Commentators also see in them elements of the baptismal rite and admonitions given in the context of baptism (Roloff 1988: 341–42). It is probably most fruitful to see the different aspects of the text as complementary. Thus 6:11–16 contains material from both baptismal and ordination rituals. Since the passage relates to the earlier discussion of healthy or sound doctrine, it should also be regarded as a more general description of doctrine and godliness.

Timothy is addressed as "man of God." This phrase connects him with Moses (Deut. 33:1), Samuel (1 Sam. 9:6–7), David (Neh. 12:24), and other people with a specific divine task. As a man of God, Timothy should avoid the desire for riches and the problems it brings (1 Tim. 6:11). Instead, he is to "pursue" six exemplary virtues that have all been introduced in the body of 1 Timothy.

"Righteousness" (*dikaiosynē*) and "godliness" (*eusebeia*) are general virtues that comprise the whole character of a Christian. They also connect civil virtues with the life in Christ. Thus they characterize the ethos of a Christian in a comprehensive manner.

"Faith" (*pistis*), "love" (*agapē*), and "endurance" (*hypomonē*) are similar to "faith, hope, and love" especially in 1 Cor. 13 but also in Rom. 5:1–5 and 1 Thess. 1:3; 5:8. The virtue of endurance is closely connected with hope in both Rom. 5:3–5 and

1 Thess. 1:3. It is likely that endurance and "gentleness" (*praupatheia*) here together replace "hope," but the intention of this replacement is less clear. Whereas hope is eschatological, the two other virtues are more concrete and civil and can thus adjust the Christian to the less eschatological situation of the emerging church.

On the other hand, eschatology is strongly present in 1 Tim. 6:14–15, and, since endurance is central already in the early Pauline epistles (Rom. 5:3–5; 1 Thess. 1:3), endurance and gentleness may in 1 Tim. 6:11 just point to specific dimension of the eschatological hope. "Gentleness" (*praotēs*) complements the ordinary virtue of being friendly (2 Tim. 2:25; Titus 3:2) with the notion of *pathos* ("desire"). In this manner 1 Tim. 6:11 shows that there are positive desires and good emotions, a view with regard to which Christianity has remained at variance with the Stoic ideal of *apatheia* (see appendix B and positive *epithymia* in 3:1 and *makrothymia* in 1:16).

Understood in this sense, the six virtues can be organized into three pairs: righteousness and godliness comprise the overall moral character of the person; faith and love point out the constitutive theological virtues (cf. 1:5); whereas endurance and gentleness refer to the manner of organizing one's internal desires and external behavior in view of eschatological hope. This moral pattern contrasts with the list of vices mentioned in 6:4–5. It further witnesses to the comprehensive health present in a Christian as a result of healthy doctrine (6:3).

This mental and spiritual strength or health is put into use in the "fight of the faith" (*agōn tēs pisteōs*). The apostle now returns (cf. 4:7–10) to the imagery of training and struggle. The virtues are, as in Greek ethics, understood as skills that help the trained person to fight against vices, bad desires, and other temptations. Paul describes himself as a spiritual athlete (1 Cor. 9:24–27; Phil. 3:12–14); now his followers should have the same self-understanding.

Since faith here depicts a virtue and relates it to a personal struggle, 1 Tim. 6:12 does not refer to the controversy with the false teachers concerning doctrinal faith. The personal fight is fought in order to achieve "eternal life" so that the training would be useful for both the present life and the life to come (4:8). Mentioning eternal life also alludes to the baptismal rite, especially through the latter part of 6:12. God has called Timothy, who has responded to this call in his baptismal confession (*homologia*) in front of many witnesses, that is, in the presence of the congregation.

The latter part of 6:12 can also be understood as referring to the ordination of Timothy (Marshall 1999: 660–61). Maybe the interpreter should regard the two rites as complementary in the sense that both are here alluded to. In his baptism, Timothy has confessed his faith in the presence of witnesses. In a similar manner, he has been called and has made the good confession in his ordination. Confessing the faith occurs at various turning points of one's life, as also the reference to the testimony (*homologia*) of Jesus before Pontius Pilate (6:13) shows. According to this complementary reading, 6:12 primarily refers to the baptism, whereas the focus is consciously shifted toward the duties of the ordained church leader in 6:13–14.

In 6:13 Paul points out that the presence of witnesses in the event of confession has a deeper theological background in the presence of God. God is described as "giver of life." The phrases of 6:13–14 follow a creedal order: first comes the reference to God as creator, then the confession of Jesus before Pontius Pilate, and finally the eschatological manifestation of Christ as Lord. The point of making a confession is thus embedded in the structure of the creed. Jesus Christ is both the one who testifies and the one who is testified.

The literary skill of the author is again visible. One may draw the conclusion that Paul here employs liturgical material, but this material is arranged to suit his purpose. Thus it is very difficult to conclude which phrases come from liturgical tradition. At least the characterization of God as the giver of life, the reference to Jesus before Pontius Pilate, and the eschatological manifestation of Lord Jesus Christ belong to a broader creedal tradition of the church.

Paul now addresses Timothy in the first-person singular and charges (*parangellō*) him to keep the commandment (*entolē*) without spot or blame. *Parangellō* here clearly refers to a binding order or command (cf. 1:3–4; 5:7). The precise meaning of *entolē* is less obvious. The word can mean commandment or task. If it is interpreted as the concrete tasks that Timothy is expected to fulfill as church leader, the connection with ordination ritual is strong. If *entolē* also refers to the institution of the teaching office entrusted to him (6:20), an impression of apostolic succession emerges. "Keep the commandment" may, however, simply refer to the ethical commandments of the Christian faith.

It is not necessary to play the alternatives against one another, but they can be regarded as complementary. The addition "without spot or blame" refers to the expectations that the church leader should lead a morally blameless life (cf. 3:2). If he holds fast to "healthy words" (6:3), his life should also be healthy and virtuous. Since sound doctrine and moral godliness always belong together in 1 Timothy, "keep[ing] the commandment" extends the task of this ministry to both teaching and setting an example. The liturgical and creedal context of this admonition makes the allusion to the ordination plausible.

The final part of 6:14, "until the manifestation [*epiphaneia*] of our Lord Jesus Christ," indicates that the commandment will last until the epiphany. "Keep[ing] the commandment" may thus extend beyond the life of Timothy, a feature that gives the idea of succession more weight. In 3:14–15 the apostle still hopes to return, but 6:14 shows that the church should not wait for the his return, but for the eschatological epiphany of Jesus Christ. The Greek notion of epiphany means an appearance in light and shining (Marshall 1999: 287–96, esp. 293; Roloff 1988: 363–65). In 2 Thess. 2:8 and 2 Tim. 4:1, 8 *epiphaneia* is employed as an eschatological notion. Elsewhere the term is connected with the saving work of Christ (2 Tim. 1:10; Titus 2:11, 13; 3:4). Similarly, in 6:14 the "manifestation" of Jesus Christ is understood as an eschatological saving act.

The thought of two manifestations or two advents of Jesus Christ, namely, in his incarnation and in his parousia, appears here for the first time (Roloff 1988:

353–54). The *epiphaneia* of Christ in 2 Tim. 1:10; Titus 2:11; 3:4 (but not Titus 2:13!) refers to the past, whereas 1 Tim. 6:14 refers to the future. The Vulgate translates the future *epiphaneia* as *adventus* (here and Titus 2:13), whereas the advent in Christmas is translated *illuminatio* (2 Tim. 1:10) or *apparuit* (Titus 2:11; 3:4).

In 1 Tim. 6:15 the divine initiative becomes emphasized. The verb *deiknymi* ("to show") connotes the idea of actively bringing about the event that is shown. God makes visible and brings about the manifestation of Christ in the parousia. As in 2:6, the phrase "right time" connects Timothy's mission with broader salvation history. "Keep[ing] the commandment" (6:14) until this time is essential for the manifestation of Christ in the last days.

The eschatological statement is followed by a doxology in which a list of majestic characterizations becomes ascribed to God. Some of them have their origin in Hellenism, whereas others derive from Jewish sources. Thus the titles most likely stem from the liturgical practices of Hellenistic Judaism and identify the God of Jesus as the God of Judaism. At the same time, this God has titles that are meaningful in both Hellenistic and oriental traditions. God is a ruler or "Sovereign" (*dynastēs*; cf. Luke 1:52; Sir. 46:5–6, 16) who is "blessed" and "only" God. Philo also uses the two attributes (*On the Sacrifices of Abel and Cain* 101 [LCL 227.171]; *Unchangeableness of God* 26 [LCL 247.23]; Oberlinner 1994: 299).

Both "King of kings" and "Lord of lords" are employed of God in the Old Testament (e.g., Deut. 10:17; Ps. 136:3). They are oriental expressions for earthly rulers (Ezek. 26:7; Dan. 2:37). When used of God, the expressions set limits on the earthly rulers. This tendency is clearly visible in the doxology, since God is also said to be the "only" sovereign (1 Tim. 6:15) and the "only" immortal being (6:16). The next phrase, "it is he alone who has immortality" (*ho monos echōn athanasian*), continues this critical tendency, since the title "immortal" was used commonly of oriental and Hellenistic kings and rulers. Here we see the only appearance of the title in the New Testament, although the adjective *aphthartos* in 1:17 and Rom. 1:23 comes close. God is not only immortal, but incorruptible and eternal.

The uniqueness of God becomes even more strongly emphasized in the next phrases. The "unapproachable [*aprositos*] light" is said to be the place in which God dwells. The glory of God appears as unapproachable in the Old Testament (Exod. 33:18–23). Together with the next phrase, "whom no one has ever seen or can see," the connection with Moses in Exod. 33 is strengthened, but at the same time the statement attempts to present an almost philosophical theology. The manifestation of God's will can be seen in the *epiphaneia* of Jesus Christ, whereas God as God remains unapproachable.

The closing line of the doxology states that God deserves our "honor and . . . dominion" (*timē kai kratos*). Similar liturgical formulas often use "honor and glory" (1 Tim. 1:17; Rev. 4:9–11). The word for power and dominion strengthens the idea of God's unique power over the whole creation. The word "eternal" (*aiōnion*) is an abbreviated form of "forever and ever" (1 Tim. 1:17).

The doxology underlines the incomparable uniqueness and sovereignty of God. Such descriptions always face the logical problem of having to make this statement with the help of available concepts. Although the statement attempts to stress the unique reality of God, the concepts reveal their Hellenistic, Jewish, and oriental origins. Statements that define Christian uniqueness often need to assume a language that is commensurable with other cultures and worldviews. This observation need not relativize the claim of uniqueness, but a theological interpreter should be aware of the complex nature of the phenomenon (for the hermeneutical assessment of doctrinal statements like "God is immortal," see the postscript).

Although the doxology of 6:15–16 strengthens the admonition given to Timothy in 6:11–14, it also continues the tone of other doxologies that appear at the end of various thematic passages, in particular 1:17; 2:5; and 3:16. They can be read as creedal and liturgical statements that formulate the sound doctrine of the church. In this sense they are autonomous parts that mark the transition from one issue to another. They may strengthen the aforesaid passage but do not aim to add new content to the instruction given.

Instructions about Rich People (1 Tim. 6:17–19)

In his last instruction Paul adds some words concerning rich Christians. The statement is an attempt to moderate the criticism of greed expressed in 6:9–10. If the love of money is the root of all kinds of evil, what can be said of good Christians who are rich but neither false teachers nor particularly greedy? Such people are commanded not to be exalted or haughty (*hypsēlophroneō*), but they should also exercise the Christian virtue of humility (*tapeinophrosynē*; Phil. 2:3; Rom. 12:16). The word employed here may have been invented by the apostle; in Rom. 11:20 *hypsēla phroneō* means exalted sophistication in the sense "becoming proud." The Vulgate translates Rom. 11:20 literally: *altum sapere* ("thinking sublime things").

Rich people tend to rely on their riches. But riches are uncertain and cannot offer a true basis of hope. Like all Christians, rich people should set their hope on God. The idea of uncertainty of riches is here linked to 1 Tim. 6:7. A truly wise person understands that riches do not offer hope beyond death and remain uncertain even during this life. The Vulgate translates *hypsēlophroneō* in 6:17 with *sublime sapere*, thus connecting the argument explicitly with wisdom and with Rom. 11:20. Rich people should give up their exalted wisdom and set their hope in the same reality of God from whom ordinary poor people receive what they need. Exalted wisdom with false hope appears to be foolishness and arrogant boasting. Even if the allusion to "lofty words or wisdom" in 1 Cor. 2:1 remains uncertain, the apostle presupposes the same kind of paradoxical interplay between Christian truth and philosophical wisdom. Exalted philosophy becomes refuted, but this refutation is done with the help of philosophical vocabulary, although for a theological purpose.

God is here depicted as the generous giver and benefactor. When God provides us "richly" (*plousiōs*) with everything, the riches become a positive reality and an enjoyment for people. If one strives for riches and makes virtues a means of gain, then one's love of money is extremely blameworthy (1 Tim. 6:5, 10). But when God gives away riches, they are a source of enjoyment (6:17). Following this paradigm, rich people need to be generous and rich in giving, imitating the model given by God (6:18). The issue of dealing with money may lead a person to the vice of greed, but it may also provide an opportunity to practice the virtue of generosity. Finding an adequate middle way between the extremes is important.

In 6:18 four concrete recommendations are given to the rich Christians. The verb used in the first of these, *agathoergeō* ("to do good"), is employed in Acts 14:17 of God's giving, whereas human good works are normally referred to as *agathopoieō* (Luke 6:33–35; 1 Pet. 2:15, 20). The analogy to God's benevolent giving is here obvious (see appendix C and Seneca, *On Favors* 4.9.1 [Seneca 1995: 280]).

The exhortation "to be rich in good works" plays again with the metaphor of richness. The virtue of being "generous" (*eumetadotos*) points toward the right path between being stingy and being ostentatious. "Ready to share" (*koinōnikos*) is likewise a Greek virtue. This use of the ecclesiological word *koinōnia/communio* (Vulgate: *communicare*) connects the virtue of generosity with the believers' *koinōnia* as a community of sharing.

A person who has property is expected to be generous, that is, to give gifts in an adequate manner, to share goods with others, and to exercise charity. In a society in which taxes and other obligatory payments did not provide social security, rich people were morally obliged to be generous in this manner. When rich Christians behave in this way, they are not doing anything exceptional, but they practice an exemplary civil godliness, even if they rightly think that in doing this they imitate God's goodness.

Paul connects the exercise of this civil virtue with his eschatological vision. Rich people have treasure in the present age, but real treasure is found in the salvific participation in future life. When rich people give away riches, they also obtain riches, namely, the spiritual treasure that awaits them in the future. In giving, one also receives something, namely, the gratitude of recipients. This gratitude transforms into the favor of God, who is in charge of our future life. In this gift exchange the "uncertain" capital becomes transformed into a "good foundation."

The apostle is thinking of this life, of death, and of the future life (cf. 1 Tim. 4:8; 6:7, 17). Rich people tend to focus their mind on this life. A wise person understands that no riches can be taken beyond death. Therefore he or she uses riches in this life so that they can be transformed into a new kind of treasure that stretches its existence to the future life. In this way the topic of richness becomes connected with salvation and eschatology. This closeness with many other topics of the epistle shows that 6:17–19 is not merely an addition, but basically applies the same instructions to a new group of people.

I note briefly that the motivation of doing favors in 6:19 differs from Seneca's *On Favors*. Whereas Seneca emphasizes disinterested giving (see appendix C), Paul says that the giver is rewarded in the future life. Philosophically speaking, this view downplays the free gift and approaches the idea of economic exchange. First Timothy 6:19 should, however, be read in its eschatological context, which probably includes Luke 12:33–34. The eschatological ideal fits well together with the fundamental criticism of riches in 1 Tim. 6:5–10. The point is not to say that a similar return is to be expected in a future life, but that any real and lasting richness is possible only in a future life.

Excursus 5: Chrysostom on Generosity

John Chrysostom is again instructive on the dynamics of giving material aid and receiving spiritual rewards. When Chrysostom discusses hospitality in the context of 1 Tim. 5:10, he stresses that the hospitality in question is not primarily a practical arrangement but a phenomenon that "teaches you philosophy." "The hospitality here spoken of is not merely friendly reception, but one given with zeal and alacrity." Welcoming a stranger entails a reward, if the hospitality is genuine: "If you receive the stranger as Christ, be not ashamed, but rather glory: but if you receive him not as Christ, receive him not at all. . . . If you do not so receive him, you have no reward" (NPNF[1] 13.454–55).

Chrysostom points out that receiving a stranger requires much attendance. Receiving a favor makes the stranger ashamed. The person showing hospitality should therefore counteract these reactions so that the roles are reversed: We are to "show by words and actions, that we do not think we are conferring a favor, but receiving one. . . . For as he who considers himself a loser, and thinks that he is doing a favor, destroys all the merit of it; so he who looks upon himself as receiving a kindness, increases the reward" (NPNF[1] 13.455).

Chrysostom is well aware of the complex philosophy of favors. A giver needs to disguise the act of giving, to act as if he or she were the recipient. This concealment is no illusory simulation, since the giver in fact does become the recipient of merit or reward: "You are rather indebted to the poor man for receiving your kindness. For if there were no poor, the greater part of your sins would not be removed. They are the healers of your wounds. . . . Thus you receive more than you give. . . . But if you do not lessen it by giving, then it is indeed diminished!" (NPNF[1] 13.455). Circulation, concealment, and counteracting are necessary parts of the gift of hospitality.

As in Seneca's discussion on favors (*On Favors* 1.5.2–3 [Seneca 1995: 201]), the real and fundamental transaction takes place in the mind. Chrysostom points this out by saying that it is important to give personally in order that the giver's mind can be transformed:

Give with your own hands.... You sow in souls, where no one takes away what is sown, but it is firmly retained with care and diligence. Cast the seed yourself, why deprive yourself of your reward....

This refreshes the soul, this sanctifies the hands, this pulls down pride. This teaches you philosophy, this inflames your zeal, this makes you to receive blessings. Your head, as you depart, receives all the blessings of the widows. (NPNF[1] 13.455)

Like Seneca, Chrysostom is aware of the difference between the material vehicle of gift and the personal act of giving. In the personal or mental act of hospitality, a complex network of reciprocal, nonmaterial benefits is involved. When the giver realizes this to be the case, the bestowal of hospitality is not merely a utilitarian arrangement, but it becomes an act of manifold character formation.

Training the acts of hospitality makes a person more virtuous and teaches him or her to exercise a genuine care for others. The act of showing hospitality reveals a person's true character. This is one reason why hospitality is a virtue required from various Christian groups, from bishops and widows alike. Chrysostom advises Christians to train this virtue by visiting the desert fathers and, in giving to them, to perform an act of identification as follows: "Do you see the desert? Do you see the solitude? Often when you have gone to bestow money, you give your whole soul. You are detained, and have become his fellow captive, and have been alike estranged from the world" (NPNF[1] 13.455). In this act of identification, the mental act of giving one's soul accompanies the material donation and thus merits the reward of becoming similar to the holy person. In this way the giver receives a refreshed soul or mind.[6]

Final Admonition to Timothy (1 Tim. 6:20–21)

The ending of 1 Timothy is unique among the Pauline Epistles, since no greetings are included. Instead of making remarks of a more personal nature, the apostle here recollects the central message of his instructions to Timothy. Since 2 Timothy and Titus end with greetings, some interpreters assume that these three epistles were compiled as a unity in which the greetings of 2 Tim. 4:19–22 can be understood as pertaining also to 1 Timothy (Roloff 1988: 370–71). But this remains speculation.

Timothy is asked to guard the *parathēkē* ("what has been entrusted") (Vulgate: *depositum*). A deposit is a legal term, meaning a thing that can be entrusted or transferred to another party while remaining the property of the original owner. The entrusted person is responsible for keeping the deposit in good condition until the return of the owner. This idea was employed metaphorically by Philo and

6. For Chrysostom, similar reciprocal character formation or mental training also occurs in many other relationships, e.g., between Christian slave and pagan master (NPNF[1] 13.533), between boy and slave (Knuuttila 2004: 136), and between husband and wife (Brown 1988: 309).

other Hellenistic authors of a teaching that is passed on to pupils (*Worse Attacks the Better* 65 [LCL 227.247]; Marshall 1999: 675; Oberlinner 1994: 309–10; 1995: 49–50). The main idea is thus clear and recollects the earlier emphasis of 1 Timothy: Timothy is entrusted with the "sound doctrine" that he ought to guard and pass on in good condition, without bending toward the false teachers.

Given this, some further questions emerge. The relationship of 6:20 to "keep[ing] the commandment" in 6:14 is relevant. But whereas 6:14 refers immediately to teaching and morals, the deposit of 6:20 has to do with the whole legacy or heritage of Paul. Thus the *parathēkē* emphasizes the legal and apostolic dimension of both faith and church order. Another important issue concerns the relationship between *parathēkē* and the concept of *paradosis* ("tradition"), which occupies a similar role in earlier Pauline epistles (e.g., 1 Cor. 11:23; 15:3).

The issue is complicated and demands a closer look at the concepts. One important clue is to note that in *paradosis* Paul is handing over the gospel that he himself has received from the Lord. The *parathēkē* of 1 Timothy is primarily the deposit of Paul to Timothy and to the church. In 1 Tim. 1:18 Paul underlines that he himself is giving these instructions. The original tradition (*paradosis*) comes from the Lord and is identical with the gospel, but the deposit of sound doctrine reflects the authority of Paul as true apostle. In some sense, then, one could say that *paradosis* is theologically higher than *parathēkē* or that *parathēkē* represents a lower but more structured authority than *paradosis* (see Roloff 1988: 371–72 and excursus 6).

The difference between tradition and deposit should not, however, be exaggerated. Both terms remain descriptions of the gospel and of the role of the church in proclaiming the good news. Both concepts depict the idea of a chain of true witnesses. In 1 Timothy *parathēkē* is closely connected with the ordination of Timothy in which he is entrusted with the task of teaching sound doctrine (4:13–16) as a custodian of Pauline property.

In 6:20b–21 the false teachings become recollected. "Profane chatter" (*kenophōnia*) refers to senseless talk (cf. 2 Tim. 2:16). The phrase may refer back to the widows' gossip (1 Tim. 5:13), but also to the idea that the disturbed minds of the false teachers "understand nothing" (6:4). The "contradictions" (*antitheseis*) likewise point toward the controversies and disputes mentioned in 6:4. Marcion later published a book with the title *Antithesis* (Marshall 1999: 677), but the occurrence of the term here cannot yet refer to Marcion. The term points out that whereas the true deposit is consistent, the false teachings evoke a number of contradictions. Therefore the false teachers just chase controversies instead of seeking understanding.

All this can be summed up as thinking that is "falsely called knowledge" (*pseudōnymos gnōsis*). From this phrase we can read that the false teachers called themselves those who have *gnōsis*. Without entering into the extensive debates about the nature of gnosticism, I note that the characterizations of *heterodidaskaloi* in 1 Timothy offer one historical source for the understanding of this many-sided phenomenon. The adherents to the variant of *gnōsis* described in 1 Timothy are interested in myths and genealogies (1:4) and probably in the Jewish Bible in general. The *gnōsis* meant here further appeals to women or at least to young widows (5:13–15). The followers of this *gnōsis* practice ascesis with regard to marriage and foods (4:3).

The apostle judges this *gnōsis* in very negative terms throughout 1 Timothy. The idea that the false teachers are not just wrong but that their minds are disturbed (6:4–5) plays a role also in 6:20b–21. Their teaching is not real knowledge, but the word "knowledge" remains a pseudonym. When this *gnōsis* is professed, the people actually "miss the mark" (*astocheō*). As in 1:6, this verb contains the idea of intellectual error and turning to "meaningless talk." When the mental disturbance reading is assumed, a modern interpreter should be aware that the description of one's opponents as foolish and disturbed is not meant to be the most derogatory accusation. If the heretics are in error and their mind does not work properly, the possibility of intellectual therapy and new learning remains open (cf. 1:20; 4:16).

The final greeting (6:21b) is similar to Col. 4:18, with "you" in the plural (cf. 2 Tim. 4:22; Titus 3:15). Some manuscripts correct this to the singular, assuming that only Timothy is addressed. But most likely the greeting was used in the plural form and is written down in this more solemn wording.

SECOND TIMOTHY

OPENING OF THE LETTER

2 Tim. 1:1–5

Second Timothy begins with an opening that is more extensive than that of 1 Timothy. The opening consists of a greeting (1:1–2) and thanksgiving (1:3–5). Both parts contain traditional Pauline phrases, but especially 1:3–5 also adds materials that are not found elsewhere in Pauline writings. Whereas in 1 Timothy the whole first chapter can be understood as an introductory part, 2 Timothy moves to its actual themes already in 1:6.

Greeting (2 Tim. 1:1–2)

The greeting follows the tripartite form found in other Pauline and Hellenistic letters: it names the sender and the recipient and expresses a benevolent salutation. It employs materials that can also be found in the greetings of Romans, 1 Corinthians, and 1 Timothy. Special emphasis is here, as elsewhere in the Pauline Epistles, laid on the role of Paul as apostle. As in 1 Cor. 1:1 and 2 Cor. 1:1, Paul is apostle "by the will of God." Whereas in some epistles, in particular Gal. 1, Paul defends his apostolicity against dissidents, here his role is unquestioned. The phrase "Christ Jesus" is typical of the Pastoral Epistles, in which it appears twenty-five times, whereas the phrase "Jesus Christ" occurs six times. No clear shift of emphasis between the two expressions needs to be assumed. Both are confessional formulas that underline Christ's role as messianic Savior.

The apostolicity of Paul serves a clear purpose, namely, the "promise of life" found in Christ. Romans 1:1–2 speaks of the gospel as God's promise, and obviously the phrase is here meant to be a shorthand of the gospel proclaimed by Paul. First Timothy 4:8 says that the practice of godliness holds "promise for both the present life and the life to come." A life in Christ refers to the ecclesiastical aspect of the apostolic proclamation. The church is the body of Christ, and the promise of life dwells in this body.

Timothy is named as recipient. As in 1 Cor. 4:17, he is called Paul's "beloved child." In the Pastoral Epistles (1 Tim. 1:2), this phrase emphasizes Timothy's position as legitimate heir of the apostle. Timothy is worthy of taking care of the legacy of the Apostle Paul. The metaphor of being "child" is to an extent ambivalent, since it can also refer to a subordinate or a nonautonomous person. But here the opposite of subordination is meant. Timothy inherits the theological legacy of Paul and is thus supposed to have authority in the church.

The second part of 2 Tim. 1:2 is identical with 1 Tim. 1:2b. Many other Pauline writings employ a bipartite salutation: "grace and peace" (also Titus 1:4). The inclusion of mercy refers to the motivation of God's salvific action. The Pauline "autobiography" in 1 Tim. 1:13–16 describes how Paul the sinner received mercy. Paul the apostle can now salute the recipients of his epistle with wishing mercy. Later (2 Tim. 1:16–18), he also expresses the same wish concerning the household of Onesiphorus.

Thanksgiving (2 Tim. 1:3–5)

Unlike 1 Timothy, but in accordance with many other Pauline epistles, 2 Timothy continues with a thanksgiving. It resembles in particular Rom. 1:8–11, but also 1 Thess. 1:2–3. The author of 2 Timothy knows many other Pauline epistles and consciously employs them in his composition. At the same time, the thanksgiving has accents that remain peculiar to this epistle.

Already the first phrase, *charin echo* ("I am grateful"), replaces the use of the verb *eucharisteō* ("I thank") in Rom. 1:8 and elsewhere in the Pauline Epistles (e.g., 1 Cor. 1:4; Phil. 1:3; 1 Thess. 1:2). One reason for this replacement is that *eucharisteō* has already become closely connected with the Eucharist. In order to avoid this connection, another phrase is preferred. Another reason may be that *eucharisteō* is linked with the worshiping community, whereas 2 Timothy addresses an individual (Oberlinner 1995: 13–14).

In an impressive but also somewhat puzzling manner, 2 Tim. 1:3–5 emphasizes the value of tradition with the help of previous generations. Paul has received the names of Timothy's mother and grandmother, Eunice and Lois (1:5), from an unknown source. These women are said to have shared the faith of Timothy. It is obvious that the Christian faith is meant. Parallel to this, Paul himself claims to worship in the same manner as his "ancestors did" (1:3). As we have no reason to assume that Paul's parents were Christians, the assumed continuity has taken place between Jewish and Christian worship. Another challenge is given by the observation that whereas 1 Tim. 1:12–16 presents the apostle's own past in self-critical terms, Paul in 2 Tim. 1:3 looks back with satisfaction.

The verb *latreuō* ("to worship") in 1:3 comprises both Jewish and Christian worship, whereas the "faith" in 1:5 refers to the Christian faith (Weiser 2003: 88–90). Thus both Paul and Timothy can highly appreciate their ancestors, but for slightly different reasons: Timothy for his Christian upbringing, Paul for the learning of the worship of the one God. Moreover, 1:3 does not relate to Paul's self-critical recollections, but to his earlier life as a "blameless" Pharisee (Phil. 3:6).

Given this, we can see an important recognition of Jewish worship taking place in 2 Tim. 1:3. This is particularly significant because the so-called false teachers are sometimes (1 Tim. 1:4; Titus 3:9) accused of Judaizing tendencies. But, as with regard to the "good law" of the Decalogue (1 Tim. 1:8–11), Paul here shows his appreciation of the Jewish faith. The unconditional trust in Jesus Christ is therefore not in theological conflict with the heritage of Judaism. Such an attitude in early Christianity contributed to the formation of the Christian Bible as a distinctive unity of the two Testaments. In 2 Tim. 3:15 Paul even regards that the reading of the Jewish Bible can instruct for salvation through faith in Christ.

Paul is continuing the tradition of good worship, and Timothy has the same sincere faith as his mother and grandmother. The authority of these two leaders stems from tradition, and they have received their personal integrity from this tradition. The "clear conscience" refers to this integrity with regard to the past. The phrase is similar to the "good/clear conscience" of 1 Tim. 1:5, 19; 3:9. It expresses an awareness that one's own moral life is in accordance with God's commands and that Paul thus lives a life of piety and godliness. This moral meaning can be connected with Paul's Jewish ancestors: they had as clear a conscience as their Christian descendant. Thus a connection between worship and continuous moral tradition is assumed in 2 Tim. 1:3.

Paul emphasizes that Timothy is constantly in his prayers. Similar sayings are found in Hellenistic letters as parts of friendly correspondence (Marshall 1999: 692; Weiser 2003: 30–34). The absence of the important mentor is relieved through the assurance that the mentor constantly thinks of his pupils and prays for them. The next verse, 1:4, strengthens this impression through expressing the wish to see again the beloved person. The literary style serves the purpose of joining Paul and Timothy intimately together in order that Timothy can be entrusted with the necessary authority.

The "sincere faith" (*anypokritos pistis*) of Timothy constitutes the other focus of the above-mentioned comparison. The phrase relates to 1 Tim. 1:5, in which it is also coined with conscience. In earlier Pauline epistles, *anypokritos* is used of love (Rom. 12:9; 2 Cor. 6:6). As in 1 Tim. 1:5, faith here comes closer to the idea of a moral virtue. Such a genuine, nonhypocritical faith was already present in Timothy's mother and grandmother, and now the exemplary church leader shares in this virtuous faith. The nature of faith as gift, a central feature of other Pauline writings (Rom. 10:17) has not disappeared. The idea that faith dwells or "lives" in Timothy's family expresses the view that the sincere faith is not their own achievement but something received from God.

The ideas of tradition and continuity from one generation to another are especially important for the overall purpose of 2 Timothy. The epistle is composed to describe the inalienable possession (see appendix C and excursus 6) of Paul that is handed over to Timothy. Paul's words aim at pointing out the necessary continuity. Therefore tradition is highlighted and allusions to previous generations are made.

We do not know from which sources the author of 2 Timothy received the names Eunice and Lois (Weiser 2003: 328–39 offers a summary of all names in 2 Timothy, their possible sources as well as their later reception history). In Acts 16:1–3 we read that the Jewish mother of Timothy was a believer, but no names are mentioned. Both Acts 16:1–3 and 2 Tim. 1:5 employ the same tradition. Through mentioning these names and the circumstance that the faith "first" lived in the grandmother Lois, Paul wants to say that Timothy belongs to the third generation of Christians to whom already a great tradition has been entrusted.

WITNESS AND SUFFERING IN THE FOOTSTEPS OF PAUL

2 Tim. 1:6–2:13

After the introductory part, 2 Timothy turns to its main theme, namely, the legacy of the apostle and its defense by Timothy. Various pieces of advice are given to Timothy. This advice is further illuminated with exemplary events from the life of Paul as well as with other proverbial and exemplary stories. The first part of the main body of the text can be divided into three smaller units: (1) Timothy is encouraged to give fearless testimony of God and to join Paul's suffering (1:6–14); (2) some good and bad examples of early Christians are given (1:15–18); and (3) Jesus Christ is displayed as the paradigm of the way of salvation (2:1–13).

Gospel as Testimony and as Tradition (2 Tim. 1:6–14)

The first phrase, "for this reason" (*di' hēn aitian*), connects the opening part with the thematic body of the epistle. The reason referred to is probably Timothy's family tradition. Timothy is admonished to "rekindle" (*anazōpyreō*) the "gift" (*charisma*) of God given to him in the ordination performed by Paul himself. Timothy is asked to behave like his courageous mother and grandmother so that the sincere faith would be alive in him.

The charism mentioned here is not merely faith but also ministry and leadership. The laying on of hands clearly refers to ordination. It is assumed that this act transfers a specific charism. Since 1:6 is the only place in the Pauline Epistles in which Paul says that he himself ordains people and since Timothy's ordination in 1 Tim. 4:14 is said to have occurred "by the council of elders," the verse remains somewhat enigmatic. In Acts 14:23, however, Paul is said to have appointed elders.

The different sayings can theoretically be harmonized by holding that Paul was one of the elders mentioned in 1 Tim. 4:14.

More important than this kind of circumstantial coherence are, however, the different theological emphases of the different texts. Whereas 1 Tim. 4:14 probably reflects the actual practice of many congregations, 2 Tim. 1:6 underlines the intimate relationship between Paul and Timothy. Timothy is made the heir of the apostolic legacy in many complementary ways. He has received his ordination from the apostle, an event that enables him to "rekindle" the special gift given to him by God.

Reason for the encouragement of Timothy is spelled out in 1:7. The gift of God should lead to activity and virtuous behavior; therefore Timothy is asked to rekindle his gift. A certain problem in 1:7 concerns the range of "us." In principle it is possible to understand this pronoun to concern only Paul and Timothy or only a limited number of church leaders. It is more likely, however, that all Christians are meant by "us," since all should have the spirit (cf. 1:14).

The three virtues of spirit, namely, spirit "of power and of love and of self-discipline," allude to Rom. 8:15–17. But whereas in Rom. 8:15 the "spirit of adoption" remains soteriological, the three virtues of 2 Tim. 1:7 resemble Hellenistic ethics and basically describe the moral character of a person who is not fearful or cowardly. The three virtues are strongly embedded in the moral vision of the Pastoral Epistles. According to 1 Tim. 1:5, the right instruction aims at bringing forth love. In Titus 2:11–12 the practice of self-discipline characterizes trained Christians who can renounce impiety and bad passions. "Spirit of power" is vaguer, since having spirit already means to become empowered to exercise virtues.

In the larger context of the Pastoral Epistles, 2 Tim. 1:7 stresses the overall ideal of *metriopatheia* as a model of the good Christian life (see appendix A). A good leader can exercise self-discipline and thus moderate his passions so that a right mean is found. If the problem is cowardice, the good alternative is not simply its opposite, an excessive courage or rashness, but the proper middle between them, a spirit in which the person is empowered to do good, paying attention to love and self-control. Paul holds that the proper standard of a person's good life is finally found in the external standard of sound doctrine (1:13). *Sōphronismos* does not mean only self-discipline, but it approaches the virtue of *sōphrosynē* ("modesty"; cf. 1 Tim. 2:9, 15; Titus 2:4–12). *Sōphronismos* in 2 Tim. 1:7 means therefore also "balanced judgment" or even "clear and reasonable understanding" (Weiser 2003: 110; Marshall 1999: 182–91; and appendix A).

Second Timothy 1:8 alludes to Rom. 1:16, in which Paul says that he is not ashamed of the gospel that is the power of God. Neither should Timothy be ashamed of the testimony about our Lord or of Paul the prisoner, but he should rely on the power of God. The idea of not being ashamed (*epaischynomai*) belongs intimately together with the tasks of Christian witness and the proclamation of the gospel (Mark 8:38; 1 Pet. 4:16). It is thus an aspect of the virtue of boldness (*parrēsia*; Phil. 1:20; 1 Tim. 3:13), calling for the testimony of personal faith.

Because of the background of Rom. 1:16, the "testimony" (*martyrion*) about our Lord is the most likely translation. This testimony refers to the proclamation of the gospel or "suffering for the gospel." At the same time, 2 Tim. 1:8 employs motives that incline toward martyrdom. Paul is depicted as prisoner, and Timothy is asked to join with his sufferings. In earlier Pauline epistles (Rom. 8:17; 1 Cor. 12:26), Paul suffers with Christ. Here Timothy and other readers of the epistle are asked to join with Paul's sufferings. The chain of witnesses is thus prolonged. No inclination toward conscious martyrdom needs to be presupposed, but the whole picture of 2 Tim. 1:8 becomes more dramatic than that of Rom. 1:16. A situation in which Christians are convicted and persecuted can be assumed (Weiser 2003: 112–13).

A prominent expression of this witness and testimony is given in 2 Tim. 1:9–10. Although the apostle has probably given these verses their final shape, they reflect a traditional confession of faith. They can be regarded as the thematic focus of the passage. Following the usage typical of the Pastoral Epistles, God is said to have "saved" (*sōzō*; 1:9) us and Jesus is called "Savior" (*sōtēr*; 1:10). In 1:9–10 these words are clearly employed as a shorthand of the gospel message, whereas in many other texts they can describe a singular event of healing (Mark 6:56; Luke 8:36) or a particular case of forgiveness (Luke 7:50; Matt. 1:21). The various meanings of "saving" are analogically related to one another. The Pastoral Epistles employ "Savior" as prominent title and the verb "save" as a shorthand of the topics that theologians later called salvation or soteriology (Weiser 2003: 114–16 and Roloff 1988: 358–65 offer summaries).

The parallelism of "saved" and "called" (*kaleō*) in 2 Tim. 1:9 expresses the event of salvation from two slightly different angles. Whereas the saving act of God is monergistic, that is, a sovereign act of God, the calling pertains to the human beings who are saved. The event of saving implies a duty or calling: Christians should not be ashamed or quiet, but they are to behave boldly and give testimony about God and their faith. The calling is "holy" because it comes from God. The phrase "holy calling" may also allude to baptism (cf. 1 Tim. 6:12).

The human involvement present in this call is differentiated in 2 Tim. 1:9b, in which God's initiative becomes underlined. This part contains materials found in earlier Pauline epistles, in particular Gal. 2:16 and Rom. 3:20–26. The saving act is basically the act of justification. The "works of the law" in Romans and Galatians are now called "our works." This change probably reflects the new situation of the Pastoral Epistles. The apostolic writer is no longer confronting the Jewish law, but more generally the human efforts of achieving perfection. This need not mean a theological change in the view of salvation, but a generalization of Pauline theology in the Hellenistic environment.

God has his own "purpose and grace" (*prothesin kai charin*; Vulgate: *propositum suum et gratiam*). The purpose means literally "predecision" and is connected with the phrase "before the ages began." The idea of God having formed this decision reflects Pauline usage in Rom. 8:28–29, but also Old Testament passages like Isa.

14:26 and 25:1 (Weiser 2003: 119). The question here is whether the expression "in Jesus Christ before the ages began" entails the view of the preexistence of Christ. Whereas Rom. 8:28–29 speaks of divine foreknowledge, 2 Tim. 1:9 says that the grace was "given" (*dotheisan*) to us in Christ. This phrase can be understood to refer to the divine predecision before the creation, although the grace was only "revealed" (1:10) in the life of Christ.

It is nevertheless possible to understand 1:9 in keeping with Rom. 8:29 so that God's purpose or foreknowledge includes the sending of Christ. Thus no preexistence of Christ need be assumed. On the other hand this verse does offer biblical background for the later doctrinal development (Oberlinner 1995: 40; Marshall 1999: 706). The readers' response to 2 Tim. 1:9–10 was the doctrine of the preexistence of Christ. Exposition of the passage therefore depends on whether the interpreter emphasizes the most probable historical intention of the author or the understanding of the text among its early readers.

In 1:10 the christological theme is expressed with the term "appearing" (*epiphaneia*). Unlike in 1 Tim. 6:14, *epiphaneia* now refers to an event in the past, namely, the events recorded in the Gospels. Both *epiphaneia* and the phrase "brought life" (*phōtisantos de zōēn*) relate to the gospel mentioned in the end of 2 Tim. 1:10. The phrases need not presuppose a preexistence of Christ, but, again, it is natural to read 1:10 so that Christ existed in God before appearing and enlightening the life of the faithful. The verb *phōtizō* means "to enlighten, bring to life, instruct." This impression is strengthened by the passive verb "has been revealed" (*phanerōtheisan*) in the beginning of 1:10. God had the distinct purpose of saving, but this predecision was only fully revealed in the epiphany of Jesus Christ (Marshall 1999: 293–95; Weiser 2003: 116–18).

In addition to this, 1:10 expresses the work of Christ by saying that he "abolished death and brought life and immortality." This phrase resembles what was later called the "classical idea of atonement" (see Aulen 1969 and excursus 9). The theological reception of 1:10 has broadened its scope to become a theory of atonement, especially since 1:10–11 refers to the preceding phrases as the "gospel."

The idea of conquering death and enlightening our life with a view toward immortality relates to the Hellenistic worldview in which everything was subject to corruption and death. God's grace in the Savior Christ Jesus is able to overcome this natural state of affairs and transform human existence into a divine state of immortality (Weiser 2003: 121).[1] This description also relates to 1 Cor. 15:42–44 and Rom. 8:21, but, unlike in these passages, the emphasis here is not eschatological. Second Timothy 1:10 assumes that the epiphany of Christ already here and now has abolished death and enlightened the faithful with regard to their deeper life. Thus the accent is laid more on the salvific presence than on the future salvation.

---

1. In the Pastoral Epistles, the philosophical word for corruption (*phtharsia*) appears in the context of "corrupted mind" (1 Tim. 6:5; 2 Tim. 3:8; Titus 2:7).

In 1:11 the author returns from the traditional material to his present situation and role. In order to proclaim this gospel message, Paul was appointed "a herald and an apostle and a teacher" (*kēryx kai apostolos kai didaskalos*). Some manuscripts, following 1 Tim. 2:7, add *ethnōn* after *didaskalos*, and for this reason the Vulgate has the last title as *magister gentium*. The three titles do not refer to particular functions or ministries, but they all emphasize the significance of fearless proclamation of the gospel as the major task of a Christian leader. The first title obviously comes from the Pauline understanding of the gospel message as *kērygma* ("message, proclamation"; 2 Tim. 4:17 and Titus 1:3).

The title "apostle" here appears as one of the three titles that concentrate on proclamation and teaching. The leaders of the next generations were preachers and teachers, but no longer apostles. And yet, the title "apostle" appears to be closely connected with preaching. Another noteworthy issue concerns the title "teacher," which is not found in early Pauline epistles. Here and in 1 Tim. 2:7 the title *didaskalos* is connected with the overall importance of "sound doctrine" in the Pastoral Epistles. Timothy should be a good teacher of sound doctrine. It is therefore also necessary to portray Paul as the teacher par excellence.

In 2 Tim. 1:12 the author returns (cf. 1:8) to the autobiographical portrayal. He is suffering in prison because of his bold commitment to proclaim the gospel. The boldness of Paul in prison is supposed to serve as an admonition to Timothy. Paul knows whom to trust in, namely, God. Second Timothy 1:12 is not easy to understand, the difficulty being that the pronoun "he" can be taken to mean Timothy (see NRSV) to whom, in 1 Tim. 6:20 and 2 Tim. 1:14, the legacy of Paul is entrusted. But in 2 Tim. 1:12 the same "he," namely, God, is both the object of Paul's trust and the guardian of his legacy.

It is most adequate to read 1:12 proceeding from the phrase *parathēkē mou* ("my deposit"; Vulgate: *depositum meum*). The Pastoral Epistles aim at defending the legacy of Paul. Thus the *parathēkē*, which contains sound doctrine, is sometimes almost literally considered as belonging to Paul, while Timothy is its guardian (cf. 1 Tim. 6:20). At the same time, Paul is of course the recipient of the gospel message and serves Christ as apostle. Thus the deposit is not literally "his property," but Paul is the apostolic messenger of this deposit. The following generations should guard the Pauline deposit rather than the message of the false teachers.

Another problem is created by the view that God should "guard" (*phylassō*) Paul's legacy while he is in prison. This needs to be interpreted metaphorically: Paul trusts that God can protect or safeguard the gospel message until the end. God is thus not a "guardian" in the same sense as Timothy, but God acts as the providential sovereign who can protect sound doctrine even in critical times. This interpretation finds some support in the observation that 2 Tim. 1:12 employs the perfect tense *pepisteuka* ("have put my trust"), alluding to Paul's having always trusted in God in this manner (Weiser 2003: 123–24 and appendix C). Given this, 1:12 would not describe a legal deposit, but the more general trust in God who is capable of protecting the gospel message. In this sense Paul can leave his task in God's hands.

The next verses (1:13–14) proceed from this general observation to the concrete task of Timothy, to whom the literal and quasilegal *parathēkē* of Paul has been entrusted. Timothy has heard the "sound words" (*hygiainontōn logōn*) from the teacher Paul, and he should hold to this "standard" (*hypotypōsis*).[2] In 1 Tim. 1:16 Paul is himself the "example" (*hypotypōsis*); now his words become this model or standard. *Typos* is the exemplary picture; the prefix *hypo-* can be understood in the sense of an archetype. In Rom. 6:17 the phrase *typos didachēs* ("form of teaching") describes the apostolic doctrine.

As in 1 Tim. 1:3–10, "sound" is connected with healthy and opposed to vices and disturbances. In both 1 Tim. 1:5 and here, faith and love characterize the sound or healthy state of a Christian mind. Faith and love together denote the ethos, the virtuous character of good Christians. These virtues are not, however, the products of human works or efforts, but they can be found in Christ Jesus. In this way the christological motif of grace expressed in 2 Tim. 1:9 is here continued.

Second Timothy 1:14 alludes to 1 Tim. 6:20. Timothy is now the guardian of the deposit. But whereas in 1 Tim. 6:20 the chain of tradition simply goes from Paul to Timothy, in 2 Tim. 1:14 the Holy Spirit is mentioned as a helper in this process of handing over the legacy of sound doctrine. We can thus see that in 1:12–14 the matter of handing over the *parathēkē* is safeguarded and protected by God and the Holy Spirit. In this sense 1:12–14 broadens the understanding of handing over the apostolic tradition. This process of tradition does not only and primarily occur among humans, but it is supervised by God.

The deposit is now called "good treasure" (*kalē parathēkē*). Mentioning the Holy Spirit "living in us" reflects the language of the spirit in other Pauline epistles (Rom. 8:14–16; 2 Cor. 13:13). At the same time, the function of the Holy Spirit is connected with the institutional role of Paul and Timothy. In Timothy's ordination Paul laid his hands on him in order that Timothy may receive the spirit of power (2 Tim. 1:6–7). After encouraging Timothy, Paul returns to the theme of the spirit, saying that the "Holy" Spirit, that is, the spirit of God, is operative in both of them. In this way 1:14 assumes that the presence of the spirit is connected with the tasks of church leadership.

Excursus 6: Tradition

The issue of tradition plays an important role in the Pastoral Epistles. Timothy is entrusted the legacy of Paul, the sound doctrine that he ought to safeguard and propagate (1 Tim. 6:20; 2 Tim. 1:14; 3:14). Different links of this good tradition are mentioned: Lois, Eunice, and Timothy (1:5); Christ, Paul, and Timothy (1 Tim. 1:12–18; 2 Tim. 1:10–14);

---

2. Later Christian writers, for instance, Philipp Melanchthon in his 1521 *Loci communes* (1993), sometimes refer to their dogmatics with this word.

maybe also Paul and God (1:12). At the same time it should be noted that some other traditions are criticized. The false teachers spread their "myths" and "genealogies" (1 Tim. 1:4; 4:7; Titus 3:9). These false traditions are "old wives' tales" (1 Tim. 4:7), "gossip" (5:13), and "contradictions of what is falsely called *gnōsis*" (6:20). It is thus not tradition as such that is regarded as being valuable, but the tradition that serves the truth and is transmitted by reliable witnesses.

Jesus was critical of the "tradition of the elders," which he regarded as "human tradition" (Mark 7:3–8; Matt. 15:1–9). A similarly critical attitude toward the traditions of false teachers is described in the Pastoral Epistles. Given that the "genealogies" refer to Jewish sources, a critical distance to some Jewish or Judaizing customs can be observed. At the same time, however, the Pastoral Epistles emphasize the positive value of tradition more strongly than many earlier New Testament texts. This feature is historically understandable if we presuppose that Timothy already represents the third generation of Christians. When the first generation was passing away, a positive sense of tradition needed to be developed in order to safeguard the Christian message.

For a more precise theological understanding of the phenomenon of tradition, it is useful to analyze the concept of *parathēkē* (1 Tim. 6:20; 2 Tim. 1:12, 14) in terms of giving and receiving. Roughly speaking, the term *paradosis* ("tradition") expresses a more flexible and more general event of transmission, whereas *parathēkē* emphasizes the idea of keeping, safeguarding, and entrusting (Roloff 1988: 370–72; Weiser 2003: 125–30). But, as I remarked in the exposition of 1 Tim. 6:20, *paradosis* in other Pauline epistles can represent a message coming directly from the Lord, whereas *parathēkē* is the "deposit" of Paul to Timothy and to the church. In this sense *parathēkē* represents a lower but more structured event of transmission.

The topic of tradition is vast and cannot here be treated from all theologically relevant perspectives (Pannenberg and Schneider 1992–98 is a very comprehensive overview). Often we can understand structured traditions as inalienable possessions that are characterized by the event of "keeping-while-giving" (see appendix C). In such an event, the object is handed over to trusted persons so that it remains the property of a designated group, in this case the church. Thus the vehicle given and received becomes a deposit. This view is theologically helpful because it facilitates connecting the discussion of *parathēkē* with other "varieties of giving" discussed in the Pastoral Epistles. Since the theory of inalienable possessions claims to have a broad anthropological validity, it can also offer a plausible way of understanding the theology of *parathēkē* in the Pastoral Epistles.

The "deposit" (*parathēkē*) of the Pastoral Epistles is an exemplary inalienable possession. It gives a group identity to those Christians who adhere to healthy doctrine. It is transmitted through a series of reliable owners and witnesses. The *parathēkē* needs to be guarded against the false teachers, who intend to blur the necessary distinctions. Whereas *paradosis* ("tradition") depicts the general event of transmitting the gospel message coming from God, the deposit entrusted to Paul and Timothy is an inalienable possession that has emerged as a result of keeping-while-giving. The overall message of Paul to Timothy expresses this twofold pattern: on the one hand,

Timothy is to proclaim and spread the good news according to sound doctrine. On the other hand, he is to keep and safeguard this very doctrine. This twofold pattern of keeping-while-giving gives the deposit of sound doctrine its identity as an inalienable possession.

The false teachers also aim at presenting a pattern of doctrine that is authenticated with the chain of tradition. But their myths and genealogies are illusory, whereas the true deposit of faith is transmitted by reliable witnesses. The phenomenon of keeping-while-giving is, as such, a neutral designation of events; it can be practiced by all parties involved. It is not the phenomenon, but its specific content that is at stake in Paul's discussion. But the understanding of the phenomenon of keeping-while-giving is helpful in order to understand the flow of Paul's argument.

In the theory of inalienable possessions, the vehicle of transmission, the "gift" or the "deposit," is of seminal importance. The second category of favor that it expresses is not constituted only in the minds of the particular giver and the individual recipient, but its exclusive identity has been constituted over a longer period of time and series of owners (for the categories, see appendix C). In the second category of favor, the vehicle of transmission thus exemplifies a kind of collective mind. The deposit has been entrusted to many previous owners but they all share the same faith.

The significance of keeping-while-giving for the Pastoral Epistles can be further analyzed through looking at the various distinctions between alienable and inalienable possessions. In many, perhaps most, cases Paul recommends giving away or sharing one's possessions. Hospitality (the third category of favor) as a virtue of the church leader is in many ways a counterpart to keeping-while-giving. Food, shelter, and many other material goods should be treated as alienable. They need to be shared with strangers, paying attention to their needs. The disinterested giving that characterizes hospitality is proper with regard to various alienable goods and services.

Money is a particularly effective alienable good, since it fulfills all kinds of needs but is in itself totally alienable. For this reason, the desire to become rich, that is, to make the very means of exchange inalienable, is "a root of all kinds of evil" (1 Tim. 6:10). But when rich people are "rich in good works, generous, and ready to share" (6:18), they alienate from the riches and in this way use them properly. Alienation from "gold, pearls, or expensive clothes" (2:9) is also recommended. The inalienable possessions of Christians are thus not found in worldly riches, but in immaterial goods, particularly in sound doctrine.

Treating material goods as alienable does not mean that they would be despised. On the contrary, they prove to be valuable when they are not kept but are given and shared. In demanding ascesis and celibacy (1 Tim. 4:3), the false teachers do not understand the proper circulation of things. A proper payment (5:17) and food and clothing (6:8) do not create dependencies, but are rather necessary for the *autarkeia*, proper independence.

The basic contrast is thus found between (1) the inalienable possession of sound doctrine, entrusted to Timothy, and (2) various alienable possessions that are to be circulated according to the rules of hospitality and other virtues. In addition to this basic contrast, four other matters mentioned in the Pastoral Epistles may approach the borderline of inalienable possessions.

1. With regard to material things, the cloak and parchments of Paul (2 Tim. 4:13) may be understood as possessions to be preserved for the sake of memory.
2. More importantly, the various recommendations of moderation with regard to food and especially wine (e.g., 1 Tim. 3:2–3; 5:23; Titus 1:7; 2:3) may relate to the various ways of being inalienable. Paul teaches that Christians should not become addicted to wine; such vice would take wine out of the disinterested circulation. But maybe total abstinence would also take wine out of the same circulation. Another dimension of food may be relevant with regard to 1 Tim. 4:3–5. The appearance of the verb *eucharisteō* and the phrase "those . . . who know the truth" (4:3; cf. 3:15) may contain a reference to the eucharistic meal. The Eucharist would exemplify an inalienable possession of consumable goods.
3. It may also be possible to discuss procreation and bringing up children in terms of keeping-while-giving. In childbearing, women and their household are expected to "continue in faith and love and holiness" (1 Tim. 2:15) so that a sort of tradition emerges. Special attention is paid to the church leader's children (3:5; Titus 1:6). Through bearing and bringing up children who remain believers (1 Tim. 4:3; 5:14; Titus 1:6; 2:4), the church creates an inalienable possession that stretches out through time.
4. The circulation of words and arguments in general is an immaterial area with regard to which much advice is given in the Pastoral Epistles. A church leader is expected to teach according to sound doctrine. He should "proclaim the message" (2 Tim. 4:2) and at the same time avoid "controversies" (2:23) and "profane chatter" (1 Tim. 6:20; 2 Tim. 2:16). This advice can also be understood in terms of keeping-while-giving. A committed discussion regarding doctrine should not be a free exchange of ideas, but a church leader involved in such discussion should exemplify his inalienable possession with the necessary care. Often it is better not to get involved in discussions that transform the inalienable possession into an exchangeable opinion. The instructions to women to keep silent (1 Tim. 2:11–12; 5:13) seem to assume that the speaker cannot preserve her integrity but is, in the flow of talking, alienated from her proper conviction. Notwithstanding the author's misogynism, it is possible to think that keeping silent helps to preserve the conviction that is not intended to be exchangeable.

Yet another issue of verbal transmission concerns the overall genre of 2 Timothy as Paul's testament. A testament is an act of targeted giving characterized by the absence of the giver. By means of testament, the absent giver makes himself present to the recipients. At the same time, the recipients who understand themselves as legitimate heirs use the testament to legitimize their position. Understood in this broad and formal sense, 2 Timothy displays many features of a testament. With regard to the interpretation of individual passages and arguments, however, it is more fruitful to employ the different varieties of giving and the theory of inalienable possessions to understand Paul's intention. As an interpretative notion, testament manages to shed light on some features discussed in 2 Timothy. Paul is not, however, concerned with the writing of a testament, but with keeping the faith.

My decision to dispense with the notion of testament is further motivated by the very different and controversial matters ascribed to the interpretation of 2 Timothy as testament in the exegetical literature (see Oberlinner 1995: 1–5 and Weiser 2003: 34–39 on "testament"; Marshall 1999: 33–40 treats the book's genre and structure). It would be arbitrary to argue that, for instance, because 2 Timothy is a testament, it stems from a different author than 1 Timothy and Titus or that its logical place in the canon comes after Titus. It is more fruitful to compare 2 Timothy with the other farewell or testamentary texts of Paul, especially Romans and Acts 20:17–38, but the parallels remain rather general. As a name of a literary genre, "testament" is difficult because it interferes with "farewell speech" on the one hand and the manifold meanings of the New Testament term *diathēkē* on the other.

For these reasons, it is more illuminating to treat 2 Timothy in terms of keeping-while-giving and inalienable possessions. These explanatory terms bring all three Pastoral Epistles into closer interaction with one another. They are all concerned with the preservation of the sound teaching that they understand to be Paul's legacy. In this concern 2 Timothy cannot be distinguished from 1 Timothy and Titus.

In sum, I employ the theory of inalienable possessions in order to highlight in which senses the Pastoral Epistles express the idea of keeping-while-giving. The theory enables me to connect the discussion of *parathēkē*, tradition, and sound doctrine with other varieties of giving elaborated in the Pastoral Epistles. It allows me to claim that the Pastoral Epistles contain a differentiated theology of giving in which 1 Tim. 6:20 and 2 Tim. 1:12–14 represent only one dimension of the manifold acts of giving that contribute to the self-understanding and the memory of the church. The vertical dimension of theological giving is constituted in the salvific act of the self-giving of Jesus Christ (see excursus 9). Its various horizontal dimensions are manifested in the thematic field of giving and receiving favors, practicing hospitality, and showing gratitude (see exposition of 1 Tim. 3:2) as well as in the view of tradition as keeping-while-giving.

Because the present work is a theological commentary, the historical and exegetical background of this theology of giving has not been presented in full detail. Further historical work is necessary to make the claims more plausible (for background, see appendix C and Saarinen 2005). It is not my aim, however, to reduce the Pauline theology of giving to its historical or social context. Historical and anthropological points of comparison serve the purpose of understanding rather than the purpose of reduction.[3] A theological understanding should not be reduced to analogies, but it nevertheless needs some analogical background in order to be understood at all.

---

3. See the postscript for the grounds of the claim that historical analogy can be employed without compromising the main subjects of theology.

Good and Bad Examples (2 Tim. 1:15–18)

Having encouraged Timothy to be a bold witness, Paul in 1:15 mentions other people who have been "ashamed" and "turned away." The passage begins with "you are aware," which is repeated in 1:18. These phrases give the impression of an intimate relationship between Paul and Timothy. They have the same opinion of the persons concerned. The Asian Christians have turned away from the prisoner Paul, not from the Christian truth as such (cf. 4:4, 10; Titus 1:14). The author may be referring here to a conflict of loyalty rather than one of heresy.

On the other hand, we do not gain more information of this conflict. Neither do the names Phygelus and Hermogenes appear in any other New Testament texts. The names are pejorative: Phygelus connotes "flight" and Hermogenes "a descendant of pagan god Hermes." Chrysostom (NPNF[1] 13.484) thinks that Paul refers to Asian Christians living in Rome, and Theodoret (in Gorday 2000: 237) explains that they have abandoned Paul on account of the fear of Nero (Weiser 2003: 136–37). The rhetorical intention of 1:15 is nevertheless clear, namely, to give a bad example that is not to be followed by the readers of the epistle.

A contrasting good example is offered in 1:16–18. Onesiphorus, who is also mentioned in 4:19, has visited Paul in prison, refreshed him, and given a bold witness about his Christian conviction. The name Onesiphorus connotes "useful" and perhaps thus reminds Timothy of Onesimus (Phlm. 10). In addition, this person has rendered great service (*diēkonēsen*) in Ephesus. Although we cannot infer from this that he was a deacon, his example is connected with diaconic service. Allusions to Matt. 25:43–44 are probably not conscious, but 2 Timothy does mention both visiting the prisoner and giving him clothing (4:13) as examples of Christian service.

A traditional problem concerns the issue whether Onesiphorus is presupposed to be dead. Some features seem to indicate this, especially mention of the "household of Onesiphorus" (1:16; 4:19) and the eschatological wish "may the Lord grant mercy" (1:16, 18). No death of Onesiphorus need, however, be presupposed (Oberlinner 1995: 59–60). The "household" may include its master, and the eschatological phrase need not imply the death of the person, since the whole situation of Christians is eschatological. Moreover, in 1:16 the wish of mercy is addressed to the household, whereas in 1:18 it is addressed to Onesiphorus himself. Although "that day" in 1:18 refers to the parousia (cf. 1:12), it is plausible to read 1:16–18 so that Paul there prays the Lord to grant mercy to the living Onesiphorus and his household.

This issue is of theological importance since 1:18 has traditionally been used to argue in favor of the prayer for the dead. Whereas Catholics, Orthodox, and some Protestants pray for the dead, many Protestants find such prayer problematic. Thus the problem is both theological and ecumenical. Exegetically, it is not evident whether 1:16–18 describes a prayer. Paul simply expresses the wish that the Lord grant mercy. That we hear 1:16–18 as a prayer has to do with the phrases having found a later liturgical use in various rites of the Christian churches. Typically, 1:18a is employed in funeral rites (Weiser 2003: 142–45 gives an overview of the reception history).

Thus the response of the readers has legitimized a certain understanding of the text. It is also an exegetically possible understanding. Two things ought to be noticed: (1) 1:16–18 does not force the reader to understand the text as a prayer for the dead; and (2) although the tradition has broadened the original scope of 1:16–18, it has not necessarily misunderstood the theological possibilities left open by the text.

Exhortation to Be a Strong Witness (2 Tim. 2:1–7)

After the examples, Paul returns to the theme of being not ashamed but strong and bold. Paul encourages Timothy through many imperatives. The first two (2:1–2) concern primarily witness and leadership, whereas the following exhortations employ materials from everyday life and Hellenistic popular philosophy.

As in 1:2, the intimate relationship between Paul and Timothy is expressed with the phrase "my child" in 2:1. The first imperative, "be strong," relates strength to the grace in Christ Jesus. The grace (*charis*) bestows the Christian with various charisms, in this case especially strength. As the following examples of soldier and athlete (2:4–5) show, the required strength in character is both spiritual and moral, maybe even physical. Throughout 1–2 Timothy, sound or healthy doctrine is emphasized. Corresponding to this, the character of the good Christian should be healthy and strong, both mentally and spiritually. Health and strength are two aspects of the comprehensive reality of the gospel and grace in Jesus Christ.

In the second imperative (2:2), Paul briefly returns to the topic of his legacy or *paratheke*. Interestingly, another link in the chain of tradition is now made explicit. Whereas 1:14 and 1 Tim. 6:20 concentrate on Timothy's task as the guardian of the *paratheke* and 2 Tim. 1:12 describes the overall divine protection over this legacy, 2:2 tells Timothy how he should hand over this legacy to other Christians. Timothy should "entrust" (*parathou*) the deposit to faithful people who will then teach others. The chain of tradition is thus continued.

This fundamental point of 2:2 is clear. A certain problem pertains to the beginning in which Paul mentions that Timothy has heard the gospel message "through many witnesses" (*dia pollon martyron*). The simplest meaning of *dia*, adopted by the NRSV, is "through." This, however, gives the impression that Paul and Timothy are not so intimate as 2:1 and many other places presuppose. On the other hand, the theme of tradition, appearing in the context of *paratheke*, requires a chain of witnesses both before Timothy and after him. In order to express this chain, *dia* is the obvious choice.

Given the overall intention of 1–2 Timothy, one must presuppose that Timothy receives the *paratheke* immediately from Paul. The "many witnesses" of 2:2 may refer to the persons present in Timothy's ordination, namely, the "many witnesses" of 1 Tim. 6:12. Since 2 Tim. 1:6 assumes that Paul himself has ordained Timothy, 2:2 may also serve the purpose of underlining that the event of ordination was a public and ecclesial event. Thus *dia* could be translated "in front of" or, following 1 Tim. 6:12, "in the presence of" many witnesses. Given this, the expression "what you have heard from me" would also refer to Paul's words spoken at the ordination. These words express the central content of the *parathēkē*. They are also heard by many witnesses, who thus guarantee the sound doctrine of Paul (Weiser 2003: 157–58; Marshall 1999: 725 does not think that a "formal occasion" need be assumed).

This is not a compelling explanation, but especially because of 1 Tim. 6:12 it may be the most likely one. This explanation further assumes that the handing over of the *parathēkē* is not an individual event between two persons, but an ecclesiastical event that requires a synodical responsibility. This is indicated by the three plural forms of 2 Tim. 2:2, namely, "many witnesses," "faithful people," and "others." They establish a certain contrast to the phrase "you . . . from me." In this way 2:2 broadens the scope of 1 Tim. 6:20 in an important manner. Handing over a tradition is on the one hand a matter between the recognized leaders. On the other hand, it is at the same time a matter of the wider community that witnesses this event and participates in it. Both 2 Tim. 1:12 and 2:2 extend the scope of handing over the tradition in an important manner.

The third imperative (2:3) compares Timothy to a soldier. Both are to "share in suffering" (*synkakopatheō*). The apostle now moves to comparisons taken from his environment. It was a commonplace in Hellenism to describe the life of a soldier as one of suffering (Marshall 1999: 727–28; Oberlinner 1995: 70). In 1:8 Timothy is asked to join in suffering. A soldier is an apt point of comparison with regard to both suffering and strength. This and the next comparisons employ motives found in 1 Cor. 9:7–10, 24–27. The service of Jesus Christ may be compared with the life of a soldier or an athlete. Images of struggle, competition, training, and suffering were employed in Stoicism as examples of inner training, self-control, and aspiration. The purpose of inner training was to control the emotions with the same mastery as the soldier or athlete controls his body (Weiser 2003: 160–61, referring to Epictetus, *Discourses* 2.18.22 [LCL 131.355]; 4.4.30 [LCL 218.325]).

A more elaborated military illustration is formulated in 2 Tim. 2:4. The person serving in the army should not get entangled "in everyday affairs" (*tais tou biou pragmateias*). The Greek phrase may mean many things, for instance, earning a living or enjoying the comforts of ordinary life. The point of comparison is nevertheless clear. Timothy should please his enlisting officer even when this is uncomfortable. Since Timothy is the soldier of Christ, it is Christ and not Paul who is here thought to have "enlisted" Timothy. The obedience of a good soldier is required. Given the context of 2:6 and 1 Cor. 9:9, one may see here a reference to the church leader's right to be paid.

The next comparison (2 Tim. 2:5) concerns Timothy as athlete. In order to win the "crown" he should compete according to the rules. Here the self-control of an athlete, mentioned in 1 Cor. 9:25, is consciously assumed. Competing "according to the rules" employs the word *nomimōs* ("lawfully, legitimately"), which is also used in 1 Tim. 1:8. The "law" of 1 Timothy is both the Decalogue and the Hellenistic moral law. In the comparison of 2 Tim. 2:5 both the external rules and the inner sense of morality and sound judgment are assumed. Not only external rules, but above all the inner moral integrity of Timothy should be preserved. In this sense 2:5 is concerned with the godly character of the leader as well as his sound judgment. Thus 2:5 resembles the athletic comparisons of 1 Tim. 4:7–8 and 6:12. Paul himself has already won the crown (2 Tim. 4:8).

The final comparison (2:6) describes the laborious suffering of the farmer. As the farmer has the right to the first share of the crops, so the person who suffers in witness to Christ is entitled to a remuneration. The comparison is consciously formed after 1 Cor. 9:10–11. Whereas in 2 Tim. 2:5 the "crown" is an eternal reward, in 2:6 the "share" is a material reward in this life. The point of the comparison is not, however, the reward, but the original point of departure (2:3): Timothy is called to a laborious work, which means suffering. Other aspects of this work are mentioned in the three comparisons.

Taken together, all three comparisons emphasize the hard and unselfish work of the church leader. Witness to Christ requires obedience, moral integrity and self-control. Mentioning "crown" and "first share of the crops" may motivate Timothy, but they also appear here because materials from 1 Cor. 9 are used. In spite of this rhetorical coherence, the actual content of the three comparisons remains cryptic. Taken literally, Timothy is advised (1) to please Christ, (2) to compete "legitimately" (*nomimōs*), and (3) to have the first share of the crops. We may ask whether these three points relate to any general moral idea or merely serve the purpose of underlining the necessity of hard work and bold witness?

The three points may also be understood in terms of moderation. The context here speaks of self-control (2 Tim. 1:7; 1 Cor. 9:25) and youthful passions (2 Tim. 2:22), but the desires are not to be eradicated. Timothy can please Christ and enjoy the fruits of his work. He should not detach from ordinary life but involve himself in hard work and competition, as long as this is done "legitimately," that is, with proper integrity and sound judgment. Thus no *apatheia* or hard ascesis is recommended, but rather such moderation of inner life that keeps the person both active and obedient at the same time. For this purpose, the virtues expressing *metriopatheia*—like contentment (*autarkeia*; 1 Tim. 6:6), self-discipline (*sōphronismos*; 2 Tim. 1:7), and steadfastness (*hypomonē*; 3:10)—are needed.

This ethos of 2:4–6 is also underlined in the fourth imperative, which is formulated in 2:7 as "think over" (*noeō*). When Timothy thinks over or meditates on what Paul is saying, the Lord will give him "understanding in all things" (*synesin en pasin*). *Synesis* is a philosophical term that occurs only here in the Pastoral Epistles. In Col. 1:9 it is paralleled with wisdom, both terms denoting a deeper insight into God's will, paralleling the Septuagint version of Isa. 11:2: "spirit of wisdom and understanding" (*pneuma sophias kai syneseōs*). In secular Greek, *synesis* often results from hearing or, in other words, receiving external information properly (Marshall 1999: 731; H. Conzelmann in *TDNT* 7.888–96). The comparisons given in 2 Tim. 2:3–6 thus call for further meditation, which may lead to increased insight and proper balance.

Promise of Salvation (2 Tim. 2:8–13)

The fifth imperative admonishes Timothy to remember a brief rule of faith that Paul calls "my gospel." Similar to "my deposit" in 1:12, this expression does not claim any specific authorship, but formulates what the apostle thinks to be an adequate expression of sound doctrine. The rule of faith is taken from Rom. 1:3–4, in which the same phrases are called "the gospel." Only the order of christological descriptions is reversed: 2 Tim. 2:8 first says that "Jesus Christ [is] raised from the dead" and then that he is "a descendant of David." Whereas Rom. 1:3–4 employs the order of salvation history, 2 Tim. 2:8 names the items in the order of importance.

Although the remembrance of the resurrection is the most important point in this admonition, it is significant that 2:8 pays attention to descendance from David. As in 1 Tim. 2:5, the confession to Christ as human being here plays a role. The Pastoral Epistles emphasize incarnation and counteract docetic tendencies. Maybe 2 Tim. 2:8 also contains an idea of extending the tradition backward: the deposit of faith came from Christ to Paul and from Paul to Timothy. But Christ himself is also a link in the historical tradition extending back to Judaism.

The point of Paul's suffering is again (1:8, 16) mentioned in 2:9. This time the description is dramatic: Paul suffers in chains "like a criminal." The words *kakopathō* ("suffer hardship") and *kakourgos* ("wrongdoer") underline the deplorable state of this condition. They also express a strong contrast to 2:9b. Paul is in chains, but the word of God remains free. The "word of God" here relates to "my gospel" in 2:8: it is the gospel "for which" Paul suffers. Human beings can chain Paul, but not his gospel, since it is the word of God that, having been entrusted to God (1:12), cannot be chained. When Timothy remembers this gospel and its inherent freedom, he is encouraged to serve it even when his teacher is in prison.

In 2:10 a final motivation and reason for Paul's suffering is given. He endures "everything for the sake of the elect [*eklektoi*]." In the Pauline Epistles, this word depicts those who believe in Christ (Rom. 8:33; 16:13; Col. 3:12). Here as well as in Titus 1:1 the word emphatically refers to those Christians who conform to the Pauline gospel, sound doctrine, and godliness (Oberlinner 1995: 81). Although Paul in 2 Tim. 2:8–10 draws the attention of the reader to himself, he nevertheless points out that salvation and eternal glory are found in Jesus Christ.

The phrase "the saying is sure" (*pistos ho logos*) appears often in the Pastoral Epistles (1 Tim. 1:15; 3:1; 4:9; Titus 3:8), marking the beginning of a new and important passage. In 2 Tim. 2:11–13 Paul recites a traditional Christian formula that is most likely connected with the gospel mentioned in 2:8. As in 1:9, here also a short liturgical rule of faith is expressed. This rule extends the sufferings of Paul and Timothy toward the death of Christ, but also toward the suffering and death of all faithful.

Second Timothy 2:11b alludes to Rom. 6:8. Dying with Christ brings about a new life with Christ. The sentence can probably be understood as referring to both Christian baptism and martyrdom. At the same time 2 Tim. 2:11b is connected with the present sufferings of the faithful. Christians who join the labor and sufferings of Paul must in a way die to the world, but in this labor they receive a new life with Christ. This last thought is essential for the understanding of the second line (2:12a). The new life began in baptism, but the Christian must still endure the hardship of earthly life. This endurance in obedient labor leads to the future reign in which we are crowned (2:5). The verb "to endure" (*hypomenō*), employed in both 2:10 and 2:12a, connects Paul's example with all the faithful. This connection may also presuppose the persecution of Christians (Weiser 2003: 172–73).

The third line (2:12b) points out the opposite of 2:12a. If Christians do not endure and deny Christ, he will also deny them. The line is probably connected with Luke 12:8–9. Thus the problem of apostasy, or at least of falling away from sound doctrine, is addressed. The author presupposes that even the elect of 2 Tim. 2:10 may fall if they do not endure in the time of hardship and suffering. The line is dramatic since it employs "we" as if Christians would collectively deny Christ.

The fourth line makes an unexpected, but at the same carefully composed dramatic turn. Even if Christians were unfaithful, Christ remains faithful. The word *apistos* means "untrue, unfaithful." It does not mean apostasy or a complete lack of faith, but rather a lack of trust in God. Although a dramatic contrast to 2:12b is intended, 2:13a does not contain a real paradox or contradiction. The sentence intends to point out God's immutable promise and trust in the covenant with humans. Even if human beings lack trust and break their promises, Christ remains true and the salvation provided in his death and resurrection remains available. This idea resembles Rom. 3:3–4, in which the faithlessness of some people does not nullify the faithfulness of God. God or Christ cannot be untrue.

This idea is underlined in 2 Tim. 2:13b. Although humans can deny Christ (2:12b), Christ cannot "deny himself." The absolute fidelity of Christ provides a firm foundation to the comforting thought that the promise of salvation remains. The possibility of human denial admonishes us to work hard and to endure, but at the same time the impossibility of divine denial gives a lasting consolation.

The third and fourth lines (2:12b–13a) thus express a contrast that is no contradiction. The problem of apostasy is real and may lead to the denial of salvation. At the same time, God cannot be unfaithful but his promise endures all shortcomings of human beings. It is not, however, possible to press these two contrasting points into a rigid system. Probably 2:13a alludes to the lack of trust and to moral shortcomings, whereas in 2:12b a direct denial is at stake. We cannot define precisely where the mere lack of trust ends and a denial begins.

Although the imperatives to Timothy continue, the concise and hymnic lines of 2:11–13 bring the first thematic part of the epistle to a close. This first part is characterized by the encouragement to be a bold witness and by the emphasis on suffering for the sake of the gospel. Paul's imprisonment is portrayed as an example to all Christians to suffer for the sake of Christ and his apostle, Paul. Through enduring this suffering, Christians may obtain salvation. This major tendency invites the reader to assume that both the author and the recipients of 2 Timothy were in a situation of hardship and suffering.

FALSE TEACHERS
AND THEIR CONDUCT

2 Tim. 2:14–3:9

The second thematic part of 2 Timothy concerns the false teachers and their conduct. Paul employs examples, comparisons, and extensive lists of vices to portray
the false teachers. The passage displays many affinities with 1 Timothy. As in
1 Timothy, the false teachers are contrasted with the good behavior of exemplary
Christians. In particular, Timothy is encouraged to display such a good example.
The passage also contains materials from the Old Testament and other traditional
sources.

Right Conduct as Purification (2 Tim. 2:14–26)

In the imperative in 2:14 Timothy is asked to "remind" his fellow Christians
of the aforesaid words of Paul. In addition, Christians are warned of "wrangling
over words" (*logomacheō*). This warning closely resembles 1 Tim. 6:4, in which
logomachia is attributed to the false teachers who obstinately seek controversies.
Such controversies are in 2 Tim. 2:14 said to lead to the "ruin" (*katastrophē*) of
the listeners. In the exposition of 1 Tim. 6:4 I argue that for Paul *logomachia* is an
expression of pathological behavior. This passage leads toward a similar conclusion.
Whereas sound doctrine promotes a healthy character and moral integrity, false
teaching is portrayed as leading to confusion and ruin of character. In addition,
2 Tim. 2:14–16 argues, in keeping with 1 Timothy, that sound doctrine does not
need too many words but appreciates silence.

Instead of quarreling, an exemplary leader should take care of his approval
by God (2:15). The command "do your best to present" has a moral sense,

meaning moral exertion and intensive involvement (Quinn and Wacker 2000: 673–74). Instead of many words, a leader should pay attention to his own moral and personal integrity. Being "approved by" God can also be translated "mak[ing] yourself a fit offering to God" (Quinn and Wacker 2000: 674). In any case, moral integrity is vitally important, as the next phrase, "no need to be ashamed," also points out. It is enough for a church leader to explain "the word of truth" (*logos tēs alētheias*) "rightly" (*orthotomeō*). The word of truth refers to the sound doctrine that is the "truth" in 2:18. The verb *orthotomeō* means "to build a straight road"; the metaphorical use here points out the necessity of teaching rightly.

The detached and even quiet attitude of the exemplary leader is highlighted in 2:16. As in 1 Tim. 6:20, "profane chatter" (*kenophōnia*) is to be avoided. The reason for this imperative is that chatter has a contagious effect. "Making progress in impiety" (*prokopsousin asebeias*) employs the verb *prokoptō* ("to make progress"), a Stoic term that Philo ascribed to the practitioners of *metriopatheia*. For Philo, the perfect ideal requires the eradication of emotions (*apatheia*), but for ordinary people successful moderation already demonstrates good progress (*Allegorical Interpretation* 3.114, 128–29 [LCL 226.377, 387, 389]; see appendix A and Sorabji 2000: 386). For Paul, the verb here has a sarcastic connotation, since it denotes a "progress" toward something disreputable. In 1 Tim. 4:15 Timothy's progress (substantive *prokopē*) is positive, whereas here and below (2 Tim. 3:9, 13) negative "progress" is indicated.

Profane talk "will spread like a gangrene" (2:17). Gangrene was in medicine an expression of a rapidly growing cancerous tumor. It alludes to sickness, whereas sound doctrine alludes to health. The vice of vain talking appears in many places in 1 Timothy (1:6; 3:3; 4:7; 5:13; 6:4–5, 20). It always refers to the persons who are not capable of living according to proper godliness. Paul here adheres to the biblical and Greco-Roman idea that a trained character manages to keep silent, whereas chatter is a symptom of the person's lack of self-control (Epictetus, *Encheiridion* 33 [LCL 218.517]; G. Wohlfart and J. Kreuzer in *HWP* 8.1483–95). Chatter is harmful because it provokes more of the same and thus easily leads to *logomachia* ("wrangling over words"). For these reasons, it can be compared with impiety and morbid gangrene.

Hymenaeus and Philetus are mentioned as bad examples of such impious behavior. In 1 Tim. 1:19–20 Hymenaeus is a person who has "reject[ed] conscience," an expression that may connote the lack of control and sound judgment. In 2 Tim. 2:18 the two persons are said to have "claim[ed] that the resurrection has already taken place." Given the context of *logomachia* and vain talking, it is plausible to interpret this false doctrine as an expression of exaggerated enthusiasm. If someone feels that the new life in Christ and the presence of salvation is completely overwhelming, that person may claim that he or she is already resurrected. Some Pauline sayings (Eph. 2:4–6) may move in this direction. Here, however, this interpretation of the "new life in Christ" is clearly rejected.

Hymenaeus and Philetus may have been gnostics who claimed that they have already left the material world and their body in their conversion and are thus resurrected (Weiser 2003: 210–25 gives an extensive overview of this heresy and its interpretation history). A more definite knowledge of their position cannot be deduced from 2 Tim. 2:17, but it is clear that Paul moderates the exaggerated enthusiasm. This is significant, since he also encourages Timothy to be a strong witness about Christ and eternal glory (2:10). Paul's advice thus moves between two extremes. A Christian should not be ashamed of his or her conviction (2:15), but also needs to avoid exaggerated enthusiasm and doctrinal statements that become empty *logomachia* without any corresponding reality. A Christian should examine his or her reality and integrity rightly and truthfully.

As 2:18b shows, the false doctrines have caused confusion in the "faith of some." This may be the contextual background of 2:14–3:9. In 2:19 Paul aims at convincing his readers of God's "firm foundation" (*stereos themelios*), which remains unshaken by false doctrines. As in 1 Tim. 6:19, *themelios* refers to solid ground on which the good and healthy personal character of the Christian can be built. In 2 Tim. 2:19 the role of God as establisher and guarantee of this foundation is underlined by two quotations. The first is from the Septuagint version of Num. 16:5, but the source of the second is less clear. It may be taken from Num. 16:27 or it may be a combination of Sirach 17:26 and Isa. 26:13 (Marshall 1999: 755–59). More important than the precise source is, however, seeing that, for Paul, God guarantees the firm foundation amidst all false teachings.

In 2 Tim. 2:20 the "large house" is a metaphor of the church. In the Pastoral Epistles the church is primarily compared to an *oikos* ("house"). The bishop's task is compared to that of leading a household (1 Tim. 3:5). This image of *oikos* is now broadened to include the utensils that are, motivated by Rom. 9:21, compared to the members of the church. The comparison is not altogether coherent and may give rise to misunderstandings. In 2 Tim. 2:20–21 it is assumed that the utensils can cleanse themselves. In addition, Paul is not aiming to say that there are first-class and second-class Christians. The point of the comparison is to argue against false teachers. In this specific context, 2:20–21 wants to point out that those who adhere to sound doctrine can also avoid impiety and wickedness (2:16, 19).

The aim of the comparison is formulated in 2:21. All who "cleanse themselves" (*ekkatharē heauton*) will become special utensils. The author presupposes an anthropology in which harmful emotions and passions (2:22) engender bad behavior and false beliefs. The metaphor of cleansing alludes to both the cleansing of God's *oikos* (the church) and the personal purification of harmful passions. There is a many-sided dynamic of activity and passivity involved in this purification of character. A "utensil" is in itself passive and is used by the master of the house. "Profane chatter" and "wrangling over words" (2:14, 16) refer to the wrong activity, which should be replaced with quietness and simple explanations. In this training a person becomes more passive and able to receive the truth. This training is in itself a cleansing of the character and a purification of the heart (2:22). The renunciation of false activities is an aspect of cleansing oneself.

This flow of thought is assumed in 2:21b. A purified vessel or utensil is "useful to the owner." It is "dedicated" or, in fact, "sanctified" (*hēgiasmenon*; 1 Tim. 4:5). Instead of lending itself to false activities, it is available for every good work. The dynamics of activity and passivity is complex, since the utensil is also assumed to be capable of purifying itself. In this cleansing, the right activity is seen as self-reflection, presenting oneself to God (2 Tim. 2:15), in order that God may use this person as an utensil.

Excursus 7: Ecclesiology and Ordained Ministry, Part 2

In the context of 1 Timothy I discussed ecclesiology and ordained ministry in general (see excursus 2). Here is a proper place to continue the ecclesiological discussion, with a special focus on the character formation of the Christians in the church. Although the metaphor of *oikos* in 1 Tim. 3 relates to the abstract and universal church, I stress the proximity of household ethics to the individual character formation, especially in the view of *oikeiōsis* ("familiarization" or "genuine care for others"). The church is a "large house" (2 Tim. 2:20) in which some utensils are for ordinary use, others for special use. Christians are to be "cleansed" (2:21) so that they may become useful to the owner of the house. The process of cleansing means a moderation of passions. It leads to the knowledge of the "truth" (2:25) that is inherent in the church. When a member of the household knows the truth, he or she has a sound mind and can practice love, peace, and gentleness, that is, exercise a genuine care for others (2:22, 25). This Christian also realizes that the false teachers have not progressed from their egoism toward reason and altruism, but have remained in their folly (2:23, 25–26).

In this way the church-as-household is a laboratory of character formation, a space in which the process of *oikeiōsis* may proceed. This process presupposes a relatively small community, a nuclear church or an *ecclesiola* in which genuine care for others can take place. It is important to notice that the emphasis on "the knowledge of the truth" (2:25; Titus 1:1) as an aspect of the church's existence is not only connected with the universal truth of sound doctrine, but it also sets the agenda for individual aspiration. The individual Christian should seek the truth in order to be able to renounce egoism and shameful passions and to replace them with such genuine care for others, which is accompanied by the virtuous emotions of joy, gentleness, and contentment.

This program of character formation is ecclesiological because it is expressed with the help of the ecclesiological concepts "household" and "truth." As a community in which the process of *oikeiōsis* can take place, the church is a "social ethic" (this famous expression is from Hauerwas 1983: 99). Obviously, this does not mean that ecclesiology should or could be reduced to morality. The Pastoral Epistles rather aim at arguing that the comprehensive virtues of godliness and self-control are to be realized in the church. Christians should know the truth and practice good works. But although these goals are also known to philosophers, Christians realize that a "household of God" (1 Tim. 3:15) or "God's economy" (1:4) is needed to attain these well-known goals. In its stress on communitarian and individual aspiration, the household ecclesiology displays an affinity to the later trends of evangelical Pietism.

An important aspect of ecclesiology is the task of handing over the tradition that Paul entrusts to Timothy. In this event of temporal succession, the theological phenomenon of tradition emerges. I treated this phenomenon in excursus 6. Here it suffices to say that, with the help of the Pastoral Epistles, later theologians can develop the concepts of succession, apostolicity, and orthodoxy. Relying on these concepts, the church of our day can be called the same church to which Paul and Timothy belonged.

With regard to both ecclesiology in general and to the doctrine of ministry in particular, the most obvious interpretative problem of the Pastoral Epistles concerns the theological role of character formation. Extensive requirements concerning the personal character of bishop, elder, deacon, and widow are given, whereas the concrete tasks of these roles or offices are not spelled out. This puzzles and even frustrates a modern theologian, who is often more interested in finding out the nature of their office and the institution that they represent.

In appendixes A–B, I attempt to solve this problem through a systematic concentration on the issues of sound mind and virtuous character. The church, depicted as an ideal household, takes the role of a seedbed in which the formation of sound judgment and the proper moderation of emotions can take place. I have not, however, developed this view toward a consistent pedagogical ecclesiology in which the church would resemble a seminary. Since the household is not only a place of nourishment, rest, and security, but also a place of learning and socialization, such a "pedagogical ecclesiology" may nevertheless be a promising theological undertaking.

Theologians have traditionally turned to the Pastoral Epistles in order to find solutions to the matters of church order, doctrine of ministry, apostolicity, and succession. Therefore my extensive treatment of character formation may seem odd or secondary. But when we look at some of the most influential expositions of the Pastoral Epistles, we can see that this pedagogical and "therapeutic" concentration is not an entirely new idea.[1]

Apart from this concentration, I have for the most part preferred such ecclesiological insights that are both Catholic and evangelical at the same time. Marshall (1999) succeeds in showing that the ecclesiological material of the Pastoral Epistles is not sufficiently well organized to justify a Catholic ecclesiology or to rule out an evangelical one. At the same time, the strongly Protestant attempts to show either (1) that there is hardly any institutional structure or (2) that the existing institutional structure is already

---

1. See, in particular, Chrysostom's homilies, discussed in excursus 5. Among recent commentators, Johnson 2001 has some awareness of this, although he, following Malherbe 1989, downplays the therapeutic approach by interpreting it as metaphorical imagery.

at variance with Jesus and Paul remain unconvincing (see the research histories of Schenk 1987 and Hahn 1986: 39–56 and excursus 2). With regard to ecclesiology, the "early Catholic" paradigm, moderated with the flexibilities of the household metaphor, still yields good exegetical results.

The imperatives continue in 2:22: Timothy is to "shun youthful passions [*neōterikas epithymias*]." In the Pastoral Epistles, Timothy is often assumed to be young (e.g. 1 Tim. 4:12), and in Hellenistic ethics it was a commonplace to think that young people cannot yet master their emotions properly (Weiser 2003: 227–28). It is therefore plausible to read 2 Tim. 2:22 in the light of 2:15 and 2:20–21. A faithful church leader should manage to keep a distance to the emotions proper to young persons. This does not mean mortifying all passions or a state of *apatheia*, but rather a mature control and moderation of various desires. Although *epithymia* in Christian tradition often connotes sexual passions, the word in this context has more to do with rash, impatient, and talkative behavior. False teachers do not control their passions but are led by them. Timothy should develop his self-control to become a golden utensil employed by God.

The mature behavior is characterized as being in pursuit of four virtues: "righteousness, faith, love, and peace." Similar, though not identical, catalogues appear in 1 Tim. 4:12 and 6:11. In 2 Tim. 3:10 Timothy is said to follow Paul in faith and love. The two virtues appear in all these catalogues and constitute the central characteristics of Christian existence. As in 1 Tim. 6:11, the catalogue opens with righteousness, a concept that is contrasted to *adikia* ("injustice") in 2 Tim. 2:19. Righteousness is further connected with peace in many biblical texts (e.g., Rom. 14:19; Heb. 12:14; 1 Pet. 3:11).

"Those who call on the Lord" (cf. 2 Tim. 2:19) are the sincere Christians. The phrase "pure heart" (cf. 1 Tim. 1:5) underlines the importance of good character, which becomes expressed by the practice of the four above-mentioned virtues. The phrases echo the requirement of cleansing (2 Tim. 2:21) one's character of impious behavior in order that the person may behave in an exemplary manner.

In 2:23 Timothy is again (2:14–17) warned of following the false teachers. They are characterized as bringing forth "stupid and senseless controversies" (*mōras kai apaideutous zētēseis*). While *mōria* is simply foolishness, *apaideutos* connotes the idea of a household in which members receive good education (*paideia*). False teachers do not give proper education, but they provoke senseless misbehavior.

As in 1 Tim. 6:4, *zētēsis* refers to pointless quarrels that reflect the person's stupidity or even a psychopathic obsession toward myths and genealogies (1:4). Timothy should know that these only give birth to new controversies. Paul does not aim at giving instructions about the content of the argument, but he focuses on the practical and therapeutic side of a proper reaction. A responsible church leader should exercise caution; he is not to engage in unnecessary debates. This is another aspect of silence and detachment recommended in the passage (e.g., 2 Tim. 2:16).[2]

The advice is thus concentrated on strengthening the good character of Timothy and questioning the character of his opponents. In 2:24 a good leader is presented as "the Lord's servant" (*doulos kyriou*). Like the similar statements regarding Paul (Acts 16:17; Rom. 1:1; Gal. 1:10), this phrase depicts the master as a servant of a higher lord. Paul here alludes to earlier texts in order to say that Timothy should be regarded in this quasiapostolic manner.

The catalogue of good properties (2 Tim. 2:24–25) resembles closely 1 Tim. 3:2 and Titus 3:2. The requirement not to be "quarrelsome" but rather to be kind continues the theme of responding to the provocation of false teachers with necessary detachment, patience, and silence. This detachment does not, however, rule out the requirement to be a good teacher. It is important that opponents be corrected with "gentleness" (*prautēs*). This term is synonymous with *praupatheia* in 1 Tim. 6:11. Gentleness is the outcome of moderating one's *pathos* in order that unnecessary controversies can be tamed through the display of mature character. It further relates to the proclamation of Jesus, according to which "the meek" (*praus*) will inherit the earth (Matt. 5:5). Thus gentleness is both a very radical virtue and a virtue that expresses a proper mean between anger and indifference (see exposition of 1 Tim. 3:3).

In 2 Tim. 2:25b–26 Paul points out that the false teachers are in reality not using their capacity to know things freely, but they have been held captive by the devil. The picture of the "snare of the devil" appears in 1 Tim. 3:7. Here the picture again underlines the obsessive and foolish character of the false teachers: they behave as if their free reason were held captive. They are not to be encountered with arguments, but with kind and gentle behavior. Maybe God will grant that they turn their mind or "repent" (*metanoia* in 2 Tim. 2:25b). The truth may some day make them free.

In sum, I interpret 2:22–26 in much the same manner as 1 Tim. 6:3–16. I presuppose that the false teachers are persons held captive by their own harmful passions. Therefore their arguments display foolishness and should not be met with intense doctrinal debate. Instead, Paul recommends a treatment in which the responsible church leader detaches himself from debate and acts with gentleness. The church leader is supposed to moderate his passions and set an example of good conduct and apt teaching rather than aim at convincing his opponents in open debates. This recommendation employs ideas taken from the Hellenistic treatment of the passions (see appendix A).

---

2. See appendix B and Epictetus, *Discourses* 4.5.1–4 (LCL 218.331–33): "The wise and good man neither himself fights with any person, nor does he allow another. . . . [Socrates] remembered well that no man has in his power another man's ruling principle."

Folly of False Teachers (2 Tim. 3:1–9)

The character of a good leader (2:20–25) is dramatically contrasted with an extensive list of the vices of the false teachers. Their appearance is an eschatological phenomenon, as 3:1 points out, again using the imperative form "you must understand." This eschatological vision is employed to communicate the essential features of good character here and now. The list of vices (3:2–4) is no eschatological prophecy, but it describes the sins to be avoided by sincere Christians.

In addition, the vices express a bondage to harmful desires (*epithymiai* in 3:6), a corrupted mind (*katephtharmenos ton noun*; 3:8), and a kind of foolishness or mental incapacity (*anoia* in 3:9). These phenomena are not merely vices or sins, but disorders that stem from harmful passions. The extensive list of eighteen vices is collected from both Jewish and Greco-Roman sources. It employs materials from the Decalogue, but refers predominantly to Hellenistic vices. Thus it differs from 1 Tim. 1:9–10, which is predominantly Jewish material. Moreover, many of the vices in the Greco-Roman world are conceived in terms of mental disorder. The list of 2 Tim. 3:2–4 may be dependent on Philo (*Flight and Finding* 81 [LCL 275.53]; *Sacrifices of Abel and Cain* 3 [LCL 227.97]; *Worse Attacks the Better* 32 [LCL 227.223]; see Oberlinner 1995: 123).[3]

"Lover of oneself" (*philautos*) appears in many Greco-Roman catalogues of vices. It can be contrasted with the Christian ideals of unselfishness and neighborly love as well as with the Stoic theory of *oikeiōsis*. "Lover of money" is likewise prominent in philosophical catalogues. In Stoa and the Cynical school, the love of money is often considered to be the root of all evil. Paul shares this opinion in 1 Tim. 6:10. The first two vices are the generic roots of other and more particular disorders.[4]

"Boaster" and "arrogant" also appear in Greco-Roman and Jewish lists of vices. Arrogance is condemned in Rom. 1:30. "Blaspheming" (*blasphēmos*) can mean both despising God and spreading bad rumors about other people. It relates to the Decalogue, as does the next topic on the list, "disobedient to parents." Respecting one's parents also belongs to the practice of *eusebeia* ("godliness"; 1 Tim. 3:4).

"Ungrateful" (*acharistos*) can relate to God and to other people. Thanksgiving and gratitude are essential in both biblical ethics and Greco-Roman texts (see appendix C and excursus 3). "Irreligious" (*anosios*; cf. 1 Tim. 1:9) is likewise connected with the respect for God and one's own parents. Proper obedience to higher authorities is thus highlighted in several different ways.

"Unaffectionate" (*astorgos*; Vulgate: *sine affectione*) shows that not only positive desires, but also the lack of emotional affection can be harmful. It is paired with "irreconcilable" (*aspondos*; Vulgate: *sine pace*). The underlying idea has to do with

---

3. In the following I do not always use the NRSV.

4. Weiser 2003: 261–63 gives an overview of the catalogues, of which Philo may be the most important. For *oikeiōsis*, see appendix A; for the love of money, see Diogenes Laertius 6.50 (LCL 185.53); Polycarp, *Philippians* 4.1 (Ehrman 2003: 1.337); and exposition of 1 Tim. 6:10.

the strength of proper affections. On the one hand, life without affection is cold and inhuman. On the other hand, without the capacity to moderate affections a person is led to irreconcilable conflicts. In this way the pair of two opposite vices again expresses the idea of moderating affections rather than eradicating them. Both vices appear in some Greco-Roman texts; in Rom. 1:31 they are mentioned together in many manuscripts. "Diabolic" (*diabolos*; Vulgate: *criminator*) can mean a liar. As many other vices on the list, it appears in Philo.[5]

"Incontinent" (*akratēs*; Vulgate: *incontinens*) is a person who acts against his or her better knowledge. This vice was discussed in philosophical ethics since Aristotle. Also the next two terms may be related to Aristotle's threefold categorization of moral vices. Being "wild" (*anēmeros*) may refer to Aristotle's brutishness, which is the most inhuman moral state, whereas being a "hater of good" (*aphilagathos*) may refer to Aristotle's moral baseness, which is a worse state than incontinence, but nevertheless more human than brutishness. Although *aphilagathos* and *anēmeros* are not Aristotle's terms, the three terms match Aristotle's tripartite division of bad moral characters. In Aristotle, all three vices are connected with the failure to use practical reason properly (*Nicomachean Ethics* 1145a15–17 [LCL 73.375]; Saarinen 1994: 8; Weiser 2003: 271 gives other possible sources).

"Treacherous" and "rash" persons are both characterized by the inability to persevere in proper decision and corresponding conduct. They may also be related to the Aristotelian discussion on incontinence, especially because rashness can be a subspecies of incontinence. But treacherous behavior is a common vice that can be connected with false teachers in general. Rashness appears in some philosophical catalogues of vices.[6]

"Blinded" or "conceited" (*tetyphōmenos*) is related to the verb *typhoomai*, which in 1 Tim. 3:6 is used of a recent convert who may not see the trap of the devil. In 6:4 the verb is employed of false teachers who remain blind to sound doctrine and thus understand nothing. In this way the vice of blindness is connected with treachery and falling away from sound doctrine, a theme that is again highlighted in 2 Tim. 3:5–9.

Together with being "conceited," the last vice—being a "lover of pleasure" (*philēdonos*)—prepares the examples given of false teachers in 3:5–9. As the first vices of the catalogue, this last vice of "hedonism" is not just a particular disorder, but a summary notion that comprises different sins. Both Philo (*Sacrifices of Abel and Cain* 32 [LCL 227.117]) and Greco-Roman popular philosophy regard the love of pleasure as a comprehensive vice (Weiser 2003: 272). All vices—from the love of oneself in 3:2 to the love of pleasure in 3:4—are finally contrasted to the "love of God" (*philotheos*), which is the root of all virtues.

5. See Philo, *Sacrifices of Abel and Cain* 32 (LCL 227.117) for *aspondos* and *diabolos*. See also Weiser 2003: 270 and appendix A.
6. Saarinen 1994: 8–17 gives an overview of Aristotle's *akrasia* and related notions. Weiser 2003: 171 gives Epictetus, *Discourses* 4.4.16 (LCL 218.319) for rashness.

In 3:5 a temporal change from the future to the present tense signals that the vices mentioned do not belong only to the eschatological future, but they trouble the Christians in the here and now. The people captured by these vices may hold to the "outward form of godliness" (*morphōsis eusebeias*) but in reality they deny its "power" (*dynamis*). By this distinction between matter/power and form, Paul points out that the true content of *eusebeia* is found in virtuous conduct. The "form" probably refers to the verbal profession (cf. Titus 1:16) that is contradicted by the actions. Timothy and other sincere Christians should avoid such people.

False teachers do not respect the proper structure of the *oikos* ("household"; 2 Tim. 3:6). They enter households and "captivate silly women." Given the witness of 1 Tim. 5:13 and the greater difficulty for men to enter other households in this manner, it can probably be assumed that both men and women were among the false teachers.

In a somewhat unexpected fashion, 2 Tim. 3:6b–7 deviates from the actual topic in order to make the point that the silly women (using the pejorative *gynaikaria*) have many vices. They are sinners who cannot control their desires. Even though they are instructed, they do not really learn the truth. This negative description resembles the treatment of younger widows in 1 Tim. 5:11–15. At the same time it does not refer to any particular group of women, but remains a paradigmatic characterization. In 2:11–12 it is said that, within the proper structure of the household, women can learn in silence. In the paradigmatic example of 2 Tim. 3:7 women do not learn properly because the false teachers do not respect the proper order but "make their way" into households and apparently teach "wrangling over words" (2:14).

In 3:8 Paul returns to false teachers and compares them to "Jannes and Jambres." These two Egyptian sorcerers, whose names are received from rabbinic traditions (Strack and Billerbeck 1922–61: 3.660–64; Charlesworth 1985: 2.427–42; and Weiser 2003: 267–68), compete with Moses in Exod. 7:8–13. The purpose of making the comparison remains unclear; maybe Paul only wants to associate false teachers with false religion. Important in 2 Tim. 3:8 is that the false teachers are said to be "of corrupt mind [*katephtharmenoi ton noun*] and counterfeit faith [*adokimoi peri tēn pistin*]." *Adokimoi* means literally "untested, unfit" (Titus 1:16) and in this sense unreliable.

The phrase "of corrupt mind" is similar to 1 Tim. 6:5 and Titus 1:15. In the exposition of 1 Tim. 6:5 I argue in more detail that Paul is not only making an invective but also attempting to say that the loss of healthy doctrine goes together with the loss of a clear mind and good reason. Thus the false teachers are not only wrong but also in a sort of pathological state. The same line of thought can be applied to 2 Tim. 3:8b–9 and its context, particularly the list of vices (3:2–4). The verb *kataphtheirō* does not appear elsewhere in the New Testament, but it is basically synonymous with *diaphtheirō* in 1 Tim. 6:5 (see appendix B and the expositions of 1 Tim. 6:3–10 and Titus 1:10–16).

If the *nous* ("mind") of a person gets corrupted, he or she remains opposed to the truth. Although the rhetorical skill and the obsessive affection of such persons toward details and disputes (2 Tim. 2:14; 1 Tim. 6:4) may captivate some people, in the long run their *anoia* ("lack of mind" or "folly"; 2 Tim. 3:9) will become plain for all listeners. Given this interpretation of false teachers, the list of vices in 3:2–4 is not only slander or a catalogue of vices, but also a diagnostic list. Persons who suffer from *anoia* or corrupted mind are likely to display those vices. In addition, wrangling over words (2:14) and the craving for controversies (2:23) are diagnostic characterizations.

Besides making a polemical point that casts a doubt over the opponents, Paul is thus attempting a diagnosis. The opponents have not moderated their desires, but they act with rashness and self-love. Their desires drive them to controversies and heated involvement. In this activity their minds have become corrupted and they even suffer from *anoia*. This state of mind is captivity under evil powers (2:26). An adherent to healthy or sound doctrine should encounter these people with necessary detachment. They are to be corrected with gentleness, without entering into debate.

In 3:9 the verb *prokoptō* ("to make progress") appears again. As we saw in 2:16, this Stoic concept can mean successful moderation of emotions (see appendix A), but Paul can use it either positively (1 Tim. 4:15 and maybe here) or ironically (2 Tim. 2:16; 3:13). One way to explain this usage is to say that the real progress in the moderation of emotions was a matter of controversy between Paul and his opponents. Both sides were claiming progress, but Paul aims at showing that real progress is achieved with the help of sound doctrine, godliness and detached behavior. The false teachers claim to have progressed, but they succeed only in provoking controversies. Therefore their "progress" leads from bad to worse, toward impiety (2 Tim. 2:16; 3:13).

CONCLUDING ADVICE TO TIMOTHY

2 Tim. 3:10–4:22

The third major part of the epistle opens with a concluding statement, saying that Timothy has now observed the teaching of Paul. The final part of 2 Timothy consists of several relatively independent passages. First, the author briefly recollects the exemplary life of Paul (3:10–14). Then, in a theologically important passage he digresses over the importance of sacred writings for sound teaching and good conduct (3:15–17). In 4:1–8 Paul speaks in a solemn and eschatological tone. He refers to his own death and reflects his past activities with satisfaction. Timothy is admonished to defend Paul's legacy. The last passage (4:9–22) contains an extensive list of greetings and remarks on other people.

Paul's Example and Scriptures (2 Tim. 3:10–17)

In 3:10 Paul appreciates Timothy as his true follower. Whereas the first part of 2 Timothy encourages Timothy to follow in Paul's footsteps (e.g., 1:8), Timothy is now contrasted to the false teachers (3:8–9) as a true teacher of sound doctrine. The point of comparison is Paul himself: it is his conduct and his faith that provide the norm. Although the authority of the apostle is highlighted, Paul remains a servant of the Lord (3:10; 2:24).

The verb *parakoloutheō* ("to follow, observe") echoes *akoloutheō*, the verb employed by the Gospels (Mark 1:18) of following Jesus. A longer chain of tradition is probably intended. The apostles followed Jesus, Timothy is following Paul, and Timothy himself should set an example to future Christians. A short catalogue of exemplary virtues is given. Paul is an example in orthodoxy, namely, teaching and faith. But he is also the example of right conduct and virtuous attitude. These attitudes—"patience," "love," "steadfastness"—appear in many Pauline writings (e.g., 1 Tim. 6:11) and are here presented in a summarizing fashion.

As in 2 Tim. 2:9–10, Paul is depicted in 3:11 as an example of suffering for the gospel. The place names "Antioch, Iconium, and Lystra" match well the description of Acts 13:14–14:19. But 2 Tim. 3:11 does not refer to any particular persecutions. Instead, Paul now sees in retrospect the totality of his sufferings. The phrase "the Lord rescued me from all of them" sounds like a liturgical formula. It alludes to Ps. 34:18–20 and may also have christological connotations.[1] Like Christ, Paul suffers although he is righteous.

The christological dimension becomes explicit and is presented as universal truth in 2 Tim. 3:12. All who "want to live a godly life" (*thelontes eusebōs zēn*) in Christ will suffer. The concept of *eusebeia* particularly prominent in 1 Timothy appears here as a summarizing virtue of right conduct. Here *eusebeia* is not merely a civil virtue, but it describes the life in Christ, and yet in some way it connects with the philosophical virtues.

This connection becomes more evident in 2 Tim. 3:13, which again refers to the false teachers and wicked people. These people will "progress from bad to worse." In 2:16 these people were said to progress toward impiety (*asebeia*). In both verses, the verb *prokoptō* is employed, a verb that derives from Stoicism. In Philo, it means the state of those who practice *metriopatheia*. The word *goēs* ("impostor") is also prominent in Philo as a description of false teachers (*Special Laws* 1.315 [LCL 320.283]; Oberlinner 1995: 142). One can thus read 2 Tim. 3:13 to mean that although the false teachers claim to make progress in moral conduct, they only deceive themselves and others.

In this way 3:12–13 aims at contrasting true Christian *eusebeia* with the illusory progress of the false teachers. Paul teaches throughout 2 Timothy that successful moderation and self-control of desires can be reached and that Timothy should exemplify this kind of right conduct. But patient, gentle, and yet courageous behavior is possible only in the footsteps of Jesus Christ and Paul the apostle. Other ideologies may claim to make progress, but in reality they go only from bad to worse. True *eusebeia* is found only in Christ. In sum, Paul both criticizes the view of "progress" toward "godliness" and employs it himself in a theologically qualified fashion.

The contrast turns back to Timothy in 3:14. He is to follow the path of sound teaching. In a way, the chain of tradition is now continued from the idealized Timothy described in 3:10 to the present and future Christian church. The church leader ought to know from whom the tradition comes, namely, from Paul, who has taught the gospel to Timothy and advised him in many ways.

---

1. Marshall 1999: 785 notes that "Lord" here probably refers to Christ, whereas in the psalm it refers, of course, to God.

Instead of trusting the false individual progress, one should maintain the traditional teaching.

Another important aspect of this tradition is introduced in 3:15, namely, "the sacred writings" (*ta hiera grammata*). Most biblical interpreters today are convinced that this phrase, as well as the "scripture" (*graphē*) of 3:16, pertains to the Jewish Bible (Marshall 1999: 789; Oberlinner 1995: 145; Weiser 2003: 177). Related to 1 Tim. 5:18, there may be some discussion whether the sayings of Jesus or the Epistles of Paul already could be called "scripture," but it is certain that the Jewish Bible is meant in 2 Tim. 3:15–16.

This is of major theological importance, since 3:15b claims that the sacred writings "are able to instruct you for salvation through faith in Christ Jesus." The word "salvation" probably belongs together with the phrase "through faith in Christ Jesus." In other words, it is not the instruction that effects salvation but the faith in Jesus Christ (so Weiser 2003: 278, against Oberlinner 1995: 146). Nevertheless the scriptural instruction in some way contributes "for salvation" (*eis sōtērian*). The preposition *eis* probably contains the idea that the instruction aims at bringing forth an understanding of salvation that may, in practical terms, be more or less identical with the salvation itself. In this sense the aim of scriptural instruction is to bring people into the reality of salvation.

Understood in this way, it is not absolutely necessary to assume that Paul here finds Christ in the Jewish Bible. He may simply think that the knowledge of the sacred writings disposes the Christian mind so that it can receive the gospel. The Jewish narrative would in this sense prepare the mind with the necessary vocabulary needed to understand the gospel. On the other hand, it is reasonable to assume that the Christian congregation interpreted the prophetic sayings of the Jewish Bible as referring to Jesus Christ and employed them in this way in its catechesis and liturgy.

Although the nuances of 3:15 can be understood in slightly different ways, the basic intention is clear. Through reading the Jewish Bible, Christians receive an understanding that is highly relevant and practically useful for receiving Jesus Christ as well as for the entire Christian formation. At the same time 3:15 says that a Christian should read the Jewish Bible in this fashion: we should read it not for the sake of myths, genealogies, or ascetic rules (1 Tim. 1:4; 4:3), but for the sake of salvation through faith in Christ. The apostle is giving a hermeneutical rule. We must read the Jewish Bible for the sake of present salvation in Christ.

It may be a rhetorical exaggeration to say that Timothy knew the Jewish Bible "from childhood," especially since *brephos* means an infant (Vulgate: *ab infantia*; cf. 2 Tim. 1:5). The point is that Timothy's character and knowledge have been adequately prepared by the biblical narrative. The importance of many-sided character formation is highlighted in 3:16–17. The knowledge of the Bible is "useful" for many different but related purposes. In addition to "teaching," this knowledge can be effectively employed "for reproof" (*pros elegmon*) and "for correction" (*pros epanorthōsin*). All three notions refer to the battle with heresies and false teachers. In this sense they pertain to the intellectual mastery of sound doctrine. The fourth phrase, "training in righteousness," refers to the moral conduct of good character.

The first phrase of 3:16, "all scripture is inspired by God" (*pasa graphē theopneustos*), has had an enormous theological influence and continues to be debated. Recent studies show, however, that 3:16 was not central for the patristic authors who wrote on biblical inspiration. But at least since Thomas Aquinas, the Vulgate phrase *scriptura divinitus inspirata* was employed as a proof-text of inspiration. At least since the Vulgate, *scriptura* was understood to refer to the Christian Bible. In this sense 3:16 could be employed to say that the Bible proves its own inspiration (Weiser 2003: 286–97 provides an excellent interpretation history of this important matter from patristics to contemporary ecumenism).

Exegetically, the meaning of *pasa graphē* is not obvious. Today's interpreters tend to prefer the meaning "every scriptural text" rather than "the whole scripture." This means that *pasa graphē* is synonymous with *ta hiera grammata* (3:15). Neither phrase presupposes a fixed canon of texts. On the other hand, *pasa graphē* should probably not be read to mean "everything in the sacred writings" so that the inspiration of every word or sentence should be assumed. Understood in this way, the inspiration would neither pertain to the most comprehensive unit (the canon) nor to the smallest unit (word or sentence), but to the middle-sized unit (*graphē* as text or individual book; so Weiser 2003: 279–81, with a summary of the research history).

The word *theopneustos* should be taken in the passive sense "is inspired" rather than active. Almost all church fathers understand the word in its passive sense. The exception is Ambrose, who can say that "every scripture breathes the divine grace of God" (*De spiritu sancto* 2.16.122 [Corpus scriptorum ecclesiasticorum latinorum 79.198]). Paul takes it for granted that the Jewish Bible is inspired and useful for many purposes. The Jews also thought that God's spirit works in the sacred writings of Israel (2 Pet. 1:21; Weiser 2003: 280–81; Marshall 1999: 794). Being *ōphelimos* ("useful"; cf. 1 Tim. 4:8 and Titus 3:8) is an important criterion of doctrine or teaching (Marshall 1999: 333, with many Greco-Roman parallels; see also Cicero, *De finibus* 3.33 [LCL 40.253]).

Second Timothy 3:17 continues the "training in righteousness," which expresses the formation of good character. The subject is *ho tou theou anthropos* ("the man of God"), a Jewish expression that refers to the church leader (Marshall 1999: 796). The leader should be "proficient" or "adapted" or maybe even "perfect" (*artios*; Vulgate: *perfectus*). The word *artios* here refers to the end result of training: a trained character is suitable or "equipped" (*exērtismenos*) for bringing forth good works. The church leader should present "a model of good works" to everybody (Titus 2:7).

Excursus 8: Scripture and Tradition

At this point the mutual relationship between "sacred writings" (2 Tim. 3:14–16), "apostolic deposit" (1:12–14) and the "gospel" (e.g., 2:8) can be briefly discussed from the perspective of later Christian theology. The three notions occupy slightly different meanings in the Pastoral Epistles. The sacred writings refer predominantly, though not exclusively, to the Septuagint as the Jewish Bible. The apostolic deposit refers to the doctrinal tradition that Paul hands over to Timothy. The gospel is certainly an essential part or the core of this deposit, but the term "gospel" refers more directly to the salvific action of God in Jesus Christ as the fulfilment of the divine plan (1 Tim. 1:4, 11, 15).

When the canon of the Christian Bible is authorized, the theological meaning of the three terms is enriched so that they become more synonymous. The sacred writings now clearly include the Four Gospels and the Pauline Epistles. The apostolic deposit entrusted to Paul and his followers can be interpreted to mean those Pauline epistles that are now included in the biblical canon. The meaning of the gospel can now be grasped by hearing and reading the canonical texts. In this theological sense the three terms cover the same extension, namely, the Scripture.

Given this, the remaining theological problem can be formulated as the problem of Scripture and tradition: does the apostolic deposit consist of canonical texts only or does it include the broader tradition of the church? My commentary cannot answer this perennial problem. But it is important to give some attention to the difficult hermeneutical issues that emerge when a text is canonized. The Pastoral Epistles refer to the sacred writings, to the apostolic deposit, and to the gospel as the authoritative sources of sound doctrine. What happens when the Pastoral Epistles themselves become authoritative?

There are different speculative ways to answer this question. One can claim that the apostolic deposit is a higher authority than the canonical text. Or one can claim that the sacred writings and their inspiration from now on refer to the Pauline texts as well. One can also hold that it is simply impossible to treat such speculative matters in any responsible manner. Although it may be impossible or futile to answer such questions, the fact remains that the Christian church has made authoritative decisions with regard to them. It is, for instance, not very rare to claim that the Bible proves its own inspiration through referring to 2 Tim. 3:16.

Because later Christian theology in any case argues with the canonical texts, using them canonically, it may be better to take some stance with regard to the "authority claims made inside an authority." My very modest proposal is to hold that the three above-mentioned terms become more synonymous as a result of canonization. The matters that Paul said were entrusted to him are certainly included in the canonical texts. It is also beyond doubt that the eminent main subject of the Christian Bible is the gospel message of God's plan of salvation in Jesus Christ. In this very simple and straightforward sense the Protestant view of *sola scriptura* can be seen as consonant with the authority structure that emerges from the Pastoral Epistles as canonical texts.

This result does not deny that Catholic and Orthodox authority structures can probably be argued with a similar degree of plausibility.

Final Words of the Apostle (2 Tim. 4:1–8)

Paul now moves to the final part of his message to Timothy.[2] "I solemnly urge" (*diamartyromai*) underlines the great responsibility connected with the legacy of the apostle. The verb *diamartyromai* appears also in 2:14 (cf. 1 Tim. 5:21), in which Paul warns of the pathological phenomenon of *logomachia* ("wrangling over words"). The responsible Christian leader should not waste words or speculate, but is to be content with the solemnly expressed witness.

The solemn character of 2 Tim. 4:1 is further emphasized by the mention of the presence of God and Jesus Christ. As in many other New Testament texts (Rom. 2:16; 14:9; 2 Cor. 5:10), Jesus Christ here appears as a judge. The phrase "to judge the living and the dead" expresses an already recognized conviction of orthodox Christians and thus underlines Paul's sound doctrine. It should further be noted that 2 Tim. 4:1 contains an eschatology in which several different but related aspects of the presence of God are emphasized. Paul already here and now speaks before God (Vulgate: *coram Deo*). Christ will perform a second epiphany (*epiphaneia*) with which the kingdom of Christ will appear.

As we have seen, *epiphaneia* in 1:10 refers to the past, whereas here and in 1 Tim. 6:14 it refers to the future. The concept of epiphany need not, however, be understood in a merely punctual fashion, but as an expression of the increasing presence of God in eschatological times (Weiser 2003: 299; Marshall 1999: 293–95). In 2 Tim. 4:1 it is assumed that Christ is present but Christians still wait his appearance. The final epiphany becomes related to the final judgment. But the present time is also characterized by another kind of presence of Christ. As in 1 Tim. 6:13, this presence of Christ is related to Paul's handing over of the apostolic legacy to Timothy. Although we cannot draw too far-reaching ecclesiological conclusions from Paul's phraseology, it is evident that he relates the eschatological presence of Christ to the apostolicity of his message.

In 2 Tim. 4:2 a list of the tasks of Timothy in the leadership of the church is given. As Paul has proclaimed the message (1:11; 1 Tim. 2:7), so should Timothy. The five tasks of 2 Tim. 4:2 are characterized by the situation that so many false teachers now spread their opinions; among them, but in clear contrast to them, Timothy is to teach healthy doctrine. For the successful accomplishment of this task it is necessary that Timothy can "convince" the hearers, "rebuke" the false teachings, and "encourage" the Christians. For the task of convincing it is necessary that he exercise the utmost patience (*makrothymia*; cf. 1 Tim. 1:16) and not get into heated arguments (cf. 2 Tim. 2:14–16).

2. For reasons explained in excursus 6, I consistently avoid the concept "testament," which in some ways fits 4:1–8 well, although not 2 Timothy as a whole.

The second admonition to be persistent "whether the time is favorable or unfavorable [*eukairōs akairōs*]" is not self-evident. The Greek concepts come from rhetoric (Marshall 1999: 800) and point out that the speaker should find the proper moment (*kairos*) for reaching the recipients of his message. But Paul here advises Timothy to ignore this rule and to speak the truth irrespectively of the right moment. Commentators tend to explain this strange advice either by referring to the unchanging character of Christian truth or by holding that Paul requires a special steadfastness in order to rebuke the false teachers and their rhetorical skill (see Weiser 2003: 301 and Oberlinner 1995: 155–56; Malherbe 1989: 137–45 points out that the Cynics were famous for their "unfavorable" comments).

Although both of these explanations may contain a grain of truth, there is probably more that can be said with regard to this advice. The advice resembles Jesus's parable of the sower (Matt. 13:3–30). It further resembles such practices of gift-giving and generosity in which the gift is tailored not according to the needs and wishes of the recipients or with a view to the expectations of the giver; rather, a free and disinterested giving is intended (see appendix C and Saarinen 2005). If the second advice of 2 Tim. 4:2 is read in the light of such practices, it does not express the stubbornness of the speaker, but rather the moderation of his expectations and rhetorical skills. In this sense, Timothy is expected to serve the word of truth, distributing it in a democratic fashion to everybody but not bending it to suit the expectations of either himself or his hearers. It is the false teachers who bend the word in this fashion, waiting for a proper *kairos* to influence their listeners. But Timothy is to proclaim the message without too much regard for rhetorical purposes. He should put his trust in the word rather than in his rhetorical skills and timing.

This reading is supported by 4:3. In the *kairos* of the last days, sound or healthy doctrine (cf. 1 Tim. 1:10) does not fulfill the rhetorical needs and other desires of people. Paul here again polemicizes against the false teachers, but he also attempts to make a more general point concerning desire-based motivation and rhetorical skills. Because the rhetorical expectations (or "itching ears") of so many people are based on the search for entertainment and the satisfaction of desires, it would be highly problematic to exercise a rhetoric that would subsume its *kairos* under this horizon of expectations. This is precisely what the false teachers do: they suit their message to match the desires of the people. The real problem is, however, that these desires need to be educated. Paul is confident that the patient proclamation of the truth will be able to do this. It is not the proclamation that should suit itself to the desires of the listeners, but the desires that should be moderated and educated.

Paul thus in 2 Tim. 4:2–3 criticizes such rhetorical practices for which the right moment and the selfish desires of the people are decisive criteria. At the same time we can note that he is not simply pleading for the opposite model, that is, to mold people to suit the criteria of an otherwise incomprehensible doctrine. He is rather aiming at moderation: on the one hand, Timothy is to exercise patience and to encourage people; on the other hand, he is not to compromise doctrine for the sake of appeal. As a leader, he should educate the desires of other people, neither extinguishing the desires nor accommodating his message to them.

When people merely listen to their own desires, they turn away from the truth and "wander away to myths [*mythoi*]" (4:4). In the Pastoral Epistles, "myths" designate the false alternative to Christian truth (1 Tim. 1:4; 4:7; Titus 1:14). Although the concept of myth is of Greek origin, the myths of the false teachers have clearly Jewish features, for instance, the interest in genealogies (1 Tim. 1:4; Titus 1:14). Here, myths are connected with the fiction and the wishful thinking emerging from people's "own desires."

In contrast to the harmful myths, another set of positive imperatives is given in 2 Tim. 4:5. Timothy is expected to "be sober" (*nēphō*). This verb is metaphorical and means awareness and the capacity for clear judgment (cf. 1 Thess. 5:6, 8; 1 Pet. 1:13). In 1 Tim. 3:2 the corresponding adjective *nēphalios* is translated "temperate" in the NRSV. This term, as well as the capacity to endure suffering, points out that the desires of an exemplary leader are to be moderated so that the leader's mind is not shaken by varying external circumstances and internal affections, but remains firm.

The "work of an evangelist" probably does not refer to a specific ministry in the church, but simply highlights the task of preaching the gospel. An allusion to Phil. 2:22 can be assumed. The last imperative of 2 Tim. 4:5 is also expressed in general terms. The "ministry" (*diakonia*) comprehends the whole activity of Timothy and thus summarizes the two sets of imperatives in 4:2 and 4:5.

In 4:6–8 the focus shifts to Paul. The dramatic description of Paul's approaching death is meant to strengthen the force of the above-mentioned imperatives. The verses allow for an understanding that Paul has already given his legacy over to Timothy and his followers. Paul's self-description as "libation" that is being poured out (*spendomai*) gives the impression that Paul's death is imminent. In Phil. 2:17 Paul already employs this picture as referring to his own death. In the cultic act of libation, a part of a drink is poured out as a sacrifice or, maybe, "over the sacrifice," as 2:17 holds.[3] The other metaphor of death, "departure" (*analyō* and *analysis*), also appears in Phil. 1:23.

With these two metaphors, 2 Tim. 4:6 wants to make a connection with Phil. 1–2. A portrayal of Paul's death as a sacrifice is not intended (see excursus 9), nor is the departure described as a transition to another form of existence. What is intended, however, is the portrayal of Paul as a martyr. The passive form *spendomai* underlines Paul's role as an object of other powers. Paul concedes to his imminent death as a martyr who suffers death at the hands of his captors.

---

3. On libation, see Weiser 2003: 305–6 and Marshall 1999: 805. Philo, *Allegorical Interpretation of the Laws* 2.56 (LCL 226.259) speaks of pouring out one's blood as sacrifice.

In 2 Tim. 4:7 Paul reminds the reader of his earlier words to Timothy, now applying them to his own person. Timothy should "fight the good fight" (cf. 1 Tim. 6:12), but Paul has already fought the good fight. Timothy should keep the commandments until the end (cf. 6:14), but Paul has already finished the race. Timothy should keep his sincere faith (2 Tim. 1:5–6), as Paul has kept the faith (1 Tim. 6:20). The phrases are carefully composed: "I have finished" (*teteleka*) and "I have kept" (*tetēreka*) rhyme with one another, and so do the words in the phrase "I have fought the good fight" (*agōna ēgōnismai*).

The next verse, 2 Tim. 4:8, shifts the focus to the future. A "crown of righteousness" (*ho tēs dikaiosynēs stephanos*) is reserved for Paul. The picture of crown or prize also appears in 2:5 as well as in 1 Cor. 9:24–25 and Phil. 3:14, but one also recalls Jesus's words concerning the reward in heaven in Matt. 5–7. The Lord Jesus, the righteous judge (cf. 2 Tim. 4:1), will give this crown not only to Paul, but "to all who have longed for" the final appearing (*epiphaneia*; cf. 4:1) of Christ. In this way 4:8 rounds out the eschatological vision of 4:1. The "longing" (*agapaō*; Vulgate: *qui diligunt*) expresses Paul's love toward the second epiphany.

Certain theological problems are connected with the understanding of the "crown of righteousness." Semantically, the phrase probably means both "the crown that will bring final justification" and "a crown that is appropriate for a righteous person," with a stronger emphasis on the first meaning. For those churches that stress unilateral justification by faith, the second meaning may be problematic since it includes a thought of reward. Yet it must be said that the whole metaphorics of "finishing the race" and receiving a prize assumes some sort of accomplishment from the person obtaining the prize. In addition, the use of the verb *apodidōmi* in the phrase "the Lord . . . will give me" also expresses the idea of recompense (Marshall 1999: 808–9).

For a proper understanding of 4:8, some sort of reciprocity must be assumed. If this reciprocity is understood in similar terms as the "reward in heaven" in the Sermon on the Mount, churches that teach monergistic justification can relate to this verse. On a deeper level, one needs to analyze in which theological sense even a "gift" includes some kind of reciprocity (see appendix C and Saarinen 2005). A deeper theological understanding of righteousness must seek ways to explain in which sense Paul may claim to be righteous.

Personal Communications (2 Tim. 4:9–18)

The concluding part of 2 Timothy opens with a long list of personal communications. That 1 Timothy includes neither such communications nor greetings has given rise to speculation whether 1–2 Timothy (and maybe Titus) at some point belonged together. A better explanation for the long list of personal matters is, however, that it underlines the specific character of 2 Timothy as Paul's farewell speech. Although it may seem somewhat odd that the solemn 4:1–8 is followed by a rather diffuse list of details, 4:9–18 is nevertheless typical of Greco-Roman letters. It also alludes in a more or less consistent manner to the different phases of Paul's activity (Weiser 2003: 314). In this sense it can be read as a part of Paul's literary farewell.

In 4:9 Paul repeats (cf. 1:4) the wish to see Timothy. Now he stresses that Timothy should come soon. Although this is a proper literary convention, it does not fit well together with Paul's overall advice that Timothy should be a faithful servant of his local church. The wish should not, however, be seen in this light of logical consistency, since its dramatic purpose is to evoke the reader's sympathy toward the dying apostle.

The next verse, 4:10, strengthens this impression by telling that three persons have deserted Paul. They have left Paul alone not only in a literal, geographical sense, but they, or at least Demas, have also forsaken him. Together with Mark and Luke (4:11), Demas appears in Phlm. 24; all three and Tychicus are mentioned in Col. 4:7–14. It is reasonable to assume that the names are here taken from these and maybe other similar sources (Weiser 2003: 328–39). The characterization of Demas is particularly problematic, since in other epistles he is mentioned positively. We have no criteria to decide whether Demas is here blamed for dramatic literary purposes or whether some historical incident has caused this state of affairs.

More important than this matter is the meaning of the phrase "in love with this present world" (2 Tim. 4:10). The phrase is employed by Polycarp of apostles who were not in love with the present world but with Christ (*Philippians* 9 [Ehrman 2003: 1.345]). In the last days, Christians should love the epiphany of Christ (2 Tim. 4:8), not this world. Although the phrase is clearly negative, we cannot say how negative it finally is. The phrase need not refer to apostasy or heresy, but to Demas's having found it inconvenient to stay with the prisoner Paul and preferring other duties. Timothy, however, should prefer to visit Paul as soon as possible.

In 4:11 it is remarked that Luke is with Paul. This may reflect Col. 4:14. In contrast to Col. 4:10, Mark is no more in Rome, but Timothy is advised to bring Mark with him. Paul wants to communicate that even in his last days in prison the Christian ministry and mission proceed. The word *diakonia* refers to "ministry" in the sense of service for Christ, as in 2 Tim. 4:5 and 1 Tim. 1:12. It is not meant that Mark should serve Paul. The disagreement between Paul and Mark in Acts 15:36–39 is not mentioned. Thus 2 Tim. 4 evaluates both Demas and Mark in a manner that differs from some other New Testament texts.

No reason is given for the sending of Tychicus (4:12) to Ephesus, where Timothy is also supposed to be. Mentioning this underlines Paul's missionary activity. In addition, many important places of Paul's activity are successively recollected in 4:10–20 for the purpose of giving a summary of the apostle's range of influence.

The admonition to bring Paul his cloak, books, and parchments (4:13) may just evoke the impression of accidental needs for the coming winter (4:21). Commentators have seen a number of hidden and symbolic meanings connected with these items. Wandering philosophers had cloaks, and some New Testament texts mention simple clothing as proper for the evangelist (1 Tim. 6:8; Acts 20:33). It is also suggested that the cloak and the books could be handed over to Timothy as a sign of succession (Oberlinner 1995: 172–73).

The "books" (*ta biblia*) and the "parchments" (*hai membranai*) have also given rise to speculation. It can be assumed with some plausibility that the "books" refer to the books of the Jewish Bible that Paul needs in prison to carry on his work (cf. 2 Tim. 3:15–17). The distinction between books and parchments could theoretically mean that the term "parchment" refers to some other genre of writings. But this is highly uncertain, since the construction "above all" (*malista*) need not contain any clear distinction between the two but may simply refer to the set of books, among which the parchments are most valuable. Even though some commentators see a new genre of important writings already emerging here, other explanations seem to be more likely (Marshall 1999: 819–20). In any case, the importance of books as necessary equipment of the apostle is here underlined.

The series of loose remarks continues with a warning in 4:14–15. Alexander the coppersmith is probably not related to the Alexander mentioned in Acts 19:33, but he may be the person spoken of in 1 Tim. 1:20. In any case, Alexander here serves as paradigmatic opponent to Paul's message. We do not obtain any information of the nature of the harm done to Paul. In opposing Paul, Alexander has also opposed God, who "will pay him back for" this. Alexander nevertheless seems to have remained connected with the life of the church, since Timothy is asked to avoid him. Thus he may be a non-Pauline Christian who belongs to the group of false teachers.

The nature of "first defense" (*prōtē apologia*) in 4:16 has caused considerable exegetical debate (Marshall 1999: 823; Mounce 2000: 594–95). One possibility is to assume a distinction between the first and the second imprisonments of Paul in Rome (Acts 28). It is more likely, however, that Paul here refers to the first phase of the continuing judicial process. As a forensic term, *apologia* means the speech given in defense of the prosecuted person. The point of 2 Tim. 4:16 is not to give an account of Paul's process, but to underline his heroism. Although all his followers deserted him during the public occasion of his first apology, Paul wishes them well. The crucial issue in the text is not the process in the Roman court, but the fidelity of Paul's followers. The internal danger of false teachers poses a greater problem to the church than the external problems connected with the Roman law.

In contrast to the lack of support from other Christians, Paul counts on the Lord and on his own strength. Second Timothy 4:17 appears somewhat odd, because Paul here says that the occasion of his first defense became an event in which the gospel message was proclaimed to all the Gentiles. The Roman court officials now appear as representatives of all Gentiles, and the forensic process is transformed into an event of proclamation. Paul may here have various scenes from Acts 26 in mind, scenes in which a defense is turned into a sermon. "Hearing" the message does not imply that the hearers would have accepted it. In this sense 2 Tim. 4:17 underlines Paul's courage and the importance of "fully" proclaiming the message, that is, taking every opportunity to speak in both proper and improper (4:2) settings.

The last part of 4:17 is also somewhat enigmatic and has given rise to symbolic interpretations. The "rescue from the lion's mouth" is a picture employed in the Old Testament (1 Maccabees 2:60; Dan. 6:22; Ps. 22:21). Paul is not alluding to any specific power as a "lion," but he wants to give the impression that his sermon was finally in some way successful and rescued him from an immediate sentence.

Continuing the topic of trusting the Lord, 2 Tim. 4:18 turns toward the future and expresses the thought that, even in the face of death, Paul confidently looks toward the "heavenly kingdom." The beginning of 4:18 displays a resemblance to the Lord's Prayer (Matt. 6:13b). At the same time, the phrase "evil works" (*ergou ponērou*) continues the theme of "good works," which is prominent in the Pastoral Epistles (1 Tim. 2:10; 5:10, 25; 6:18; 2 Tim. 2:21; 3:17; Titus 2:7, 14; 3:8, 14). An exemplary Christian who puts his trust in the Lord avoids evil deeds and remains "equipped for every good work" (2 Tim. 2:21; 3:17). Good works indicate that their performer remains in the sphere of sound doctrine.

With the mention of "heavenly kingdom," 4:18 alludes to 4:1 and thus rounds out the last thematic part of the epistle. Paul waits for the epiphany of this kingdom and remains confident of his salvation. Both Paul's reference to the kingdom and his final doxology, followed with "amen," may contain allusions to the Lord's Prayer. This need not be a conscious intention of the author, since similar doxologies are found in the Pauline Epistles (Gal. 1:5; Rom. 9:5; 11:36) and were most probably employed in various local settings of early Christianity (*Didache* 8.2 [Ehrman 2003: 1.429]). As elsewhere in the Pastoral Epistles (e.g., 1 Tim. 3:16; 2 Tim. 2:11–13), liturgical elements coming from tradition mark the end of a thematic passage.

Final Greetings (2 Tim. 4:19–22)

The last verses express several greetings in conventional Pauline style. Whereas the first list of persons in 4:10–15 contains strong evaluations, the second list of greetings remains neutral. Some names are known from other New Testament texts, whereas others are mentioned here for the first time (Weiser 2003: 328–39).

Prisca and Aquila are well known from many sources (Acts 18:2, 26; Rom. 16:3; 1 Cor. 16:19). The positive relationship to them is also assumed here. Onesiphorus and his household were already described in 2 Tim. 1:16–18. The characterization of Trophimus does not match very well with Acts 20:4 and 21:29, in which he is supposed to have traveled to Jerusalem. Erastus we know from Rom. 16:23 and Acts 19:22, in which he travels with Timothy to Macedonia.

In 2 Tim. 4:21 the wish expressed in 4:9 and further motivated in 4:10–13 is repeated. Because of storms, wintertime was not suitable for sea travel. As in many other Pauline writings, Paul's companions send their greetings. After Paul's complaint of his loneliness (4:10–11, 16), the sudden presence of many friends in 4:21 sounds surprising. The dramatic purpose of 4:21 is, however, to underline that the community of Roman Christians to an extent supports Paul. At the same time, 4:21 imitates other similar endings of the Pauline Epistles.

The names Eubulus, Pudens, Linus, and Claudia do not appear elsewhere in the New Testament. In Irenaeus (*Against Heresies* 3.3.3 [ANF 1.416]) and Eusebius (*Ecclesiastical History* 3.2; 5.6.1 [NPNF² 1.133, 221]), Linus follows Peter as the bishop of Rome. *Apostolic Constitutions* 7.46 (ANF 7.478) mentions that Claudia was his mother. Pudens is sometimes understood to be the husband of Claudia. Eubulus is mentioned in the apocryphal Third Corinthians (Weiser 2003: 335). With the possible exception of Linus, the historical value of these later literary witnesses is very uncertain. The NRSV translation of *hoi adelphoi pantes* ("all the brothers and sisters") is in this case well founded, since *adelphoi* clearly comprehends both male and female Christians.

The final greeting (4:22) is more extensive than in 1 Timothy and Titus, but it is similar to Gal. 6:18; Phil. 4:23; and Phlm. 25. In this context, "spirit" (*pneuma*) refers to the spirit of the human being. The first "you" is singular, the second plural. Some manuscripts end with "amen," reflecting not only Gal. 6:18 but, more generally, the closeness of Pauline greetings with the emerging liturgical phrases.

TITUS

APPOINTMENT OF ELDERS
IN CRETE

Titus 1:1–16

The first part of the Letter of Paul to Titus is concerned with the appointment of elders "in every town" (1:5) in Crete. Paul greets Titus, whom he has left in Crete, the important island mentioned in Acts 27:7–14, 21. The epistle does not, however, reveal anything more of this particular situation. Paul gives general rules for the church in the area for which Titus is responsible.

These rules are similar to those given to Timothy in 1–2 Timothy. As in the letters to Timothy, healthy or sound doctrine is emphasized and false teachers are criticized. The negative characterization of Paul's opponents is extensive and may alienate a modern reader. The use of phrases like "their very minds and consciences are corrupted" (1:15) does not merely serve polemical purposes, but it is related to Paul's overall aim of describing the balanced faith and life of an exemplary Christian.

Greeting (Titus 1:1–4)

The introductory greeting of Titus is longer than the similar greetings of 1–2 Timothy. One reason for this may be that Titus 1:1–4 employs Rom. 1:1–7 as its model. In both passages, Paul is a slave (*doulos*) and an apostle. Both epistles teach the foreknowledge of God in promising the gospel or eternal life (Titus 1:2; Rom. 1:2–3). At the same time, the greeting employs words and phrases that are peculiar to the Pastoral Epistles, in particular "godliness" (*eusebeia*; Titus 1:1) and the proclamation with which Paul has been "entrusted" (*episteuthēn*; 1:3; 1 Tim.

1:11). The greeting thus shows both a continuation with earlier Pauline epistles and an affinity to the language of 1–2 Timothy.

There is no compelling reason to think that Titus is written after 1–2 Timothy. Its place in the canon reflects that it is shorter than 1–2 Timothy. It is also possible to understand Titus as a "first attempt" to deal with the problems that are then elaborated in more detail in 1–2 Timothy (Marshall 1999: 1–2). We need not take a stance on the chronological order of the Pastoral Epistles, since it is in any case obvious that all three epistles deal with similar problems.

"The faith of God's elect" in Titus 1:1 reflects the self-understanding of orthodox Christians (Rom. 8:33; Col. 3:12; 2 Tim. 2:10). The election by God is witnessed in the faith that Paul teaches, not in the talk of the deceivers (Titus 1:10). This faith relates to the "knowledge of the truth" (*epignōsis alētheias*; cf. 1 Tim. 2:4) and to godliness. "Truth" is one of the key concepts of the Pastoral Epistles. The false teachers reject the truth (Titus 1:14; cf. 2 Tim. 2:25; 3:7) and call their contradictions knowledge (1 Tim. 6:20). But God's church is the pillar and bulwark of the truth (3:15; see excursus 2). In Titus 1:1 the knowledge referred to is related to God as Savior (1:3–4). As in 1 Timothy, the word "godliness" is employed to make the point that true faith manifests itself as exemplary Christian life. The various catalogues of virtues and vices in Titus exemplify the good life of orthodox Christians and the blameworthy behavior of false teachers.

The theme of truth is also highlighted in Titus 1:2. God "never lies," whereas deceivers are known for their lies (1:10–12). Christian "hope of eternal life" is grounded in God's truthful promise. The hope of eternal life is a central aspect of the faith and knowledge of orthodox Christians who believe in God our Savior. It is hardly possible to read any elaborate theology of election or predestination into the phrase "before the ages began" (*pro chronōn aiōniōn*). The phrase highlights the sovereign role of God in guiding God's people through history. Thus no particular promise is meant in the phrase, but rather the salvific intent of God in its totality (Oberlinner 1996: 8–9).

The phrase "in due time" (*kairois idiois*) is plural and specifies the recent and present events in which God's "word" (*logos*) was revealed. This revelation is connected with the proclamation (*kērygma*) of Paul. The apostle on the one hand makes the point that Paul's proclamation essentially belongs to the event of revealing God's word. On the other hand, this *kērygma* is not, strictly speaking, Paul's *kērygma* but a task with which Paul has been entrusted. As in 1 Tim. 1:11, the verb *pisteuō* ("to believe, entrust") is used in the passive sense "to be entrusted with." The English translation overlaps with the idea of the deposit (6:20) entrusted to Paul, whereas the Vulgate, for instance, has a more differentiated wording: *in praedicatione quae credita est mihi*. Titus 1:3 ascribes the authority of gospel transmission to Paul; the Pauline proclamation transmits the knowledge of the truth.

Like Timothy (1 Tim. 1:2), Titus is called "my loyal child in the faith." This wording does not intend to say that Titus would be childish, but, on the contrary, it emphasizes the right succession of the apostolic faith. Titus is legitimized to represent the Pauline message in Crete. The phrase "according to a common faith" (*kata koinēn pistin*) employs the idea of *koinōnia*, a common spiritual fellowship. The use of *pistis* further connects Titus with the idea of being entrusted: in their *fides communis* (Vulgate), Titus shares in the task and authority of Paul.

The greeting (Titus 1:4b) imitates other similar greetings (Rom. 1:7b; 1 Cor. 1:3). The words "our Savior" appear twice in Titus 1:3–4. Paul wants to underline his knowledge of the truth that is expressed in this elementary confession. The truth need not become formulated with many words. It is God's will that all people are to be saved (1 Tim. 2:4; 4:10).

Requirements for Elders and Bishops (Titus 1:5–9)

As in 1 Tim. 1:3, Paul briefly describes the assumed situation of the recipient. Crete is connected with Paul's activity in Acts 27, but no closer relationship to Acts 27 can be found. Because of its central location in the Aegean sea, Crete was an important island influenced by many different cultures of the Mediterranean area. At the same time, the book of Titus contains no concrete information about the Christian congregation in Crete. The rules given to Titus are assumed to be generally valid irrespectively of geographical location.

Interestingly, the rare verb *epidiorthoō* ("to put in order"; Titus 1:5) is found only in texts dealing with Crete (Marshall 1999: 151). Together with 1:12, it may give some local color to the epistle. Paul's command to "appoint elders in every town" already presupposes a situation in which local congregations are geographically distributed and together constitute a larger body. We are not told which ecclesiastical title Titus may have, but he is supposed to have the authority, by the command of Paul, to appoint elders. The Pauline authority is once more emphasized by the clause "as I directed you." Thus an organized network of local churches is portrayed as emerging in Crete.

We are not told any further details about the structure of this network or its offices. It is unclear whether "elder" is an office in the ecclesiological sense of the word. Paul is not interested in the structure, but he aims at characterizing the personal ethos of the church leaders. A short catalogue of requirements of an elder is given in Titus 1:6, which resembles 1 Tim. 3:2–5 and other Greco-Roman catalogues of virtues and occupational duty codes (Marshall 1999: 154–55).

"Blameless" (*anenklētos*; Titus 1:7; cf. 1 Tim. 3:10) is a general virtue that conveys the view that the person cannot be accused of clear moral or other failures. "Married only once" (*mias gynaikos anēr*) means that the elder approves the monogamous moral code in his own household (see exposition of 1 Tim. 3:2 and 3:12). The third requirement concerns the exemplary behavior of the children of the elder. Again, the requirement resembles 1 Tim. 3:4–5. The household of an elder should give a good testimony of the moral character. This reflects the virtue of *eusebeia* ("godliness"), which especially in 1 Timothy means both good citizenship and the practice of Christian piety.

The requirements concerning one's family are further related to the Stoic view of *oikeiōsis* ("familiarization, genuine care for others"). A person who has a healthy mind and can care for others has progressed in *oikeiōsis*. The welfare of one's household witnesses to a person's progress in this regard (see appendix A).

In Titus 1:7–9 a longer catalogue regarding the moral characteristics of an *episkopos* ("bishop") is given. The beginning of 1:7 is much debated, since it is not clear whether 1:5–6 is continued or a new, slightly different catalogue is introduced. The first words, *dei gar* ("for . . . must"; Vulgate: *oportet enim*), seem to indicate that an explanatory specification of 1:5–6 is given, in which case the "oversight" would be just one task of the elders. As a whole, however, the second list seems to be independent of the first one and cannot be understood as being merely its qualification. The plain sense of 1:7–9 is that much more is required of bishops than of elders.

Although two different lists must be taken into account, it does not follow that "elders" and "bishops" would be two very different offices in 1:5–9. According to John Chrysostom (NPNF[1] 13.524) and Jerome (Gorday 2000: 285), this passage shows that the two titles were interchangeable in the earliest churches. The longer list of episcopal virtues is not sufficient to conclude that the author intends to make a conscious distinction between the two titles. And yet, the longer list of 1:7–9 may witness and even contribute to the emergence of an episcopal office in the third and fourth generations of Christianity.

Most vices and virtues of the second catalogue are likewise found in 1 Timothy and in philosophical texts. The bishop needs to be "blameless" (cf. Titus 1:6). As "God's steward" (*theou oikonomos*), the bishop ought to display the virtues connected with household and *oikeiōsis* in general. With regard to the five vices mentioned in 1:7, being "arrogant," "quick-tempered," and "violent" (cf. 1 Tim. 3:3; 2 Pet. 2:10) refer to the lack of the most important social skills that emerge in the process of *oikeiōsis*. The person who is rude and indifferent to the feelings of others actually resembles the pathological character of false teachers presented in the Pastoral Epistles (see appendix B).

Being "addicted to wine" or "greedy for gain" (cf. 1 Tim. 3:3, 8; 6:5; Titus 1:12) shows a weakness of character with regard to passions and temptations. These two vices also mean that a person does not have a sound judgment. Greed in particular is a vice of false teachers.

The virtues of 1:8 display the presence of social skills and sound judgment. As in 1 Tim. 3:2–4, no particularly Christian virtues are mentioned, but the general Hellenistic virtues of good life. A "hospitable" person can take care of others in a proper manner (3:2; see appendix C and excursus 3). "Lover of goodness" (*philagathos*; cf. 2 Tim. 3:3) likewise signals a classical virtue that is the opposite of egoism (Marshall 1999: 163). A "prudent" (*sōphrōn*) person does not engage in passionate and pointless debates but preserves his or her detached judgment.

An "upright" (*dikaios*) person defends fairness and justice. A "devout" (*hosios*; cf. 1 Tim. 2:8) person worships properly, and a "self-controlled" (*enkratēs*—the good counterpart of *akratēs* in 2 Tim. 3:3) person can resist his or her bad impulses (Marshall 1999: 182–91).

Taken as a whole, these virtues are not individualistic but refer to the proper behavior in a community. A bishop who is to oversee a local church must possess social skills and virtues. Even the more individual traits of character, like being devout or self-controlled, serve the purpose of setting an example for others (cf. 1 Tim. 3:8; 4:12). Attachment and neighborly love are central in Christian life.

In Titus 1:9 the focus shifts from communal virtues to the specific Christian skills of a church leader. The expression *tou kata tēn didachēn pistou logou* can be understood as a reference to "the word that is trustworthy in accordance with the teaching" (NRSV) or "the preaching which is reliable as regards doctrine" (Marshall 1999: 166). The "word" is related to both the "word" of 1:3 and the "sound doctrine" of 1:9b and 2:1. Since the faithfulness of the bishop is contrasted with the deceivers (1:10), the doctrinal orthodoxy of the bishop is primarily at stake here (cf. Vulgate: *amplectentem eum qui secundum doctrinam est fidelem sermonem*).

The twofold purpose of this requirement is given in 1:9b: the bishop must be able to preach with sound or "healthy" doctrine (*en tē didaskalia tē hygiainousē*; cf. 1 Tim. 1:10; 2 Tim. 4:3), and he must be able to "refute" false teachers. As in 1–2 Timothy, the idea of healthy doctrine that promotes sound judgment and right conduct is employed here. The false teachers are not only wrong, but they have lost their mental health and virtues (see appendix B and the expositions of 1 Tim. 6:3–10 and 2 Tim. 3:1–9). The bishop, as a paradigm of orthodoxy, should set an example of both sound doctrine and right conduct. Thus he displays the state of comprehensive health and virtue.

False Teachers Are Corrupted Liars (Titus 1:10–16)

In contrast to the requirements for elders and bishops, the vices of the deceivers are portrayed extensively. The overall purpose of 1:10–16 is to show that false teachers have corrupted minds (1:15) and deny God in their shameful actions (1:16). Whereas orthodox Christians possess sound judgment and can therefore act virtuously, the deceivers have deviated in both their thought and their action. The overall characteristics presented here resemble similar descriptions in 1 Tim. 1:3–11; 6:3–10; and 2 Tim. 2:14–18, in particular with regard to mental disorders and Judaizing tendencies. More than in 1–2 Timothy, the false teachers are here accused of lying. This may relate to the Cretan "local color," since otherwise the opponents display the same psychopathology as the false teachers in 1–2 Timothy.

The opponents are identified as "rebellious people" (*anypotaktoi*; cf. Titus 1:6), "idle talkers" (*mataiologoi*; cf. 1 Tim. 1:6), and "deceivers" (*phrenapatai*). They display a lack of communal virtues, an inability to pay attention to proper household rules and care for others. In Titus 1:10b these vices are related to the Jewish-Christian character of the opponents. In 1 Tim. 1:4–7, as well as in Titus 1:14 and 3:9, the Judaizing tendencies of the opponents are criticized. Although we cannot explain away the problematic anti-Judaism of these verses, the main point is not Jewish features as such, but the rigid and obstinate manner in which these features are displayed. In 1:10 Paul is not focusing on circumcision, but on the rebellious and deceitful character of the opponents.

The lack of genuine care for others is emphasized in 1:11. The behavior of deceivers is "ruining entire households." The NRSV's "upsetting whole families" is too mild: *anatrepō* here means "to ruin" or even "to destroy." It is also important to see that the welfare of Christian households is tightly connected with the communal virtues of successful *oikeiōsis*, as they are portrayed in 1:6–9. Because of the catastrophic consequences, the opponents need to be "silenced." False doctrine destroys the social fiber of Christian community; therefore it must be stopped. Paul's point is not to control teaching for teaching's sake, but to preserve the basic virtues of Christian households.

Paul does not give a description of the content of false doctrine, but says only that his opponents are teaching "for shameful gain" (*aischrou kerdous charin*; cf. 1 Tim. 6:5) "what . . . is not right" (*ha mē dei*; cf. 5:13). Paul wants to say that both the motives and the character of his opponents are profoundly wrong and therefore cause harm to the people who listen to them. A responsible person who has grown in his or her *oikeiōsis* and can think of the common good does not appeal to personal gain. Personal gain as a motif of conduct is shameful and shows that the speaker striving for it cannot care for others.

In Titus 1:12 the opponents are described as typical "Cretans [who] are always liars." The hexametric verse quoted by Paul in 1:12 has given cause for extensive historical and philosophical comments. Already Clement of Alexandria and Jerome claimed the Cretan poet Epimenides as the author of this verse. Epimenides was also regarded as a prophet by Plato, Aristotle, and Cicero. In the Greco-Roman world, Cretans had a widespread reputation as liars (Oberlinner 1996: 38–39; Marshall 1999: 200–201). For these reasons, the assimilation of false teachers with Cretans was illuminating for many readers of Titus.

Together with 1:13a, 1:12 contains a logical problem that is widely known as the "paradox of the liar." If a Cretan claims that all Cretans are "always liars," how can this "testimony" be true? Commentators tend to deny that Paul would have been conscious of the logical problem. But there may be some point in the claim that Paul is here showing that the futile nature of idle talk leads only to self-refuting contradictions, whereas a true virtue is not verified by words but in actions (cf. 1:16). According to this interpretation, verbal statements concerning one's own character tend to be misleading and even self-defeating. Thus a truly virtuous and self-controlled person should not speak of his or her own virtues, but let them be visible in actions (Thiselton 1994; Oberlinner 1996: 39–40; Marshall 1999: 203).

The Stoic doctrine of *oikeiōsis* presupposes that the person who observes the world from a "first-person" perspective cannot reach the truth. Only when the subject turns toward reason and other people does he or she begin to grasp the world as it is (see appendix A). Although the evidence is too scarce to read this doctrine from 1:10–16, it is consistent with Paul's basic tendency. Adherents to sound doctrine should prove their orthodoxy by displaying virtues rather than by extensive lip service (cf. 1:16a).

Irrespectively of whether we think that the liar paradox is intended in 1:12, Paul's general point is sufficiently clear: his opponents do not manage to prove their character, but their words remain idle and deceptive talk. For this reason, they can "become sound in faith" (*hygiainōsin en tē pistei*; 1:13) only when their thoughts are sharply refuted. A cognitive therapy is to be offered that does not nurture false thoughts but effectively refutes them and shows that sound doctrine is to be preferred. The verb *elenchō* ("to rebuke") refers to the therapeutic intervention of the bishop. At least since Aristotle, *elenchos* means the refutation of the opponent's position (*Sophistical Refutations* [LCL 400.11–155]).

In this process of cognitive therapy and doctrinal refutation, the attention should be shifted away from "myths" (*mythoi*) and "commandments" (*entolai*). The attribute "Jewish" in 1:14 belongs to both terms, but Paul is most likely not referring to the Jewish law or to the central stories of the Jewish Bible. Myths and commandments are explicitly said to be "of men," that is, not from God. What Paul has in mind are teachings that are added to God's commandments. Most likely these are similar to the ascetic rules mentioned in 1 Tim. 4:1–3 and the myths in 1:4; 4:7; and 2 Tim. 4:4. In refuting false teachers, no appeal to such rules and myths should be made.

The next verse, Titus 1:15, applies to this situation the words of Jesus ("everything will be clean for you" in Luke 11:41) and Paul ("everything is indeed clean" in Rom. 14:20; cf. 14:14). Such words relativize the Jewish rules concerning food (cf. 1 Tim. 4:3). In addition to human rules concerning food, Paul may here have Christian baptism in mind (cf. Titus 3:5–7). But probably the view that orthodox Christians are "pure" serves an even broader argumentative purpose. Because the Pauline Christians adhere to sound doctrine, they are "healthy" in a comprehensive sense. They have the right judgment of all matters and can thus evaluate other persons, opinions, actions, and created things in a proper way. Pure Christians are not obstinate or rigid in the sense that their mind would be trapped by some idiosyncrasy related to myths, commandments, or genealogies. A pure mind can preserve its *autarkeia* and, at the same time, care for others in an unselfish manner (see appendixes A–B). In this sense being pure or clean means the ability to judge "all things" properly.

In contrast to this, those who are "corrupt" (*memiammenoi*) cannot receive or grasp anything that would remain pure. This is because "their very minds and consciences are corrupted." The capacity of right judgment, or the power of sound reason, is not working properly. The pollution or corruption of the mind colors everything so that nothing remains pure. Therefore the false teachers remain trapped by their idiosyncrasies and lack real interaction with the external world. In this way Paul is not only mocking his opponents, but he tries to explain their behavior by referring to the damaged mind and conscience.

The verb *miainō* ("to defile") can mean moral defilement (Jude 8; Heb. 12:15) and ritual defilement (John 18:28). In the *Testaments of the Twelve Patriarchs: Issachar* 4.4 [Charlesworth 1985: 1.803]) and Titus 1:15b, it means the corruption of the mind. As in 1 Tim. 6, Paul here claims that his opponents are mentally disturbed. In terms of Stoic therapy, mental disturbance means that a person has false opinions and has to be liberated from them. Cretan false teachers are disturbed by the various lies that they are spreading to the ruin of Christian households. The lies stem from false judgments that, in turn, are connected with worldly passions (Titus 2:12; 3:3). As in 1–2 Timothy, the passions of envy, hatred, and greed (Titus 1:11; 3:3) cause rebellious and untruthful behavior.

In order to cure people from this corrupt state of mind, Titus is asked to refute the false judgments of Paul's opponents. By means of this refutation, they can be "silenced" (1:11) and may still become "sound in the faith" (1:13). Since the disease is rooted in false judgments and opinions, it can be cured in the process of therapeutic refutation. This argumentation approaches the Stoic idea that harmful passions are false judgments (see appendixes A–B).

Although the root cause is thus found at the level of teachings, the corruption manifests itself in actions. The person may "profess" (*homologeō*) to know God but deny him in concrete action (1:16; cf. 2 Tim. 3:5). Christians are to be identified by their good works, which emerge as fruits of their faith. At the same time, Titus 1:16 gives a differentiated picture of sound doctrine. It is possible to make an elementary confession, a kind of lip service, and yet not possess sound doctrine. Sound doctrine is a judgment that makes and keeps a person pure and illuminates the mind so that a person is capable of both *autarkeia* and caring for others. Paul aims at emphasizing both sound doctrine and the virtues of character. The latter are rooted in the former, but sound doctrine is not a merely propositional profession, but a conviction that illuminates the mind so that it can become operative in virtuous behavior (doctrines are, however, also propositions that can represent the judgment; see the postscript).

The closing words highlight the other side of this coin. A merely propositional assent to know God that is not manifested in action leaves the person in a detestable and disobedient state. Titus 1:16b may in some way be related to the paradox of the liar in 1:12. A first-person propositional confession, be it "I am lying" or "I know God," is vulnerable to self-refutation. In the latter case, greedy or hateful actions can refute the proposition. Maybe for this reason Paul in Titus 1 admonishes the elders and bishops to witness by their character. This admonition is not in tension with the primacy of sound doctrine. It rather gives a differentiated picture of sound doctrine, right judgment, and good works as they become contrasted with lies, a corrupted mind, and lip service.

VIRTUES AMONG CHRISTIANS

Titus 2:1–15

The second chapter of Titus is a literary unit that outlines good Christian life in accordance with sound doctrine. Different groups in the church are addressed successively: older men, older women, younger women, younger men, and slaves (2:2–10). Each group should perform virtues that are proper to their role in both church and household. Most virtues can be understood in terms of moderation, that is, they avoid harmful extremes and aim at finding the virtuous mean. In addition, most virtues are communal and display the fruits of a successful *oikeiōsis*, that is, both a genuine care for others and a self-controlled *autarkeia* (see appendixes A–B).

The latter part of the chapter (2:11–15) outlines "the doctrine of God our Savior" (2:10b). This is the essence of sound doctrine. The soteriological outline contains elements that relate to the virtues of moderation, especially in 2:12 and 2:14. Although the chapter concentrates on the portrayal of virtues, they in turn serve the fundamental gospel message that becomes sound doctrine.

Virtues of Older Men, Older Women, and Younger Women (Titus 2:1–5)

The first verse (2:1) has a dual purpose. First, the task of Titus is contrasted with the behavior of deceivers who "profess ... God, but ... deny him by their actions" (1:16). The teaching of Titus should not be idle talk or lip service, but it must be consistent with "healthy" doctrine, that is, it should be accompanied with proper conduct. This admonition may contain some criticism of first-person oral professions. The point is not to downgrade doctrine, but to show what a serious adherence to "sound doctrine" means. In addition, 2:1 introduces the theme of the passage. Paul wants to describe the virtues that are consistent with sound doctrine; Titus is entrusted with the task of explaining them to the Cretan Christians.

The following catalogue resembles similar lists in 1 Tim. 2:8–10; 3:1–13; 6:11; 2 Tim. 2:22–24; 1 Pet. 2:18–20; 3:1–8. The lists are similar in their appreciation of household values and typical Greco-Roman virtues (Collins 2002: 337). At the same time, Titus 2:2–9 is more comprehensive than its counterparts elsewhere in the Pastoral Epistles. In particular, this list is not directed to the church leader or to a special group, but it comprises more or less all relevant groups in the local church. Thus it is significant as a universal code of ecclesiastical ethics.

Older men are advised to be "temperate" (*nēphalios*) and "serious" (*semnos*). The same virtues are recommended to bishops (1 Tim. 3:2) and deacons (3:8, 11). The advice to be "prudent" is especially significant, because *sōphrōn* and related concepts are central for the catalogues in the Pastoral Epistles and in particular here. Young women and younger men also are asked to be "self-controlled" (*sōphrōn* in Titus 2:5; *sōphroneō* in 2:6). Older women are asked to "encourage" (*sōphronizō*; 2:4) young women. The grace of God trains us to live "self-controlled" (*sōphronōs*; 2:12) lives.

The concept of self-control occurs twenty-six times in the Pastoral Epistles, with twelve occurrences in Titus, thirteen in 1 Timothy, and only one in 2 Timothy (1:7) (Marshall 1999: 182). The most condensed group of occurrences is here, and all groups in the church are commanded to display prudence and self-control. *Sōphrōn* is a typical virtue in philosophical texts, in which it means "rational" and "self-controlled," referring generally to a sound mind. As self-control it can be translated into Latin as *moderatio cupiditatum* (Cicero, *De finibus* 2.60 [LCL 40.149]; Marshall 1999: 182). The Vulgate here uses *prudentia*, which is also the translation of Aristotle's *phronēsis*, meaning the capacity of practical reason to find adequate particular actions. *Sōphrōn* has no clear equivalent term in Jewish tradition.

Marshall relates the terms *semnos*, *nēphalios*, and *enkrateia* ("discipline"; Titus 1:8) to the *sōphrōn* word group, since they all express self-control and moderation. As a result of his analysis, he presents the following theological problem that bothers several modern commentators. If self-control and prudent behavior were the proper way to display good life and sound doctrine, does this not mean that the Pastoral Epistles are "over-concerned with a dull respectability"? Marshall answers this challenge by holding that, because of the false teachers, the church was becoming an object of ridicule and therefore needed the necessary respectability (1999: 189–90).[1]

This may also be true, but my exposition proceeds from different premises. I argue that the virtues at stake here need to be understood in terms of *metriopatheia* ("moderation of emotion"; Heb. 5:2; see exposition of 1 Tim. 3:3). This tradition

---

1. Collins 2002: 13 speaks of the "overly accommodating" tendency of the Pastoral Epistles.

is more consistent with Judaism and Christianity than many other philosophical doctrines. The tradition of *metriopatheia* ascribes a positive value to the emotions and does not plead for their eradication. It rather aims at evaluating the often simultaneous opposite emotions in a proper and balanced manner, so that the person may express his or her emotional self in a way that is not distorted. Although such conduct needs reason, one basic role of reason is to provide for the emergence of *oikeiōsis*, the social capital that is needed for the genuine care for others. This is very different from "dull respectability." The conduct aiming at balance and moderation is an affirmation of the elementary created gifts of human beings: reason, emotions, and the ability to love and care for others. Such gifts belong essentially to Jewish and Christian religious traditions, but they can also be spelled out with the help of the view of *metriopatheia* and *oikeiōsis* (see appendixes A–B).

According to this approach, the same virtue of being self-controlled, *sōphrōn*, is required from all groups in a Christian church, but it may manifest itself in different ways. The prudence of an older man may relate to his eating, drinking, and anger; the prudence of a young woman may relate to her household tasks. Such an approach allows a theological interpreter to say that the particular issues considered to be prudent in Crete at the time of Titus may not be prudent in an identical fashion in other contexts. This reconsideration opens up possibilities to deal with the submission of women and slaves in the household. As a virtue of balance and moderation, prudence weights the circumstantial matters differently in different times.

In Titus 2:2 the basic virtues of moderation become connected with the most important Christian virtues of being "sound in faith, in love, and in endurance." This statement echoes 1 Cor. 13:13; 1 Tim. 6:11; and 2 Tim. 3:10 (in the latter two cases the virtue of hope is replaced with the idea of perseverance). Faith and love are in most cases mentioned together in the Pastoral Epistles. In Titus 2:2 the argumentative purpose is to connect the well-known Christian virtues with the idea of being "healthy" or "sound." The three civil virtues of a sound mind (2:2a) go together with sound Christian doctrine (2:2b).

The older women are advised to be "reverent in behavior" (2:3). The term *hieroprepēs* relates to priesthood or "what is fitting for a priest." Although this most likely means "reverent" in a general sense, it should be noted that the older women are here advised to teach young women and to set an example to them in various ways. While women are prohibited from teaching men (1 Tim. 2:12) because such a situation would be against the moral codes of household, it remains possible for them to teach younger women "what is good." The term *kalodidaskalos* ("teacher of the good") stresses the comprehensive nature of this exemplary task (Collins 2002: 341–42).

In Titus 2:4 the verb *sōphronizō* ("to make of sound mind, encourage") again illustrates the metaphor of health and reasonable balance in the virtue of *sōphrōn*. Teaching by example is a proper means of transmitting this virtue. As young people are only proceeding from "I" to "we" in their *oikeiōsis* (see appendix A), the teaching should emphasize the social skills of being "lover of husband" (*philandros*) and "lover of children" (*philoteknos*). It is evident that Paul again stresses the values of household and family. A modern reader easily considers that women are here defined in terms of their husband and children. But it is also important to see the movement from "I" to "we." The social skill of love concerns, at least in principle, both women and men, and male bishops are also commanded to pay attention to their families (1 Tim. 3:4–5). In Titus 2:6 young men are commanded to exercise similar self-control.

The list of virtues to be taught to young women is continued in 2:5. As are other groups, they are to be "self-controlled" (*sōphrōn*). This general virtue is specified as a set of traditional household values: "chaste" (*agnē*) refers to blameless and sincere character in a broad sense; "good managers of the household" and "submissive to their husbands" describe the ethos of a balanced home. As in 1 Tim. 3:7 and elsewhere, Paul is interested in the outward manifestation and good witness of various Christian groups. When they display the proper virtues of moderation and care for others, the "word of God" is not discredited. Whereas preaching is primarily the matter of church leaders (Titus 1:9), other groups should witness by their virtuous character and good behavior, in contrast to the false teachers, who are characterized by idle talk and lip service.

Virtues of Young Men, Titus, and Slaves (Titus 2:6–10)

Young men are only briefly and generally advised to exercise the virtue of moderation (*sōphroneō*; 2:6). It is likely that in 2:7–8 Titus is thought to exemplify the virtues of young men. He should be a "model of good works" and, in addition, practice his teaching with the necessary virtues. Three qualities of virtuous teaching are mentioned. Titus should show "integrity" (*aphthoria*). The word is rare and means "incorruption, soundness." Interestingly, the false teachers are accused in 1 Tim. 6:5 of having a "disturbed mind" (*diephtharmenōn ton noun*; cf. 2 Tim. 3:8). In contrast to this, an exemplary teacher possesses soundness and integrity. "Gravity" (*semnotēs*) expresses again the moderated attitude of seriousness (Collins 2002: 344).

"Sound speech" (*logos hygiēs*) continues the metaphors of mental health and balance. The qualification "that cannot be censured," or "beyond reproach," emphasizes the orthodoxy of sound words. Given that such comprehensive soundness, balance, and orthodoxy is found in Titus's teaching, the opponents cannot find anything to blame. The expression "will be put to shame" (*entrepō*) contains the wish that the opponents will be converted to orthodoxy. As a result, they will no longer speak badly of Pauline Christians. The teaching thus fulfills the role of cognitive therapy. Sound words are able to cure the mind that is lost in idle talk.

Slaves are addressed as the fifth group of church members in 2:9–10. In agreement with the established household codes, Christian slaves should show a proper respect of their masters. As in 1 Tim. 6:1–2, this command may echo a situation in which Christian slaves already feel themselves liberated by the gospel message. In order to preserve the social order with the help of the idea of self-control, slaves are advised to continue in their old position. The cases of women and slaves show the limits and dangers of the ethics of moderation. The virtue of self-control can be used as an argument to stay in the old roles and legitimize the prevalent social order.

One hermeneutical strategy to deal with this phenomenon is to say that the virtue of moderation is conditioned by social surroundings and is thus itself a contextual phenomenon. The abolition of slavery in Paul's times would have led to social unrest and chaos. In our democratic society, the advocation of slavery would have similar results. As prudence, the virtue of moderation should find an adequate balance in the complex network of the surrounding society.

Concerning the duties of the slaves, *mē antilegō* (Titus 2:9; cf. 1:9) does not merely mean "to not talk back" but "to not talk against" or "to not contradict" (Marshall 1999: 169, 260). Instead of putting aside their master's property, the slaves are to demonstrate (*endeiknymi* is emphatic) their strong fidelity. Paul also wants to stress the exemplary outward appearance of Christian groups in a society: they are to witness by their good works and character.

This positive purpose is rounded out with a phrase that may alienate a modern reader: through their exemplary conduct in slavery, the slaves should be "an ornament to the doctrine of God our Savior." The phrase needs to be expounded with the necessary contextualization. The virtue of moderation becomes a decorum when it is practiced properly. In a different society, a different behavior is needed in order that it may add to the beauty of the agent concerned.

The verb *kosmeō* ("to make beautiful"; cf. 1 Tim. 2:9) is clearly positive. It may, however, also contain a moderation of the very thought of moderation. Proper behavior and good works are commanded, but finally they remain an ornament, a cosmetic addition to the underlying doctrine. The point is not that we would be saved by good works, but we are saved according to God's mercy through Jesus Christ (Titus 3:5–6). The virtues of prudence and self-control are commanded by Paul in order that Christians could witness by their good works rather than by idle talk. Teaching the virtue of moderation is not, however, the core of the gospel, but rather an ornament of the message of God as Savior.

Grace of God in Jesus Christ (Titus 2:11–15)

The last part of Titus 2 can be characterized as the apex of Paul's Epistle to Titus. The epistle for the most part deals with the Christian virtues of moderation as contrasted to the false teachers. But in this central part of the epistle, the core of sound teaching is spelled out, namely, confession of the salvific action of

God in Jesus Christ. This is the foundational event of salvation history; all human virtues and good works remain a corollary to this foundation.

The grace of God "appeared" (*epephanē*). The Pastoral Epistles typically employ the idea of epiphany in describing the revelation in Jesus Christ (1 Tim. 6:14; 2 Tim. 1:10; 4:1, 8). As Titus 2:13–14 shows, the epiphany is centered around the manifestation of Jesus Christ. In 2:11 the emphasis is on the grace that is said to bring "salvation to all human beings." The universality of salvation is also affirmed in 1 Tim. 2:4. Given that Titus 2:1–10 addresses a variety of different groups in the church, one can read 2:11 to mean that the Christian message of salvation reaches Jews and Gentiles, men and women, young and old, free people and slaves. False teachers may have wanted to limit salvation to specified groups (Collins 2002: 349–50; Marshall 1999: 268).

In 2:12 the message of salvation is connected with the program of Christian character formation described in detail in 2:2–10. The grace of God participates in this education or "training" (*paideuō*). In the course of this training, "impiety" (*asebeia*) and "worldly passions" (*hai kosmikai epithymiai*) are renounced. The qualification "earthly" entails the idea that some passions, namely, those of lower value, are to be renounced, while other, maybe spiritual or higher emotions, are not. The cultivation of passions is a central topic of Stoic therapy (see appendixes A–B).[2]

I advocate the view that the Pastoral Epistles recommend a moderation of passions rather than their complete extinction. The "training" described in 2:12 is in keeping with this view. The self-control and prudence (*sōphrōn* in 2:2–6, 12) achieved in this training do not extinguish good emotions such as love and kindness (2:4–5) but strengthen them, enabling the person to exercise a genuine care for others. In a similar way, philosophers who advocate the ideal of moderation do not require that love toward family members should be eradicated. Since this love belongs to the socially mature life, it is compatible with the ideals of moderation and self-control (Sorabji 2000: 388–89).[3]

In 2:12b this ideal is spelled out with regard to the present life of Christians. Paul asks them to live a life of self-control (*sōphrōn*). This basic virtue of moderation is connected with the Pauline and classical virtue of being just, righteous, and fair (*dikaios*). The third virtue is that of "godliness" (*eusebeia*), which is employed in 1 Timothy as an overall characterization of Christian life. In this way the three virtues summarize the discussion of the proper Christian life. It is important to see that they are not autonomous virtues, but remain connected with the epiphany of God's grace.

The epiphany of the recent past in Titus 2:13 (cf. 2:11) is connected with the final "manifestation" (*epiphaneia*) of the glory. An obvious problem of 2:11–13

2. Collins 2002: 350 considers this to comprise all passions. Marshall 1999: 270 remarks that *epithymia* is in itself neutral and can sometimes (1 Tim. 3:1) be positive.

3. According to Engberg-Pedersen 2000: 72–73, even the Stoic wise still retain the good emotion of joy.

is whether Paul here teaches two different and successive manifestations (Marshall 1999: 267, 293–95). As in 1 Tim. 6:14; 2 Tim. 1:10; 4:1, 8, the concept of epiphany can refer to both the future and the recent past. Paul is not, however, developing a view of different epiphanies; rather, his use of the term as relating to the future emphasizes eschatological hope and expectation. At the same time, however, Titus 2:11–13 already contains an idea that in the "first" epiphany God reveals the will to save, whereas the "second" epiphany in glory reveals God's final judgment of the world.

The use of the word "glory" (*doxa*) as the attribute of final epiphany alludes to the last judgment (cf. 2 Tim. 4:8). The translation of Titus 2:13b has caused a lot of debate because the two last words, "Jesus Christ," seem to relate to "God and Savior" (so NRSV). But it is also possible to read 2:13b as meaning that Jesus is the glory of God. A third possible reading is "the epiphany of the glory of the great God and of our Savior Jesus Christ." Without entering the exegetical debate in detail, it may be noted that recent commentators find the NRSV's translation to be the most convincing one (Marshall 1999: 276–82; Collins 2002: 352–53).

The saving work of Jesus Christ is spelled out in 2:14. This verse is theologically significant since it contains a view of the atonement and the redemption. At the same time, the verse summarizes earlier Pauline tradition. The self-giving of Jesus Christ as "a ransom for many" (Mark 10:45) is an early Christian proclamation to which Paul refers in Gal. 1:4 and 2:20. The idea of redemption is spelled out in Rom. 3:24 and 1 Cor. 1:30. In 1 Tim. 2:6 Christ is likewise said to have given himself as "a ransom for all." The difference between "for us" in Titus 2:14 and "for all" in 1 Tim. 2:6 is insignificant, since Titus 2:10 includes "all." If *anomia* in the phrase "from all iniquity" (*apo pasēs anomias*) signifies the recipient to whom the payment is made, this may give some support to the idea that the payment is made to evil powers in order that humans can be delivered from evil. But, as the phrase probably derives from the Septuagint translation of Ps. 130:8, it should not be interpreted as containing an elaborate view of redemption (Marshall 1999: 283–85).

The last part of Titus 2:14 again connects with the view of virtues put forward in 2:2–10. The grace of God and the redemptive work of Jesus Christ contribute to the emergence of God's people, the church. God's work "purifies" (*katharizō*) Christians, who because of redemption become God's own people. The redemptive work of Christ thus defines "God's people" in a new way that is different from Judaism. The word *periousios* ("chosen, of one's own"; Vulgate: *acceptabilis*) defines the church in terms of new election and possession by God. This chosen and purified group of Christians is eager to practice "good deeds." The phrase "good works" in both 1 Timothy (5:10, 25; 6:18) and Titus (2:7, 14; 3:8, 14) is used as a summarizing term that captures exemplary behavior.

In 2:15 Titus is admonished to spread this message using three modes of speech: he should "declare" (*laleō*), "exhort" (*parakaleō*), and "reprove" (*elenchō*). The Vulgate is very illuminating: *loquere, exhortare, argue*. In his ordinary speech (*laleō*), the church leader declares this to be the case. In exhortation and consolation (*parakaleō*), human virtues and the work of Christ set an example to be followed. Finally, in "elenchtic" argumentation Christian truth is disputed without quarrel and idle talk so that false teachings are refuted (Collins 2002: 356). "With all authority" here carries the meaning "with all impressiveness"—not the formal authority of the speaker, but the impressiveness of his words is emphasized.

The final command of 2:15b is somewhat tricky. To an extent, it resembles 1 Tim. 4:12. Paul probably wants to underline once more (cf. Titus 2:7) that the character of the church leader should be exemplary. But he also wants to point out that the teaching mentioned in 2:15a should be performed with the necessary skill and gravity. A church leader should not be an idle talker, but his speech, consolation, and argumentation should be performed with a firm grasp of the word (cf. 1:9–10). In this manner, the church leader should be thought well of by insiders as well as outsiders (cf. 1 Tim. 3:7).

▮ Excursus 9: Self-giving of Jesus

The saving work of Jesus Christ, as it becomes expressed in 1 Tim. 2:5–6 and Titus 2:14, should be put into the broader theological context of giving and self-giving. The biblical verb for giving (*didōmi*) is one of the most frequent verbs in the New Testament, occurring over four hundred times. Such a common verb is often used without specific theological aims, but it can also depict a specific theological relationship, for instance, between God, the trinitarian persons, and the world in John 3:16, 35. The general meaning "to give" is connected with other common New Testament verbs, in particular *paradidōmi* ("to hand over"), *apostellō* ("to send"), *aphiēmi* ("to forgive"), *tēreo* ("to keep"), and *paratithēmi* ("to present").

These biblical verbs have a complex theological interplay that gives rise to many classical themes of dogmatics, such as mercy, atonement, sacrifice, prayer, and charisms (Saarinen 2005). The reflexive use of *didōmi* outlines a view of "self-giving" that is essential for the theological understanding of the work of Christ. The use of *paradidōmi* in the earliest Passion Narratives (Mark 9:31; 14:10, 41; Rom. 8:32; Gal. 2:20) enables theologians to think that somebody "gives" Jesus to someone else. In addition, this "deliverance" involves a third party for whose sake the event takes place, as, for instance, the phrases "for all of us" in Rom. 8:32 and "gave himself for me" in Gal. 2:20 state (Popkes 1967 is an excellent exegetical study of such phrases).

Augustine developed these biblical thoughts into a theological view that can be called a "four-place relation." In this relation, A gives B to C in order that D may benefit from this act. In Western theology, the four-place relation of giving has found many applications related to the theology of atonement, sacrifice, and the Eucharist. It should be noted that two or more places of the relation may refer to the same agent. We can, for instance, say that the Father gives the Son to the Father in order that the humankind can be saved or that the Son gives himself (to the Father or to death). Augustine even said that Jesus Christ can fill all four places in phrases like "Jesus, God and human, gave himself to God for the sake of salvation of humans" (*De trinitate* 4.3.19 [Augustine 1991: 166–67]).[4]

Another important aspect of the four-place relation is that one or more of its places can be bracketed so that the reader does not know who (or what) is meant to fill the place. This event of bracketing is very prominent in the New Testament texts, since they do not make explicit all possible parties involved. When John 3:16 says that the Father gave his only Son, it is not obvious to whom the Son is given. In a similar vein, Rom. 8:32 does not say to whom Jesus is handed over (Saarinen 2005: 37–42).

In the Pastoral Epistles, this terminological level of "giving" is particularly relevant for the understanding of 1 Tim. 2:5–6 and Titus 2:14, in which the work of Christ is explained. In 1 Tim. 2:6 Christ "gave himself a ransom for all" (*ho dous heauton antilytron hyper pantōn*). Christ is thus the giver and the gift, whereas "all" are the beneficiaries of this act of self-giving. The recipient of this act is not mentioned, a feature that connects 2:6 with many other New Testament texts (e.g., Mark 10:45; Rom. 8:32; Gal. 2:20). The idea of ransom, however, clearly signals that a recipient is assumed. The context affirms that Jesus is human and gave this ransom for all humans and makes it plausible to think that the recipient of this act is God. At the same time, the picture remains enigmatic, because it is difficult to think that this act of self-giving would be a ransom paid to God in order to liberate people from their slavery to God.

Augustine's four-place relation is both helpful and problematic at the same time. In a useful manner, the relation makes evident the logical and semantic places that the event of giving normally presupposes. As a heuristic tool it is exegetically helpful, since it enables the interpreter to ask the inevitable questions. At the same time, the four-place relation remains problematic because the biblical text often brackets some of those logical places. A reader may ask whether all places need to be filled and whether the concealment of some placeholders is intended.

Regardless of the answer to such questions, it is clear that the practice of bracketing shifts the focus to the placeholders who are actually mentioned. It remains the task of the expositor to fill the bracketed places. In the theology of atonement and sacrifice, theologians have performed this task to a great extent. Thus we can discuss whether the ransom is paid to God or to the devil, whether God sent Jesus or Jesus himself decided to perform the redemptive act of self-giving. Many of the root causes of these controversies can be traced back to the phenomenon of bracketing in the New Testament texts (argued in more detail in Saarinen 2005: 36–45, 81–94). Without mentioning Augustine's four-place relation many, probably most, exegetical commentators also address the issue of missing placeholders in the relevant biblical texts. In this sense the four-place relation is not merely a later theological extrapolation, but an issue that almost inevitably belongs to the syntactic structure and semantic content of the text.

With regard to the theological interpretation of 1 Tim. 2:5–6, it is important to notice how the humanity of Jesus Christ is emphasized. The work of Christ as mediator

---

4. W. Simon 2003 applies the four-place relation to the theology of the Eucharist.

(*mesitēs*; 2:5) stems from the idea that the whole of humankind needs reconciliation and that Jesus Christ can act as a representative of this group. In a similar way Moses, according to Philo (*Moses* 2.166 [LCL 289.531]), was a mediator between God and Israel. The idea of mediating presupposes that two parties are involved. No third party to whom the ransom would be paid need be assumed.

The other significant text describing the work of Christ, Titus 2:14, is very similar to but not identical with 1 Tim. 2:5–6. In Titus 2:14 Jesus "gave himself for us" (*hōs edōken heauton hyper hēmōn*) in order to "redeem us from all iniquity." The immediate context further speaks of worldly passions that need to be renounced and purified in order that salvation can be affirmed. The places of the four-place relation are similar to the other texts: Jesus is the giver and the gift, human beings are the beneficiaries, but the recipient of the act of self-giving is concealed.

The thought of payment appears in the phrase "he might redeem us from all iniquity" (*lytrōsētai hēmas apo pasēs anomias*). It may be possible to interpret *anomia* ("lawlessness, sin") as the recipient of the act of self-giving, although the connection remains somewhat vague. If this interpretation is adopted, Titus 2:14 is closer to the so-called devil-ransom theory that Anselm of Canterbury opposes in his *Cur deus homo* (esp. 1.7, 22; 2.6, 16 [Anselm 1988]). According to this theory, the redemptive act of Jesus paid the ransom to the devil in order that humans can be liberated from their slavery to the devil (Hopkins 1971: 187–214 is a good commentary on this topic).

On the one hand, this phrase makes the situation of Titus 2:14 to an extent different from 1 Tim. 2:5–6. On the other hand, we should again be careful of not pressing the ransom metaphor too much. The verb *lytroō* often means "to set free" and can be used to express God's deliverance of his people from Egypt in the Septuagint (Marshall 1999: 284). The connection with a concrete ransom remains vague. As a consequence, the recipient of Jesus's self-giving also remains bracketed. The state of *anomia* may simply refer to the human condition that needs the act of mediation. Given this, no major discrepancy between 1 Tim. 2:5–6 and Titus 2:14 need be assumed. The notion of *anomia* may simply derive from the Septuagint version of Ps. 130:8.

A traditional exegetical problem of the Pastoral Epistles concerns the high position that Paul attributes to himself. The Pastoral Epistles underline Paul's central role as the guardian of the sound doctrine that Jesus Christ has entrusted to the apostle and that he is handing over to Paul. Paul emphasizes his "appointment" as herald and apostle (1 Tim. 2:6; 2 Tim. 1:11). He speaks of the gospel as a deposit that he entrusts to others, maybe even to God (1:12; 2:2). It is Paul from whom the standard of sound teaching is heard (1:13). Because of this central place in the chain of gospel transmission, some biblical scholars ask whether Paul's role in the Pastoral Epistles approaches the role of Jesus Christ (Marshall 1999: 290 and Weiser 2003: 123–29; Läger 1996 is an example of this trend).

But if we analyze these sayings with the help of the four-place relation of giving, we do not obtain a picture in which Paul would approach Christ. In his self-giving, Christ is both the giver and the gift. In the apostolic acts of transmitting and entrusting the treasure (2 Tim. 1:14) to the next generations, Paul does not, strictly speaking, take any roles other than those of giver and recipient. It is important to distinguish Paul's sound doctrine from the false teachings, but in this act of discernment the gift of the gospel, the grace in Jesus Christ, remains christocentric. Paul's commitment even unto death does not entail the idea that Paul himself would be the gift spoken of in the gospel. He is the guardian of the deposit that, in 1:12, he can call his deposit, but this deposit is not Paul's gift but the gift of God. In this sense the self-giving of Paul is clearly different from the self-giving of Jesus Christ (Weiser 2003: 127).

In addition, there are no beneficiaries of Paul's sufferings in the sense of the christological acts of self-giving described in 1 Tim. 2:5–6 and Titus 2:14. Paul can compare his own self-giving with the libation sacrifice in 2 Tim. 4:6. But here, as in 1 Tim. 1:16, an exemplary act is intended. A truly sacrificial act can be understood to "produce" or "bring about" a surplus that can be ascribed to a beneficiary. Precisely this is intended by the fourth place of the Augustinian relation: the relational place of the beneficiary is filled by the person or group "for the sake of" which the sacrifice is done. An exemplary act may influence or move others observing this act. But the exemplary act does not produce anything more than an exhortation to follow the example being observed. Therefore, the persons observing and following an example are not outsiders but simply the recipients of the act of "giving an example" (Saarinen 2005: 110–25). In this sense one can clearly distinguish between sacrificial and exemplary acts of self-giving. Paul's self-giving may resemble Christ's example and may, in turn, set an example for Paul's followers. But an exemplary self-giving is different from the christological and soteriological *pro nobis* contained in 1 Tim. 2:5–6 and Titus 2:14.

GOOD WORKS IN THE SOCIETY

Titus 3:1–15

The third and last major part of the epistle concerns mainly the behavior of Christians in the society at large. The focus is no longer on the character formation of Christians, but on the signal value that their works give to all people. Christians are to behave as exemplary citizens (3:1–3). At the same time they should not think that they are saved by their good works. In an impressive manner, Paul recollects (3:4–7) the Christian truths that relate to baptism, Holy Spirit, and justification by the grace of Christ. In dealing with opponents, these truths are to be witnessed without being caught in disputations (3:8–11). The final verses (3:12–15) contain greetings and concrete admonitions.

Christians as Good Citizens (Titus 3:1–3)

Paul now reminds Titus to give seven admonitions to all members of the church. All these requirements deal with good citizenship. The exemplary behavior of Christians is motivated by the remark (2:15b) that no one should look down on persons practicing the Christian faith.

First, Christians should "subject" themselves to "rulers and authorities." The two notions are general and overlap (cf. Luke 12:11). The point is that all secular authorities are to be obeyed, a general admonition that resembles Rom. 13:1–7 and 1 Pet. 2:13–17. In the context of the Pastoral Epistles, such admonition underlines the need to display the Christian virtues to all people. Second, Christians ought "to be obedient." This is what subjecting to authorities often means in practice (Marshall 1999: 300–301).

Third, the church members should "be ready for every good work." As in Titus 2:14, good works generally refer to the external manifestation of the virtues of moderation. Fourth, they should not "speak evil of" anyone. The verb *blasphēmeō* may mean only speaking ill, but it is probable that some kind of religious connotation can be assumed, in other words, that Christians should not speak evil of other Christians or other religious matters. Fifth, Christians should "avoid quarreling" (cf. 1 Tim. 3:3), a vice often portrayed as typical of false teachers (6:4; Titus 1:10–11).

Sixth, Christians should be "gentle" (*epieikēs*). This Greek virtue can also mean "reasonable" and "conciliatory." Seventh, they ought to show patience to everybody. The word *prautēs* may mean "courtesy" or "gentleness" (2 Tim. 2:25). In 1 Tim. 6:11 *praupatheia* ("gentleness") expresses the idea of moderating the underlying emotion in a proper manner. Gentleness thus expresses a good emotion. Friendliness and patience belong to the essential characteristics of being *prautēs*. The emphasis is here laid on "to everyone," that is, Christians are not called to behave virtuously merely among each other, but it is important to behave in an exemplary manner in the society at large. The Christian virtue has grown from a narrow group identity to the consciousness of "we" as the whole of humankind.

As a contrast to these virtues, Paul in Titus 3:3 outlines the portrait of Christians in their earlier stage of life. In some sense, this negative picture mirrors the general human condition outside Christian faith. Since Paul aims at presenting the virtues in contrast to the vices, the description should not be taken too literally. Romans 1:29 may have served as a model, but the description also resembles the sickness from which Stoic philosophical therapy aims at curing the human (see appendix B).

In earlier times, the Christians who are now virtuous were "foolish" (*anoētoi*). The lack of reason or a disturbed mind is the point of departure in philosophical therapy. False teachers are also accused of *anoia* in 2 Tim. 3:9 (cf. 1 Tim. 6:5). Being "disobedient" (*apeithēs*) refers to the lack of obeying authorities (Titus 3:1), but it also alludes to the incapacity to obey reason. "Led astray" (*planōmenoi*) likewise refers to people who are deluded and deceived. The first three characteristics thus relate to the general phenomenon of foolishness or lack of rationality.

The fourth description, "slaves to various passions and pleasures" (*douleuontes epithymiais kai hēdonais poikilais*), is again reminiscent of philosophical therapy. In Stoicism, passions and desires hold people captive and can be cured with the help of reason (see appendixes A–B; Collins 2002: 359; Oberlinner 1996: 167–68). The Stoic picture is here connected with the Jewish-Christian view of human existence under the slavery of sin. At the same time, the fourth description explains the three first characterizations: passions and desires cause the state of being disobedient and led astray.

Since the presence of reason enables the *oikeiōsis*, the transition from "I" to "we," it also enables love and care for others. The remaining descriptions illustrate the social condition outside *oikeiōsis*. A person who lacks reason in this sense is envious and hates other people. Hatred and envy destroy human fellowship and cause humans to pass their days in malice. In this way 3:3 aims to present the paradigmatic state of the foolish person who lacks reason and social skills. In Paul's Christian application, God's loving kindness can lift humans from this despicable state. But the description is also intimately connected with the basic ideas of Stoic therapy of emotions and *oikeiōsis*.

Saving Presence of God through Jesus Christ (Titus 3:4–7)

After the parenetic and therapeutic description of the universal human condition, Paul continues with a theological passage that outlines some basic doctrines of the Christian faith (cf. 2:11–14). The despicable state of human beings was dramatically changed with the epiphany of the "goodness and loving kindness" (*hē chrēstotēs kai hē philanthrōpia*) of God. *Chrēstotēs* ("kindness, goodness, generosity") is used of God (Rom. 2:4; 11:22; Eph. 2:7) and of humans (Rom. 3:12; 2 Cor. 6:6; Gal. 5:22). In Titus 3:4 the goodness of God is the paradigmatic good work that, in addition to its salvific meaning, has an exemplary character (Marshall 1999: 312–13).

The same holds true with God's "philanthropy." The term is not used in this sense elsewhere in the New Testament (cf. Acts 28:2), but philanthropy is a major virtue of Stoicism. It also plays a major role in Philo (*Virtues* 51–174 [LCL 341.195–271]; *Gaius* 67 [LCL 379.35]; *Special Laws* 2.75; 3.156 [LCL 320.355, 573]; see Collins 2002: 361). The two divine virtues are here employed to connect the two points made by Paul. On the one hand, God's example should be imitated in the good works of Christians. On the other hand, God's goodness and philanthropy motivate the manifestation of the salvific activity of God through Christ. The language of manifestation connects Titus 3:4a with 2:11–13.

In 3:5 Paul recapitulates the language of justification by faith. Parallel formulations include Gal. 2:16; 3:11; Rom. 3:20–21; and Phil. 3:9. The wording of Titus 3:5 is thus shaped by Pauline tradition. Its appearance here is especially important, since Titus otherwise so often stresses the "good works" that witness sound doctrine. Without 3:5–7, the Letter to Titus would lack much of the Pauline soteriology. "Good works" are praised in 2:7, 14; 3:1, 8, 14, but here it is emphasized that we are not saved "because of . . . works" (*ex ergōn*). At this point, some exegetes even see a radicalization of Paul's view, because it is not only works of the law that are criticized, but even the works done "in righteousness" (Marshall 1999: 315, referring to Trummer 1978).

This may, however, be an exaggerated interpretation, since the author here only intends to contrast the mercy of God with human works. The phrase "according to his mercy" (*kata to autou eleos*) is intimately connected with "grace" (2:11) and "goodness and loving kindness" (3:4). Taken together, all these expressions aim at presenting the central and genuine Pauline thought that salvation, or justification, is not by our works, but by God's grace (cf. 3:7). A minor problem concerns the past tense related to "works . . . we had done." The point is not to say that good works would belong to the past; the rest of Titus massively points toward their continuing usefulness. The past tense employed in 3:4–6 continues to the present day.

In 3:5b–7 a brief theology of baptism and the Holy Spirit is outlined. We are saved "through the washing of rebirth and renewal by the Holy Spirit" (*dia loutrou palingenesias kai anakainōseōs pneumatos hagiou*). The phrase is difficult and has prompted various exegetical debates. An obvious problem concerns the precise role of the Holy Spirit in this process. Without entering this debate in detail, it can be said that new life is effected by the Holy Spirit, which has a central role in baptism. In this way the phrase is traditional and in keeping with, for instance, John 3:5.

Another difficult issue concerns the meaning of *palingenesia*, a word used only here and in Matt. 19:28 in the New Testament, which can mean many different kinds of regeneration in philosophical and religious texts (Marshall 1999: 319–20). The word refers to two different but related contexts: on the one hand, the salvific event of baptism is certainly meant. At the same time, the event of crossing the borderline from foolishness to a sound mind, from hatred to love, and from impiety to godliness (Titus 2:12; 3:1–3), may also be implied.

Anakainōsis means the renewal of one's mind in Rom. 12:2 (cf. Eph. 4:23). In Rom. 6:4 *kainotēs* is connected with baptism. Still another problem concerns the mutual relationship of the two concepts mentioned in Titus 3:5b. Although some scholars see here two distinct acts, resembling baptism and confirmation, it is more likely that *palingenesia* and *anakainōsis* are synonymous (Marshall 1999: 321). The translation of the Vulgate, *per lavacrum regenerationis et renovationis Spiritus Sancti*, may have given motivation to later theologians to think about regeneration and renovation as two distinct aspects of salvation.

In baptism, God's saving work occurs through the Holy Spirit, which is released for Christians through Jesus Christ. Without reading too much trinitarian theology into 3:6, it is important to note that in baptismal theology all three divine agents are involved (Matt. 28:19). The pouring out of the Spirit relates to the Pentecostal promise of Joel 2:28–29 and Acts 2:17, 33. As in Acts 2:38, the saving work of Jesus Christ has made the fulfilment of this promise possible. In this way the baptismal gift of the Holy Spirit manifests God's philanthropy.

In Titus 3:7 the past tense of 3:3–6 is again shifted toward the future. Christians are "justified by . . . grace" (*dikaiōthentes tē . . . chariti*). The "grace" refers back to 2:11 and thus comprehends the whole salvific event described here. Although the phrase is Pauline and probably derives from Rom. 3:24, the emphasis here lies in the completion of the event of justification. It is not possible to read Titus 3:5–7 in terms of temporal sequence; thus we cannot conclude whether the pouring out of the Spirit precedes, coincides with, or follows justification (Marshall 1999: 323–24). At the present state, all these salvific events have been realized in those Christians to whom Paul addresses his words. Therefore, they should look toward the eschatological fulfilment and devote themselves to good works and exemplary conduct.

In 3:7b the future hope of "eternal life" is portrayed as the final goal. The Pauline phrase of "becom[ing] heirs" (Rom. 8:17; Gal. 3:29; 4:7) aims at motivating Christians to act already here and now in terms of their future hope. Because Christians are justified and have the Spirit and the hope of eternal life, they should make visible this new reality in their teaching and good works.

Dealing with Opponents (Titus 3:8–11)

The first phrase (3:8a; cf. 1 Tim. 3:1; 2 Tim. 2:11) emphasizes the certainty of what is said in the preceding doctrinal statement. It also leads to the concrete instructions that follow. In a similar manner, the next phrase, "I desire that you insist on these things," points out the necessity of defending sound doctrine.

The purpose of this activity is defined in Titus 3:8b. When Christians adhere to sound doctrine and see that the church leader defends it with great assurance, the believers will do good works in a "careful" (*phrontizō*) and "devoted" (*proistēmi*) manner. The first verb means "to think of, be intent on" and describes an activity that includes both intention and execution (Marshall 1999: 331). It relates to the overall idea of a sound and thoughtful mind that is needed for good actions. The second verb means "to exercise well" and refers to the skillful and devoted manner of performance.

The two verbs thus express an activity similar to the term "progress" in 1 Tim. 4:15. Progressing Christians train themselves in the practice of good works. The last sentence of Titus 3:8 is very general, and it is not quite clear to what "these things" refer. They may refer to sound doctrine in general, as the repetition of "these things" in 3:8 (NRSV) assumes. But it is also important to see the intimate connection between teaching and good works. Sound doctrine is "good and useful" (*kalos kai ōphelimos*) for everyone, that is, not only for orthodox Christians, but for all humans. Paul's point is that everyone who adheres to sound doctrine will progress in the practice of good works. Being *ōphelimos* is an important criterion of the authenticity of moral teaching. Chrysostom says that the Greeks "make the life and conduct the test of the doctrines" (NPNF[1] 13.533). According to Cicero's description of Greek philosophy (*De finibus* 3.33 [LCL 40.253]), *ōphelēma* proceeds from natural perfection (other parallels in Marshall 1999: 333).

In contrast to this, 3:9 lists actions that go against all progress in good works. As in 1 Tim. 6:4 and 2 Tim. 2:23, controversies are condemned as stupid, a remark that relates to the general insanity of false teachings (see appendix B). "Genealogies" and "quarrels about the law" (cf. 1 Tim. 1:4, 7–9) probably refer to the Jewish-Christian nature of Paul's opponents. The false teachers aim at presenting their own traditions, which provoke controversies. A general feature of false teachings is that they remain speculative verbal acrobatics and do not bring forth good works. Because of this they remain on the level of fruitless dispute.

Whereas sound doctrine promotes true progress and is thus useful (Titus 3:8), verbal controversies remain "unprofitable and worthless" (3:9). The word *mataios* ("worthless") is emphatically related to speech in 1:10 (*mataiologos*) and 1 Tim. 1:6 (*mataiologia*). In a remarkable manner Paul downplays the role of speech. It easily becomes "idle talk" (Titus 1:10) and leads to insane controversies. Although *logos* is highly valuable as the power of a sound mind and as the word of God, it can also be ambivalent in connection with speech that remains idle and worthless because it does not contribute to good works. Words and doctrines should contribute to the formation of character; they should lead to genuine care for others.

The advice given in 3:10 shows in its own way the limits of the power of words. A teacher of sound doctrine should engage in dialogue with false teachers. But he should not continue disputes. If two admonitions cannot alter the course of affairs, he has done his duty. It would be harmful to continue the dispute. The person "who causes divisions" is here called *hairetikos anthrōpos* (Vulgate: *homo hereticus*). Titus 3:10 is thus a classical locus telling how heretics are to be treated. They need to be corrected twice, but after that the orthodox Christians need not have anything to do with them.

The substantive *hairesis* ("choice") can also denote a school of thought in the sense having particular beliefs. Titus 3:10 is the only place in the New Testament in which the adjective *hairetikos*, derived from the word *hairesis*, is used, and here it clearly means "heretic." Pharisees are called *hairesis* (Acts 15:5; 26:5), meaning simply that they are a religious group. In Paul's early epistles (1 Cor. 11:18–19; Gal. 5:20), the word already begins to have a negative connotation, because the apostle is critical of the formation of different factions among Christians (Oberlinner 1996: 186–87). In Titus 3:10 the same idea of causing divisions is meant, but at the same time the phrase *homo hereticus* connotes the rigid, obstinate, and quarrelsome behavior of the false teachers in general. In this sense heretics begin to receive the character of eclectics who stick to an idiosyncratic set of beliefs.

In 3:11 Paul underlines his point by saying that such a person is sinful. In addition, the eclectic and idiosyncratic nature of this conviction makes this person "self-condemned" (*autokatakritos*). This word is very rare but the point is clear. The behavior of heretics witnesses to their state of mind and can, over a longer period of time, be observed by orthodox Christians. If two admonitions by a sound-minded authority cannot influence the idiosyncratic beliefs of heretics, they are beyond remedy. The state of being "perverted" (*exestraptai*) means a continuing, maybe even a permanent state of mind.

The idea of being *autokatakritos* may express a counterpoint to the process of *oikeiōsis* that proceeds from "I" to "we." The person who lacks all openness and obstinately remains in individual selfhood sets himself or herself outside the community. Neither can the community reach this person by means of rational discussion and loving care. In such a case the community cannot be blamed, for the chronically obstinate person is responsible for this immutable state. In addition to this "therapeutic" interpretation, 3:10–11 probably reflects the pastoral situation of early Christians. The advice given to Titus as church leader is a pragmatic way of dealing with problematic groups (for disciplinary measures in the earliest church, see Oberlinner 1996: 190–93).

Final Instructions and Greetings (Titus 3:12–15)

The final part of the epistle contains customary instructions and greetings. The only geographical name mentioned is that of Nicopolis, which is generally thought to refer to Actia Nicopolis, the major city of Epirus on the western coast of Greece. No other sources relate Paul to this city. Since ships do not travel during the winter season, the apostle chooses a given place to proclaim the gospel and help build the church (Marshall 1999: 341–42).

With regard to the personal names of 3:12, we know Artemas from no other sources. Tychicus is sent to Ephesus by Paul (2 Tim. 4:12). He is introduced as "dear/beloved brother" and "faithful minister" (Eph. 6:21; Col. 4:7) and also appears in Acts 20:4. We do not know why Titus should do his "best to come to" meet Paul at Nicopolis; a similar wish is expressed to Timothy in 2 Tim. 4:9. One intention of the phrase may be to underline the extending sphere of influence of the church leader.

Zenas is mentioned only in Titus 3:13. His characterization as a lawyer may relate to the quarrels about the law in 3:9 or to the controversies with regard to the church order. The skillful rhetor Apollos is mentioned in Acts 18:24–19:1; 1 Cor. 1:12; 3:4–6, 22; 4:6; 16:12. No reason is given why Zenas and Apollos should be sent on their way. One could think that they were the bearers of the Epistle to Titus and are for this reason commended by Paul. It can also be noteworthy that both pairs include one name that is fairly well known in the Pauline tradition and another name that appears only here. In this way new carriers of sound doctrine join with the well-known adherents of Paul (Marshall 1999: 342–44).

In Titus 3:14 Paul summarizes the overall exhortation to progress in good works. The "people" here means "our people," that is, the Christians in Crete. As in 3:8, Christians are to "devote [*proistēmi*] themselves to good works." The clause expressing the purpose, *eis tas anankaias chreias* ("to meet the necessary needs"), is somewhat difficult. It may mean "urgent needs" (NRSV) among Christians or "problems in the community at large" (Marshall 1999: 346). The formulation may also indicate the practice of neighborly love, the turning from "I" to "we" in general. Exercising good works thus means the progress of Christians in the *oikeiōsis*. Since good works are the fruit of faith, Christians should not be "fruitless" or "unproductive" (*akarpoi*). The parable of the sower admonishes Christians not to remain fruitless but to bear fruit (Matt. 13:22–23).

The final greetings are expressed briefly. As in Rom. 16:16b and 2 Cor. 13:12b, "all" unite in the greeting. The greeting may include some kind of group spirit in the phrases "all who are with me" and "those who love us," indicating that the group of orthodox Pauline Christians is meant. The phrase "in the faith" may strengthen this impression; there may be others who have suffered shipwreck in the faith (1 Tim. 1:19) or have wandered away from the faith (6:10). Titus 3:15b expresses a slight rhetorical contrast to this connotation. The closing benediction of 1 Tim. 6:21 and 2 Tim. 4:22 is extended with *pantōn* so that the grace is said to be with "all" of you. Thus the closing benediction of the Letter to Titus is more inclusive than that of 1–2 Timothy (cf. Heb. 13:25).

PHILEMON

Introduction to Philemon

In spite of its brevity, the Letter of Paul to Philemon continues to draw historical and theological attention in biblical scholarship. The letter is generally considered to have been written or dictated by the apostle himself. It offers a perspective to Paul's treatment of practical matters in a particular occasion. In prison Paul has converted a fugitive slave, Onesimus, to the Christian faith. Now he sends Onesimus back to his Christian master, Philemon, and asks that the master receives him as a "beloved brother" (Phlm. 16). But Paul does not explicitly ask for the release of Onesimus.

The historical and theological interest of interpreters primarily relates to the difficult and complex issue of slavery. Paul declares that in Christ "there is no longer slave or free" (Gal. 3:28). But he also advises slaves not to be concerned about their condition but to make use of it, "for whoever was called in the Lord as a slave is a freed person belonging to the Lord" (1 Cor. 7:21–22). What do these eschatological statements mean in concrete life? Is Paul in favor of the abolition of slavery, or does he mean only that Christian slaves should concentrate on their inner freedom in the realm of thoughts, feelings, and convictions? And what are the duties of Christian masters with regard to their Christian and non-Christian slaves?

Answering these questions is difficult for two reasons. The first reason has to do with the understanding of slavery. The institution of slavery in the Greco-Roman world was many-sided (for the following, see Barth and Blanke 2000: 3–103). The life conditions and careers of the slaves varied enormously. While the work in mines and on galleys was miserable and led to slow death, the life of a house slave in a city could be relatively comfortable. As teachers or otherwise specialized workers, slaves often had much better living conditions than poor free persons. Because slaves needed food, clothing, and other maintenance, slave labor was often more expensive than the work of free persons. It was therefore not necessarily economic to keep slaves for simple tasks, and it may have been a privilege to be a house slave rather than a poor freeman. As a rule, however, slaves certainly wanted to become free.

The release of slaves was a practice motivated by contractual, economic, and philanthropic reasons. Debt slaves served a certain period that gave a proper compensation for their debt. If the slave owner could no longer afford to keep slaves, they were sold or released. Slaves could sometimes buy themselves out of slavery with the money at their disposal. Humanitarian reasons and the desire for a good reputation were also known as reasons for releasing slaves. The concrete practice of release, the so-called manumission, was regulated by law. Freedmen normally signed a contract in which they agreed to serve their former master as a loyal servant for a certain period. After this period, they could gain total independence. Their legal status nevertheless remained that of a freedman or freedwoman.

I cannot here enter into the complexities of the institutions of slavery and manumission. Relevant for the understanding of Philemon is above all the awareness that slavery was a legally established institution that in many ways sustained the daily life of both society and household, providing the basic conditions of life for both masters and their slaves. Although slaves dreamed of freedom and although both Hellenistic philosophers and Jewish teachers could emphasize the humanitarian reasons and formulate some basic rights in the treatment of individual slaves, the institution of slavery was a legally and socially established pillar of society.

The second reason has to do with Paul's flow of thought in Philemon. The epistle is written in a personal and polite fashion that often avoids concrete and univocal statements. That Paul sends Onesimus back to his master indicates that Onesimus continues his life as a slave of Philemon. And yet, Phlm. 16 says that Onesimus should no longer be treated as a slave. It is possible even to wonder whether Onesimus actually is a fugitive, since this is not spelled out. Paul wants to leave the matter for Philemon to decide, but his open-ended formulations do not make clear what the apostle recommends be done.

This ambiguity has left its traces on the interpretation history of Philemon. The early interpretation history is dominated by the so-called antienthusiastic attitude. According to this view, Philemon aims at showing that Christians do not aim at a revolution of the prevailing society. A fugitive slave who has converted to Christianity should return to his legal position as slave. John Chrysostom argues that, when Christian slaves return to their masters and continue their life as faithful slaves, even the unbelieving Greeks can see that slaves and servants can have faith and that Christianity does not want to question the existing norms of the society (NPNF[1] 13.545–57). Likewise argues Theodore of Mopsuestia (*In epistolas Pauli commentarii* 2.258–86 [Theodore 1882]). The different social roles and estates are established by God, and every individual should stay in his or her proper role (Stuhlmacher 1975: 58–59; Barth and Blanke 2000: 203–5).

In his 1527 *Lecture on Philemon*, Martin Luther uses Onesimus as an example of a person who is misled by the idea of freedom. Against the Radical Reformers, Luther argues that Paul respects the prevailing legal rights of property and does not abolish slavery. Calvin likewise affirms the need to respect the prevailing order, but he also underlines Paul's wish (Phlm. 13) to get Onesimus back into his service (Stuhlmacher 1975: 61; Barth and Blanke 2000: 206–7; WA 25.69–78; Calvin, Corpus reformatorum 80.437–50).

In the eighteenth and nineteenth centuries interpreters begin to emphasize Phlm. 16, in which Onesimus is said to no longer be a slave. J. A. Bengel (1887) holds that Paul expects Philemon to manumit Onesimus. J. B. Lightfoot (1904) considers that the church fathers were too timid in their conclusions. For Lightfoot, Philemon and the New Testament as a whole tend toward a peaceful and gradual abolition of slavery. John Knox (1960) claims that the real purpose of Philemon is the release of Onesimus (Stuhlmacher 1975: 62–65; Barth and Blanke 2000: 209–12, 225–26).

The interpretation history shows that it is possible to read Philemon from a conservative as well as from an emancipatory perspective. The conservative perspective has traditionally been more influential. Today's historical scholarship again tends toward it, especially because the emancipatory view runs the risk of being anachronistically conditioned by the modern dislike of slavery. Both perspectives receive, however, important support in Paul's text. It may therefore be necessary to attempt a reading that can combine the two views: (1) the need to preserve the social order and (2) the clear affirmation of Gal. 3:28 and Phlm. 16, that is, of releasing slaves and achieving equality (Stuhlmacher 1975: 65–66). My brief commentary adheres to the second but admits that some open-ended wordings tend toward the first. I set out to explain this tendency so that it remains secondary and the actual message of Philemon is emancipatory.

Although Philemon is generally considered to be Paul's work, the place and date of the epistle remain disputed. Paul speaks of himself as an old man and as a prisoner (vv. 1, 9). It may therefore be most plausible to situate Philemon to Paul's imprisonment in Rome between 61 and 63, although earlier captivities in Ephesus and in Caesarea cannot be ruled out (Barth and Blanke 2000: 121–28, 494–95).

Philemon contains obvious resemblances with Colossians. Indeed, Onesimus is mentioned as coming to Colossae in Col. 4:9. Paul's fellow prisoner Aristarchus sends greetings in Phlm. 24 and Col. 4:10. Epaphras from Colossae is free in 4:12, but prisoner in Phlm. 23. Archippus is mentioned in v. 2 and Col. 4:17; some commentators even claim that he is the master of Onesimus (Knox 1960; Winter 1987, discussed in Barth and Blanke 2000: 227, 257). In any case, it is reasonable to suppose that Philemon was sent to Colossae and that Philemon lived in that city, which Paul himself never visited. It is not possible, however, to say with certainty whether Philemon was written before or after Colossians. If both texts stem from Paul's hand and refer to the same event in Onesimus's life, they can even be almost simultaneous.

Ignatius of Antioch mentions a certain Onesimus as a bishop of Ephesus (*To the Ephesians* 1.3; 2.1; 6.2 [Ehrman 2003: 1.221, 225]). The letter shows affinities with Philemon, and it is often claimed that (1) the fugitive slave later became bishop and (2) the reasons for the canonization of Philemon are related to that event. Although we do not have enough evidence to verify or falsify these claims, the tradition of exegesis often held that Onesimus was manumitted and later became a bishop (Barth and Blanke 2000: 141–50).

The purpose of Philemon is obvious: it is a letter of recommendation that should accompany Onesimus and create good will in Philemon so that he would not punish the returning slave. On the way home, such a letter may also to some extent protect the fugitive slave from imprisonment by the legal authorities. Other similar letters are known; the most famous is the letter of Pliny the Younger to Sabinianus from around AD 110. In this letter, quoted in many commentaries on Philemon (e.g., Barth and Blanke 2000: 86–87), Pliny appeals for a freedman who has run away and thus violated his duty of servanthood. Like Paul (Phlm. 16), Pliny pleads for a relationship of brotherly love between the servant and his master and recommends the returning servant as worthy of such love.

Although Philemon was originally composed for this practical purpose, the epistle also creates a "symbolic universe" (Petersen 1985) in which a prisoner, Paul, pleads for the release or at least for the kind treatment of another nonfree person, Onesimus. Neither Paul nor Onesimus is free, but their being Christian transcends external boundaries. In a paradoxical manner, the epistle stresses joy, love, and confidence between people in chains. Christians have become prisoners "of" and "in" Jesus Christ (Phlm. 9, 23). Although Philemon is a practical and occasional piece of writing, it also contains a deeper message. In the exposition, this deeper message relates to freedom, love, and gratitude as the motivational grounds of Christian behavior. It is further noteworthy that Philemon is addressed not only to Philemon but to the church (vv. 2, 25).

Philemon is included in Marcion's canon as well as in Canon Muratori (Barth and Blanke 2000: 202–3). The epistle is extensively commented on by many church fathers. Although they often present the argument that the occasional nature of Philemon raises some doubts with regard to its place in the canon, they more or less unanimously defend the canonicity of this epistle. Thomas Aquinas (1888), Martin Luther (WA 25.69–78), and Calvin (Corpus reformatorum 80.437–50) also commented on Philemon (see the reception history in Stuhlmacher 1975: 58–66 and Barth and Blanke 2000: 200–214). One of the most interesting later expositors is Hugo Grotius. In his 1642 commentary, Grotius uncovers the legal and social background of slavery in the Roman Empire. According to Grotius (1756: 2/1.831–37), Paul's intervention remains within the boundaries of the Roman law: the apostle does not question the legal right of the master over the slave (Stuhlmacher 1975: 61–62; Barth and Blanke 2000: 207–8). Given that a letter of recommendation may need to be shown to various authorities, it is prudent to formulate it in accordance with existing laws. Among contemporary commentators, Markus Barth and Helmut Blanke (2000) present extensive background information on virtually all historical matters relevant for the understanding of Philemon.

Philemon consists of three parts. Paul first addresses the epistle in his usual manner and recollects the exemplary faith and love of Philemon (vv. 1–7). He then presents a friendly intervention for Onesimus, underlining the usefulness of this slave for both Paul and Philemon and hoping that the fugitive would be well received and eventually released (vv. 8–21). The concluding part of the epistle deals with Paul's travel plans and customary greetings (vv. 22–25).

Address and Expressions of Gratitude (Phlm. 1–7)

The epistle begins with naming the sender and addressee, as is customary in the letters of the Hellenistic period. As in several Pauline letters (1–2 Thessalonians, 2 Corinthians, Philippians, Colossians), Timothy is mentioned as cosender. From these letters as well as from Acts we know that Timothy frequently accompanied Paul in his missionary travels. Timothy is regularly called "brother" (Col. 1:1; 2 Cor. 1:1).

Paul's self-description as "a prisoner of Jesus Christ" (*desmios christou iēsou*) underlines his position under legal bondage. Thus his situation resembles that of Onesimus. The repetition of the words *desmios* and *desmoi* ("chains") in Phlm. 1, 9, 10, 13 strengthens the impression of bondage and evokes sympathy in the reader. At the same time, Paul's imprisonment does not diminish his being in Christ. The deeper truth of his existence is that he is Christ's prisoner in the same sense as he is "prisoner in the Lord" in Eph. 4:1. The description is also applicable to the case of Onesimus: the worldly bondages are secondary, since Christian slaves and prisoners nevertheless remain in Christ.

Philemon is described as "beloved friend" (*agapētos*) and "co-worker" (*synergos*). In the New Testament, his name appears only in Phlm. 1. Given the resemblances with Colossians, it is plausible to assume that Philemon was sent to Colossae. *Apostolic Constitutions* 7.46 (ANF 7.478) mentions Philemon as bishop of Colossae (see the introduction to Philemon and exposition of Phlm. 23–24). Philemon 4–7 describes Philemon as a benefactor to the "saints," that is, Christians. He even has a church in his house (v. 2) and can thus be considered a committed Christian and a relatively wealthy man as well as an important friend and coworker of Paul.

The name Apphia appears only in v. 2, whereas Archippus is also mentioned in Col. 4:17. Later tradition, for instance, John Chrysostom, held the two persons to be Philemon's wife and son (NPNF[1] 13.547; Barth and Blanke 2000: 255–56). A spurious postscript to Philemon available in the NA[27] apparatus calls Archippus a deacon, and *Apostolic Constitutions* 7.46 (ANF 7.478) lists him as bishop of Laodicea. Because the house church is mentioned immediately after Archippus, it is possible, though very unlikely, that Paul primarily addresses Archippus and his house church (so Knox 1960: 49–61; see Barth and Blanke 2000: 258). All these interpretations suffer from lack of evidence. It is most reasonable to say that Apphia and Archippus are fellow Christians related to the church in Philemon's house. The designation of Archippus as "fellow soldier" echoes Phil. 2:25.

The "house church" (*hē kat' oikon ekklēsia*) is a typical phenomenon of the Pauline Epistles. In the biblical narrative, this phenomenon grows from the shared meals in Jerusalem (Acts 1:13; 2:46; 5:42; 12:12). Romans 16:5 and 1 Cor. 16:19 mention the church that meets in Rome in the house of Prisca and Aquila. It is reasonable to assume that some of the early Christians were relatively wealthy homeowners who could offer a spacious meeting place for the congregations. The meeting room of the most prominent extant house church at Dura Europos, a first-century private home converted into a house church in the second or early third century, measures five meters by thirteen meters. Around forty persons could assemble in such rooms (Stuhlmacher 1975: 70–75; Barth and Blanke 2000: 260–62). Through addressing the letter to the church, Paul counts on a broader reception. Philemon is not a private letter, but an epistle that was to be read by a larger community. This may have put a certain amount of pressure on Philemon (Barth and Blanke 2000: 493).

The apostolic blessing (Phlm. 3) is found in many Pauline letters as well as in 1–2 Peter. While "peace" alludes to the Jewish greeting, "grace" emphasizes the Christian message of God's free gift of salvation and life. In a similar manner, "God our Father" applies to the God of Israel who reveals himself as the God of Christians in Jesus Christ. The apostolic blessing thus expresses a nonidentical repetition of Jewish traditions in Christianity.

Philemon 4–7 aims at preparing Philemon for the actual intervention of Paul in vv. 8–21. By appealing to his own intercession as well as to the Christian virtues of Philemon, Paul attempts to create an atmosphere of gratitude that is needed for his intervention. In addition to this rhetorical purpose, vv. 4–7 contain several informative details concerning the faith and life of the early Christians.

The atmosphere of gratitude begins to be effectively outlined in v. 4. Paul thanks his God when he remembers Philemon in his prayers. Paul is thus himself grateful when he prays for the recipient of Philemon. The reason for this gratitude is spelled out in v. 5. Paul hears of Philemon's love for all Christians; he also obtains information regarding Philemon's faith. A modern reader is often ignorant of the great importance of the virtue of gratitude in classical Christian texts. Thomas Aquinas (*Summa theologiae* 2/2 QQ. 106–7) and the Heidelberg Catechism (Müller 1999: 682–719), for instance, treat thankfulness as a major virtue and regard ingratitude as an elementary vice.

In the ancient economics of giving and receiving favors, the proper amount of gratitude was important. Favors are to be received with proper gratitude, without a feeling of indebtedness, but with a willingness to give favors to persons from whom favors are received. Mutual favors and mutual gratitude create permanent but voluntary liaisons within a group of persons. Expressions of gratitude serve the purpose of strengthening these liaisons in order that the exchange of favors may continue in the future. At the same time, the freedom of both partners is underlined when gratitude is expressed. Favors are not calculated by means of bookkeeping, but each favor and each expression of gratitude is a unique event.

The next favor is not added to the old account; instead, it initiates a new account. At the same time, however, the successive favors become a chain of voluntary giving and receiving (the classical discussion is Seneca's *On Favors*, esp. books 1–2 [Seneca 1995: 193–241]; see also appendix C).

Paul plays with the subtleties of this voluntary economics. In Phlm. 4–5 he says that he is grateful for the faith and love of Philemon. In v. 6 Paul reverses the order of gratitude: Philemon is encouraged to realize the goodness around him so that he also can be grateful. The text of v. 6 is very difficult. My interpretation largely follows the translation of Barth and Blanke, but with some amendments. I prefer to translate v. 6 as follows: "I ask that your faith communion [*hē koinōnia tēs pisteōs sou*] be a source of energy [*energēs genētai*] to recognize all the good that is found in us [*en hēmin*], toward Christ."[1]

It is not possible to discuss here all details of this translation. I prefer the NA²⁷ reading, "in us," over its alternative, "in you." The NRSV also prefers *en hēmin*, but it interprets this phrase and the idea of *koinōnia* in an actualistic fashion. It is not "our doing for Christ" that is at stake here. Rather, the good found in Paul's party is supposed to evoke Philemon's gratitude so that both parties finally become oriented toward Christ. *Koinōnia tēs pisteōs* does not mean an operative "sharing of faith" (NRSV) but rather the communion of faith present in Philemon's house church. Given this, it is plausible to assume that while v. 5 and v. 7 describe Paul's gratitude, v. 6 focuses on the emergence of gratitude in Philemon.

In v. 5 Paul expresses his gratitude because of what he has heard of Philemon. In v. 6 he wishes that Philemon's own house church enables him to become grateful for the goodness found in Paul and his coworkers. Maybe some Pauline members of Philemon's house church, for instance, Epaphras (Col. 4:12), exemplify this goodness. In Phlm. 7 Paul returns to his own gratitude vis-à-vis Philemon. This gratitude finds emphatic expression in Paul's joy and encouragement, attitudes that are very much needed in prison. The theme of mutual gratitude based on free exchange creates a dramatic contrast to the conditions of slavery and imprisonment. Love and gratitude define the being of Paul and Philemon as Christians, whereas many external constraints define their being as worldly people.

Through Philemon "the hearts of the saints" are "given rest" (*anapauō*). This phrase resembles 1 Cor. 16:18 and 2 Cor. 7:13, which also speak of the rest of the spirit. This way of speaking relates to the Jewish Sabbath and to the use of *anapauō* and *anapausis* in the Septuagint. In Phlm. 7 and 20 Philemon appears as the giver of this rest. In other words, Philemon is supposed to perform acts of hospitality toward "the saints," that is, Christians. At the same time, the idea of giving rest also embraces the broader dimensions of security and spiritual nourishment. Paul is grateful for this comprehensive *anapausis* provided by Philemon.

1. "Few passages in the New Testament have been interpreted and translated in so many different ways," says Riesenfeld 1982: 251. For textual and other problems, see Barth and Blanke 2000: 280–91 and Fitzmyer 2000: 98–100.

This refection and recreation consist of all that a house church can provide: food, shelter, security, spiritual nourishment.

Appeal for Onesimus (Phlm. 8–21)

Paul continues his rhetorics of persuasion in Phlm. 8–9. "For this reason" refers to vv. 4–7, meaning that the relationship of Paul and Philemon is based on mutual love and gratitude. Paul mentions in passing that he would have the *parrēsia* ("boldness") simply to command Philemon to act properly, but he prefers to make an appeal based on love and gratitude.

The theme of love goes through Philemon. Philemon's love for all Christians (vv. 5, 7) is transformed in v. 9 into an argument based on love. Paul calls both Philemon and Onesimus "beloved" (vv. 1, 16). Although Paul's use of *agapē* in some way always entails the love of God in Christ, his appeal to love in Philemon underlines the social and interhuman dimension. The relationship among Christians is not based on duties and economic exchange, but it is characterized by a loving mutual trust. Because Christians experience both the love of God and the love of their neighbors, they are equipped with a surplus of gratitude that prompts new voluntary actions motivated by the same love. In this manner love both creates and sustains the atmosphere of treating one's neighbors as brothers and sisters.

The end of v. 9 is difficult for several reasons (for more detail, see Barth and Blanke 2000: 319–24 and Fitzmyer 2000: 105–6). The NRSV assumes that Paul undertakes a brief self-reflection, maybe in order to evoke sympathy in Philemon. When an old man and prisoner appeals to love it is difficult not to concede to his wishes. This is the most probable understanding of v. 9b. It is also possible to understand *presbytēs* to refer to an office: Paul, ambassador of Christ. Another difficulty is raised by the Vulgate's *cum sis talis ut Paulus* ("because you are the same kind as Paul"). This would be a very logical reading, since Philemon is asked to act for love's sake, as does Paul. But the Vulgate reading is not supported by any extant Greek manuscripts. These variant readings have, however, been influential in the interpretation history.

In v. 10 the actual appeal that is the main purpose of the epistle is made. The verb *parakalō* used in vv. 9–10 generally means "to ask"; the preposition *peri* here clearly indicates that Paul is asking for a favor on behalf of Onesimus. The end of v. 10 is again difficult. A literal translation would be as follows: "my own child whom I have begotten/born in chains, Onesimus." The basic idea is clear enough: Paul has converted Onesimus to Christianity in prison, thus becoming his spiritual father. The verb *gennaō* can refer to both the male and female contribution in creating a child. We therefore obtain theological sentences in which the father gives birth to a child. This inclusive language of procreation has found a rich use in Christian spirituality (for historic and linguistic background, see Barth and Blanke 2000: 329–35).

The word *onēsimos* is synonymous with *euchrēstos* ("useful"; v. 11). Onesimus has gone through a transformation from potentiality (*achrēstos*, "useless") to actuality. When he is now sent back to his master, Philemon receives more than he has lost. The text of v. 12a is very difficult and several variant readings are possible (Barth and Blanke 2000: 351–62; Gnilka 1982: 46–47). The basic idea is the sending back of Onesimus, saying that he is in some sense Paul's "own heart." Here (cf. v. 7) *splanchna* ("bowels, heart") also connotes womb and the embryo; the expression continues the picture of giving birth. In Paul's bosom, Onesimus has been born or transformed from a mere potential to an actually useful person.

In vv. 13–14 Paul formulates a complicated wish. He would have liked to keep Onesimus, because he needs service for the gospel during his imprisonment. The phrase *hyper sou* probably means an act of substitution: Philemon is in fact obliged to render this service himself, but Onesimus could act in the place of his master. Paul does not want to undertake such a decision, but he wants Philemon to act voluntarily in this matter. Therefore he sends the slave back to his legal master.

Philemon 13–14 employs three words that emphatically denote a voluntary action: first *boulomai* ("to want"), then *thelō* ("to will, consent"), and finally *hekousion* ("voluntary"). All these words play a role in philosophical contexts (Sorabji 2000: 319–40 and Chappell 1995 are particularly helpful), but here their use is conditioned by the idea that the services taking place out of love and gratitude need to be voluntary. Paul does not appeal directly to duties and needs, but he points out that both parties are supposed to act on the basis of free will. The obvious problem following from this usage is that the recipient of Paul's letter does not necessarily obtain a clear picture of what the sender actually wants.

The most probable message of vv. 13–14 is that either Onesimus or Philemon himself should be available to help Paul in prison. This message is, however, obscured by vv. 15–17. Philemon 15 is relatively clear in its purpose. The verb *chōrizō* ("to separate") means local separation, whereas *apechō* ("to hold properly") relates to possession. The flight of Onesimus has caused a relatively brief loss that is amply compensated by the return of a new Onesimus, a Christian who is bound with new ties to his master. The logical problem of this meaning is that it suggests, in seeming contrast to vv. 13–14, that Onesimus will permanently stay with Philemon.

In v. 16 Paul spells out the nature of the new bond between the slave and his master. Onesimus should no longer be treated as slave, but as "beloved brother." Paul calls Philemon his "brother" (vv. 7, 20); Philemon should likewise treat Onesimus as a brother. Given the overall atmosphere of Philemon, which stresses the voluntary character of relationships among Christians and underlines the idea of acting out of love, it is natural to interpret v. 16 in its literal and plain meaning. Philemon is to be treated "no longer as a slave," that is, he needs to be manumitted and eventually set free.

The relationships among Christians should not be based on coercion or even on legal and moral obligations. Christians should act out of love; this sometimes means renouncing the service and help available. Paul can voluntarily send Onesimus back and thus give up the help he needs. Philemon is, in turn, subtly advised to act according to the same paradigm of voluntary altruism. In other words, he should act out of brotherly love toward Onesimus and give him his freedom. This reading also alleviates the tension between vv. 13–14 and v. 15.

My exposition of v. 16 departs from the antienthusiastic strain of interpretation tradition and approaches the emancipatory view (see the introduction to Philemon). Because Philemon is formulated in a very polite and open-ended manner, one cannot logically rule out the alternative interpretations. My grounds for the emancipatory view are related to the overall emphasis of gratitude, freedom, and love in Philemon. With his polite and open-ended formulations, Paul sets an example of freedom. Philemon should realize that this is the example to be followed in the case of Onesimus.

The overall purpose of Philemon is to be a recommendation letter accompanying Onesimus so that he would be treated well on his way back to the house of Philemon as well as after arriving there. Paul is not primarily asking Onesimus to be sent back to the apostle. He is primarily persuading Philemon to release Onesimus.

The more abstract and theological purpose of Philemon has to do with the teaching of freedom, love, and gratitude. Christians should be able to renounce their legal and moral claims and learn to act out of love and gratitude. In sending Onesimus back to Philemon, Paul sets an example of this behavior. He cannot command directly that his example should be followed, because such a command would be self-contradictory. Voluntary actions, loving deeds, and the state of being grateful cannot be commanded. But these phenomena can be imitated and learned through following the example. In 1 Cor. 4:16 Paul asks Christians to imitate him. A similar appeal of voluntary imitation is now made to Philemon.

There may, in addition to this, be a more concrete reason for Paul's open-ended or disguised formulations. If Onesimus is arrested on his way home, and if Paul's letter is to provide any help in such a case, it would not be prudent to write recommendations that directly challenge the existing Roman laws. Given this, the letter contains a double message: whereas a Roman official can read it as a harmless recommendation letter of a slave returning to his legal master, Philemon discovers the deeper meaning that urges him to do more than Paul says directly (cf. Phlm. 21).

Philemon 16b–17 underlines the point of equality among Christians and among humans in general. Onesimus is loved "most of all" (*malista*) by Paul and "how much more" (*posō mallon*) by Philemon. This characterization is not altogether consistent, but it nevertheless aims at emphasizing the voluntary love toward Onesimus. More importantly, this love is applicable to both "the person he is"[2] (*en sarki*, "in the flesh") and "in the Lord." In other words, voluntary love does not only exist within the faith communion, but is concerned with the person as he or she is.

In v. 17 Philemon is addressed as Paul's "partner" (*koinōnos*). This word can refer to a legal circumstance of partnership that obliges the partners to act in a certain manner (Barth and Blanke 2000: 474–75; Fitzmyer 2000: 116). It is more likely, however, that Paul refers to the partnership that exists in the faith communion (*koinōnia*; v. 6) among Christians. Since Paul and Philemon share the same faith communion, Philemon should receive Onesimus as he would receive Paul. In a somewhat concealed and polite sense, Paul continues to make the point of equality: Christians should love their neighbors and treat them as brothers and sisters.

Philemon 16–17 thus contains the central message of Philemon. The message of love and equal treatment is rooted in the attitude of voluntary gratitude. This message softly but consistently urges Philemon to release Onesimus. Paul's message appears in a somewhat concealed fashion, which may be due to his need to comply with the Roman law. The more obvious background reason for his polite formulations is, however, that gratitude and free will cannot be commanded.

In vv. 18–19a, Paul offers to provide compensation for the eventual harm caused to Philemon through the flight of Onesimus. The sentences are hypothetical, that is, there is no evidence of actual harm done by Onesimus. The purpose of Paul may be twofold: on the one hand, he wants to create additional good will in Philemon; on the other hand, if a Roman official were to read this recommendation, he would see that Paul aims at providing legal compensation. Through mentioning his personal signature, the so-called *cheirographon* (Barth and Blanke 2000: 482–83), Paul gives in v. 19a a sort of receipt that obliges him to give this compensation.

After providing this seemingly generous legal security, Paul returns to the deeper exchange of favors and gratitude that occurs among Christians. Onesimus in fact owes Paul his "own self" (v. 19b). Although the verb *prosopheilō* ("to owe") can indicate a financial obligation, it here relates to the idea that Philemon's status as a Christian owes to Paul's activities. One can assume that Paul has met Philemon, maybe even converted him to Christianity, and thus become Paul's spiritual "child" (1 Cor. 4:14; Gal. 4:19). At this deeper level of exchange, Paul in turn wants to "profit" (*oninēmi*) from Philemon. This verb relates to the name Onesimus.

The words of Phlm. 20b, "give my heart rest in Christ," continue the play with words. Onesimus was in v. 12 called the "heart" of Paul; this heart should now find a rest at the household of Philemon. The verb *anapauō* ("to give rest") again (cf. v. 7) has a rich spiritual meaning, referring to the Sabbath rest and to the spiritual

---

2. So translated in Barth and Blanke 2000: 450–51. See also Gnilka 1982: 52–53, who remarks that this is the only Pauline verse in which *en sarki* does not spell out a contrast to the Christian life but complements it.

nourishment. It should be clear to Philemon that this wordplay points toward the release of Onesimus. "In Christ" there are no longer slaves (Gal. 3:28).

Paul subtly advises Philemon to release Onesimus. His open-ended wordings are conditioned by the circumstantial need to comply with Roman law, but also and primarily by the need to spell out the voluntary character of Christian behavior. Given this argument, Phlm. 21 still belongs to Paul's actual appeal, in particular because it concludes with the words "you will do even more than I say." In this way Paul underlines that he has not said everything openly. The key word *hypakoē* ("obedience") refers to the proper hearing; the corresponding verb *hypakouō* means "to give ear."

One difficulty of v. 21 is that it seems to undermine the overall idea of Philemon's free decision (cf. v. 14). This difficulty is alleviated when *hypakoē* is understood as hearing and understanding properly what Christianity requires. It is thus not Philemon's obedience to Paul that is at stake here, but his correct attitude in the faith communion. This attitude calls Philemon to act lovingly and to renounce his legal rights with regard to a Christian brother. Paul is confident that Philemon recognizes this attitude and is obedient to its claims. Thus Paul knows that Philemon will do more than what Paul explicitly says.

In spite of this result one cannot claim that Philemon aims at abolishing all slavery. The letter deals with a particular case in which it is argued that a Christian master should no longer treat a Christian slave as an ordinary slave. The argument is not entirely based on the relationship among Christians, since Onesimus is a "brother" also "in the flesh" (v. 16). For this reason, Philemon displays a slight tendency to regard persons in general as brothers and sisters. But it is obvious that Paul does not say explicitly that all slavery should be abolished. He may have circumstantial reasons for not saying this: in the hands of a Roman official such a statement would be a disservice to Onesimus. But there is enough textual evidence to say that the so-called antienthusiastic reading misses the deeper message of Paul, which is emancipatory.

Travel Plans and Greetings (Phlm. 22–25)

Paul asks Philemon to prepare a "guest room" for him. If the letter is sent from Rome, Paul was most probably not able to fulfill the wish expressed in Phlm. 22. As in Phil. 1:19, he thinks that the prayers of the recipients of the epistle will help in his release. The main purpose of this wish is to be mindful and grateful for the prayers of the faithful.

The names mentioned in Phlm. 23–24 also occur in Col. 4:10–14. Instead of Aristarchus (4:10), Epaphras is now the fellow prisoner of Paul. The list of persons in Col. 4 is longer. Reasons for these slight differences remain hypothetical; in any case, Philemon and Colossians are closely related. Epaphras is a Colossian (Col. 1:7; 4:12), and it is likely that Philemon is sent to Colossae. In 4:9 Onesimus, "the faithful and beloved brother, who is one of you," is mentioned as coming to Colossae. This characterization makes it obvious that the same Onesimus is meant. If the two letters were composed simultaneously, it is somewhat odd that the status of Epaphras and Aristarchus has changed. Maybe Colossians has been written some time after Philemon.

The final benediction (Phlm. 25) is similar to Phil. 4:23. "The Lord Jesus Christ" alludes to Phlm. 3. Plural "your" underlines that the letter is sent not only to Philemon but to the faith communion. The "spirit" (*pneuma*) refers to the highest human faculty that is employed when will, consent, and voluntary conduct (v. 14) are being referred to.

JUDE

Introduction to Jude

The Letter of Jude has not drawn much attention in historical scholarship. It has been called the "most neglected book of the New Testament" (so the title of Rowston 1974). The same can be said with regard to its consideration by contemporary systematic theology. And yet, this epistle offers a fascinating window on the Jewish-Christian issues that continue to stimulate theological reflection.[1] Because Jude uses the motifs of the Jewish Bible to argue its Christian theology, the epistle offers a model of how Christians can use the Old Testament. The culmination point of this intertestamentary theology occurs in Jude 5, in which it is stated that "Jesus saved a people from the land of Egypt" (so the Vulgate [following many Greek manuscripts] and Neyrey 1993: 58).

Jude also employs two noncanonical Jewish texts, *1 Enoch* (Charlesworth 1985: 1.5–89) and the *Testament of Moses* (also called the *Assumption of Moses*; Tromp 1997), to argue that Christ will judge the world (vv. 14–15) and that Christians should leave the final judgment to the Lord (v. 9). This strategy may evoke some hermeneutical speculation. Does a noncanonical text become canonical when it is quoted in a canonical text? Such questions easily become pointless sophisms. When Paul quotes Epimenides in Titus 1:12, no canonical upgrading of Epimenides can be assumed. In addition, most of the Jewish examples used in Jude depict prominent themes of the Old Testament. Jude's didactic application of Jewish texts to a contemporary Christian situation, a sort of Christian midrash (Bauckham 1983: 4), sets an example that has been followed by many church fathers and later theologians.

My exposition of Jude differs from the exposition of the Pastoral Epistles and Philemon. I do not present a verse-by-verse exposition. Instead, I lay out the basic content of Jude through focusing on two theological main subjects of the epistle: Jesus Christ and the Christian faith. This procedure is designed to illustrate and to exemplify my postscript, arguing that a theological exposition aims at identifying the main subjects illuminated by various explanatory predicates.

I understand subject and predicate to be the two grammatical functions that constitute a sentence. The subject identifies the person or thing of which something

1. Jenson's *Systematic Theology* (1997–99), for instance, consistently interprets the Old Testament in the light of Jesus Christ in the same manner as Jude—though Jenson never quotes Jude.

is said. The predicate makes a statement about the subject. In a sentence, something is thus "predicated" of the subject. Given this, the predicate typically mediates between the subject named and the conceptual world of the reader, allowing him or her to learn something concerning the subject at stake.

The "main subjects" are the most important theological themes of a text. As I argue in more detail in the postscript, the main subjects cannot simply be presupposed, but they should be worked out as the end result of detailed expository work. In the case of Jude, however, I make an exception to this general rule. After the necessary introduction, I proceed directly to the two main subjects and their explanatory predicates.

This procedure has the advantage of showing, with regard to one short and exemplary text, what the hermeneutical end result argued in the postscript actually looks like. With respect to Jude, however, this procedure leaves at least three other expository aspects in its shadow. First, the exceptionally large number of uncertain and alternative readings preserved in the different manuscripts cannot be taken into account. A brief look at the footnotes of the NRSV or NA[27] shows the unusual number of Greek text variants. Second, I cannot discuss the precise sources of various Jewish quotes (in particular, Old Testament versus *1 Enoch*) employed in Jude. Current commentators like Richard Bauckham (1983) and Jerome Neyrey (1993) consider the various textual possibilities in more detail and offer English translations of many relevant sources. Third, minor theological terms and issues of the text remain unmentioned.

Jude was composed in the second half of the first century. The Jude mentioned as author in v. 1 claims to be the brother of James in a way that also makes him the brother of Jesus (Matt. 13:55). We do not have any comparative evidence to either verify or falsify this claim. The author employs good literary Greek, and he is obviously well trained in both Jewish tradition and Greek language. This observation need not disclaim the possible authorship by the brother of Jesus (contrary to Bauckham 1983: 15–16 and Neyrey 1993: 31). The brothers of Jesus are mentioned as missionaries in 1 Cor. 9:5. The Judas referred to in Acts 9:11 is sometimes identified with Jude the brother of Jesus. The Jewish-Christian themes of the epistle support the traditional conviction that this brother of Jesus was a missionary among the Jews. Eusebius preserves this tradition (*Ecclesiastical History* 3.19–20, 32 [NPNF[2] 1.148–49, 164]). Bede identifies Jude with Thaddeus (Matt. 10:3; Mark 3:18; Bray 2000: 246).

The purpose of the epistle is to combat "certain intruders" (Jude 4) who spread false teachings, exaggerate Christian freedom (v. 4), and "reject authority" (v. 8). As "worldly people" (v. 19) these false teachers are different from their ascetic counterparts in the Pastoral Epistles. But they nevertheless share some similar traits of character, being "ungodly" (vv. 4, 15), "grumblers and malcontents," and "bombastic in speech" (v. 16). They blemish the agape meals (v. 12) and cause divisions within the church (v. 19) (for the identity of these people, see Martin 1994: 68–75). Jude considers the root cause of such behavior to consist in the denial of the Lord Jesus Christ and in unbelief (vv. 4–5). Jude emphasizes the lordship of Christ (vv. 1–2, 4–5, 17, 21, 25) and the true nature of Christian faith (vv. 3, 20–23).

The final judgment and the issue of condemnation are important theological topics related to this overall aim. False teachers are guilty of "slander" (vv. 8, 10), whereas true Christians leave the final judgment to the Lord (v. 9). The opponents are among the sinners who have spoken against the Lord; but it is the Lord "who execute[s] judgment on all" (vv. 15–16). While true Christians should keep away from the false teachers and even hate the clothes they wear, Jude also recommends that they save their opponents and have mercy on them (v. 23). This double strategy stems from the view that all final judgment must be left to the Lord. If good Christians begin to condemn and slander their opponents, they make themselves guilty of the sin of the opposing party.

Although Jude criticizes the intruders, he does not consider this criticism to be a form of slander or condemnation. Unlike his opponents, Jude prefers "mercy, peace, and love" (vv. 2, 22–23). To understand Jude's own intention properly, it is important to see his double strategy of nonjudgmental criticism. A modern reader easily regards Jude as returning the slander to the opponents who have first slandered his party. But such a view is not consonant with the self-understanding of Jude, who leaves all final judgment to the Lord.

The epistle does not offer clues that could relate it to any geographical place or to a controversy known from other sources. Given the extensive use of Jewish texts, it is plausible to locate the epistle within Jewish Christianity in either Palestine or the Diaspora. Stylistic evidence makes it probable that Jude is a "genuine letter" in the sense that it is composed for the purpose of solving a real controversy. It is not a treatise against heresy in general, but is targeted to attack a group of real opponents (so Bauckham 1983: 3–4). But we do not know who these opponents were, nor where they exercised their influence.

The epistle contains three parts. In vv. 1–4 Jude greets his readers and presents the aim of his letter. In the body of the letter, vv. 5–23, Jude studies some Jewish texts and applies their message to the present situation of the recipients. The closing passage of this second part, vv. 17–23, underlines the importance of central Christian truths and virtues. The final part, vv. 24–25, presents a doxology in which God and Jesus Christ are praised.

The text of Jude is employed in 2 Pet. 2. Most commentators today think that 2 Peter borrows from Jude (Martin 1994: 138–39; Bauckham 1983: 8). I agree with this view and do not compare Jude and 2 Peter in more detail. For the attestation and later reputation of Jude, it is important that it is extensively quoted in another canonical text. Jude was accepted as authoritative by Tertullian, Clement, and Origen. It is also included in the Canon Muratori. The Syrian church accepted Jude into its canon only in the sixth century, but otherwise this epistle was considered authoritative at least from the late second century onward (Bauckham 1983: 16–17; Chaine 1939: 263–67). The church fathers commented on Jude fairly often, paying attention to his role as the brother of Jesus according to the flesh (Bray 2000: 245–59 presents an extensive collection).

The later reception history of Jude in the Christian church has remained somewhat marginal. Martin Luther, for instance, held that Jude is dependent on and contained in 2 Peter (WADB 7.386–87). Some European Reformers claimed Jude to be Deuterocanonical (Martin 1994: 82, quoting Metzger 1987: 244). On the other hand, Jude provided an important canonical model for the use and interpretation of Jewish texts in the Christian church. The modern exegetical view according to which Jude is older than 2 Peter gives this epistle a new prominence as one of the essential sources of early Jewish Christianity.

Although Jude has often been counted among those New Testament texts that represent the so-called early Catholicism, it is not helpful to treat Jude in too close a connection with, for instance, the Pastoral Epistles (Bauckham 1983: 8–11). The proximity of Jude to Jewish Christianity and its emphasis on divine judgment lend this epistle a theological color that may be better understood in the context of Matthew and Mark. This does not mean, of course, that Jude would not be a "catholic" letter. Although its Jewish style of making didactic comparisons sometimes appears peculiar, Jude fundamentally defends a theology in which Christians "pray in the Holy Spirit; keep [them]selves in the love of God; [and] look forward to the mercy of our Lord Jesus Christ" (vv. 20–21). Jude offers an important early witness to the trinitarian faith of the early church.

Jesus Christ

The most frequent and most important explanatory predicate of Jesus Christ is that he is Lord (*kyrios*; Jude 4, 5, 17, 21, 25). As a "servant" (*doulos*; v. 1) of Christ, Jude recognizes his lordship. The title *kyrios* is employed frequently of Jesus in the Gospels. Jude's use of this title brings Jesus Christ into a close connection with God as *kyrios*. Since a predication does not imply identity, different understandings are theoretically possible: God is *kyrios*, but not every *kyrios* is God. It is significant that the word "God" in Jude always appears in the context of Jesus Christ (vv. 1, 4, 21, 25). The intimate connection between God and Jesus Christ is further expressed by the word "only": Jesus Christ is "our only Master and Lord" (v. 4); majesty and other divine virtues are ascribed to "the only God our Savior, through Jesus Christ our Lord" (v. 25).

The title *kyrios* is a predicative term with two hands (see the postscript). Its one hand holds its main subject, creating the canonical rule and usage, while the other hand reaches out toward the ordinary meanings of the word. Within the canon of the New Testament, God and Jesus Christ are prominently called "the Lord." This intracanonical rule shapes the theological language of the Christian faith: God is the Lord, Jesus Christ is the Lord. At the same time, *kyrios* in ordinary language means master, the *dominus* to whom other people relate as servants or subjects. These two meanings or "hands" of the term are interconnected, for instance, in Eph. 6:5–9. The "Master in heaven" shows no partiality between earthly masters and servants (6:9). This Ephesians passage shows that the lordship of Christ can, to some extent, be compared with the so-called patron and client relationships of the ancient world (Neyrey 1993: 61–62). And yet, this comparison is insufficient, since it focuses on only one hand of the term *kyrios*. The other hand, which is intracanonical, tells in which ways Christianity predicates the *kyrios* of Jesus Christ. These ways do not only resemble, but they also significantly differ from the secular uses of the term.

With its two hands, the predicative term *kyrios* performs a task of semantic mediation: Christians are related to God and Jesus Christ in a way that resembles the relationship between earthly servants and their master but that also differs from this relationship. The main subject of the epistle, Jesus Christ, thus becomes illuminated from two directions: the intracanonical use teaches the new rule of Christian usage, whereas the extracanonical analogy shows to which old rule the term is related. Jesus Christ is the Lord, but he is a new and different Lord, a better Lord than our old masters.

These rudimentary linguistic observations become more interesting in Jude 5, in which it is claimed that "Jesus/the Lord . . . saved a people out of the land of Egypt." The manuscript evidence between the two words continues to divide exegetical opinions. Neyrey (1993: 61–62) argues that "Jesus" should be preferred (the Vulgate also employs this word). Bauckham and the NRSV translate "the Lord," but Bauckham concludes that this term refers to Jesus (1983: 49). Martin reads "the Lord" but adds that the work of Jesus is also associated (1994: 77–78). Without going further into the problems of manuscript abbreviations and the different possible understandings of the preexistence of Christ, it can be stated that most scholars find the reading preserved in the Vulgate, but not the one in the NRSV, to be very plausible. Jude teaches that our Lord Jesus Christ led the Jewish people in their exodus.

Let us focus on the interpretative role of the Jewish examples provided by Jude more closely. In v. 5 the Lord Jesus Christ and his work—in other words, Christology—remain the main subject. The Jewish stories, which for the Jews were (and are) the main subjects of their faith, now become predicative demonstrations that shed light on the person and work of Jesus Christ. This is in many ways a fascinating and bold hermeneutical move. The Jewish narratives are supposed to mediate between Jesus Christ and the phenomenal world of Jude's readers. Readers are assumed to be familiar with the essential narratives that depict God's action with Israel. Jude claims that Jesus Christ is involved in this action.

It would be misleading to say that the Jewish texts are, as a result, upgraded or downgraded. The Jewish stories are looked at from a new angle. Jude claims that a deeper meaning in those texts can be seen when they are rearranged so that they are predicated of our Lord Jesus Christ.

Two other Jewish texts are employed in the same manner of rearrangement. The archangel Michael said to the devil: "The Lord rebuke you!" (Jude 9; cf. Zech. 3:2), meaning, according to Jude, that our Lord Jesus Christ will accomplish the final judgment.[2] This christological meaning is detected only when the Jewish narrative is predicated of Christ, who is the hidden main subject behind the term "Lord." In a similar manner, "the Lord [who] is coming with ten thousands of his holy ones" (Jude 14; cf. *1 Enoch* 1.9 [Charlesworth 1985: 1.13–14]), is for Jude our Lord Jesus Christ (Bauckham 1983: 96). Thus the term "the Lord," which in the New Testament generally expresses a title predicated of God and Jesus Christ, now becomes the main subject in order that the essential Jewish narratives can be predicated of Jesus Christ. This move occurs in Jude 5, 9, 14. In the case of v. 5, it has even led to manuscript variants, although the basic idea is clear: essential Jewish narratives witness to Jesus Christ.

Jude's Christology thus operates with a paradigm in which essential Jewish narratives are predicated of Jesus Christ. The concept of *kyrios* offers a terminological bridge to accomplish this move. As result we obtain a view of preexistence (v. 5) and a strong emphasis on Jesus Christ as the one who "execute[s] judgment on all" (v. 15).

Is it legitimate to interpret older texts in the manner of Jude? This is a difficult hermeneutical problem that should be addressed with proper care. An obvious danger is present in this interpretative strategy, namely, the postulate of successive revelations so that a new authoritative text can be used to reinterpret the older one. Christianity approves this postulate to an extent with regard to Judaism, but it disapproves the Islamic application of the same postulate. From the perspective of abstract fairness, this seems to be inconsistent.

And yet, there simply is no way of avoiding such a postulate. A theological interpreter needs an authoritative text in which some main subjects are illustrated by means of predicates that have two hands and thus can mediate between the main subject and the phenomenal world of the already known language, the old rule. At the same time, the mere presence of a new authoritative text with its new main subjects already generates a new rule that revises the old rule. The old rule remains a necessary point of departure, the beginning of the mediation leading to the adoption of the new rule. In this sense Christianity needs Judaism, although it needs it in a manner that is different from the Jewish faith.

The Epistle of Jude performs its christological rearrangement of Jewish texts in a manner that is clear and provocative. The Lord, who saved a people out of Egypt and will come to execute a judgment on all, is Jesus Christ. We must leave all judgment to him. The false teachers or "intruders" (v. 4) do not understand this, but they think that they can judge matters autonomously. Because they

---

2. Bauckham 1983: 62 thinks it exegetically "probable" that *kyrios* here, as in Jude 5, refers to Christ in Jude's didactic use of the Jewish text.

exercise that final power of judgment, which belongs to Jesus Christ, they in fact deny their master and Lord.

When Jesus Christ is portrayed as a judge in this manner, on the one hand, he takes the traditional role of divine judge. On the other hand, due to this intracanonical attribution, the very event of final judgment also receives new, christological aspects that reflect the new rule of the gospel. The theme of mercy exemplifies this new rule.

Mercy (*eleos*) appears together with peace and love already in Jude's greeting (v. 2). In v. 21 mercy is attributed to Jesus Christ and love to God; it is also possible to think that the Holy Spirit mentioned in v. 20b exemplifies peace (cf. Rom. 8:6). In this quasitrinitarian group of major Christian virtues, mercy is attributed to the judge who comes to "convict everyone of all the deeds of ungodliness" (Jude 15). The task of executing judgment thus appears together with the "mercy of our Lord" (v. 21). In Christ, justice and mercy can coexist without the "licentiousness" (v. 4) of which the false teachers are found guilty.

Although Christians are not supposed to execute judgment, Jude advises his readers to imitate the mercy of Christ (vv. 22–23). The readers should have mercy on those who go wrong. Although they are advised to hate even the polluted clothes of the wrongdoers (v. 23), they should at the same time be merciful on the people wearing them. This somewhat complicated advice becomes meaningful when it is seen in terms of imitation: our Lord Jesus Christ condemns sin and executes judgment on sinners; at the same time, he is merciful. We cannot execute judgment, but we should stay away from sin while being merciful to others who have fallen. This is the example given us by Christ.

The new rule that the canonical text teaches is, therefore, that justice and mercy go together in Christ. If the christological act of judgment is looked at only from the perspective of the old rule, justice primarily appears as condemnation and even destruction of the unfaithful (vv. 5, 10). Although this old rule remains a part of the canonical text, it is supplemented by the new rule of mercy. Following Christ, Christians should have mercy on others. At the same time, the virtue of mercy does not allow the execution of final judgments. The liberal judgments that the intruders make in fact "pervert the grace of our God into licentiousness" (v. 4). Christians are called to perform nonjudgmental acts of mercy.

This inner logic of christological mercy is complex. Jude does not give much practical advice regarding how to stay away from sin and have mercy without being judgmental. His hard words concerning "worldly people" (v. 19) sound very judgmental to the ears of modern readers. Both before and after pointing out that no condemnation of slander should be brought against the opponents, Jude states, paradoxically, that the opponents in fact slander others (vv. 8–10). He evidently thinks that it is possible to state this while leaving the final judgment to Christ.

The doctrinal point that Jude wants to make is that Christians should not execute judgment or condemn others. It is the task of our Lord Jesus Christ to make such judgments. In this sense Christian conduct is not characterized by the attempt to achieve justice, but rather by the ethos of having mercy and refraining from final condemnation. Thus Christians are advised to live under the new rule of the gospel and leave the final judgment to God. Jude's criticism of his opponents is counteracted by his simultaneous need to show mercy on them. Thus a complex balance of the old and the new rule of our Lord emerges.

Christian Faith

In Jude 3 Jude explains that the purpose of his letter is to "appeal to you to contend for the faith that was once for all entrusted to the saints." Jude defends the faith against "intruders" and "worldly people" (vv. 4, 19). Jude admonishes his addressees to "build yourselves up on your most holy faith" (v. 20a). This admonition is followed by a trinitarian formula (vv. 20b–21).

If we treat faith as a theological main subject, its predicate in v. 3 is "that was once for all entrusted to the saints" (*tē hapax paradotheisē tois hagiois*). The verb *paradidōmi* relates to the act of handing over and to the concept of *paradosis* ("tradition"). Although the expression in many ways resembles the language of 1 Tim. 6:20 and 2 Tim. 1:12–14, it more probably reflects an older and less structured view of the church and its tradition (Bauckham 1983: 32–34). The word "faith" (*pistis*) means for Paul in Gal. 1:23 the content that is preached and believed (cf. Rom. 10:8). In Jude 3 *pistis* likewise expresses a *fides quae*, a body of doctrine that the apostles handed over to other holy people.

The word *hapax* ("once for all") underlines the continuity and sameness that stretches from the salvific action of Jesus who died "once for all" (Rom. 6:10; Heb. 9:26) to the proclamation of the gospel and to the faith of the church. The "saints," that is, all faithful Christians, have received this salvific message, the gospel, from the apostles. Given this, the verb *paradidōmi* is related to the handing over of the content of the faith to the entire communion of saints. This event is not as structured as the "deposit" entrusted to Timothy in 1 Tim. 6:20 and 2 Tim. 1:14 (see exposition of these passages and of Titus 2:14). It rather resembles the handing over of essential gospel truths in 1 Cor. 11:23 and 15:3.

In terms of my hermeneutics, it is again important to note the "two hands" of the predicative description. On the one hand, the process of tradition resembles other ordinary acts of giving and receiving. As I note in appendix C, religious tradition can be compared with the so-called inalienable possessions, that is, the handing over of material and immaterial goods that in some way remain the property of the giver and provide the series of recipients with a distinct identity. Here, the recipients have become "saints" as the result of receiving the faith.

On the other hand, the intimate connection between faith and tradition also emphasizes the difference between the anthropological forms of exchange and the Christian faith. Faith is not merely spontaneous, but it can be handed over; thus it resembles tradition. But when faith is "handed over" or "entrusted" to somebody, the relationship between giver and recipient is peculiar and even unique. The word *hapax* underlines the difference: this event of handing over is unique and cannot be repeated, for the actual giver of the gift of faith is Jesus Christ who, through his death on the cross, made this gift possible. This gift cannot be repeated or reinvented; it can only be handed over in due fashion. Therefore Jude is not describing the handing over of faith as one tradition among others, but as Tradition with a capital T.[3] This Tradition resembles human traditions, but is also different from them.

In Jude 20b the main subject, "faith," receives a brief predicate: *tē hagiōtatē hymōn pistei* ("on the foundation of your most holy faith" or simply "most holy faith") (Bauckham 1983: 113). The faith that the saints received (v. 3) has now become their holy faith. The formulation indicates that the recipients are holy because they have received this holy faith. The faith is in some sense theirs, but it has been handed over to them by the apostles and, more importantly, by Jesus Christ.

Is it possible to analyze such a short predicate with the method of postulating the two hands? The danger of arbitrary inventions must be kept in mind. I will present only a very modest observation: the appearance of the term *hagios* in v. 3 and v. 20b is on the one hand connected with the sanctification of life, the Christian conduct. Jude describes extensively the moral failures of his opponents (vv. 7–8, 12, 16) and admonishes his readers to "stand without blemish" (v. 24). The opponents are compared to those "who [do] not believe" (v. 5); they are "devoid of the Spirit" (v. 19). The predicate of being holy thus connotes the exemplary life and the proper conduct. This can be regarded as the ordinary meaning that is comparable to other texts and even to other religious convictions of the old rule. A holy person distinguishes himself or herself from other people. This holiness often finds its expression in moral conduct.

At the same time, the intimate connection between faith and holiness also expresses another dimension: not moral conduct, but receiving the true faith has made Christians "saints." When Jude advises his readers to build themselves up in the most holy faith, he does not refer to moral conduct, but to the worship of the trinitarian God: "Pray in the Holy Spirit; keep yourselves in the love of God; look forward to the mercy of our Lord Jesus Christ" (vv. 20–21). Although holiness secondarily refers to moral conduct, it primarily has to do with other acts of faith: prayer, worship, and expectation. In this way, the intimate link between faith and holiness, the new rule, underlines that the state of being holy primarily relates to this inward life of faith.

---

3. Cf. the definition of the 1963 Montreal Faith and Order Conference §46: "We can speak of the Christian Tradition (with a capital T), whose content is God's revelation and self-giving in Christ, present in the life of the Church" (quoted from Gassmann 1993: 11).

In sum, the ordinary meaning of *hagios* relates the concept to moral progress and exemplary conduct. The intracanonical connection with faith, however, teaches that the term cannot be reduced to morality. Other aspects in the life of faith are the primary source of all external expressions of holiness.

Summary

This brief exposition of Jude focuses on two "main subjects" or *loci communes*: Jesus Christ and the Christian faith. Although for the most part I concentrated on the immediate and explicit predicates that these two main subjects receive, I also argue that the rest of the epistle, in particular the Jewish texts and the descriptions of Jude's opponents, relate to the two main subjects and can be understood as their contextual background. This is by no means an exhaustive exposition of this important text. Some features, in particular Jude's Jewish sources as well his final doxology (vv. 24–25), have not received the treatment they deserve.

With the help of these two main subjects it is possible, however, to illustrate some claims made in the postscript. I argue there that it is helpful and often necessary to read a canonical text in a manner that identifies some theological main subjects that are in turn illustrated through several different predicative descriptions. The predicative descriptions relate to both the canonical main subject and the ordinary meanings of the surrounding world. Thus the predicative descriptions have "two hands" and they can be employed as a bridge between the old rule of the ordinary language and the new rule of the canonical text. Since a predication expresses both an identification procedure and a nonidentity, it is essential to see both the historical parallels and the distinctive new rule taught by the text.

There is a further reason why Jude offers an especially interesting platform for the application of this theory of doctrine. Jude employs earlier authoritative texts in a predicative fashion, highlighting the new main subject with their help and thus allowing a differentiated mediation between the Jewish and the Christian text. The conscious use of this interpretative procedure makes Jude a particularly fascinating epistle within the canon of the New Testament.

AFTER THE WORD

Hermeneutical Postscript

A Lutheran collection of sermons is sometimes called postilla. The name comes from the Latin phrase *post illa verba* ("after these words"), meaning that the sermon follows and expounds the text of the Gospel reading. Martin Luther's *Kirchenpostille* (1522) is often considered to be the paradigmatic model of later postillas (L. Friedrichs in *Religion in Geschichte und Gegenwart* 6.1514). The name "postilla" thus underlines that the sermon remains heteronomous and receives its meaning from the text being expounded. The preacher is supposed to remain "under" the word of God and not to present his or her own, personal thoughts.

While in ordinary speech, thought precedes word, the word of God should be expounded in a reverse order: first comes the external word, and only after receiving it are the internal thoughts allowed to emerge. This old practice of involving the mind only "after the word" is already formulated in the rule of Saint Benedict.[1]

In this postscript, I will briefly reflect on the hermeneutical procedures that can accompany the exposition of the Pastoral Epistles, Philemon, and Jude. I did not set any hermeneutical method or agenda in advance, but simply expounded the text with the help of available means. This was a conscious decision motivated by both practical and theoretical reasons. The practical reasons are concerned with the limits of hermeneutical strategies in the detailed expository work. While some strategies, for instance, the speech-act theory or the cultural-linguistic understanding of doctrine, may be helpful in abstract and systematic reflection, they do not

---

1. In "praying the Psalms and liturgical prayer . . . the word, the voice, goes ahead of us, and our mind must adapt to it." So Pope Benedict XVI 2007: 131, referring to Saint Benedict's Rule §19.7.

offer much concrete help in understanding particular words and sentences.[2] In the worst case, hermeneutical constructs can become empty abstractions that prevent the detailed understanding of the text.

My theoretical reasons relate to the primacy and immediacy of the biblical text in the process of understanding. All understanding may be conditioned by some hermeneutical decisions, but an open-minded reading of and listening to the text nevertheless remains the approach to be taken. Taking this approach, we need not worry too much whether the meaning of the text represents the author's intention or some other reality behind the text or whether it is the construction of the reader and his or her community (Oeming 2006 is a helpful overview of these matters). Close reading is "catch-as-catch-can"; it is a style of wrestling in which any hold is allowed. The expositor need not state his or her hermeneutical rules in advance. The relative usefulness of each "hold" will be judged by the readers of the commentary.

In the long process of reading and explaining, however, certain rules emerge. If the exposition is to remain consistent, some procedural rules and content-defining theses are preferred, while others remain in the background. It may be prudent not to press the preferred rules and theses into a too rigid system, since the polyphony of the text also needs to be heard. The preferred rules and theses should not be fixed in advance, but they emerge only in the process of understanding.

Since hermeneutics in this sense is not a method but a gradually growing self-awareness of what is going on in the interpreter's mind, its proper place is after the actual exposition, *post illa verba*. A hermeneutical postscript reports on the nature of the more general rules and practices that have emerged in the interpreter's mind.

Although hermeneutical reflection follows the exegesis, it need not be a merely documentary report. It can also be "after" in the sense of "following in search of," since it attempts to make systematic conclusions on the basis of the accomplished exegesis. When the expositors realize that their exposition follows a certain pattern, they can reflect on the nature of this pattern in more detail. And when they learn to understand this pattern, they have not only increased their own self-understanding but have also been "in search of" the biblical word of God that has given impetus for the emergence of this pattern in the first place.

The following reflections have, to a great extent, emerged during my exposition of the Pastoral Epistles and relate to them as *postexegetical* hermeneutics. To make my position as clear as possible, I applied the results of this reflection to my exposition of Jude. Thus the following model relates to my exposition of Jude as *preexegetical* hermeneutics, and the commentary on Jude can be read as an illustration of this postscript.

---

2. This is not meant as criticism, but as an indication of how difficult it is to construct interpretative methods. See Richard S. Briggs in Vanhoozer 2005a: 763–66 and, for cultural-linguistic theory, Vanhoozer 2005b.

The Pastoral Epistles contain a number of key ideas that can be expressed in terms of short statements:

1. Sound doctrine brings forth a sound mind, virtuous character, and good works.
2. False doctrine is accompanied with disordered mind and problematic conduct.
3. The church is the household of God.
4. Christians should progress in true godliness.
5. Godliness is contentment and moderation.

Such statements are essentially theological in the sense that their subject is a theological term that is elucidated by the predicative part of the statement. The predicative parts include terms and phenomena that resonate with our ordinary language and nontheological ways of understanding the world.

Without entering the philosophy of language in detail, I understand the subject and the predicate discussed here to be the two grammatical functions that constitute a sentence. The subject identifies the topic so that the subject is the person or thing about which something is said. The predicate ascribes some description to the subject so that the predicate is the statement made about that person or thing (see more detail in Lyons 1977: 334–37). The predicate typically mediates between the subject named and the conceptual world of the reader, allowing him or her to learn something concerning the subject at stake.

The five statements can also be understood as instances of the old rule of explaining Scripture by Scripture (see the essays by Timothy Ward and Daniel J. Treier in Vanhoozer 2005a: 730–34). The key ideas expressed in the statements are either explicitly present in the text, or they can be formulated as the obvious summary of the biblical text. In some rather simple and straightforward sense, the process of interpreting Scripture by Scripture defines the subject terms and illuminates their content with a number of predicates. When theological key subjects become attached to biblical predicates that stem from more ordinary types of language, a particular light is shed on the theological subjects.

Since the predicative terms of the Pastoral Epistles resonate with ordinary language as well as with medical and philosophical language, the interpreter is called to compare them with other historical and linguistic contexts. How was the moderation of emotion conceived in philosophical schools? What were the defining characteristics of a Greco-Roman household? Conclusions drawn with the help of historical analogy and extracanonical references play a major role in understanding the complex field of nontheological and semitheological predicative terms.

It seems to me, however, that the meaning of the most important theological subject terms is not established by the same procedure as that of its nontheological predicates. The meaning of key terms such as "Jesus Christ," "sound doctrine," and "the church" is established through a network of intracanonical predications in which the subject is highlighted from various directions. A series of such predications can be labeled "identification narrative" or description, using Jenson's term (1997: 42–89). When we know that Jesus Christ was born of the Virgin Mary, that he suffered under Pontius Pilate, was crucified and risen, we begin to know who Jesus Christ is.

The semantic matters involved in this process are very complex. Identification, for instance, is only a relative concept, since the cluster of different predicates by no means "exhausts" the meaning of the subject term.[3] Predications help identification, but they do not establish the full identity. A predicative term normally also expresses the remaining difference with regard to its subject: thus a household is not a church, "the one who suffered under Pilate" need not be Jesus, and so on (Ian Paul in Vanhoozer 2005a: 508). Another complex issue pertains to the possibilities and dangers of reducing the complex biblical text to the simplified subject-predicate models that are at stake here (for discussion of the so-called kernel sentences, see Peter G. Riddell in Vanhoozer 2005a: 428–31). We must leave these difficult issues undiscussed.

My aim is to make the following three points: in the hermeneutics of a canonical biblical text, (1) the interpreter distinguishes between central theological subjects and their explanatory predicates through interpreting Scripture by Scripture. (2) He or she further realizes that the meaning of theological key subjects is elucidated by their intratextual predicates. Thus the understanding of central theological subject terms proceeds in a "canonical-linguistic" (this concept is elaborated in Vanhoozer 2005b) fashion in which the intratextual rules of biblical language remain decisive. (3) The interpreter further realizes that the predicative terms to a large extent resonate with the ordinary language as well as with other language types and the phenomenal world of human beings. The predicative terms are then interpreted with historical-critical methods and, in fact, with the whole inventory of "catch-as-catch-can."

This hermeneutical self-awareness cannot dispense with the notion of doctrines as propositional sentences.[4] The propositional structure sustains the subject-predicate order. It further enables the twofold semantics (the second point versus the third) that accompanies the ordering of theological key concepts as the subject terms of doctrinal propositions.[5] The twofold semantics can be illustrated as

3. This is developed as a philosophical idea in Hintikka 1996: 20–45. For a down-to-earth theological statement, see John Webster in Vanhoozer 2005a: 724–27 at 727: "Because the text is authoritative, the text will be inexhaustible by any one reading . . . because the text's claim upon the church's attention is perpetual and cannot be disposed of in a single act of interpretation."

4. In my discussion, the syntactic and relational-pragmatic features of propositions are highlighted, not the problematic idea that a proposition would be a "picture" of reality. One can, I think, find this idea problematic but nevertheless hold that we need propositions to discuss the nature of doctrine.

5. Within the propositional structure, the truth value can nevertheless be determined by the use of the theological terms that give us rules of the second type. An obviously irregular use of the subject term renders the whole proposition false, even when the predicate is correctly understood. Thus a crusader who

follows: while the predicative term has two hands, one holding the subject term and the other reaching out to the phenomenal world of the interpreter, the subject term has only one hand, which holds the predicative term. The theological subject is concealed in the sense that it does not lend itself to the ordinary phenomenal world. Its meaning can thus be learned only through its biblical uses or "canonical handshakes" with the predicative terms.[6]

In my exposition of Jude, the New Testament usage (the second point) is consistently called the new rule, whereas other ordinary meanings of the predicates (the third point) are called the old rule. I will not, however, reflect on the difficult issue in which precise sense a "rule theory" of doctrine is presupposed. Since subject and predicate are in linguistics called the basic "grammatical functions," the label "functional theory of doctrine" could perhaps also be used.[7]

Given the enormous discussion on theological hermeneutics, it is easy to make critical remarks on these guidelines. An imaginary opponent may present the following three observations. First, it is clumsy to presuppose two different semantics. This I admit, but add that the ascent from the ordinary meaning of the predicates toward the canonical meaning learned through the canonical use may also occur in other linguistic contexts. Reflection on metaphorical language offers examples.[8]

Second, any ordering of subjects and predicates in the first point is arbitrary, since any term can function in both roles. Contrary to this I claim that this ordering already takes place with sufficient clarity in the Scripture (Protestantism's *sola scriptura*). One could alternatively hold that it has been de facto established in the ecclesial interplay of Scripture and the Nicene tradition of faith (Catholic "Scripture and Tradition"). Both evangelicals and Catholics thus deny the view that Scripture is only raw material from which very different doctrinal sets can be composed. The distinction between biblical key subjects and other terms is not arbitrary but factual. Theological key subjects are relatively few, and, as their fundamental meaning is concealed, they stand in need of further elucidation. At the same time it is true

---

shouts "Christ is Lord" while killing an opponent utters a false sentence. The crusader may understand the predicate "Lord" correctly, but still use the sentence in an improper context, which makes this use of the subject term irregular and, in turn, falsifies the whole sentence. Given this, the propositional structure sustains the subject-predicate order while the truth of the statement stands and falls with the regular (canonical) use of the theological subject term. See Lindbeck 1984 and B. Marshall 1989.

6. The idea of concealment can, of course, be interpreted in various ways: that natural reason cannot grasp theological truths, that God reveals himself in two distinct ways (e.g., law and gospel, nature and grace), that theological matters can be approached only metaphorically, or that a genuinely religious-language game remains different from ordinary language. These interpretations need not concern us here.

7. Lyons 1977: 334 concludes that "it is a fundamental principle of traditional grammar, and also of much modern syntactic theory, that every simple, declarative sentence consists of two obligatory major constituents, a *subject* and a *predicate*."

8. See the metaphor theories of Max Black (1962: 25–47; 1979) and Paul Ricoeur (1978). I am not claiming, however, that doctrinal sentences are to be read as metaphors.

that they can sometimes also serve as grammatical predicates. It is further to be conceded that some theological concepts are borderline cases.[9]

Third, if the predicated meaning (the third point) is established by means of human reason and if the nexus of canonical handshakes elucidates the subject meaning (second point), it follows that the subject meaning finally becomes determined by the dictates of human reason and historical analogy. To meet this objection, the following qualification is necessary: in each biblical predication, an added value emerges and is attached to the subject. In terms of our illustration, the phenomenon of handshake does not merely mean the presence of a hand. When the church is called household, it does not mean simply that the domestic features are carried over to the church as one additive item in the process of identifying the church. It is rather the case that each metaphorical predicate becomes attached to the subject so that a new entity emerges, for instance: church-as-household, church-as-pillar-and-bulwark, church-as-body-of-Christ. The ordinary meaning of bodies, households, and pillars in this cluster remains secondary, though not insignificant. Thus an ecclesiologist does not study bodies and bulwarks. He or she studies the constructed phrases by referring to their canonical use rather than to the ordinary meanings of the predicative terms (see textual examples in the exposition of Jude).

As this modest hermeneutic is not a method, but a systematized and simplified account of some governing principles of my exposition, it can be made more concrete through referring to the five exemplary statements above. Concerning the first two, the interpreter's problem is that Paul does not define very clearly the content of sound and false doctrine, but describes extensively the character of their adherents. As the predications relate to the world of Greco-Roman emotion theory and medicine, they can be understood with the help of historical analogy. This analogy also sheds some light on the subject matter but, at the same time, the interpreter remains aware of the nonidentical character of the predications. Sound doctrine brings forth good works, but good works remain very different from sound doctrine. The interpreter's challenge is not the resemblance between subject and predicate, but their remaining difference and heterogeneity.

With regard to the fourth and fifth statements, godliness appears first as predicate and then as subject. The subject matter of the fourth is Christian existence, which becomes elucidated as "progress in true godliness." The predicates appear in Hellenism and can be understood with the help of analogy. If the fifth statement is taken as an explanatory note on the fourth, then the subject matter of godliness can be understood in terms of other Hellenistic virtues. It should again be noted, however, that the predications do not express synonymity but they keep the door open for remaining differences. Godliness may be contentment, but contentment is not godliness. In order to understand godliness, it is not necessary to consider

9. For instance, "the law" is on the one hand a theological main subject, but it is also a predicate that resonates with many different but related ideas of rule, command, duty, etc.

that it be synonymous with some of its predicates. Thus we may meaningfully debate whether *eusebeia* is a specific Christian subject matter, as its prominent role in 1 Timothy indicates, or merely another Hellenistic virtue that can be predicated of Christian life. My simple hermeneutics cannot settle this predominantly exegetical matter, but the subject-predicate order can to some extent elucidate the different options available in the debate.

In the framework of dogmatics, my hermeneutics bears some resemblance to the so-called *loci* method (for historical background, see F. Nüssel in *Religion in Geschichte und Gegenwart* 5.511). Philipp Melanchthon's 1521 *Loci communes*, based on the subject terms of Romans, is the classical example of this approach. In the *loci* method, the most significant biblical concepts are understood as basic notions that become elucidated with the help of manifold auxiliary terms employed in the narrative description. The basic notions and biblical rules guiding their use in the theological sentences thus constitute the backbone of dogmatics. Understood in this fashion, the *loci* method combines the mystery and the rule of faith, expressed by the basic notions, with the pedagogical interests of their narrative exposition taking place through the manifold predicates.

What contemporary hermeneutical models does my view resemble? George Lindbeck's 1984 theory of doctrine as developed in Kevin Vanhoozer's 2005 canonical-linguistic approach to theology offers a point of departure. This approach underlines the canonical uses and linguistic practices in a helpful manner. Vanhoozer's description of "canonical practices" resembles the intratextual emergence of meaning of the subject terms in my view (the second point). My focusing on the subject-predicate order modifies, however, the canonical-linguistic approach in several ways. Doctrinal statements have permanent propositional features that cannot be reduced to uses, rules, and practices. Lindbeck's refusal to regard doctrines as propositions may have heuristic value, but a consistent "post-propositionalism" (Vanhoozer 2005b: 266–72)[10] confuses more than clarifies. It is useful to focus on rules, but the so-called grammatical functions of doctrinal sentences must also receive proper attention.

Because the meanings of the predicative terms are illustrated with the inventory of human reason (third point), my approach is quite friendly toward critical exegesis and its use of historical analogy. My approach employs significantly more historical exegesis than many other theological hermeneutics of the Bible. It needs to be argued that the thematic material of the New Testament is historically close to the Nicene views.[11]

It could even be argued that points one and two do not represent methodologically anything more than a philosophical and rational ordering of the biblical material. If this is the case, then my hermeneutical principles would be more or less

10. Needless to say, I have never encountered doctrines that are not communicated with the help of propositional sentences.

11. This means that a theological interpreter has a definite historical burden of proof. For the Christian application of the subject-predicate order to the Old Testament, see the exposition of Jude.

entirely philosophical and historical. But I hesitate to claim this, since there may nevertheless be some "invisible hand" that allows us to discover the main subjects of the Scripture as well as to grasp their meaning with the help of canonical handshakes. Since we do not have immediate cognitive access to the theological main subjects, they cannot be understood with direct historical analogies. The invisible hand may do something to unfold their meaning through the canonical usage. It may be the easiest solution to claim that the established canonical practices enable us to perform points one and two and that the invisible hand is at work in these practices.[12]

Generally speaking, my aim is to avoid hermeneutical models that rely strongly on the concept of tradition. If we claim that the presence of tradition safeguards the proper cultural and linguistic practices, we easily remain blind to the immense pluralism that is inherent in traditions and weakens their regulative value. An interpreter can hardly avoid these questions: which tradition? whose tradition?[13] The idea of tradition is fascinating and helpful, as I show in appendix C and in excursus 6. But it is not the most helpful as a hermeneutical directive. The concept of a canonical rule of faith is a better directive, although it also has its problems.[14] When a canon can be presupposed, it is also possible to discover the main subjects within the canon.

In which ways does my concrete exposition proceed "after the word"? The hermeneutical disclosure progresses from the first point to the second and the third. The hard labor of the exegete, however, normally advances from the third point slowly toward the second. The exegetical procedure (the third point) attempts to grasp the meaning of ordinary speech available in the text. It focuses on the handshakes between the predicative terms and our phenomenal world. But, in the New Testament, even ordinary speech revolves around theological subjects, such as Christ, the gospel, the church, and healthy doctrine. Thus the new rule is always at stake, modifying and changing the old rule of ordinary meanings.

The theological subjects are beyond the immediate reach of ordinary language. At the same time, they constitute the final "word" that we are "after." The meaning of this constitutive word can be approached only indirectly, with the help of more ordinary predicates and through the canonical uses and liaisons of these words. In our search for the meaning of the final word, we therefore always remain behind and after it. Its meaning can be approached and elucidated, but not exhausted. In this process of searching and learning, the word of God discloses itself as the life-giving word. Thus it turns out to be the active subject of the entire process, the word of God.

12. This claim would be in keeping with the "canonical handshake" illustration as well as with the above-mentioned qualification that the event of handshake is more than the sum of its parts. But I would not rule out other opinions; e.g., that the tradition (and even the office) of the church steers the interpretation or that the Holy Spirit inspires the understanding of interpreters as well as the Scripture itself.

13. I am not making this point primarily because I happen to be a Lutheran theologian. The Pastoral Epistles are themselves selective with regard to traditions: they advise avoiding genealogies while approving sound doctrine.

14. The much-discussed issue of plurality within the canon is perhaps the most obvious problem (Dunn 2005; Vanhoozer 2005b). It is, however, a smaller problem than the existing plurality within and among traditions and different traditionalisms.

APPENDIX A

Moderation of Emotion

Aristotle's *Nicomachean Ethics* can be regarded as the starting point of the tradition of moderation of emotion. Aristotle (384–322 BC) teaches that a virtue lies between two problematic extremes. Thus a virtuous person needs a moderated and right amount of the active power in question, for instance, courage or pride. This doctrine of the right mean concerns both the emotions and the actions of a virtuous person. Aristotle criticizes the view that virtue would consist in liberating oneself from emotion (*Nicomachean Ethics* 1104b25, 1106a13–1107a26 [LCL 73.81, 89–97]; Sorabji 2000: 194–95).

Later Stoic philosophers, however, preferred to proclaim a freedom from emotions (*apatheia*). This freedom meant different things for different philosophers, but the Stoics generally developed intellectual strategies and therapeutic exercises aimed at eradicating the harmful emotions. Through philosophy and ascesis, a wise person can reach the state of *apatheia* in which he or she is not affected by the changing perceptions and passions emerging from them (for an overview of the complex phenomenon, see Knuuttila 2004: 47–80).

In his *De finibus*, Cicero (106–43 BC) compares Stoic and Aristotelian ethics. He shows sympathy with the idea of freedom from emotions (*De finibus* 3.35 [LCL 40.255]), but he also advocates many Aristotelian ideas of good life and right conduct. Cicero mentions Aristotle's comparison of action with the art of archery (*Nicomachean Ethics* 1094a23–24 [LCL 73.5]), in which the middle of the mark is to be hit with the help of knowledge and skill (*De finibus* 3.22 [LCL 40.241]). He further discusses in great detail the Epicurean, Stoic, and Aristotelian philosophy of emotions. Although Cicero can hardly be regarded as a direct source of the Hellenistic topics mentioned in the New Testament, his

De finibus witnesses to the continuing actuality of Aristotelian ethics and their mixture with Stoicism.

The traditions of moderation and eradication had their advocates in the Greco-Roman philosophy. Many thinkers also attempted to outline a combination of both traditions, including a compromise between them. Some Epicurean philosophers believed that a wise person can make a selection between good and harmful emotions. But others, like Philodemus (110–40 BC), taught that one can moderate one's agitation (*On Anger* 37–41; *On Death* 34 [quoted from Sorabji 2000: 202]). He also approached the Stoics by holding that some things remain indifferent for a wise person. The Skeptics, as reported by Sextus Empiricus (second century AD) (*Outlines of Pyrrhonism* 3.235–36 [LCL 273.483]; *Against the Mathematicians* 11.161 [LCL 311.463]), believed that it is possible to control one's beliefs and in this manner also moderate the feeling of pain. In this context, Sextus employs the terms *metriopatheō* and *metriopathōs* (Sorabji 2000: 195–203).

The Middle Platonist Alcinous (second century AD) uses the term *metriopathēs* in the context of describing how the virtues of the spirited and the appetitive part of the soul are able to moderate the emotions and make them submissive to the reason (*Didaskalikos* 30.5 [Alcinous 1990: 60–62]). He recommends a moderation of emotions in proper contexts. In mourning one's dead relatives, for instance, it is improper to show too much or too little grief. A moderate emotion of grief is virtuous. Neoplatonists tended to regard *metriopatheia* and *apatheia* as two successive stages of progress. According to Plotinus (AD 205–70), in political life one should develop the civic virtues through moderation of emotions (*Enneads* 1.2.2–3 [LCL 440.131–37]). But the individual purification of the soul means that the soul becomes free of emotion (Knuuttila 2004: 88–91; Sorabji 2000: 203).

Early Christian authors adopted this discussion in a differentiated fashion. According to Heb. 5:2, the high priest should be able to "deal gently" (*metriopatheō*) with ignorant persons. The model of such conduct, Jesus Christ, is also able to "sympathize" (*sympatheō*; Vulgate: *conpati*) with human weaknesses (4:15). These verses create a positive appreciation of emotions in Christianity. The NRSV translation of *metriopatheō*, "deal gently," further indicates the important connection with the words *praus*, *prautēs*, and *praupatheia*. In the New Testament, these words describe the Christian virtue of being "meek" and "gentle" (see exposition of 1 Tim. 3:3).

Clement of Alexandria (150–215) teaches that the reason should keep the lower parts of the soul within narrow limits. He calls this view *metriopatheia* and claims that the Christians should moderate all their emotions to a very elementary level. At the same time, Clement holds that the moderation of emotions is not yet the final perfection (*Paedagogus* 1.2.4 [ANF 2.210]; *Stromata* 2.8, 10; 6.9; 7.1 [ANF 2.356, 358, 496–98, 523–24]). Christ was apathetic, and the final perfection requires an eradication of emotions. *Metriopatheia* is the lower level that may be valid in everyday life and for most humans, but the progress of ascetics should finally lead to *apatheia*. The ideal of *apatheia* was even more strongly held by Origen (185–254) in *On Matthew* 15.17; 395.8–398.28 (Origen 1933: 395–98; Knuuttila 2004: 117–23).

Richard Sorabji points out that Clement can nevertheless make some concessions. With regard to love, a certain family affection called *oikeiōsis sterktikē* is necessary. This affection stems from the relationship between parents and children; it belongs to the household, but is also a relevant aspect of love for God. Another exception for Clement is the emotion of pity (*eleos, misericordia*, "mercy") (*Stromata* 2.16 [ANF 2.363–64]). This emotion is compatible with *apatheia* and can be predicated of God, who has no passions (Sorabji 2000: 386–91; on *misericordia Dei*, see Saarinen 2004).

The interplay of *apatheia* and *metriopatheia* is also visible in the Cappadocian fathers (e.g., Basil, *Extended Rules* 8, 16–17 [Patrologia graeca 31.934–42, 958–65]; Gregory of Nazianzus, *Letter* 165 [Patrologia graeca 37.274–75]; Gregory of Nyssa, *On the Soul and Resurrection* 53c, 61c, 68a [Patrologia graeca 46:88–96]). They often teach the model of *apatheia*. On the other hand, they also say that some emotions should be felt. Ordinary people are not to react with apathy, but they should, for instance, feel grief at the loss of their loved ones. But there are exceptional people who are capable of the higher virtue of *apatheia*. In later monastic traditions, often influenced by Evagrius Ponticus (346–99), the ideal of *apatheia* continues (*Practical Treatise* [Sources chrétiennes 170], 35, 38, 81, 84, 89, 91), although it may be qualified by thoughts of the moderation of the emotions (Sorabji 2000: 392–97; Knuuttila 2004: 127–44; Williams 1993). In medieval times, the emergence of Latin Aristotelianism revitalizes the old idea of virtue as a mean between vicious extremes.

The most important connecting link between the ancient and Christian traditions of *metriopatheia* is Philo of Alexandria (30 BC–AD 45). Since Philo is relevant in discussing the background of the Pastoral Epistles, I will analyze his thoughts on *apatheia* and *metriopatheia* in more detail.

Philo's texts are among the earliest extant sources in which *metriopatheia* and *apatheia* are combined so that the moderation of emotion represents a lower stage of "progress," whereas a complete eradication of emotions belongs to the final state of perfection. In addition, he considers the two to be different ideals for different people. When Abraham lost Sarah to death, reason advised him "neither to toss about beyond measure as if at an entirely novel and spontaneous disaster, nor to be emotionless, as if nothing painful had happened, but to choose the mean rather than the extremes, and try to be moderate in emotion [*metriopatheō*]" (*Abraham* 257 [cited from Sorabji 2000: 345]).

Moses, on the other hand, was a perfect man who completely eradicated the passions of the breast, as Lev. 8:29 allegorically points out by saying that the breast was cut off: "No moderation of passion [*metriopatheia*] can satisfy him [Moses]; he is content with nothing but complete absence of passion [*apatheia*]" (*Allegorical Interpretation* 3.114, 128–29 [LCL 226.377, 387, 389]). In Philo's anthropology, breast is the seat of anger, whereas belly is the seat of other passions.

No one, Philo claims, can completely eradicate the passions of the belly, since they are indispensable for life. Therefore the belly is to be "cleansed" (Lev. 9:14), not exscinded. The desires of the belly need to be kept to a minimum, since "desire is never filled up, but continues always thirsty and in want of more." But the desires of the belly remain and the person has to learn to cope with them (*Allegorical Interpretation* 3.147, 149 [LCL 226.401]).

In this manner Philo teaches both *metriopatheia* and *apatheia*, although he considers the eradication of emotions to be the higher goal. Because of our bodily existence, however, some desires necessarily remain. They are to be cleansed with the strategies of *metriopatheia*. Philo distinguishes between the ideal, perfect person and the one who "makes progress" (*prokoptōn*). The category of progress is important, for within this category *metriopatheia* can be practiced. The companion of Moses, Aaron, could not cut away the seat of the anger, the breast. But he was able to control it by "schooling it by well-tested speech [*logos kekrimenos*], attended by two virtues, clearness [*saphēneia*] and truth [*alētheia*]." The progressing person exercises moderation, "welcoming simple and unavoidable pleasure, while declining that which is excessive and overelaborate" (*Allegorical Interpretation* 3.140 [LCL 226.395]). Three important features of moderated behavior are thus given: (1) avoidance of uncontrolled speech, (2) the virtue of truth, and (3) welcoming simple pleasure while avoiding excess.

Philo develops the distinction between the progressing and the perfect person as follows:

> He [Moses in Lev. 1:9] lays further stress upon the mere moderating of passion [*metriopatheia*] in the man of gradual advance [*prokoptōn*], by representing the wise man as declining without any bidding all the pleasures of the belly, while the man of gradual advance acts under orders.... For it must needs be that while the perfect man moves of himself towards virtuous actions, the man who is practising [*askētēs*] should do so with the aid of reason which gives him guidance what he should do, obedience to whose directions is a noble thing. (*Allegorical Interpretation* 3.144 [LCL 226.397, 399])

According to this passage, the use of reason and the practice of giving advice are relevant for the progressing person, as the perfect person does not need advice. Moderation and the state of progress are the normal case among practicing ascetics, although they strive for perfection. Philo continues the discussion on the belly with an emphasis on moderation. In parties we should consume food with the help of reason, which commands moderation. Reason acts like a shovel with which one can dig and lay bare the nature of passions. In the case of eating, only "useful and necessary" foods are recommended: "It is good to take what is fixed by strict measure [*memetrēmenon*]" (*Allegorical Interpretation* 3.155–58, 166 [LCL 226.405, 407, 413]).

Although Philo thinks of *apatheia* as the highest goal, he develops a theology of the body in which moderation and successful control of the passions can be practiced in various ways. We cannot cut away our breast or belly; therefore we remain in the state of progress. This state is characterized by the use of reason as well as by the normative advice given in the law in order to be practiced by humans. Reason can recognize and follow this advice and thus moderate the passions. Philo summarizes his discussion on the belly as follows:

> We get this result. The lover of pleasure moves on the belly; the perfect man washes out the entire belly; the man who is making gradual progress washes out the contents of the belly; the man who is just beginning his training will go forth without, when he intends to curb passion by bringing reason (figuratively called a shovel) to bear upon the demands of the belly. (*Allegorical Interpretation* 3.159 [LCL 226.407])

Troels Engberg-Pedersen attempts to systematize the ideals of progress and reason in Stoicism. A simplified account of this systematization can be presented as follows. When we discover the power of reason and learn to transform individual subjectivity through the use of reason, our identity changes and we learn to understand ourselves and the world in an objective manner. This cognitive or philosophical awakening can be described as the first and fundamental aspect of *oikeiōsis*, a realization of oneself as part of the whole and as social being.

The second aspect of *oikeiōsis* concerns the moral responsibility of a person toward other persons, a development from "I" to "we." The discovery of reason is a requirement for this second aspect and, theoretically, already contains it. In concrete reality, however, a person needs to disclose the social responsibility inherent in the rational and objective grasp of the world. This second aspect is not thought in terms of temporal succession. Basically, when a grown-up person realizes the objective character of the world, he or she can transform selfish social skills to an unselfish care for others. The children who have been loved by their parents can, as adults with the use of reason, perform a similar love for their children (Engberg-Pedersen 2000: 34–40, 53–70).

Oikeiōsis is a complex topic of Stoic ethics. Engberg-Pedersen studies its appearance in Cicero's *De finibus* 3.16–21 (LCL 40.233–39), using the Latin word *conciliatio*, and in Diogenes Laertius 7.85–89 (LCL 185.193–97). I will restrict discussion to the social dimensions of the concept, which offer parallels with the Christian idea of neighborly love. In this commentary, I employ rather free translations of *oikeiōsis* as "attachment, familiarization, genuine care for others." It should be remembered that the Stoic doctrine of *oikeiōsis* contains both an "indifference toward the world" and a "concrete involvement in it" (Engberg-Pedersen 1990: 140).

The concept of progress belongs intimately to the process of development occurring in the *oikeiōsis*. Basically, a progressing person is on his or her way from the "I" toward "reason" and "we." Although this person may be less stupid than many others, he or she is not yet wise. Engberg-Pedersen suggests that we nevertheless should distinguish a stage in which the progressing person is "basically wise . . . but not quite so." In other words, this advanced stage of progress allows the person to listen to the reason and to perform good acts, although the person is not yet perfect but still needs more progress (Engberg-Pedersen 2000: 70–71). This advanced state of progress goes well together with Philo's above-mentioned exposition of Aaron and other examples of the "moderating of passion in the man of gradual advance," whereas the less advanced stage resembles the "man who is just beginning his training." According to Epictetus, a person who exercises his or her will to make it "conformable to nature, free, unrestrained, unimpeded, faithful, modest" and who daily practices this modesty is a person who makes progress (*Discourses* 1.4 [LCL 131.27–37]). Epictetus thus describes the advanced state of progress.

Engberg-Pedersen further argues that his systematization of *oikeiōsis* and progress is applicable to Paul, although with one major change. In the Pauline Epistles, "reason" is substituted by "Christ."[1] The Christian thus performs his or her *oikeiōsis* in following Christ and in participating in the life of Christ (Engberg-Pedersen 2000: 35). A proper discussion of this fascinating but controversial proposal would require an extensive treatment of the major Pauline epistles and cannot be undertaken here. The above-mentioned rather standard and uncontroversial characterization of *metriopatheia*, *prokopē*, and *oikeiōsis* is sufficient for the purposes of this commentary. My claim that these concepts are helpful for the understanding of the Pastoral Epistles remains open for further exegetical and theological debate.

In 1 Timothy, the general setting and topics already characterize the epistle as a text addressed to a person who is progressing. Timothy is a young church leader who needs instruction and advice from a person who is already very advanced in "divine training" (*oikonomia theou*; 1:4). As in many Pauline texts, the metaphor of *oikos* ("household") creates a connection with the process of *oikeiōsis* ("familiarization, care for others"). The church is God's *oikonomia* and *oikos* (3:15). At the same time, it is also "the pillar and bulwark of the truth." Those who "know the truth" need no celibacy or abstinence from foods (4:4). As in Philo, the persons who progress in this community should, according to Paul, practice the virtue of truth. The many regulations of speech in 1 Timothy (e.g., 2:2; 4:12; 5:1, 13, 19; 6:20) likewise stress the moderation and control of words in a manner similar to Philo's *metriopatheia*.

Paul's appeal to reason appears most prominently in an indirect manner. Timothy's opponents are blamed for the lack of reason and even of insanity (see appendix B). The virtue of *eusebeia* appears, as is proper in the context of *oikeiōsis*, to be both a rational and social virtue, leading both to the intellectual grasp of the situation and to adequate social skills in the leadership of the church. Other virtues related to reason include good conscience (1:5, 19), understanding (1:7–9), and

1. Engberg-Pedersen 2000 does not discuss the Pastoral Epistles but earlier Pauline texts. Nor does he connect *metriopatheia* with *oikeiōsis*; this connection remains the view of my commentary. For his view on *oikeiōsis* and passion, see Engberg-Pedersen 1990: 170–206.

right judgment (5:21–25). As in Philo, reason is connected with an understanding of the law, especially in 1:6–9. The enigmatic sentence "the law is laid down not for the innocent" (1:9a) resembles Philo's idea that reason and the law give guidance to the "progressing" people, whereas the perfect man who "moves of himself toward virtuous actions" does not need external norms against which to measure his behavior.

Even if the nature of this resemblance remains, due to the brevity of 1:9a, rather general, the close connection between "healthy doctrine" and morally good works in 1:3–11 and elsewhere indicates more strongly that this doctrine is addressed to the progressing Christians in order that they can consider the law in the proper manner and thus understand its goodness (1:8). In this manner, reason guides intellectual learning and moral behavior during the process of *oikeiōsis*. The virtue of "godliness" (2:2) promotes a peaceful and moderated life. This life does not contain anger (2:8), but it is compatible with good desire (*epithymia* in 3:1).

The second half of the epistle offers more concrete evidence of *metriopatheia*. In 4:1–10 Paul fights the false teachers who require celibacy and abstinence from foods. Paul is less ascetic and says even that "nothing is to be rejected" (4:4). On the other hand, he regards the practice of godliness to be a "training" (*gymnasia*) in which a person toils and struggles (4:7–10). Paul thus attempts to find a proper mean in which the necessary and useful passions of hunger and procreation can be understood positively, although a trained moderation of emotions is consciously practiced. In 4:8 the aspect of usefulness, which also appears in Philo, is mentioned (cf. 2 Tim. 3:16 and Titus 3:8). The admonition of 1 Tim. 4:15, mentioning explicitly the idea of progress, sounds like an encouragement to the practice of *metriopatheia* and mentions the second aspect of *oikeiōsis*, namely, the dimension of "we." A wise person does not only think of his or her own salvation, but has a genuine care for others.

The fifth chapter of 1 Timothy contains many instructions that moderate the norms of early Christianity and emphasize the importance of right judgment in varying situations. Some widows are to be supported, whereas others are not (5:3). Widows are allowed and even encouraged to remarry (5:14). Accusations are to be accepted only in very serious cases (5:19). Wine can be consumed for reasons of health (5:23). In all different situations, partiality is to be avoided and purity is commanded (5:21–22). In addition to the moderation of certain rules, Paul wants to highlight the complex interaction between reason and the law. The law is good (1:8), but it becomes really beneficial when it is applied lawfully or "considered as" pertaining to relevant cases. Reason and the overall progress of Christians serve here as helpers in the interpretation of the law. Whereas the false teachers demand strict rules and elaborate interpretations, Paul recommends a moderation in which the good of the community and personal progress are intended. In this manner, *metriopatheia* becomes applied to many different issues related to the progress of Christians.

Finally, many other virtues mentioned in 1 Timothy are also connected with the discussion of the moderation of emotion. In particular, *autarkeia* (6:7–8) is a key term of this discussion. False teachers are trapped by harmful desires (6:9), whereas the sound teacher preserves his right judgment and thus his *autarkeia*. Thus a church leader should be capable of both familiar attachment and impartial detachment. The sound teacher is not apathetic, but can control himself or herself with the help of reason and thus preserve the necessary integrity. Other virtues like endurance, gentleness (6:11), hospitality, temperance (3:2), good reputation (3:7), and patience (1:16) also display the ideal of self-control and the ability to keep in balance.

In 2 Timothy, the idea of *metriopatheia* first appears in connection with the ideal of "self-discipline" and "balanced judgment" (*sōphronismos*) in 1:7. The importance of sound judgment and balance is also emphasized in 2:4–6. The aspiration to win the crown requires self-control, which does not eradicate emotions but cultivates and moderates them. In 2:16 a detachment from illusory progress is recommended. The overall vision of 2:14–26 is concerned with the purification of the household from disturbing passions (2:22). As a "large house" (2:20), the church needs to be cleansed. In this process of *oikeiōsis*, good works, love, and peace (2:21–22) are emphasized.

Second Timothy mentions the term "progress" three times (2:16; 3:9, 13). Whereas 1 Tim. 4:15 refers to Timothy's progress in a positive fashion, 2 Tim. 3:9 and 3:13 are critical of the false progress of the heretics. Also, 2:16 speaks of problematic progress, but 3:16–17 again recommends the good training in righteousness. Truth (3:13) and a sound mind (3:8–9) are criteria of genuine progress; thus real progress means turning from egocentrism toward objective reason. Unaffectionate people are criticized (3:3); true godliness is described as a path in which patience and love (3:10) are observed. Gentleness (2:25) becomes a good emotion that displays both attachment and detachment. The requirement to be sober (4:5) or temperate (1 Tim. 3:2) also underlines the importance of right judgment between the harmful extremes.

In Titus, the moderation of virtue is connected with the extensive use of the term *sōphrōn* in 2:1–15. Various groups of the church should live a life of self-control. This may mean different outward behavior, since the right judgment of prudent mind adapts the human actions to suit particular needs. Thus older men should be temperate and serious (2:2), whereas younger men are called to self-control and integrity (2:6–7). In the same context of rational self-control, women should be good managers of the household (2:5), and slaves should show fidelity to their masters (2:9). In spite of the slightly different shape of self-control, all groups display the same virtue of proper moderation.

In Titus, the goal of this advice is the good of the household and the church. This is realized when Christians show genuine care for others and renounce "worldly passions" (2:12). Love, kindness, and good works manifest this spirit of *oikeiōsis* (e.g., 2:2–5). Interestingly, all three Pastoral Epistles mention the positive emotion of *praupatheia* (1 Tim. 6:11) or *prautēs* (2 Tim. 2:25; Titus 3:2). As a good emotion of Christians, the virtue of being gentle witnesses to the view that Paul is not aiming at eradication of emotions, but emphasizes their proper moderation and nurture. At the same time this virtue relates to the proclamation of Jesus in which the virtue of being "meek" (*praus*) is of great importance. Gentleness was already the virtue of Moses (Num. 12:3) and the coming king of peace (Zech. 9:9–10).

The presence of *metriopatheia* and related ideas in the Pastoral Epistles is significant for both exegetical and theological reasons. The recognition of this pattern of thought allows us to understand the proper meaning and context of these epistles more precisely. In particular, the relationship between Philo and the Pastoral Epistles should be studied in more detail. Theologically, it is important to see that the New Testament contains the idea of virtue as a mean. This feature connects the Pastoral Epistles with the thought of Aristotle (*Nicomachean Ethics* 2) and Thomas Aquinas (*Summa theologiae* 2/1 Q. 64), but also, as the virtue of gentleness shows, with Jesus and the Jewish Bible. Since the patristic tradition and especially the monastic tradition is overwhelmingly permeated by the idea of a complete eradication of emotion, it is remarkable that the New Testament canon also contains writings that advocate a moderation of emotion and a proper display of positive emotions.

APPENDIX B

Mental Disorders

First Timothy employs terminology that is related to health and illness. In particular, the word *hygiēs* ("healthy") is employed as a characterization of correct teaching or doctrine (*didaskalia*; 1 Tim. 1:10; 2 Tim. 4:3; Titus 1:9; 2:1) and the words (*logoi*; 1 Tim. 6:3; cf. 2 Tim. 1:13; Titus 2:8) of Jesus Christ. In keeping with this metaphorical usage, the representatives of false doctrine are described as being ill, in particular with regard to their mental state. My commentary argues that Paul does not do this only for polemical purposes, but he also has a more general aim of presenting a portrayal of healthy and sick minds.

This portrayal is rather closely related to the ideas of *metriopatheia* and progress toward objective reason and care for others (see appendix A). Paul is not, however, saying that the false teachers are stupid and ignorant of the idea of progress. On the contrary, the false teachers also claim to make progress toward higher aims (cf. 2 Tim. 3:9, 13) and in this sense apply Stoic thoughts. Paul, therefore, must point out that their claim of progress is false and does not in reality lead toward reason and goodness. The false teachers are not simply wrong, but they are "depraved in mind" (1 Tim. 6:5) or "of corrupt mind" (2 Tim. 3:8). The background of *metriopatheia* and progress is thus assumed, but it does not provide sufficient explanation of the state of false teachers. In addition, Paul makes use of the language of mental disorders and their therapy.

Madness and mental disorders in the ancient world is a vast topic that has been treated in many studies (B. Simon 1978; Pigeaud 1981, 1987; Ahonen 2005). The field of different therapies, both medical and philosophical, has likewise been discussed by specialists (Rabbow 1954; Nussbaum 1994; P. Hadot 1995, 2002; Sorabji 2000). At the same time it must be said that we do not yet know the full picture and that much work remains to be done. I will in the following ignore many basic discussions, for instance, those relating to mania and melancholia as well as many clearly medical cases of madness. Paul's characterization of his opponents resembles what is today called psychopathic or obsessive behavior. The false teachers proclaim rigid ascesis but they exhibit no real care for others (1 Tim. 4:2–5). They do not trust others but remain suspicious. They love controversies and disputes about words (6:3–5). At the same time, they seem to be clever and at least temporarily successful in their activities. Because of this description, I focus on similar characterizations in philosophy, in particular Stoicism as represented by Seneca. It is not claimed that the Pastoral Epistles are dependent on Seneca.[1] Rather, I attempt to say two things: (1) that Seneca represents in an exemplary manner the popular picture of mental disorders in the Stoicism of the first century AD and (2) that this popular picture is assumed in the Pastoral Epistles.

One popular Stoic paradox (by Chrysippus) states that all people are mad (Ahonen 2005: 100–101; von Arnim 1903: 3.658–68). The paradox points toward the need for adopting reason and renouncing the passions. If grave madness is a medical phenomenon, passions were not seldom regarded as a milder form of mental disorder that can and should be treated with philosophical therapy. Normally, however, some distinctions are made even though Stoics regard passions or bad desires as the root cause of those diseases of mind, which can be treated with philosophical therapy.[2]

A very typical and relevant definition of the relationship of mental disease and passions is given in Seneca's *Epistle* 75, entitled "The Diseases of the Soul":

> To give a brief definition: by "disease" we mean a persistent perversion of the judgment, so that things which are mildly desirable are thought to be highly desirable. Or, if you prefer, we may define it thus: to be too zealous in striving for things which are only mildly desirable or not desirable at all, or to value highly things which ought to be valued but slightly or valued not at all. "Passions" are objectionable impulses of the spirit, sudden and vehement; they have come so often, and so little attention has been paid to them, that they have caused a state of disease; just as a catarrh, when there has been but a single attack and the catarrh has not yet become habitual, produces a cough, but causes consumption when it has become regular and chronic. Therefore we may say that those who have made most progress are beyond the reach of the "diseases"; but they still feel the "passions" even when very near perfection. (*Epistle* 75.11–13 [LCL 76.143])

Several matters are relevant. First, we see the idea of "progress" again at work (see appendix A). People who have advanced enough in their striving for reason

---

1. For more authors and texts, see Sorabji 2000; Knuuttila 2004; Long and Sedley 1987: 410–23; and Malherbe 1989: 121–36. Barth and Blanke 2000: 92 consider that "it is not impossible that the apostle knew of the writings of Seneca . . . and was influenced by them." But this is a minority opinion among the exegetes.

2. Knuuttila 2004: 71–80 offers an overview of Stoic therapy. See also Long and Sedley 1987: 419–23.

need not be cured of the diseases of the soul. Second, although passions can be said to be the cause of disturbances, they are not simply synonymous with mental diseases. Third, for the closer understanding of passions and mental disorders it is very important to realize that, for many Stoics, emotions (*pathos, passio*) are themselves certain judgments of reason. They are, in other words, not irrational desires or instincts that emerge without or contrary to reason, but in order to have an emotion a person must have evaluated the object to which the emotion relates (for the Stoic view of emotions as judgments, see Sorabji 2000: 17–155 and Knuuttila 2004: 47–71).

According to the so-called judgment theory of emotion, a view often connected with Chrysippus and later Stoic cognitive therapy, emotions have objects that are regarded as good or bad (Knuuttila 2004: 59). Basic therapeutic treatment, aiming at freedom from emotions, assumes that emotions are false judgments. The initial evaluation leading to the judgment that constitutes the emotion has to be renounced. When the reason learns to behave in accordance with virtue, it leaves the self-centered realm of emotions and begins to care for the general good of all people. Given this, the wise person no longer has emotions, since he or she does not judge particular matters on the basis of individual benefits. Since emotions are judgments, they are subject to reason, and an educated reason can, at least in theory, rise above the realm of making affective personal judgments. In this way it can reach the state of *apatheia*. This state of indifference and tranquility is useful, since it allows the person to see the universe in a truthful and just manner (Sorabji 2000: 181–84).[3]

Without entering this complex view in more detail, we can note that Seneca defines the disease of the soul as "persistent perversion of the judgment." The person who obstinately clings to a false belief and to the false object of desire can be compared to a chronically sick person. Whereas passions are transitory, persistent false judgment makes the soul chronically ill. The judgment and its corresponding emotion can relate to very different external things. It was common in both Stoicism and Cynicism to regard the love of money as a root disease leading to different selfish emotions.[4] Love of money is a good example of "judgment theory," since it certainly presupposes intellectual calculation and abstract judgment. But the Stoics taught that even the more instinctual desires are, in the human mind, represented as judgments.

In his letter Seneca offers a threefold theory of progress with regard to diseases and passions. The most advanced class of people has put aside all diseases and passions, but they have not yet been tested. Thus "they have not put their good into practice." These people who are "very near to perfection" may "still feel the 'passions'" although they will not slip back into faults. The second class of people

---

3. This is merely a simplified outline of a complex subject.

4. Ahonen 2005: 129, referring to Stobaeus (von Arnim 1903: 3.421; Long and Sedley 1987: 418) and Galen, *De placitis Hippocratis et Platonis* 4.5.24–26 (Galen 1978–84: 265). Cf. Seneca, *On Anger* 3.33.1 (Seneca 1995: 108).

have also laid aside diseases and passions, but they "can still slip back into their former state." The third class has laid aside the greatest vices, but may still feel many passions, for instance, anger. Seneca further holds that "it will be well with us if we are admitted to this [third] class" (quotations from *Epistle* 75.9, 12, 13, 15 [LCL 76.141, 143, 145]; I. Hadot 1969). It is important to see that the highest classes of progress are almost unreachable and that even in them some passions are still felt. In this sense passions and diseases of the mind continue to haunt even very serious and firm people, who consciously aim at progress. It is prudent to be realistic and humble with regard to the eradication of vices.

To give a concrete picture of how the Stoic therapy of emotions works, we can briefly look at Seneca's treatise *On Anger*, a classical manual of anger management. Many forms of anger typically represent the definition of mental disease quoted above. Seneca teaches that anger is often provoked by the false expectations:

> We are upset by empty trifles.... Any creature fierce and furious by nature is unsettled by things of no substance. The same occurs with restless and brutish characters: they are wounded by mere suspicions of how things are.... We are angry with those whom we love most because they have granted us less than we had imagined that they would or less than others have got from them. (*On Anger* 3.30.1–2)[5]

For Seneca, the start of "insane anger" lies in the attachment of "great value to little things." Among such false judgments, disputes about money play a prominent role. Other things include, for instance, "food and drink and the pretentious refinements" as well as "suspicions and the malign misconstructions of what someone else has said" (*On Anger* 3.33–34). More than other emotions, anger has to be discussed in terms of health and sickness: "Other failings are a departure from reason; ... anger is a departure from sanity." Anger is "lunatic and ever resorting to its own force, arrogant in success, crazy when frustrated" (3.1.5). In this manner a false judgment of exceptional gravity is at stake.

The cure of anger consists in recognizing the false judgment and attempting to correct it. A person should examine the difference between great and little things; he or she should not be easily provoked and should admit that he or she may be wrong. Seneca emphasizes the value of delaying one's reactions: "The greatest remedy for anger is postponement, which allows its initial heat to abate and the darkness that oppresses the mind to subside or thin out" (*On Anger* 3.12.4). Instead of fighting others, the angry person is advised to "fight with yourself" (3.13.1). This means self-control when anger is being provoked (3.13.5).

Several different virtues convey the ideas of postponement, inner struggle, and self-control in Stoic texts. The virtue of moderation and self-control (*sōphrosynē*) relates the capacity of practical reason (*phronēsis*) to the virtuous moderation. The terms *constantia* and *eupatheia* denote the state of balanced detachment in

5. Quotations of Seneca's *On Anger* are taken from Seneca 1995: 76–116.

which mild or good parts of the passions may still be felt but they are stripped of false beliefs (Knuuttila 2004: 69–70; Sorabji 2000: 49). Caution, modesty, and piety are subspecies of *eupatheia* (Sorabji 2000: 47–48; cf. Engberg-Pedersen 2000: 73).

In the Pastoral Epistles we find many concepts that underline the idea that a preacher of healthy doctrine should express self-control and detachment.[6] These concepts are connected with popular philosophy. The church leader ought to be experienced in life and able to exercise moderation (*sōphrōn*; 1 Tim. 3:2; cf. Titus 1:8; 2:2–5, 12). The absence of anger is characteristic of the leader, who is to be "not violent but gentle, not quarrelsome, and not a lover of money" (1 Tim. 3:3). The term "gentle" (*epieikēs*) here denotes the classical virtue of *epieikeia* ("moderation, fairness"). The term "gentleness" in 6:11 translates as *praupatheia* ("friendly emotion"; cf. 2 Tim. 2:25). This term approaches both *eupatheia* and Aristotle's *praotēs* ("feeling mildly"). *Praupatheia* expresses a good emotion that is compatible with detachment and inner peace, not contrary to the Hellenistic ideas, but in accordance with them.[7]

The eschatological concept of endurance (*hypomonē*; 1 Tim. 6:11; 2 Tim. 3:10) and the broader idea of patience (*makrothymia*; 1 Tim. 1:16; 2 Tim. 3:10; 4:2) also underline the idea of postponement. *Makrothymia* further means "an ability to control one's anger" (Collins 2002: 256). The two notions define the character of an advanced and exemplary teacher. Seneca's idea of inner fight as a good alternative to vicious quarreling appears in 1 Tim. 6:12 and 2 Tim. 4:7. In 2:24 the good teacher is characterized as being "not quarrelsome but kindly to everyone." The Stoic concept of *autarkeia* ("contentment") in 1 Tim. 6:6 also underlines the importance of balanced detachment.

This terminology of virtues in the Pastoral Epistles thus matches well with the Stoic recommendations that are offered as prevention, cure, and alternative to the state of mental disease, especially anger. It may be even more instructive, however, to look at Paul's description of the false teachers and their corrupted mind.

As I argue in more detail in the exposition (esp. 1 Tim. 6:3–10), the description of Paul's opponents reveals a certain psychopathology. The false teachers claim to be very progressive (2 Tim. 3:9), and they practice an advanced ascesis (1 Tim. 4:3). In reality, however, their folly and depraved mind (6:5; 2 Tim. 3:9) is evident for true Christians. At least four observable characteristics of their behavior allow this diagnosis:

---

6. Some attention is paid to medical language in Johnson 2001: 393–94; see also Malherbe 1989: 121–36 and Seid n.d. My approach does not, however, consider medical language to be primarily "imagery" and "metaphors," but this language serves, in addition to polemics, the aims of diagnostics and therapy. While I recognize the importance of the parallel material discussed by Malherbe 1989: 121–36, I cannot share his conclusion that in the Pastoral Epistles "there is no picture, as in the moral philosophers, of the intellectually and morally ill person who will be cured."

7. So slightly different from Roloff 1988: 347. Cf. Knuuttila 2004: 32, expounding Aristotle, *Rhetorics* 2.1–11. For *sōphrōn* and related concepts, see Marshall 1999: 182–91 and Johnson 2001: 393–95.

1. False teachers are talkative to the extent of meaningless talk, controversies, quarreling, and profane chatter (1 Tim. 1:6–7; 5:13; 6:4–5; 2 Tim. 2:14–17, 23–24; Titus 1:10; 3:9), whereas a wise person calmly stays away from disputes and often prefers silence (1 Tim. 2:2; 3:3; 4:7; 6:11, 20; 2 Tim. 2:16, 23). The ability to keep quiet and talk only at the right moment was trained in therapeutic exercises (Rabbow 1954; Nussbaum 1994; G. Wohlfart and J. Kreuzer in *HWP* 8.1483–95; F. von Lilienfeld in *Theologische Realenzyklopädie* 15.282–89). Silence characterizes a wise person.

2. False teachers are trapped by harmful desires, in particular anger (1 Tim. 6:9; 2 Tim. 3:6; cf. Titus 3:3). Although good teachers also have passions (2 Tim. 2:22), they have learned to control and moderate them. Paul's descriptions of harmful desires are astonishingly similar to Seneca's terminology in *On Anger*. This similarity does not mean literary dependence, but only that both represent a commonplace treatment of certain desires and emotions. Among the harmful desires, the love of money is prominent in both 1 Tim. 6:10 (cf. 2 Tim. 3:2) and Seneca (*On Anger* 3.33). Much popular philosophy identified this desire as a particular root cause. Because the love of money presupposes the view of emotion as judgment, it matches particularly well with the Stoic paradigm of emotions. In addition, both Seneca (*On Anger* 3.31–34) and the Pastoral Epistles (1 Tim. 6:4; Titus 3:3) identify envy and base suspicions as harmful desires. These emotions also involve a judgment in order to be actual. For Seneca, love of money, envy, and base suspicions are the most common causes of anger. Among the vices of the Pastoral Epistles, anger and hate (1 Tim. 2:8; Titus 3:3), violence (1 Tim. 1:13; 3:3; Titus 1:7), and quarrelsome behavior (e.g., 1 Tim. 3:3; 6:4; 2 Tim. 2:24; Titus 3:9) are especially to be avoided by the Christians. Seneca's *On Anger* is aimed at rulers whose anger had especially drastic consequences (see the editors' introduction in Seneca 1995: 3–16). In keeping with this aim, the Pastoral Epistles stress that particularly bishops and other leaders should be gentle and patient. Anger, with its root causes, related desires, and social implications, is thus the main example of harmful passion discussed in the Pastoral Epistles. The mental disorders treated by the apostle are related to the general problem of anger.

3. False teachers are characterized by obstinate and rigid behavior. In his abovequoted letter Seneca distinguishes passions from mental diseases by saying that, whereas passions are transitory, mental disease means a persistent perversion of the judgment. Such a chronic state effectively prevents the person from using reason for the purpose of understanding the real nature of the universe. A person who is a fool in this sense cannot proceed in the *oikeiōsis* but remains in the subjective state of his or her individual understanding. In 1 Tim. 6:4 (cf. 3:6; 2 Tim. 3:4), the verb *typhoomai* describes precisely this kind of idiosyncrasy in which the person aims to be original in a stupid

manner.[8] A typical such idiosyncrasy would be to think that "godliness is a means of gain" (1 Tim. 6:5; cf. 6:6–10; 5:18; Titus 1:11). This thought can be used as accusation against others or as a selfish motive, but supporting it in any case reveals one's inability to progress toward reason and genuine care for others. Abstinence from foods, celibacy (1 Tim. 4:3), an exaggerated interest in genealogies (1 Tim. 1:4; Titus 3:9), masochism (1 Tim. 6:10), and the obstinate defense of controversial positions (e.g., 1 Tim. 6:4; 2 Tim. 2:18; 4:24; Titus 3:9) also witness to the mental disease in which a person's judgment is chronically ill because it remains self-centered and incapable of reaching the objective world.

4. The vice of lying is connected with idle talk and obstinate behavior. Especially in Titus (1:2, 10–13, 16; 3:9–11), the phenomenon of lying exemplifies the problems of first-person oral confessions. Such talk may remain a self-centered lip service. Those orthodox Christians adhering to sound doctrine should perform the move from "I" to "reason" and "we" so that their witness becomes manifest in their good works, proper emotions, and genuine care for others. The phenomenon of conscious or half-conscious deception is to an extent also present in 1 Tim. 1:10; 4:1; 6:5, 21; 2 Tim. 2:18; 3:13; 4:3. Paul's aim is not, however, to claim that his opponents would be very clever and conscious liars. He rather points out that because his opponents are so stupid, obstinate, and self-centered they become carried away by their myths and idle talk. An adherent to sound doctrine can discern that this is the case.

In sum, we can see that both the virtuous characteristics attributed to the adherents of healthy doctrine and the problematic traits present in false teachers and their supporters reveal an affinity with the Stoic description of mental disturbances, especially with anger. It is too easy to read Paul's description of his opponents as merely polemical defamation. Obviously, one can speculate about the fairness of the picture given by Paul. In expounding these passages, however, I consider it more important to disclose the terminological and argumentative affinities with the ideals on mental health, good understanding, and genuine care for others, as they are advocated in Hellenistic philosophy. Showing these affinities does not mean that Paul's teaching would be reduced to philosophy. But it is important to see that Paul is not merely doing unfair rhetorical polemics, but he aims rather at outlining a diagnosis on the basis of which he can argue why the healthy doctrine and good character required of church leaders are so important. For Paul's contemporaries, this diagnosis was in keeping with the general knowledge of harmful passions and their effects on people; therefore it could fill its argumentative purpose.

8. See Collins 2002: 155, 249. The literal meaning of *typhoomai* is "to be surrounded by smoke"; 2 Tim. 3:4 uses the substantive *tetyphōmenoi* ("those surrounded by smoke").

APPENDIX C

Varieties of Giving

In order to understand the various acts of interhuman giving in the Pastoral Epistles, I need to outline the "phenomenology" of giving in more detail. Although the verb *didōmi* need not always appear, the phenomena discussed presuppose acts of giving and receiving. In order to grasp this field of reciprocity, I will draft a theory that employs features of both Hellenistic philosophy and the cultural anthropology of gifts and services. It is not my intention to press or to reduce the material of the Pastoral Epistles to suit these features, but simply to apply the theory in order to make visible the issues discussed.

The practice of hospitality is a paradigmatic example of interhuman giving and receiving. Hospitality means sharing one's food and perhaps shelter with persons in need, with friends but also with strangers. In the practice of hospitality, the gifts or the services given are normally consumed. What remains is not the gift, but a memory of the favor received, a feeling of gratitude but also a sense of reciprocity in which the host is, in turn, welcomed to receive hospitality from the guest. In this manner hospitality is different from caritative aid, although it also resembles the phenomenon of helping others.[1]

The phenomenology of giving, gifts, and favors has remained a vital discussion topic from the time of Jesus and Paul until today. Seneca's highly influential study *On Favors* can be regarded as a major starting point of this discussion. I do not aim to show direct dependencies between Paul and Seneca, but want, using Seneca as a representative example, to outline the general atmosphere in which gifts, favors, and hospitality were discussed toward the end of the first century AD.

---

1. For the different conceptual dimensions of hospitality, see Sutherland 2006; Godbout 1999; Dufourmantelle and Derrida 2000. For early Christianity, see Oden 2002.

For the understanding of favors and gifts it is essential to distinguish them from the economic exchange of buying and selling. Seneca makes this point as follows:

> "Pay back what you owe!" is an utterly reasonable maxim, affirming a universal law. But it is utterly shameful when applied to a favour. "Pay back!" Yes, but what? The life which one owes? One's status? One's security? One's health? The most important things cannot be repaid. "Well, in their place, put something of the same value." But that is just what I was saying! All that is excellent in such a precious activity will come to an end, if we turn a favour into a business deal. (*On Favors* 3.14.3–4)[2]

Although Seneca in this manner stresses the importance of "free gifts" that cannot be reduced to the economic exchange, he also affirms that some reciprocity between giver and recipient exists and is proper. The recipient should give thanks and show a proper gratitude. As recipients "we should express our delight and make it obvious to our benefactor so that he gets an immediate reward" (*On Favors* 2.22.1). But this is already enough. "To accept a favour gladly is to have repaid it" (2.31.1). No further dependence should be assumed by either side. Because of this, the giver should expect that the recipient should feel indebted. "Anyone drawn to act kindly . . . will be still more pleased to give to people who will only be indebted to the extent that they wish" (3.13.2). A strong moderation of emotions is thus expected from both giver and recipient. This moderation is not indifference, but a proper favor should approach indifference in order to remain distinct from the economic transactions in which the gains and losses are calculated.

One corollary of this basic idea is that a favor can be identified as favor only if we know the intention of the giver. If I find your book on my desk, (1) you may simply have forgotten it, (2) you may have paid back an old debt, or (3) you may have given it to me as a gift. In order to grasp the meaning of your act, I need to know your intention. Therefore, the true meaning of gifts and favors does not depend on external and material things, but on the intention of the giver:

> A favour cannot possibly be touched by the hand; the transaction takes place in the mind. There is a great difference between its material and the favour itself. So it is not the gold or the silver, or any of those things which are accepted as so important, that constitutes the favour, but rather the good will of whoever bestows it. . . . The favour, even when its vehicle is lost, remains. It is a right action and no force can undo it. (*On Favors* 1.5.2–3)

Although Seneca concentrates on interhuman giving, he also speaks of God and gods as exemplary givers. He regards nature, fate, and fortune as being names that also refer to God as giver of all kinds of favors (*On Favors* 4.8). This kind of god is exemplary because it does not think of receiving anything in return:

2. Quotations of Seneca's *On Favors* are taken from Seneca 1995: 193–308.

God confers on us the greatest and most important favours without any thought of return. He has no need for anything to be conferred, nor could we confer anything on him. Doing a favour is, therefore, something to be chosen for its own sake. The one advantage to be considered is that of the recipient, and we should approach it by putting aside any interests of our own. (*On Favors* 4.9.1)

Exemplary giving is thus disinterested and does not pay attention to whether anything is given in return. Divine giving can achieve this ideal. But Seneca obviously thinks that even many humans can offer a truly free lunch to people in need. In Greco-Roman society, in which the economic exchange was important but limited, many important services depended on favors both given and received (Oden 2002). Although Seneca downplays the importance of material gifts and favors, anthropologists, historians, and philosophers have paid attention to this dimension. Without entering this discussion in detail, I will outline a model that I consider to be useful for the understanding of the phenomenology of giving in the Pastoral Epistles. All elements of this model appear in the academic discussion on gifts; it is only my combination of them that may, to some extent, be innovative.[3]

One can distinguish between gifts and services by saying that gifts remain the property of the recipient, whereas services are consumed immediately or during a short period of time. Seneca's term "favors" (*beneficia*) is very comprehensive and may comprise acts that are not covered by either of these words, but most favors are clearly either gifts or services. The criterion of consumption is a rather sharp one, but some items nevertheless remain in the gray area between them. Giving a cloth to keep my friend warm is a service, but the cloth is also a gift that remains. But cloth is not as permanent as a necklace, which can be characterized as a typical gift. Food and shelter are typical expressions of services, as are most acts that fall under the concept of hospitality. Helping another person can consist of both gifts and services.

It is obvious that gifts are, as a rule, more permanent than services. Some anthropologists, employing the classical legal distinction between movable and immovable goods, divide gifts into these two categories (Weiner 1992: 32; Godelier 1999). A necklace can be freely circulated and is thus a typical movable gift, whereas land represents a typical immovable good. The circulation of land is much more limited than the circulation of many other gifts. Following this idea, we may obtain three categories of noneconomic transactions: (1) services in which the favor is consumed, (2) gifts that remain a property of the recipient but can be further circulated, and (3) immovable gifts that are permanent and resist circulation. The second and third need not be material items. I may tell you a joke that you can freely circulate. But I may tell you a family secret that is not supposed to

---

3. The following does not appear in Saarinen 2005, but my reflections there may be helpful as background information.

be spread further. Neither the joke nor the secret are extinguished in the event of transmission. But they differ in the mode of circulation.

The distinction between more and less movable gifts is helpful. Basically, this distinction does not extend the dimension of consumption versus endurance, but it rather expresses another and independent distinction. In understanding the manifold field of favors in which A gives the thing or renders the service B to C, the transferred item B may be (1) consumable or inconsumable and (2) freely circulated or have a restricted circulation. Moreover, the two pairs are distinguished quantitatively rather than qualitatively. Food is consumed rapidly, a cloth does not last very long, but a necklace may endure almost infinitely. A joke can be freely circulated, a family secret can have a restricted circulation, whereas a password to personal files, having been given once, is not to be circulated afterward.

Given this, we obtain four basic categories of favors:

1. Inconsumable goods that are freely circulated: material presents and immaterial stories are frequently of this kind. The anthropological notion of "gift exchange" often presupposes this category of favors.
2. Inconsumable goods that have restricted circulation: this category approaches the important phenomenon of inalienable possessions (discussed below).
3. Consumable goods that are freely circulated: such favors and services, for instance, food, shelter, and clothing, are closely related to hospitality. Often it is practical to define hospitality as the generous sharing of consumable goods.
4. Consumable goods that have restricted circulation: targeted social aid, for instance, helping a limited number of widows (1 Tim. 5:3–16), exemplifies this kind of favor. Interestingly, it can further be asked whether the Eucharist belongs to this category.

The inward essence of the favor is not constituted by the material or immaterial vehicle of transaction. As Seneca points out, the favor is constituted in the minds of giver and recipient. At the same time, the material vehicle, the gift itself, is highly important and carries a variety of different connotations. These connotations can be better understood when we focus on the second category of inalienable possessions. This category approaches the meaning of tradition in theological language.

Annette Weiner pays attention to Western legal history in which things are defined as either movables or immovables. Whereas buying, selling, and consuming movable goods is relatively easy, many prohibitions and limitations concern the exchange of immovable property, for instance, land and buildings. Weiner argues that the Western distinction between movable and immovable things is a part of the larger anthropological picture in which portability is not the final criterion. Anthropologically, some things are to be kept all the time. They are inalienable possessions that are to be distinguished from the goods that are subject to exchange and in this sense alienable. Inalienable possessions are handed over only within an exclusive series of ownership: "What makes a possession inalienable is its exclusive and cumulative identity with a particular series of owners through time. Its history is authenticated by fictive or true genealogies, origin myths, sacred ancestors, and gods. In this way, inalienable possessions are transcendent treasures to be guarded against all the exigencies that might force their loss" (Weiner 1992: 33).

Weiner does not discuss theology. She attempts to contribute to the long sociological and anthropological discussion concerning the exchange of gifts. Since Marcel Mauss's 1990 seminal work *The Gift* (see Saarinen 2005), sociologists have regarded the exchange of gifts as a basic form of economic and social structure of human society. Weiner's specific contribution to this discussion is to hold that not all items in a society are subject to exchange in a similar manner. She attempts to define the category of inalienable possessions and to claim that it represents the "oldest economic classification in the world" (1992: 43). Earlier anthropologists claimed that reciprocity forms the basis of society, but Weiner holds that reciprocity is finally motivated by "the desire to keep something back from the pressures of give and take. This something is a possession that speaks to and for an individual's or a group's social identity and, in so doing, affirms the difference between one person or group and another" (1992: 43).

There is an obvious and straightforward way of understanding Weiner's basic distinction. In a museum, we can buy items at a gift shop, whereas the museum objects are not for sale. In a shop, we are not supposed to buy the shopkeeper's wedding ring. In the larger context of discussion, however, even the inalienable possessions have once been given and received, but this transmission is "exclusive" and stretches over a "particular series of owners." Some furniture in a home may derive from the grandparents, and the owner intends to leave it to his or her children. Other pieces of furniture may be sold or thrown away, whereas the inherited items are carefully repaired and handed over to the next generation. In this act of handing over, the owner in a way also keeps the inalienable furniture. This is meant by Weiner's phrase "keeping-while-giving."

In addition to the particular series of owners, the story and genealogy related to the inalienable possession is of seminal importance. The museum piece and the family furniture come with an attached story that reveals its origin. A relic points toward the legend concerning a particular saint and can thus actualize the legend here and now. It is important to notice that the inalienable possession need not be a material item. A prayer, a confession of faith, or a liturgy can similarly be transmitted from one generation to another. For the purpose of constituting group identity, a verbal confession or prayer may even be more effective than a material item, for a confession can be said by many and it nevertheless strongly affirms the "keeping" of the inalienable possession. Immaterial acts of confession may constitute the tradition that is continued over a long period of time.

To illustrate this phenomenon, we may compare (1) reciting the creed, (2) singing a hymn, and (3) singing an ordinary song. As an act of affirmation, the first act is clearly inalienable. It gives witness, but at the same time it keeps the faith. The third act is normally a form of alienable exchange. The second act can be inalienable or alienable, depending on the circumstances.

Whereas durable material items and committed verbal performances can exemplify the phenomenon of keeping-while-giving, it is less clear whether consumable material goods can belong to the category of inalienable possessions. Weiner discusses in particular the examples of food and clothing and comes to differentiated conclusions. Ceremonial garments, handed over to one's successors, clearly represent inalienable possessions. Food is, on the one hand, the "most ineffectual inalienable possession" because it perishes in consumption. But Weiner documents cases in which food is decorated or otherwise transformed and preserved "to prompt memories from past events" (1992: 38). But it is obvious that food and clothing have to be specifically treated and designated in order to become inalienable possessions. In this limited sense, the fourth category can also, in some cases, approach the idea of keeping-while-giving.

In addition to some comments about hospitality and social aid in the passage on widows (1 Tim. 5:3–16), different varieties of theological giving are discussed in excursuses 3, 5, 6, 8, and 9.

BIBLIOGRAPHY

Ahonen, Marke. 2005. "Antiikin filosofien käsitykset hulluudesta" [Madness in ancient philosophy]. Licentiate thesis in philosophy, University of Helsinki.

Alcinous. 1990. *Enseignement des doctrines de Platon*. Paris: Belles Lettres.

Anselm of Canterbury. 1988. *Basic Writings*. Translated by S. N. Deane. La Salle, IL: Open Court.

Arnim, H. von, ed. 1903. *Stoicorum veterum fragmenta*. Leipzig: Teubner.

Augustine. 1991. *The Trinity*. Translated by E. Hill. New York: New City Press.

Aulén, Gustaf. 1969. *Christus Victor: An Historical Study of the Three Main Types of the Idea of Atonement*. New York: Macmillan.

Barrett, C. K. 1969. "Titus." Pages 1–14 in *Neotestamentica et semitica: Studies in Honour of Matthew Black*. Edited by E. E. Ellis and M. Wilcox. Edinburgh: T. & T. Clark.

Barth, Markus, and Helmut Blanke. 2000. *The Letter to Philemon*. Eerdmans Critical Commentary. Grand Rapids: Eerdmans.

Bauckham, Richard J. 1983. *Jude, 2 Peter*. Word Biblical Commentary 50. Waco: Word.

Bauer, Walter. 2000. *A Greek-English Lexicon of the New Testament and Other Early Christian Literature*. 3rd edition. Revised and edited by Frederick William Danker. Chicago: University of Chicago Press.

Benedict XVI, Pope. 2007. *Jesus of Nazareth*. Translated by Adrian J. Walker. New York: Doubleday.

Bengel, J. A. 1887. *Gnomon Novi Testamenti*. 8th edition. Tübingen: Schramm.

Black, Max. 1962. *Models and Metaphors*. New York: Cornell University Press.

———. 1979. "More about Metaphor." Pages 19–43 in *Metaphor and Thought*. Edited by A. Ortony. Cambridge: Cambridge University Press.

Bray, Gerald, ed. 2000. *James, 1–2 Peter, 1–3 John, Jude*. Ancient Christian Commentary on Scripture: New Testament 11. Downers Grove, IL: IVP.

Brown, Peter. 1988. *The Body and Society: Men, Women, and Sexual Renunciation in Early Christianity*. New York: Columbia University Press.

Bruce, F. F. 1988. *The Canon of Scripture*. Downers Grove, IL: IVP.

Burigana, Riccardo. 1986. "Caspar Cruciger: In epistolam Pauli ad Timotheum priorem Commentarius (1540): Edizione e commento." Diss., University of Florence.

Calvin, John. 1960. *Institutes of the Christian Religion*. 2 vols. Edited by J. T. McNeill. Translated by F. L. Battles. Library of Christian Classics 20–21. Philadelphia: Westminster.

———. 1996. *Commentaries on the Epistles to Timothy, Titus, and Philemon*. Translated by William Pringle. Reprinted Grand Rapids: Baker (also available at http://www.ccel.org/ccel/calvin/calcom43.html).

Chaine, Joseph. 1939. *Les epîtres catholiques: La seconde epître de saint Pierre, les epîtres de saint Jean, l'epître de saint Jude*. Paris: Gabalda.

Chappell, T. D. J. 1995. *Aristotle and Augustine on Freedom—Two Theories of Freedom, Voluntary Action, and Akrasia*. New York: St. Martin's Press.

Charles, R. H. 1995. *The Book of Enoch, Together with a Reprint of the Greek Fragments*. Reprinted Whitefish, MT: Kessinger.

Charlesworth, James H., ed. 1985. *The Old Testament Pseudepigrapha*. 2 vols. New York: Doubleday.

Chrysostom. 1890. *Homilies on Timothy, Titus, and Philemon*. Translated by J. Tweed (slightly modernized). NPNF[1] 13.399–557. Reprinted Grand Rapids: Eerdmans. (Latin text in Patrologia graeca 62.501–720.)

Collins, Raymond F. 2002. *1 and 2 Timothy and Titus: A Commentary*. New Testament Library. Louisville: Westminster John Knox.

Doriani, Daniel M. 1995. "History of Interpretation of 1 Timothy 2." Pages 215–69 in *Women in the Church: A Fresh Analysis of 1 Timothy 2:9–15*. Edited by A. J. Köstenberger, T. R. Schreiner, and H. S. Baldwin. Grand Rapids: Baker.

Dufourmantelle, Anne, and Jacques Derrida. 2000. *Of Hospitality*. Translated by Rachel Bowlby. Stanford: Stanford University Press.

Dunn, James D. G. 2005. *Unity and Diversity in the New Testament*. 2nd edition. London: SCM.

Ebeling, Gerhard. 1982. *Dogmatik des christlichen Glaubens*, vol. 3. Tübingen: Mohr.

Ehrman, Bart D. 2003. *The Apostolic Fathers*. 2 vols. Loeb Classical Library 24–25. Cambridge: Harvard University Press.

Engberg-Pedersen, Troels. 1990. *The Stoic Theory of Oikeiosis*. Aarhus: Aarhus University Press.

———. 2000. *Paul and the Stoics*. Louisville: Westminster John Knox.

Fitzmyer, Joseph A. 2000. *The Letter to Philemon*. Anchor Bible 34C. New York: Doubleday.

Galen. 1978–84. *De placitis Hippocratis et Platonis*. Edited by P. de Lacy. Berlin: Akademie-Verlag.

Gassmann, Günther, ed. 1993. *The Documentary History of Faith and Order*. Geneva: WCC.

Girard, René. 1977. *Violence and the Sacred*. Translated by Patrick Gregory. Baltimore: Johns Hopkins University Press.

———. 1996. *The Girard Reader*. Edited by J. G. Williams. New York: Crossroad.

Gnilka, Joachim. 1982. *Der Philemonbrief*. Herders theologischer Kommentar zum Neuen Testament 10/4. Freiburg: Herder.

Godbout, Jacques. 1999. *The World of the Gift*. Translated by Donald Winkler. Montreal: McGill-Queens University Press.

Godelier, Maurice. 1999. *The Enigma of the Gift*. Translated by Nora Scott. Chicago: University of Chicago Press.

Gorday, Peter, ed. 2000. *Colossians, 1–2 Thessalonians, 1–2 Timothy, Titus, Philemon*. Ancient Christian Commentary on Scripture: New Testament 9. Downers Grove, IL: IVP.

Grosshans, Hans-Peter. 2003. *Die Kirche: Irdischer Raum der Wahrheit des Evangeliums*. Berlin: Evangelische Verlagsanstalt.

Grotius, Hugo. 1756. *Annotationes in Novum Testamentum*. Erlangen: Tetzscher.

Hadot, Ilsetraut. 1969. *Seneca und die griechisch-römische Tradition der Seelenleitung*. Berlin: de Gruyter.

Hadot, Pierre. 1995. *Philosophy as a Way of Life*. Edited by Arnold I. Davidson. Translated by Michael Chase. Oxford: Blackwell.

———. 2002. *What Is Ancient Philosophy?* Translated by Michael Chase. Cambridge: Harvard University Press.

Hahn, Ferdinand. 1986. *Exegetische Beiträge zum ökumenischen Gespräch*. Göttingen: Vandenhoeck & Ruprecht.

Hanson, A. T. 1982. *The Pastoral Epistles*. New Century Bible Commentary. London: Marshall Pickering.

Häring, Bernhard. 1964. *Das Gesetz Christi: Moraltheologie*. Freiburg: Wewel.

Hauerwas, Stanley. 1983. *The Peaceable Kingdom*. Notre Dame: University of Notre Dame Press.

Hintikka, Jaakko. 1996. *Lingua Universalis vs. Rationalis Calculator: An Ultimate Presupposition of Twentieth-Century Philosophy*. Dordrecht/Boston: Kluwer.

Hopkins, Jasper. 1971. *A Companion to the Study of St. Anselm*. Minneapolis: University of Minnesota Press.

Jenson, Robert W. 1997–99. *Systematic Theology*. 2 vols. Oxford: Oxford University Press.

Johnson, Luke Timothy. 2001. *The First and Second Letters to Timothy*. Anchor Bible 35A. New York: Doubleday,

Käsemann, Ernst. 1964. *Essays on New Testament Themes*. London: SCM.

Knox, John. 1960. *Philemon among the Letters of Paul*. New York: Abingdon.

Knuuttila, Simo. 2004. *Emotions in Ancient and Medieval Philosophy*. Oxford: Clarendon.

Läger, Karoline. 1996. *Die Christologie der Pastoralbriefe*. Münster: Lit.

Lightfoot, J. B. 1904. *Saint Paul's Epistles to the Colossians and to Philemon*. 14th edition. London: Macmillan.

Lindbeck, George. 1984. *The Nature of Doctrine: Religion and Theology in a Postliberal Age*. Philadelphia: Westminster.

Lohse, Eduard. 1977. "Die Ordination im Spätjudentum und im Neuen Testament." Pages 501–23 in *Das kirchliche Amt im Neuen Testament*. Edited by K. Kertlege. Darmstadt: Wissenschaftliche Buchgesellschaft.

Long, A. A., and D. N. Sedley. 1987. *The Hellenistic Philosophers*, vol. 1: *Translations of the Principal Sources, with Philosophical Commentary*. Cambridge: Cambridge University Press.

Lyons, John. 1977. *Introduction to Theoretical Linguistics*. Cambridge: Cambridge University Press.

Malherbe, Abraham J. 1989. *Paul and the Popular Philosophers*. Minneapolis: Fortress.

Marshall, Bruce. 1989. "Aquinas as a Postliberal Theologian." *Thomist* 53:353–402.

Marshall, I. Howard. 1999. *A Critical and Exegetical Commentary on the Pastoral Epistles.* International Critical Commentary. London: T. & T. Clark.

Martin, Ralph P. 1994. *Jude.* Pages 65–86 in *The Theology of the Letters of James, Peter, and Jude*, by Andrew Chester and Ralph P. Martin. Cambridge: Cambridge University Press.

Mauss, Marcel. 1990. *Essay on the Gift.* London: Routledge.

Melanchthon, Philipp. 1993. *Loci communes 1521: Lateinisch-Deutsch.* Translated by H. G. Pöhlmann. Gütersloh: Gütersloher Verlagshaus.

Metzger, Bruce M. 1987. *The Canon of the New Testament: Its Origin, Development, and Significance.* Oxford: Oxford University Press.

Mounce, William D. 2000. *Pastoral Epistles.* Word Biblical Commentary 46. Nashville: Nelson.

Müller, E. F. K., ed. 1999. *Die Bekenntnisschriften der reformierten Kirche.* 2 vols. Nachdruck der Ausgabe Leipzig 1903. Waltrop: Spenner.

Neyrey, Jerome H. 1993. *2 Peter, Jude.* Anchor Bible 37C. New York: Doubleday.

Nussbaum, Martha. 1994. *The Therapy of Desire: Theory and Practice in Hellenistic Ethics.* Princeton: Princeton University Press.

Oberlinner, Lorenz. 1994. *Die Pastoralbriefe*, vol. 1: *Kommentar zum ersten Timotheusbrief.* Herders theologischer Kommentar zum Neuen Testament 11/1. Freiburg: Herder.

———. 1995. *Die Pastoralbriefe*, vol. 2: *Kommentar zum zweiten Timotheusbrief.* Herders theologischer Kommentar zum Neuen Testament 11/2. Freiburg: Herder.

———. 1996. *Die Pastoralbriefe*, vol. 3: *Kommentar zum Titusbrief.* Herders theologischer Kommentar zum Neuen Testament 11/3. Freiburg: Herder.

Oden, Amy G. 2002. *And You Welcomed Me: A Sourcebook on Hospitality in Early Christianity.* Nashville: Abingdon.

Oeming, Manfred. 2006. *Contemporary Biblical Hermeneutics.* Translated by Joachim F. Vette. Aldershot: Ashgate.

Origen. 1933. *Commentarius in Matthaeum.* Edited by E. Klostermann and E. Benz. Leipzig: Hinrichs.

Pannenberg, Wolfhart, and Theodor Schneider, eds. 1992–98. *Verbindliches Zeugnis.* 3 vols. Freiburg: Herder.

Pelikan, Jaroslav. 2005. *Acts.* Brazos Theological Commentary on the Bible. Grand Rapids: Brazos.

Petersen, Norman R. 1985. *Rediscovering Paul: Philemon and the Sociology of Paul's Narrative World.* Philadelphia: Fortress.

Pfnür, Vinzenz. 1970. *Einig in der Rechtfertigungslehre: Die Rechtfertigungslehre der Confessio Augustana und die Stellungnahme der katholischen Kontroverstheologie zwischen 1530 und 1535.* Wiesbaden: Steiner.

Pigeaud, Jackie. 1981. *La maladie de l'âme: Étude sur la relation de l'âme det du corps dans la tradition médico-philosophique antique.* Paris: Belles Lettres.

———. 1987. *Folie et cures de la folie chez les médecis de l'antiquité greco-romaine: La manie.* Paris: Belles Lettres.

Popkes, Wiard. 1967. *Christus traditus.* Zürich: Zwingli Verlag.

Quinn, Jerome D., and William C. Wacker. 2000. *The First and Second Letters to Timothy*. Eerdmans Critical Commentary. Grand Rapids: Eerdmans.

Rabbow, Paul. 1954. *Seelenführung: Methodik der Exerzitien in der Antike*. Munich: Kösel.

Raunio, Antti. 2001. *Summe des christlichen Lebens: Die Goldene Regel als Gesetz der Liebe in der Theologie Martin Luthers*. Mainz: Zabern.

Ricoeur, Paul. 1978. *The Rule of Metaphor*. Translated by Robert Czerny. London: Routledge.

Riesenfeld, Harald. 1982. "Faith and Love Promoting Hope: An Interpretation of Philemon v. 6." Pages 251–57 in *Paul and Paulinism: Essays in Honour of C. K. Barrett*. Edited by M. D. Hooker and S. G. Wilson. London: SPCK.

Roloff, Jürgen. 1985. "Pfeiler und Fundament der Wahrheit." Pages 229–47 in *Glaube und Eschatologie*. Edited by E. Grässer and O. Merk. Tübingen: Mohr.

———. 1988. *Der erste Brief an Timotheus*. Evangelisch-katholischer Kommentar zum Neuen Testament. Neukirchen: Neukirchener Verlag.

Rowston, D. J. 1974. "The Most Neglected Book in the New Testament." *New Testament Studies* 21:554–73.

Saarinen, Risto. 1994. *Weakness of the Will in Medieval Thought: From Augustine to Buridan*. Leiden: Brill.

———. 2004. "In sinu Patris: Die barmherzige Trinität in Luthers Gebrauch von Joh. 1,18." *Neue Zeitschrift für systematische Theologie und Religionsphilosophie* 46:431–47.

———. 2005. *God and the Gift: An Ecumenical Theology of Giving*. Collegeville: Liturgical Press.

———. 2006. "The Pauline Luther and the Law: Lutheran Theology Reengages the Study of Paul." *Pro ecclesia* 15:64–86.

Schenk, Wolfgang. 1987. "Die Briefe an Timotheus I und II und an Titus (Pastoralbriefe) in der neueren Forschung (1945–1985)." *Aufstieg und Niedergang der römischen Welt* 2.25.4:3404–38.

Schlier, Heinrich. 1958. *Die Zeit der Kirche*. Freiburg: Herder.

Schulz, Siegfried. 1976. *Die Mitte der Schrift*. Stuttgart: Kreuz.

Schüssler Fiorenza, Elisabeth. 1983. *In Memory of Her: A Feminist Theological Reconstruction of Christian Origins*. London: SCM.

Seid, Timothy W. n.d. "Psychagogy in Paul: What Is It, How Does It Help Us Understand Paul, and Why Does It Matter?" Available online at esr.earlham.edu/~seidti/psychagogy.pdf (accessed November 2006).

Seneca. 1995. *Moral and Political Essays*. Edited and translated by John M. Cooper and J. F. Procopé. Cambridge: Cambridge University Press.

Simon, Bennett. 1978. *Mind and Madness in Ancient Greece*. Ithaca: Cornell University Press.

Simon, Wolfgang. 2003. *Die Messopfertheologie Martin Luthers*. Tübingen: Mohr.

Sorabji, Richard. 2000. *Emotion and Peace of Mind: From Stoic Agitation to Christian Temptation*. Oxford: Oxford University Press.

Spicq, C. 1969. *Les épitres pastorales*. 4th edition. Paris: Gabalda.

Strack, Hermann, and Paul Billerbeck. 1922–61. *Kommentar zum Neuen Testament aus Talmud und Midrasch*. Munich: Beck.

Stuhlmacher, Peter. 1975. *Der Brief an Philemon*. Evangelisch-katholischer Kommentar zum Neuen Testament. Neukirchen: Neukirchener Verlag.

Sutherland, Arthur M. 2006. *I Was a Stranger: A Christian Theology of Hospitality*. Nashville: Abingdon.

Theodore of Mopsuestia. 1882. *In epistolas B. Pauli commentarii*, vol. 2. Edited by H. B. Swete. Cambridge: Cambridge University Press.

Thiselton, Anthony. 1994. "The Logical Role of the Liar Paradox in Titus 1:12–13: A Dissent from the Commentaries in the Light of Philosophical and Logical Analysis." *Biblical Interpretation* 2:207–23.

Thomas Aquinas. 1888–. *In omnes S. Pauli epistolas commentarii*. Opera omnia: Editio leonina. Vatican City: Vatican Polyglot Press (available at www.corpusthomisticum.org).

Thurston, Bonnie B. 1989. *The Widows: A Women's Ministry in the Early Church*. Minneapolis: Fortress.

Tromp, Johannes. 1997. *The Assumption of Moses: A Critical Edition with Commentary*. Studia in Veteris Testamenti Pseudepigrapha 10. Leiden: Brill.

Trummer, Peter. 1978. *Die Paulustradition der Pastoralbriefe*. Frankfurt: Peter Lang.

Vanhoozer, Kevin J. 2005a. *Dictionary for Theological Interpretation of the Bible*. Grand Rapids: Baker.

———. 2005b. *The Drama of Doctrine: A Canonical-Linguistic Approach to Christian Theology*. Louisville: Westminster John Knox.

Vermes, Geza. 2004. *The Complete Dead Sea Scrolls in English*. London: Penguin.

Vorgrimler, Herbert. 1994. *Geschichte der Hölle*. Munich: Fink.

Weiner, Annette. 1992. *Inalienable Possessions: The Paradox of Keeping-While-Giving*. Berkeley: University of California Press.

Weiser, Alfons. 2003. *Der zweite Brief an Timotheus*. Evangelisch-katholischer Kommentar zum Neuen Testament 16/1. Neukirchen: Neukirchener Verlag.

Wengert, Timothy. 2005. "Georg Major as Exegete of First Timothy." Pages 69–92 in *Georg Major (1502–1574): Ein Theologe der Wittenberger Reformation*. Edited by I. Dingel and G. Wartenberg. Leipzig: Evangelische Verlagsanstalt.

Westerholm, Stephen. 2004. *Perspectives Old and New on Paul: The "Lutheran Paul" and His Critics*. Grand Rapids: Eerdmans.

Williams, Rowan. 1993. "Macrina's Deathbed Revisited: Gregory of Nyssa on Mind and Passion." Pages 227–46 in *Christian Faith and Greek Philosophy in Late Antiquity: Essays in Tribute to George Christopher Stead*. Edited by L. L. Wickham and C. P. Bammel. Supplements to Vigiliae Christianae 19. Leiden: Brill.

Winter, Sarah. 1987. "Paul's Letter to Philemon." *New Testament Studies* 33:1–15.

Wöhle, Andreas. 1998. *Luthers Freude an Gottes Gesetz*. Frankfurt: Haag & Herchen.

SUBJECT INDEX

SCRIPTURE INDEX